THE DAY
OF
YAHWEH

A Biblical Eschatology

With a Study on the Book of Revelation

By Albert James Dager

Cover Art
Carrie Nelson

Image of Moon on Cover from NASA

First Printing   January, 2013

THE DAY OF YAHWEH
A Biblical Eschatology
With a Study on the Book of Revelation

Copyright 2012 by Albert James Dager

Sword Publishers
PO Box 290
Redmond, WA 98073-0290

www.swordpublishers.com

Library of Congress Control Number: 2012953234
Trade Edition ISBN 978-0-9626632-5-3

Dedicated to the One who is at the center of this study on eschatology, our Blessed Savior and Lord, Jesus Christ.

With thanks to the many friends who have helped in diverse ways, even though who disagree with some of the conclusions in this book.

Special thanks to my wife and faithful companion, Jean.

THIS BOOK IS WRITTEN WITH THE HOPE THAT IT WILL NOT BE MERELY A MEANS FOR BELIEVERS IN CHRIST TO ATTAIN MORE INTELLECTUAL KNOWLEDGE, BUT WILL ENCOURAGE SUCH TO CONSIDER THEIR WALK WITH CHRIST AND TO DRAW CLOSER TO HIM AS THE DAY OF HIS RETURN APPROACHES.

FOR THOSE WHO DO NOT KNOW HIM AS LORD AND SAVIOR, IT IS MEANT TO IMPEL THEM TOWARD EXAMINING THE SCRIPTURES IN ORDER TO KNOW THE TRUTH THAT CAN SET THEM FREE.

All Scripture quotations are from the King James Version of the Bible, rephrased in modern U.S. English, unless otherwise stated.

CONTENTS

PART I
A BIBLICAL ESCHATOLOGY

PREFACE

What does the future hold? What will be my place in the future? These and similar questions are on the minds of many, both disciples of the Lord Jesus Christ and non-believers. People are naturally fascinated with the prospect of understanding the future. Christians find fascination with the future no less than do non-believers who search out ungodly sources, hoping to discover what the future holds for them.

The Lord has placed in His Word many prophecies meant to help us understand the signs of His return during what is called "the last days." Among theologians, the study of biblical prophecy related to the last days is called eschatology (Greek: *eskhatos* "last," "furthest," "remote" [from *ex* "out of" + *logia* "a speaking"]).

Biblical prophecy is germane to the true Gospel. The focal point of all biblical prophecy is the redemption and eternal destiny of God's creation, including the destiny of mankind. For believers in Christ, understanding biblical prophecy gives assurance of our blessed hope. It answers questions related to the resurrection—how and when that will occur. Does the resurrection mean spiritual regeneration only? Does it mean the physical resurrection of the body? How many resurrections will occur? Will only the righteous be resurrected, or will there be a resurrection of the unrighteous as well? And who, exactly, are the righteous?

A proper understanding of eschatology will provide answers to these and other questions about the Second Coming of Jesus. Will He return physically to establish His reign on the earth? Or is He already reigning over the earth from Heaven, waiting for man to establish righteousness on the earth and bring an end to evil? There are untold numbers of theories about these and other issues regarding the future of mankind.

As much as the study of eschatology reveals terrible events to occur in the future, it also brings good news to those who are in Christ. It reveals the end of evil and the eternal life that will result.

Essential to the study of eschatology is the resurrection of the saints and its related events. Without the resurrection everything else comes to nothing:

> But if there is no resurrection of the dead, then Christ has not risen. And if Christ has not risen, then our proclamation is vain, and your faith is also vain.
>
> Yes, and we are found false witnesses of God because we have testified about God that He raised up Christ (whom He did not raise up, if it is true that the dead do not rise).
>
> For if the dead do not rise then Christ is not raised. And if Christ is not raised, your faith is vain; you are still in your sins....
>
> If I have fought like men with animals at Ephesus, what advantage is it to me if the dead do not rise? Let us eat and drink, for tomorrow we die. (1Co 15:13-32)

Books on eschatology are among the best sellers in Christian bookstores. With the publication in 1970 of Hal Lindsey's book, *The Late Great Planet Earth*, eschatology began to fascinate Christians as never before. By May, 1977, it was a national best seller with more than seven million copies in print—a phenomenal sales record. The book is still a strong seller today. The best selling fiction series, *Left Behind*, authored by Jerry B. Jenkins and Tim LaHaye, is an example of how fiction has been used to convey eschatological beliefs. To date sixteen volumes of the *Left Behind* series have been published.

The art of motion pictures has also been utilized to present eschatological beliefs. As far back as the early 1970s, movies such as *A Thief in the Night* made the rounds of churches eager to find out how the very last days will play out. Since then there have been several imaginative speculations put to film, including the film versions of *The Late, Great Planet Earth* and *Left Behind*. These and other movies, such as *The Moment After*,

The Moment After 2, Revelation, Image of the Beast, A Distant Thunder, and Trinity Broadcasting Network's *The Omega Code* and its sequel *Megiddo,* present in dramatic fashion one particular eschatological theory called "the pre-tribulation secret rapture theory," which we will be examining. This theory speculates that there is coming a seven-year period of great tribulation on the earth concurrent with the rise to worldwide power of an evil man commonly referred to as "the anti-Christ," but that Christians will escape that tribulation by being caught up or "raptured" to Heaven before it occurs.

The popularity of biblical end-times prophecy has become such that even Hollywood has jumped onto the financially lucrative bandwagon with movies such as *The Omen, The Omen II, The Omen III,* and *The Rapture,* which speculated on the rise and fall of the anti-Christ. Of course, these were mere fantasy, but not much more so than most of the Christian movies dealing with the same theme.

The word "rapture" in eschatological terms refers to an event coincident with the resurrection of the saints as described in the apostle Paul's first letter to the believers in Thessalonica:

> But I would not have you be ignorant, brethren, concerning those who are asleep, so that you do not sorrow as others who have no hope. For if we believe that Jesus died and rose again, even so those also who sleep in Jesus, God will bring with Him.

> For we say this to you by the Word of the Lord: that we who are alive and remain until the coming of the Lord shall not go before those who are asleep. For the Lord Himself shall descend from Heaven with a shout, with the voice of the archangel and with the trump of God, and the dead in Christ shall rise first. Then we who are alive and remain shall be caught up together with them in the clouds to meet the Lord in the air, and so shall we ever be with the Lord. Therefore, comfort one another with these words. (1Th 4:13-18)

The Greek word *harpazo* ["caught up"] was translated as *raptura* in the Latin Roman Catholic *Vulgate,* and it is from there that the English word "rapture" came to be used in relation to the catching up of the living saints at the time of the resurrection. "Rapture" is a poor translation of *harpazo,* which denotes a sudden snatching away or grabbing. The word "rapture" conjures the image of being caught up emotionally rather than physically. However, since it has been the accepted term for decades, we will use it on occasion with some reservations.

The pre-tribulation secret rapture theory is the only one put to film thus far. But views differing from it are offered in books, and we will be looking at those views.

Unfortunately, the study of the last days has been muddled greatly by authors who have misunderstood Scripture and/or have sensationalized the subject. Thus, the books and films from among the popular eschatological positions contain some truth mixed with a greater abundance of speculation, conjecture and, in some cases, downright fantasy. This makes them of no value in truly understanding what will transpire as the present age comes to a close. As we explore the Bible through the prophesies found in the writings of both the prophets of ancient Israel and the apostles of Jesus Christ we will look at various teachings and theories that have gained in popularity over the centuries. We will examine those theories as they either agree or disagree with clear statements of Scripture, and we will look at some of the more obscure and misunderstood biblical passages.

This will prove an exciting journey into the future and will reveal truths heretofore undiscerned by proponents of the popular eschatological theories of today, but perhaps understood by others with small voices unheard among the cacophony of Christian media hype.

As we proceed there will be times when redundancy is necessary simply because certain explanations and citing of Scripture apply to more than one event in the ongoing narrative of last days prophecies. As well, this will serve to impress the truths relative to those Scriptures more firmly in our minds.

The most important thing we can do when searching for truth is to willingly assess preconceived ideas. No matter how much we may have invested in time, money and admiration toward favored teachers, God's Word must prevail .

Some might question why I feel qualified to even address this deep subject. Well, I have asked the Lord the same question. The answer is that no one is qualified to handle His Word. We must trust the Holy Spirit to give us understanding, which I have done time and again. I did not take on this task lightly. My constant prayer throughout my study and research has been that the Lord not allow me to bring it to fruition if there is anything in it that might lead my brethren astray.

I have approached this writing with great fear before the Lord. And I am confident that it is true to His Word, and that it will shed light where it has been lacking while correcting some serious commonly accepted errors.

With confidence I can say that it is at the very least as credible as any other writing on eschatology. With that as our starting point, let us proceed.

1
SIGNS OF THE TIMES

The first book of the Bible, Genesis, opens with the following words: "In the beginning God created the heavens and the earth." It continues to reveal that God created man in His own image, and commanded man to have dominion over all living things on the earth. He placed man in a garden that He planted in the east of an area called "Eden," in what would become ancient Mesopotamia. But man fell from God's grace by disobedience to His one and only commandment—that he not eat the fruit from the tree of knowledge of good and evil in the midst of the garden. Because of his disobedience man was cast out of the Garden of Eden to provide for his own survival.

Early in his history man said, "Let us build us a city, and a tower whose top may reach into the heavens, and let us make us a name lest we be scattered abroad upon the face of the whole earth."

And so the infamous Tower of Babel was begun.

Realizing that a united mankind could accomplish anything they imagined (Ge 11:6), God set about to confuse men's languages and to scatter mankind across the face of the earth. So regardless how man developed his science we must question the idea that it was God-given.

Certainly God was concerned about man's technological progress early on—so much so that He stunted it. Thus we can deduce that God and/or

His faithful angels were not the ones who imparted the secret knowledge necessary for man to develop science and technology beyond the basics necessary for survival.

(I would like to interject, for those who might not understand, that God's angels are not the effeminate "fairies" and docile creatures most often portrayed. The word translated "angels" is in the Hebrew, *mal'ak* (one dispatched), and in the Greek, *angelos* (messengers). They are the "watchers" (Daniel 4:17) over the nations and individuals, consigned to do God's bidding throughout the earth. Many are in the warrior class of spirit beings.)

We know that God did use the knowledge of the sciences gained from Israel's sojourn in Egypt to help His chosen people build their cities and His temple. He even gave special talents to those He chose to work on the temple. But the knowledge they utilized came from worldly sources—the occult sciences of Egypt's mystery religion.

When God moved men away from their united purpose, mankind's scientific and technological progress was slowed to an imperceptible pace. For almost six thousand years he remained at virtually the same place of development in his science and technology. It is only recently that man has developed the ability to throw off the shackles of earth's gravity and place men on the moon. How could this be? And why, of all times in human history has such technology been developed?

Speaking of the end of this age, the Angel of the Lord told the Hebrew prophet Daniel, "Many shall run back and forth, and knowledge shall be increased" (Da 12:4).

Some who are skeptical that the Bible even addresses events past the first century say that this refers to knowledge of Bible truth, and people running back and forth in eagerness to learn His Word. Without a clear reference to this allegorical application, such a claim is not tenable, particularly in view of mankind's tremendous increase in knowledge of late that has resulted in his ability to traverse the entire globe in a matter of hours. Not to mention that men more often shrink from God's Word than eagerly seek its truths.

As we consider the tremendous increase in knowledge over the past century alone, we must identify with this prophecy. Interestingly, the increase of man's knowledge has coincided with the speed at which man has been able to move from one place to another (his ability to "run back and forth"). In Adam's day, some 6,000 years ago, man was held to a very small area in which to move about, chiefly because he did not have the means to move rapidly. His fastest means of travel was the horse. At full gallop, the fastest that man could move on horseback was about thirty miles per hour, and then for only short durations of time (well-trained race horses can approach 40 to 50 MPH.) Only because of an extensive life span in his early history was man able to migrate to distant lands and populate the whole earth.

One thousand years after Adam, around the time of Noah, man's fastest means of transportation was still the horse—about thirty miles per hour.

At the time of Abraham—some two thousand years after Adam—man had achieved little progress in technology and was still able to travel only as fast as the fastest horse. It continued this way for the next 4,000 years.

Then, during the latter part of the nineteenth century came the Industrial Revolution. Largely as a result of the freedoms granted to individuals with the founding of the United States of America, the age of technology was born, and man began to make rapid strides in science and technology. The steam engine was perfected to where it could develop enough energy to turn the wheels of giant locomotives. That spelled the beginning of man's release from time and space. Suddenly man was able to travel at over one hundred miles per hour!

Not long after, man was able to overcome the earth's gravitational pull through powered flight. When the Wright brothers achieved the first successful powered flight it was for a distance of only 110 feet and of only twelve seconds duration. But it demonstrated that man would no longer be held down in his attempt to conquer his environment; he took his eyes off the dust of the earth and turned them heavenward—toward the stars.

Yet for all his scientific and technological accomplishments, man's nature had not changed. He used his sudden increase in knowledge to fashion greater and more devastating instruments of war. His lust for conquest resulted in "the war to end all wars," the great European conflict that would come to be known as World War I.

The war spurred interest in the new flying machine that would allow men to attack their enemies from the skies. Those flying machines—aeroplanes—were built to fly faster and higher in order to gain strategic advantage. Man could now travel at some 150 miles per hour!

World War II saw the greatest conflict in the history of mankind, and man's depraved nature was manifested at its fullest when Adolph Hitler pulled all stops in an attempt to use technology to conquer the world. By then fighter planes could streak through the skies delivering death and destruction at speeds close to 400 miles per hour.

Even during World War II, Hitler's Germany had produced prototypes of the jet airplane that threatened to give the Third Reich unchallenged superiority in air combat. Fortunately the Allies were able to bring Hitler to his knees before that could happen. But after World War II the jet engine was perfected, and on October 14, 1947, Air Force Captain Chuck Yeager, piloting the rocket-powered experimental Bell X-1 aircraft, slammed his way through the sound barrier at 650 miles per hour!

The stars were looking closer.

1958 saw the rocket engine developed to where it could be trusted to carry a human perched inside the nose cone of primitive sub-orbital spacecraft. Shortly thereafter, developing millions of pounds of thrust, rockets left the earth's atmosphere and placed man into orbit. His speed suddenly increased to an incredible 17,300 miles per hour!

In 1968, man increased his speed even further to where he could actually leave the gravitational pull of the earth and utilize controlled flight to take him around the moon and back. One year later he placed his foot on the surface of the moon, and the dust of the earth mingled with the dust of its satellite.

Man's dream of the ages had become reality; he had left his home planet and stood upon another celestial body. His journey to the moon was accomplished at speeds in excess of 24,000 miles per hour!

From year one to almost A.D. 1900—a span of almost 6,000 years—man's maximum speed of travel remained at about thirty miles per hour. Within seventy years he was traveling over 24,000 miles per hour!

This sudden burst in speed is a good gauge to measure man's increase in knowledge. The greatest achievements in science and technology have been made in just the past one hundred years.

The decade of the 1940s was particularly significant, for during that short period alone the jet airplane came into its own, and man broke the sound barrier. At the same time, many new inventions were being birthed; television, refrigerators, automatic washing machines and many other wonderful, labor-saving devices began to make life easier for civilized men. And the first atomic bomb was detonated, ushering man into the nuclear age.

Fear of nuclear war was used to promote the idea of bringing the nations together once again, and a new Tower of Babel—the United Nations Organization—was formed, signifying the importance of Daniel's prophecy.

The question arises, why this sudden, exponential increase in man's knowledge? Why did God keep man ignorant of the science needed for these achievements for so many centuries?

The answer is that God knew that the greatest bulk of humanity would be living during the end times. There are more people living today than have lived in total throughout all the ages that have gone before.

It took almost the entire 6,000 years—until A.D. 1830—for the earth's population to reach one billion souls. One hundred years later—1931—it had doubled to two billion. Thirty years added another billion. In 1976 the official census figures put the total at four billion human beings. By 2012 the figure had reached over seven billion. How many people will populate the earth by the end of this century should the Lord allow mankind to continue unabated?

Every year man's knowledge increases exponentially and he runs back and forth over the face of the earth at an ever faster pace. But the result of man's increase in knowledge has not been all blessing; it has also been a curse. For with technology has come death and destruction on a scale previously undreamed of.

In truth, the increase in knowledge has not been impelled by concern for the individual's benefit as much as for the benefit of Mammon—the world's system of wealth and commerce conducted largely under the auspices of Satan, the god of this world (2Co 4:4). This will ultimately result in man's misguided attempt to prevent the Lord's return. For it is only because of his technology that man will think he can resist Christ at that time:

> And I saw the beast, and the kings of the earth, and their armies, gathered together to make war against Him who sat on the horse, and against His army. (Rv 19:19)

War has been in the heart of mankind since Cain slew Abel. Today there is more unrest among nations than ever, including the period of World War II. That war lasted some eight years. There are conflicts raging all over the planet that have gone on for centuries. Those conflicts are a continual threat to the entire world.

But beyond warfare, there are many ills plaguing mankind which exhibit the signs of the last days. Jesus gave us some of those signs:

> "...many will come in My name, saying that I am Christ, and shall deceive many. And you will hear of wars and rumors of wars. See that you are not frightened, for all these things must come to pass.
>
> "But the end is not yet. For nation shall rise against nation, and kingdom against kingdom. And there shall be famines, and pestilences and earthquakes in diverse places. All these are the beginning of sorrows." (Mt 24:5-8)

As never before, there is a plethora of false christs, and even those claiming Jesus is the Christ while perverting His Word.

Man's ability to run back and forth over the face of the earth has allowed for diseases to spread rapidly from nation to nation. And in spite of man's agricultural science, famine still plagues many nations and threatens the world due to economic depression.

The increase in the frequency and magnitude of earthquakes has risen exponentially over the past century. Many nations' economies are on the verge of collapse for varying reasons, not the least of which has been wholesale treason on the part of governments surrendering to Marxist ideology.

Personal freedom is being swept away piecemeal through never-ending legislation of laws and bureaucratic regulations. People are more and more being regarded as wards of the state.

Within advanced nations the economic establishments have implemented incredible means to track virtually every buying pattern, product preference, political thought, and even personal ideology. We are transitioning from a cash society to a credit society with the loss of privacy that allows for us to be tracked by supranational mega-corporations as well as government.

Surveillance technology allows government to keep an eye on increasing numbers of public vectors. How long before the eye-that-spies invades our homes?

The most telling sign of the times is mankind's reversion to the hedonism that characterized the days of Noah and Lot:

> "And as it was in the days of Noah, so it will also be in the days of the Son of Man. They ate, they drank, they married wives, they were given in marriage, until the day that Noah entered into the ark, and the flood came and destroyed them all.
>
> "Likewise also, as it was in the days of Lot, they ate, they drank, they bought, they sold, they planted, they built. But the same day that Lot went out of Sodom it rained fire and brimstone from the heavens, and destroyed them all." (Lk 17:26)

As it was in the days of Noah:

> And YHWH saw that the wickedness of man was great in the earth, and that every imagination of the thoughts of his heart was only evil continually. (Ge 6:5)

As it was likewise in the days of Lot:

> The men of Sodom were exceedingly wicked, and sinners before YHWH. (Ge 13:13)

So it will be in the day the Lord returns. There will be no cat[...] event (as opposed to general chaos) to warn the world of impending j[...] That judgment will come as a result of mankind's increasing ungo[...]

The increasing wickedness in the world may also be attribute[...] in some degree to the increase in knowledge which has given man h[...] and technology. Although there is no question of the temporal cor[...] have provided, many of the labor-saving devices modern technolog[...] us have proved largely frustrating.

Besides the cost of purchasing the vast array of electronic m[...] give pleasure and ease of living, there is also the cost of mainter[...] cost is not always only in money, but in time as well. Often, due t[...] for all the "good things" technology offers, families have had to [...] incomes. This has meant that many mothers—the mainstay of [...] upbringing—have abandoned their roles as keepers of the home[...] liberation groups have convinced otherwise domestic-oriented [...] there is something inherently demeaning in the role of wife and mother. As a result, the vast majority of children today are more influenced by, and learn their values from, strangers called "teachers" in government indoctrination camps called "public schools." More often than not, the "values" taught in those camps are contrary to the biblical ethics formerly held by a majority of Christians in the West.

And whereas women in the past worked diligently at home without the labor-saving devices available today, they received much reward in raising their children and being helpmates to their husbands. Few twenty-first-century women would be able to cope with living a less technologically-enhanced life at home.

One price of the wonders of technology in the home is that of divorce, which continues to plague marriages in wealthy nations far more than it does in less advanced countries. This sad turn away from the reverence with which marriage was once held may, to a large degree, be attributed to women leaving the God-ordained role of nurturer. With women working outside the home to bring in enough income to maintain the electronic marvels at their command, they have become "liberated." They are having more affairs, leaving their husbands and children, demanding "equality" in the home and generally adopting more masculine behavior patterns: smoking, drinking, cursing, adultery.

But are they any happier than their earlier, less technologically-blessed counterparts? No. And this has contributed to the breakdown of the nuclear family model that sustained western households for centuries.

This, in turn, has resulted in more children exhibiting rebellious attitudes toward not only their parents but society at large. The age at which children are becoming addicted to alcohol, drugs and sex, and engaging in crimes of violence has been steadily dropping since the 1950s.

With the breakdown of families, more and more children are being made wards of the state. According to Child Welfare Information Gateway, over half a million children in the United States were in foster care in 2008.

Throughout history Men have built civilizations, but women have been the mortar that has held those civilizations together. As women have become more mannish in their demeanor, men have become more frustrated and confused about their own role. The more masculine women have become, the more effeminate men have become. Many men have succumbed to the new psychology that attempts to force them into the more "sensitive" role of "nurturer"—a role that is primarily for women—resulting in men becoming effeminate. All this has contributed to the increase in and acceptance of sodomy, lesbianism and transgender mutilations.

No, all was not perfect in the "Happy Days" of the 1950s; it never is in a sinful world. But that's not the point. The point is that man's technological marvels have done nothing to truly ease the burdens of life which are more spiritual than physical.

Unable to cope with the stresses of life, people turn to ungodliness to ease their pain. Hedonism is increasing among the general populous in the West, largely in imitation of television and movie idols whose lifestyles are for the most part corrupt. Their screen personas reflect their real-life values, or lack thereof. And their influence among politicians and royalty is considerable. People who in the past would be nothing more than court jesters are now influencing political policy.

As hedonism among the general populous increases, society will break down, and mankind's ills will only increase as well. Yet as the enemies of God increase their work among the suffering millions on the face of this planet, we can take heart that God's Holy Spirit is abounding also. In the time that we have left we can, in a way far beyond that of natural man, lift our eyes from the dust of the earth and look heavenward, not toward the stars, but beyond—toward that "Bright and Morning Star" whose words are ever present to prompt us to live godly in this world: "Behold, I come quickly!"

2
ESCHATOLOGICAL THEORIES

Before the Lord returns, certain prophecies must be fulfilled. Some say that all prophecies relating to the end of this age have already been fulfilled, and all that remains is for the Lord to return, or for "the Church"[1] to gain ascendance in the world and establish righteousness through godly rule, or for the immediate appearance of the New Heavens and New Earth and the final judgment of mankind, or for some other scenario to take place. All eschatological theories rest on peculiar approaches to prophetic history.

Here we must consider an important rule to understanding eschatology: prophetic history (references to events that transpire in relation to biblical prophecy) is not the same as human history (all events that transpire chronologically in the course of time). All prophetic history occurs within the context of human history, but not all human history is found in biblical prophecy. As a result, biblical prophecy will often address events that appear to unfold immediately upon one another when, in truth, those events may be separated by millennia of time. Without understanding this critical rule of prophetic history, men have erred greatly in drawing conclusions contrary

---

[1] The reader will notice that throughout this writing I refer to "the Church" in quotes. For a brief treatise on my reason for this see Appendix A, "What is 'the Church'?"

to biblical truth. Worse, they have published those conclusions with the result of misleading many into misunderstanding the signs of the times.

Within Christian eschatological studies, the several theological positions taken on the subject of the resurrection and the Lord's return fall under four basic categories: Idealism, Preterism, Historicism and Futurism. Within these categories there exist many variations which would take a book in itself to cover fully. The following brief analyses of these basic eschatological categories should suffice for this study.

IDEALISM

Idealism does not take prophetic history—particularly the Book of Revelation—literally. Believing biblical prophecy to be greatly allegorical, idealists believe those prophecies merely reveal timeless principles that, if adhered to by mankind, will one day result in a better world. They believe that somehow mankind will attain to a higher level of spiritual perfection through knowledge. A form of Gnosticism, idealism teaches that human perfection may be achieved through the attainment of secret knowledge by incorporating allegorical interpretations of Scripture. Idealism is a staple of liberal Christian theology and is not a major factor in the eschatology of most true believers in Jesus, so we won't go into great detail in its regard.

PRETERISM

Preterism is a major eschatological belief system found largely within the Reformed churches. The term "preterism" comes from the Latin *praeter*, meaning "past" or "beyond." In relation to the Bible it suggests that all or a majority of Bible prophecy was fulfilled by A.D. 70 when the Jewish temple in Jerusalem was destroyed by Roman invaders.

Preterists state that all prophecies of the Bible, especially those found in Daniel and Revelation, relate events that transpired in the first century A.D. Preterism teaches "replacement theology" which says that "the Church" became the fulfillment of Israel at the destruction of Jerusalem in A.D. 70; God is finished entirely with Israel as a nation, and "the Church" is all that matters in His economy now and for the future.

Preterists claim that theirs was the original eschatology of the "early Church." This may have some basis in truth inasmuch as the "early Church" did not faithfully adhere to the faith of the original apostles. The theological system which began in the early second century eventually morphed into the Roman Catholic Church under the Roman emperor Constantine in the fourth century.

Most preterists don't know that preterism originated within Roman Catholicism with the first systematic exposition of prophecy written by the Jesuit priest Luis De Alcasar during the Counter Reformation. The Counter Reformation was a response to the Protestant Reformation and began with the Council of Trent (1545-1563). It ended in 1648 at the close of the Thirty Years War fought initially between Protestants and Catholics within the Holy Roman Empire.

Preterism became the Roman Catholic eschatological position in defense of its claim to be the Kingdom of God on earth with the pope destined to rule the nations as the Vicar of Christ—the one who replaces Christ on earth. This was the basis for the Holy Roman Empire which sought to bring all nations under its dominion. It is the first systematic realization of dominion theology. In view of this, it is quite amazing that modern Protestant preterists embrace the eschatology of those who persecuted their religious forebears.

It wasn't until as late as the 17th century that Protestantism began to adopt preterism. Dutchman Hugo Grotius, in an attempt to establish common ground between Protestantism and Roman Catholicism, was the first known Protestant to accept preterism as his eschatological position. He wrote *Commentary on Certain Texts Which Deal with Antichrist* (1640), arguing that all the texts relating to the anti-Christ had their fulfillment in the first century A.D. When this attempt was largely rejected by Protestants, he wrote *Commentaries on the New Testament* (1641-1650), in which he expanded his preterist views to include the Book of Revelation. He also said that the Lord's "Olivet Discourse" was fulfilled in the first century.

Preterism still had difficulty gaining any substantial inroads into Protestantism until English commentators Thomas Hayne (*Christ's Kingdom on Earth*, 1645) and Joseph Hall (*The Revelation Unrevealed*, 1650) were published. Neither of them, however, applied their preterist views to the Book of Revelation. It was an admirer of Grotius, Englishman Henry Hammond, a notable Protestant convert, who interpreted Revelation with a preterist bent. Earlier, in 1730, Swiss Protestant Firmin Abauzit (a devotee to Arianism) wrote *Essai sur l'Apocalypse* (*Essay on the Apocalypse*), which became part of a growing systematic preterist account of Revelation. He later recanted his position.

In America the earliest full preterist writing was *The Second Advent of the Lord Jesus Christ: A Past Event* (1845) by Robert Townley. Townley also later recanted. Yet in spite of these and other attempts by Protestant commentators who had accepted Roman Catholic eschatology, preterism gained little ground among Protestants until the end of the eighteenth century.

Preterist understanding of the New Heavens and New Earth is a transition of God's interest from the Israelite theocracy to the dominion of "the Church." According to preterism there will be no catching away of the saints and no physical reign of Christ on earth. Preterists posit that "the Church" has not done its job, and that's the reason Christ's reign over the nations has not been visibly manifested. It is only left for "the Church" to be victorious over the nations through systematic takeover of what are called "the seven spheres" of society: 1) family; 2) religion; 3) education; 4) government and politics; 5) mass communications media; 6) arts and entertainment; 7) commerce, science and technology. Then will come the New Heavens and New Earth which will be eternal.

Although some preterists deny being advocates of dominion theology, their basic teaching is a staple of the Christian Reconstructionist Movement which believes "the Church" will take dominion over the nations without Jesus present on the earth (See my book, *Vengeance is Ours: The Church in Dominion*, 1990, Sword Publishers).

Preterists do not take the Millennium (a coming age when Jesus will rule over the nations from Jerusalem for 1,000 years [Rv 20:1-7]) as a literal 1,000-year period. They also posit that the Book of Revelation was written prior to A.D. 70, and thus it has no prophetic value.

Preterism holds that the imminence of prophetic language suggests that all the events prophesied in chapter nine of the Book of Daniel (the seventy "weeks" or "sevens" [Da 9:24-27]) must have transpired in rapid succession with no gaps in time between those events. Therefore, there is nothing left to be fulfilled before "the Church" reigns supreme on the earth. The conquest of the earth by "the Church" will set the stage for the creation of the New Heavens and the New Earth.

Partial Preterism

One of two principal schools of preterism is called partial preterism. Partial preterists believe that all prophecies have been fulfilled except for the resurrection of the dead and Jesus' Second Coming or *Parousia*, with the immediate creation of the New Heavens and New Earth.

Regarding Revelation's reference to the Lord ruling the nations for 1,000 years, partial preterists are amillennial or postmillennial. That is, they do not believe in a literal 1,000 year (Millennium) reign of Christ on earth. Some partial preterists believe that Christ currently reigns from Heaven and will from there eventually destroy all His enemies, the last of which is Death. They consider this period of Christ's spiritual reign as the Millennium. Thus they may be considered post-millennial in their eschatology.

Full Preterism

The only significant difference between partial preterism and full preterism is that full preterists regard all prophecies of end-times events fulfilled, including the resurrection of the dead and Jesus' Second Coming. They believe that His Second Coming was not bodily, but rather a "return in glory" manifested through the destruction of Jerusalem and the Jewish temple in A.D. 70.

Even more aberrant beliefs are held by some full preterists who say that all the covenants and promises in Scripture pertain exclusively to a chosen remnant of Israelites in the flesh, and that these ("all Israel") were redeemed at the alleged spiritual Second Coming of Christ in A.D. 70.

Full preterism is considered heresy by many because it disagrees with the historic creeds of the established churches. Part of those creeds state a belief in the Lord's future coming to judge the living and the dead. Some critics say the full-preterist belief in a past resurrection is condemned by the apostle Paul who said that people's faith was being overthrown by Hymenaeus and Philetus who claimed that the resurrection of the dead had already occurred (2 Ti 2:17-18). Full preterists defend their position by saying that Paul's condemnation was stated prior to A.D. 70 when, they say, the resurrection actually occurred.

As to the resurrection, some preterists (full and partial) believe that it is not the raising of the physical body, but rather the resurrection of the soul from Hades, and thus all the living and the dead are raised, changed, caught up, and glorified into one New Covenant Body of Christ; thus, believers today have already been resurrected in their souls by the new birth in Christ.

Both full and partial preterists make great effort to discredit those who believe in the literal, physical return of Jesus to reign on the earth for 1,000 years before God institutes the New Heavens and New Earth. Often their tone is one of ridicule, and they dismiss as ignorant and even superstitious, those who believe in the Millennial Age of Christ's Kingdom on earth.

HISTORICISM

Historicism is the traditional Protestant interpretation of Scripture which rests on the idea that prophetic history has been, and continues to be, working its way toward fulfillment throughout the history of what it calls "the Church Age." This contrasts with other eschatological positions that place all prophecy in the past (preterism) or most prophecy in the future (futurism). The Book of Revelation is the focal point of historicism which says that we are now approaching the end of prophetic history.

Historicism formed the basis for the Reformers who claimed that the pope was the man of sin referred to in 2 Thessalonians 2:3. The Roman Catholic Church (or the pope) is considered the whore of Babylon, represented by the woman who sits on the seven mountains (interpreted as the seven hills of Rome) in Revelation 17:9.

Historicists generally believe that prophecies contained in the Book of Revelation span the time from the apostolic era to the Second Coming of Christ, which is yet future.

One of the earliest known expositors of historicism was Victorinus, who wrote the first complete commentary on the Book of Revelation in A.D. 300.

The prophecies of Daniel and Revelation are considered by historicists as an unbroken line of fulfilled prophecy, with only a small portion yet future. Chapter 20 of Revelation, which speaks of the Lord ruling the earth for one thousand years (the Millennium), and warfare at the end of that time, is viewed as referring to a future attack against the glorious city, the New Jerusalem. The Millennium is regarded as an indefinite time after the creation of the New Heavens and New Earth. In that sense, historicism would be amillennial, but not in the same manner as preterism.

FUTURISM

Futurism, as a systematic eschatology, is relatively new, having been defined as a part of dispensational theology only since around the early to middle nineteenth century. It has steadily grown to become the most popular school of eschatology. Futurists believe that prophetic history is mostly in the future, yet to be fulfilled. However, futurism is more and more giving way to preterism in popularity, largely because of failed predictions by dispensationalist teachers who have tried to pinpoint the date of the Lord's return based on faulty interpretations of last-days prophecies.

Futurists view virtually all prophecies in the Book of Revelation as yet to be fulfilled; they apply the prophecies of Ezekiel to the present age, and believe that there will be a temple built in the modern state of Israel into which the last-days anti-Christ will enter and proclaim himself God.

Dispensationalism

Dispensationalism is a major futurist theological system based on the idea that God has throughout history related to humanity in different ways under different covenants. The most famous dispensationalist—if not the actual progenitor of dispensationalism—was John Nelson Darby (1800-1882) who was influential among the Plymouth Brethren.

Dispensationalism gained tremendous popularity in the early to mid-twentieth century with the publication in 1909 of the *Scofield Reference Bible* annotated by Cyrus I. Scofield and published by Oxford University Press. Scofield's notes on the Book of Revelation form the foundation for the writings of popular end-times prognosticators such as Hal Lindsey, Tim LaHaye, Jack Van Impe, and others.

Critics of dispensationalism accuse Darby of developing his pretribulation rapture theory from a "demonic utterance" of a young Scottish lass, Margaret MacDonald, who was given to fits of ecstasy and alleged visions. But Darby himself denounced such utterances as demonic. MacDonald's account of an alleged vision from God gained notoriety through publication, first in Robert Norton's *Memoirs of James & George Macdonald of Port-Glasgow* (1840, pp. 171-176). Later, it appeared in shorter form in Norton's *The Restoration of Apostles and Prophets; In the Catholic Apostolic Church* (1861, pp. 15-18):

> It was first the awful state of the land that was pressed upon me.
> I saw the blindness and infatuation of the people to be very great. I
> felt the cry of Liberty just to be the hiss of the serpent, to drown them
> in perdition. It was just "no God." I repeated the words, Now there
> is distress of nations, with perplexity, the seas and the waves roaring,
> men's hearts failing them for fear. Now look out for the sign of the
> Son of Man. Here I was made to stop and cry out, O it is not known
> what the sign of the Son of Man is; the people of God think they are
> waiting, but they know not what it is. I felt this needed to be revealed,
> and that there was great darkness and error about it; but suddenly
> what it was burst upon me with a glorious light. I saw it was just the
> Lord himself descending from Heaven with a shout, just the glorified
> man, even Jesus; but that all must, as Stephen was, be filled with the
> Holy Ghost, that they might look up, and see the brightness of the
> Father's glory. I saw the error to be, that men think that it will be
> something seen by the natural eye; but 'tis spiritual discernment that
> is needed, the eye of God in his people. Many passages were revealed,
> in a light in which I had not before seen them. I repeated, "Now is
> the Kingdom of Heaven like unto ten virgins, who went forth to meet
> the Bridegroom, five wise and five foolish; they that were foolish took

their lamps, but took no oil with them; but they that were wise took oil in their vessels with their lamps." "But be ye not unwise, but understanding what the will of the Lord is; and be not drunk with wine wherein is excess, but be filled with the Spirit." This was the oil the wise virgins took in their vessels—this is the light to be kept burning—the light of God—that we may discern that which cometh not with observation to the natural eye. **Only those who have the light of God within them will see the sign of his appearance. No need to follow them who say, see here, or see there, for his day shall be as the lightning to those in whom the living Christ is.** (Emphasis ours)

It is from this one statement, in bold above, that the concept of a "secret rapture" seems to have developed. It is the idea that only those true believers who will be caught up to meet the Lord will actually see Him. But Scripture tells us otherwise:

Look! He comes with clouds, and every eye shall see Him, and they also who pierced him [the unbelieving Jews], and all families of the earth shall wail because of Him! Even so, Amen! (Rv 1:7)

Because Darby also espoused belief in a "secret rapture," it has been assumed, but not proven, that he received this teaching from MacDonald. Yet as I said, Darby did not believe in such utterances as emanating from the Holy Spirit, but from demonic sources. The truth remains, however, that Darby did teach a "secret rapture" which was popularized by Scofield and by Charles Henry Mackintosh, a journalist for the Brethren Movement.

Reformed Baptist pastor of London's Metropolitan Tabernacle, Charles Haddon Spurgeon, was critical of Darby and the Brethren Movement. Holding a Calvinist soteriology, Spurgeon issued a blanket condemnation of everything the Brethren Movement taught. This blanket condemnation was based on Spurgeon's conclusion that, because of its emphasis on holy living, the Brethren Movement rejected the vicarious aspect of the Lord's obedience as well as imputed righteousness. This led to Spurgeon's broad-swinging statement against all their beliefs, as evidenced by his words:

With the deadly heresies entertained and taught by the Plymouth Brethren, in relation to some of the most momentous doctrines of the gospel, and to which I have adverted at some length, I feel assured that my readers will not be surprised at any other views, however unscriptural and pernicious they may be, which the Darbyites have embraced and zealously seek to propagate.[1]

It seems as if Spurgeon's blanket condemnation of everything Brethren and Darbyish has led Reformed theologians of all stripes to reject even the truths they held.

Futurism, largely keeping with dispensational teaching, is decidedly premillennial (the resurrection and catching up will occur prior to the Millennium). Futurists expect the Lord's return in two stages: first, to take Christians (at least a remnant of faithful believers in Jesus) to be with Him before a seven-year period of great tribulation; second, to return bodily to the earth to reign for a literal 1,000-year period known as the Millennium.

Futurism has lost much credibility among many Christians because of failed prophecies by several dispensationalists who have tried to pinpoint the date of the Lord's return. Most of those failed prophecies have rested on the belief that the establishment of the modern state of Israel signaled the final generation that would be alive when the Lord returns. This belief is primarily based on an erroneous interpretation of the Lord's parable in Matthew 24:32-34, which interpretation says the fig tree represents Israel. Because Israel was granted statehood in 1948, futurists suggested that within one generation (or 40 years) the Lord would return. After 1988 came and went, the calculations have been revised to expand the definition of a "generation," but the idea that the Lord could return at any moment—known as "imminency"—has remained.

---

1 J. N. Darby, *The Doctrine of the Church of England,* Oxford, 1831.

3

'RAPTURE' THEORIES

Essential to most eschatological positions is either belief in, or denial of, the "rapture"—the catching up of the saints to meet the Lord in the air before His judgment falls on the earth. According to Scripture, this catching up of the living faithful will be concurrent with the resurrection of the saints asleep in Christ:

> Look, I show you a mystery: not all of us shall sleep, but we all shall be changed in a moment, in the blinking of an eye, at the last trump. For the trumpet shall sound, and the dead shall be raised incorruptible, and we shall be changed. For this corruptible must put on incorruption, and this mortal must put on immortality.
>
> So when this corruptible has put on incorruption, and this mortal has put on immortality, then the saying shall be brought to pass that is written, "Death is swallowed up in victory. O death, where is your sting? O grave, where is your victory?" (1Co 15:51-55)
>
> But I would not have you be ignorant, brethren, concerning those who are asleep, so that you do not sorrow as others who have no hope. For if we believe that Jesus died and rose again, even so those also who sleep in Jesus, God will bring with Him.

For we say this to you by the Word of the Lord: that we who are alive and remain until the coming of the Lord shall not go before those who are asleep. For the Lord Himself shall descend from Heaven with a shout, with the voice of the archangel, and with the trump of God, and the dead in Christ shall rise first. Then we who are alive and remain shall be caught up together with them in the clouds to meet the Lord in the air, and so we shall ever be with the Lord. (1Th 4:13-17)

Preterists deny that a literal catching up will occur, at least as it is understood by futurists and historicists. Idealists consider the Rapture more a feeling of ecstasy than a literal catching up of resurrected saints in glorified bodies.

Among historicists and futurists, however, the Rapture remains the most intriguing element of their eschatology, and there are three popular theories on the timing of the catching up of the saints: pre-tribulation, mid-tribulation and post-tribulation. There is also one less popular theory called the multiple rapture theory. All are based on the idea that there is coming a seven-year period of distress upon the earth called "The Great Tribulation," and that the body of Christ is going to either go through that tribulation or escape all or part of it by being caught up or "raptured" into Heaven.

PRE-TRIBULATION RAPTURE THEORY

The pre-tribulation (pre-trib) rapture theory posits that Christians will escape the "Great Tribulation" because the Lord Jesus is going to take us out of the earth to meet Him in the heavens before it begins.

This theory rests on the idea that our heavenly Father would not allow His children to suffer so greatly or to undergo His wrath. It is more often than not portrayed as a "secret" event—that is, those left behind will not see the Lord in the sky, and will thus not understand what has happened as millions of believers seem to just disappear from the face of the earth.

This scenario has been portrayed in films and books with scenes of cars, trains and planes crashing, people suddenly disappearing before the eyes of others, and the like. In some portrayals, the disappearing people's clothes are neatly folded where they had been standing, sitting or lying.

A fanciful idea has come forth from some dispensationalist teachers who have suggested that their videos will be the source through which the Lord will save many during the Great Tribulation.

Currently the pre-tribulation rapture theory is the most popular, although it is steadily losing ground to preterism.

MID-TRIBULATION RAPTURE THEORY

This theory suggests that at the half-way point in the Great Tribulation (three-and-one-half years) the Rapture will occur. Some would say that the Great Tribulation is a separate event from the time that the wrath of God will be poured out on the rest of humanity once the resurrection and catching up has taken place. Some mid-tribulation rapture theorists also believe in a secret resurrection and catching up.

There are a few writings that fit into this less popular view, such as *The Pre-Wrath Rapture of the Church* by Marvin Rosenthal and *The Post-Trib, Pre-Wrath Rapture* by Roland Rasmussen. These books do not sell as well as those of the pre-trib genre. This is partly because they have come relatively lately, and partly because most Christians do not want to even consider the possibility that their faith may be tried by their having to go through a period of great tribulation on the earth.

POST-TRIBULATION RAPTURE THEORY

The post-tribulation rapture theory rests on the idea that the Rapture will not occur until the entire Great Tribulation period expires. Some split the Great Tribulation into two segments: tribulation on the earth and God's wrath on the earth. Some say the Great Tribulation period is prior to the wrath of God being poured out on the earth; some say it includes the wrath of God. This is the least popular of the rapture theories.

MULTIPLE RAPTURE THEORY

There are some who believe in multiple instances of the catching up of the saints—some at the beginning of a seven-year Great Tribulation period; some throughout that period; some at the end of that period.

As we progress we will see reasons to call into question the idea of a future seven-year Great Tribulation period. This will cause some consternation, but I ask the reader to be patient and not make any premature judgments.

4

MILLENNIAL THEORIES

The question most debated among those of differing eschatological theories is whether or not there will be a literal Millennial Kingdom that will last for 1,000 years, during which the Lord will dwell on the earth as He rules over the nations with a rod of iron. Without a millennial perspective to begin with, there would be no amillennialism or postmillenialism, which are responses to millennialism. Coupled with belief or unbelief in a literal Millennial Kingdom is when the Lord's return will occur. There are four basic millennial theories:

Premillenialism: Nearly all Rapture theories fall under the category of premillennialism—the belief that the Rapture will occur prior to the Lord's return to establish His one-thousand year reign on the earth (the Millennium).

Amillennialism: There will be no Rapture and no millennial reign of Christ on earth. The only thing to look forward to is the institution of the New Heavens and New Earth concurrent with Jesus' return. Some believe that the Millennium is allegorical, or that it is spiritual, of an undetermined length.

Postmillennialism: There is a Millennium, but the saints will not be resurrected/raptured until it is over because of one of the following understandings of the Millennium: 1) Jesus currently reigns from Heaven through His "Church" which will become victorious over the nations by gaining control over the seven spheres of society. At that time the Millennium (of indeterminate duration) will commence without Jesus present; 2) we are already in the Millennium, and Jesus is already reigning from Heaven through His "Church." So the Rapture, if there is one, must come at a later time.

Latter-Rain theory: This is a Pentecostal/charismatic theory that can be classified as postmillennial. It bears a more supernatural element and posits that certain "overcomers," by submitting themselves to a "new breed" of last-days apostles and prophets, will become perfected and immortalized, and will then rule the nations supernaturally while Jesus remains in Heaven. Once they have gained dominion they will "invite" Jesus to return and rule with them.

The last three theories—amillennialism, post-millennialism and Latter-Rain—fall under the umbrella of dominion theology. They are thoroughly examined in my book, _Vengeance Is Ours: The Church In Dominion._

Students of any eschatological position will find that the authors of those positions largely draw from one another. Certain interpretations of Scripture form the bases for those positions, and careful study reveals that they all emanate from specific theological presuppositions. In many cases the study of Scripture has been used to augment the theological presuppositions held by respected teachers from the recent past. It is my intent that this writing will be different.

5
A DIFFERENT ESCHATOLOGY

By far, the most prevalent works I have read or viewed over the years have been of the pre-tribulation secret rapture position, which I at one time held very strongly. In the early 1970s I contributed at least somewhat to Hal Lindsey's best-selling success, buying his *The Late, Great Planet Earth* by the dozens and handing them out to whoever would take them.

Around 1975 I realized that Scripture proved most of the pre-tribulation rapture positions untenable. Much of what pretribulation rapture authors have written is based on conjecture, the allegorizing of Scripture, and myth. For some time I avoided addressing the subject to any great degree in *Media Spotlight*. This is because I did not want my eschatological views to be a hindrance in reaching the brethren with other truths which I felt were of more importance. Of late, however, I have become concerned that the dispensationalist pre-trib position has become the "accepted wisdom" for most American Christians, while the preterist position is steadily increasing. These are virtually the only two views that have been propagated within the Christian media and publishing industry. Just as it is erroneously believed that if you are not a Calvinist you must be Arminian, so, too, it is believed that if you are not a preterist you must be a dispensationalist, or vice versa. It's either-or, with no other positions considered, let alone understood.

I find that when I speak to people of either persuasion they tend to cite the proof texts they learned from their favorite preterist or dispensationalist teachers. They don't seem willing to consider that there is a viable, biblical eschatology that sees both the truth and the errors in those two eschatological disciplines.

I do not identify my position among those currently in vogue. Once a label is attached, preconceived judgments arise in people's minds. Therefore, I will just say that what follows is my honest assessment of what Scripture says on the subject of last things.

Whatever your eschatological position, I ask only that you consider with an open mind what is written herein. Because of their great acceptance, the dispensationalist pre-trib rapture and preterist theories are the ones that I address the most. Although some proponents of both theories choose to separate themselves from those who disagree with them, I will not make this an issue of fellowship. I recognize that there are good brethren in Christ who hold differing eschatological positions.

I do believe a period of great tribulation is coming on the earth, but not in the same way traditional eschatological theories address it. Believe me, I would much rather see the Lord come for us before we have to suffer much on this planet. But that is my flesh speaking. While most see a period of tribulation as evil, Scripture reveals it as a blessing on two fronts: 1) it will purge the earth of the present world system by preparing it for judgment; 2) it will purify the corporate Body of Christ so that it will be ready to meet the Lord "without spot or wrinkle" when He comes. And there are special rewards for those saints who remain faithful during that time.

Because of the escapist mentality fomented by pre-trib teaching, many in the Body of Christ believe that worthiness is evidenced by lack of suffering—by not having to go through any great tribulation. Many have forgotten that the more we suffer for Christ, the more worthy we are considered. We are not worthy to escape anything. That is ungodly thinking. The apostles, having been beaten by the religious leaders for proclaiming the Gospel, rejoiced that they were considered worthy to suffer for Christ (Ac 5:41). Throughout the centuries and in many parts of the world today our brethren are suffering unimaginable persecution for their faith. But today's Christians—particularly in the West—largely desire not to suffer for Christ.

One reason for this is the infusion of psychology in the form of psychoanalysis and psychotherapy of varying degrees into Christian teaching and ministry. This psychological integration focuses on "felt needs" and self-fulfillment rather than on ministry to the soul from the Word of God.

Scripture is often misinterpreted and misapplied in order to justify ungodly advice. As a result, many Christians today are focused more on solving their problems than on surrendering to the Lord's will for their lives. They have forgotten Scripture's consistent admonition to die to self and live for Christ:

> I am crucified with Christ. Nevertheless I live. Yet not I, but Christ lives in me, and the life that I now live in the body I live by faith in the Son of God, who loved me and gave Himself for me. (Gal 2:20)

Man has an inflated self-image. He thinks he has within himself the power to overcome all that bothers his flesh. But his solutions more often than not result in hollow substitutions. Is he in an imperfect marriage? Divorce is okay; God understands. Is he plagued by aberrant sexual desires? God's Word can be conveniently convoluted to allow for "committed relationships" among those of the same gender. The list is endless.

Another problem that contributes to Christians not being willing to suffer is the misconception that some "Great Tribulation" is equated with the wrath of God. Crying that we are not appointed to wrath (1Th 5:9), the pre-trib proponents insist that we will not go through "the Great Tribulation."

As for preterism, I find little with which I agree, simply because so many of its proof texts are taken out of context and applied to the wrong time and/or the wrong people. Preterists do not understand the eschatological principle that prophetic history does not equate to human history. They see all prophetic events as taking place in an unbroken chronological sequence.

It is a sad truth that God's Word is not sought after for understanding as much as is the imagination of man. Man's imagination conjures many things, both good and evil, but it does not conjure life. Only God's Word and His Spirit give life. Let us be diligent in studying God's Word and in seeking to rightly divide it. To rightly divide God's Word relative to eschatology we must practice sound hermeneutics, placing events in their proper context and understanding the times to which they pertain. We must also understand the terms used in Scripture to delineate prophetic language.

As the reader progresses he will no doubt have questions. In due time most if not all those questions will be answered.

One concern is that brethren will read this book, understand the truths it conveys, then forget them by being swayed by the many voices that present the most popular eschatologies in other books, and on radio and television. My appeal is merely that you do your own research based on the evidence presented herein to either confirm or reject that evidence. In either case, you should be well equipped to test what you hear from all sides.

6

THE DAY OF YAHWEH

One term critical to understand is what Scripture refers to as "the Day of the Lord." Two other important terms are "the last days" and "the latter days." "The last day" and "the last days" are found eight times each; "the latter days" is found eleven times. Then there is "the Day of the Lord," used 31 times. Also, a few times the term "afterward" is used as a synonym for "the last day(s)," as are "that day," and "those days." All of these are often assumed to mean the very last days of the present age. However, these terms convey different meanings at different times throughout Scripture. One very important rule in discerning the meaning is to realize that "the Day of the Lord" does not mean a single day of 24 hours, but often refers to a span of time that could cover anywhere from several days to centuries. The context in which these terms are used must be considered.

THE DAY OF THE LORD

In most English translations of the Tanakh (the canonical books of the Hebrew Bible), the name of God (generally accepted as *Yahweh*) has been translated from the Hebrew as "the LORD." This has been done in deference to the Jewish practice of substituting the Tetragrammaton (the four Hebrew consonants that correspond to "YHWH") in place of the name *Yahweh* when copying the Hebrew Scriptures. Religious Jews believe that it is wrong to actually utter or even write the name of God. Justin Martyr, in his *1 Apology* alludes to the idea that the "ineffable name" of God, as the Jews call it, should not be uttered.[1] In the Tanakh the actual phrase in Hebrew is "the Day of YHWH."

"The Day of YHWH" is used to express God's visitation, usually in judgment either on Israel or on Israel's enemies, and on the world as a whole. These terms have more than one meaning for more than one time. For example, one prophecy which uses the term, "the Day of YHWH," but does not apply to the very last days, is that of Amos telling Israel not to desire the Day of YHWH, because when that day comes it will bring judgment on the house of Israel:

"Woe to you who desire the Day of YHWH! To what end is it for you? The Day of YHWH is darkness, and not light, as if a man fled from a lion, and a bear met him, or went into the house and leaned his hand on the wall, and a serpent bit him.

"Shall not the Day of YHWH be darkness, and not light—even very dark, and no brightness in it?

"I hate, I despise, your feast days, and I will not smell [the sacrifice] in your solemn assemblies....

"Therefore I will cause you to go into captivity beyond Damascus," says YHWH, whose name is "The God ['elohiym] of Hosts." (Am 5:18-27)

This was a prophecy of God's judgment on Israel through the Babylonian Captivity.

Another Scripture mistakenly applied to future times is Joel's prophecy regarding Babylonia's destruction of Jerusalem and the captivity (Joel 1:15-2:11). The latter part of this lamentation over Israel's judgment has been misunderstood as a yet future supernatural judgment on the nations:

"Blow the trumpet in Zion and sound an alarm in My holy mountain. Let all the inhabitants of the land tremble because the Day of YHWH comes, for it is near at hand—a day of darkness and of gloominess, a day of clouds and of thick darkness, as the morning spread upon the mountains.

"A great and strong people—there has never been the like, neither shall there be any more after it, even to the years of many generations.

---

[1] Justin Martyr, 1 Apology, 61-63, "For no one can utter the name of the ineffable God; and if any one dare to say that there is a name, he raves with a hopeless madness."... "And all the Jews even now teach that the nameless God spake to Moses."

"A fire devours before them, and behind them a flame burns. The land is as the Garden of Eden ahead of them, and behind them a desolate wilderness. Yes, and nothing shall escape them. Their appearance is like the appearance of horses, and they shall run like horsemen—like the noise of chariots on the tops of mountains they shall leap, like the noise of a flame of fire that devours the stubble, as a strong people arrayed for battle.

"Before their face the people shall be very pained; all faces shall gather blackness. They shall run like mighty men; they shall climb the wall like men of war, and they shall march every one on his way, and they shall not break their ranks:

"Neither will one thrust another; they will walk every one in his path, and when they fall upon the sword, they shall not be wounded.

"They shall run back and forth in the city; they shall run upon the wall; they shall climb up upon the houses; they shall enter in at the windows like a thief. The earth shall quake before them; the heavens shall tremble. The sun and the moon shall be dark, and the stars shall withdraw their shining. And YHWH shall utter His voice before His army, for His camp is very great. For He who executes His word is strong. For the Day of YHWH is great and very terrible, and who can abide it?" (Joel 2:1-11)

Some within the Latter-Rain Movement say this is God's army of last-days perfected (sinless, glorified) saints who will bring judgment on the nations—that this is an army of immortalized "overcomers" because of the exploits described. But this warning is clearly for Israel, not the nations. The wording is metaphor, even hyperbole, connoting the army's invincibility. Another explanation for the supernatural character of this army's abilities is that behind every nation and every army stands the spiritual beings that do God's bidding—that empower the earthly armies to conquer as He wills. Thus God refers to this force as "His army."

That these verses do not refer to immortalized Latter-Rain "overcomers" is revealed in the full context which clearly shows that these verses referred to Babylonia taking Israel captive. The subsequent verses are God's appeal to Israel to turn from its sins and be healed. Had the nation done so He would have blessed it as promised. But it didn't, and it went into captivity.

The following Scriptures are others that use the term "the Day of YHWH" in addressing judgment against ancient Israel: Lamentations 2:22; Ezekiel 13:5; Amos 5:1-6:14; Zephaniah 1:1-18.

Other Scriptures use the term, "the Day of YHWH" in prophecies against ancient Egypt: Jeremiah 46:10-13; Ezekiel 30:1-11.

Isaiah 13:1-22 uses "the Day of YHWH" in prophecies against ancient Babylonia.

The references to "the Day of YHWH" that pertain to the Lord's Second Coming are: Isaiah 1:12-21; 2:1-4; 34:1–35:10 (Millennium); Joel 2:15-32 (Also Pentecost—Ac 2:17-20); Obadiah 1:1-21 (Against Esau—Arabs); Zephaniah 2:1–3:20; Zechariah 14:1-21 (the Lord's Return/ Millennium); Mica 4:1-7; Malachi 4:5-6 (partially fulfilled with the Lord's first coming).

The term, "the Day of the Lord," is used by the apostles to address the Lord's Second Coming in 1 Corinthians 5:5; 2 Corinthians 1:14; 1 Thessalonians 5:2; 2 Peter 3:10; Revelation 1:10 (the Lord's Day).

THE LAST DAYS/THE LATTER DAYS

All mentions of "latter days" and "last days" in the writings of the prophets are translated from the Hebrew, *achariyth*. But they don't always mean the very last days. The word is often better translated "future," rather than "last days" or "latter days."

So there is no empirical evidence that every usage of "latter days" means the very last days. In view of what history tells us about certain prophecies, particularly in the Book of Daniel, we should translate *achariyth* as "future."

An example of "the last days" referring to a time other than the very last days is found in Genesis 49:1-28 where Jacob gives a prophecy of his sons' destinies as patriarchs of Israel's twelve tribes. The term "the last days" does not refer to the very last days because there is no prophecy here pertaining to either Israel or any other nation(s); it refers to the future of Jacob's sons.

Another example of "the last days" referring to a time other than the very last days of this age is found where the writer of Hebrews alludes to his own time:

> God, who at different times and in different ways spoke in past times to the fathers by the prophets, has in these last days spoken to us by His Son, whom He has appointed heir of all things, and by whom also He made the worlds. (Heb 1:1)

Peter applied the Pentecost experience to Joel's prophecy of the Holy Spirit being poured out in the last days (Joel 2:23-32):

> "But this is that which was spoken by the prophet Joel: 'And it shall come to pass in the last days,' says God, 'I will pour out from My Spirit upon all flesh, and your sons and your daughters shall

prophesy, and your young men shall see visions, and your old men shall dream dreams. And in those days I will pour out from My Spirit on My servants and on My handmaidens, and they shall prophesy. And I will show wonders in the heavens above, and signs in the earth beneath: blood, and fire, and vapor of smoke. The sun shall be turned into darkness, and the moon into blood, before that great and notable Day of the Lord comes.

"'And it shall come to pass that whoever will call on the name of the Lord shall be saved.'" (Ac 2:16-21)

Notice the synonymous meaning of "the last days," "those days," and "the Day of the Lord." Peter, as did Joel, relates "the last days" to both Pentecost and the "notable Day of the Lord," which infers the Lord's return. "The last days," in this context, have already spanned almost 2,000 years.

(Preterists would say that this "proves" that the Lord already returned spiritually immediately after A.D. 70, ruling out His physical return.)

Two prophets of ancient Israel who applied the term "the last days" to the very last days were Isaiah and Micah:

The word that Isaiah the son of Amoz saw concerning Judah and Jerusalem:

"And it shall come to pass in the last days, that the mountain of YHWH's house shall be established in the top of the mountains, and shall be exalted above the hills, and all nations shall come to it.

"And many people shall go and say, 'Come, and let us go up to the mountain of YHWH, to the house of the God of Jacob, and He will teach us of His ways, and we will walk in His paths.'

"For the Law shall go forth from Zion, and the Word of YHWH from Jerusalem. And He shall judge among the nations, and shall rebuke many people. And they shall beat their swords into plowshares, and their spears into pruning hooks. Nation shall not lift up sword against nation, neither shall they learn war anymore." (Isa 2:1-4)

"But in the last days it shall happen that the mountain of the house of YHWH shall be established in the top of the mountains, and it shall be exalted above the hills, and people shall come to it. And because the Law shall go forth from Zion, and the word of YHWH from Jerusalem, many nations shall come and say, 'Come, and let us go up to the mountain of YHWH, and to the house of the God of Jacob, and He will teach us of His ways, and we will walk in His paths.'

"And He shall judge among many people, and rebuke strong nations from far off, and they shall beat their swords into plowshares, and their spears into pruning hooks. Nation shall not lift up a sword against nation. Neither shall they learn war anymore. But every man will sit under his vine and under his fig tree, and no one shall make them afraid, for the mouth of YHWH of Hosts has said so. For all people will walk, everyone, in the name of his god, and we will walk in the name of YHWH our God forever and ever.

"In that day," says YHWH, "I will assemble her [Israel] who limps, and I will gather her who is driven out, and her whom I have afflicted. And I will make her who limped a remnant, and her who was cast far off a strong nation, and YHWH shall reign over them in Mount Zion from now on, even forever." (Mic 4:1-7)

These prophecies indicate a kingdom for Israel in the future. But is that true? Or are the preterists correct when they say that Israel lost that promise when she rejected her Messiah, and now the promises of an earth covered with righteousness is for "the Church" to establish?

We will consider these questions in later chapters.

Among the writings of the apostles, the Book of Hebrews equates "the last days" with the Lord's first coming, saying that God has spoken to us by His Son in these last days (Heb 1:1-2).

There are two apostolic writings in which the words "the last days" refer to the end of this age.

Paul warns of evil men who would enter into the assemblies of the saints:

Know this also, that in the last days perilous times will come, for men will be lovers of themselves, covetous, boasters, proud, blasphemers, disobedient to parents, unthankful, unholy, without natural affection, truce-breakers, false accusers, incontinent, fierce, despisers of those who are good, traitors, heady, high minded, lovers of pleasures more than lovers of God, having a form of godliness but denying its power. Turn away from such, because this is the kind who creep into houses and lead captive silly women laden with sins, led away with various lusts, always learning and never able to come to the knowledge of the truth. (2Ti 3:1-7)

Peter also warns of false brethren in "the last days":

I now write to you this second letter, beloved, both in which I stir up your pure minds by way of remembrance so that you may be mindful of the words that were spoken before by the holy prophets, and of the commandment from us, the apostles of the Lord and Savior, knowing this first: that in the last days there shall come scoffers, walking after their own lusts and saying, "Where is the promise of His coming? For since the fathers fell asleep all things continue as they were from the beginning of the creation." (2Pe 3:1-4)

(As preterism gains influence among believers in Jesus we see this Scripture being fulfilled.)

Of course, the infiltration of false brethren has been going on for the past 2,000 years. So we see that this agrees with Peter's assessment in Acts 2:17 that "the last days" spans more than a brief period of time.

One Scripture that speaks of the very last days is James 5:1-5 which warns the rich that their wealth is corrupted and they have gathered treasure for the last days. This applies not only to the very last days, but, pertaining to individuals, the last days of their lives. In truth, this latter application may be more fitting.

Now, there is a truth about events in Israel's history which point to future fulfillment as well as past fulfillment. The Tanakh is filled with "types," and "shadows" of the future. For example, in many ways David was a type or model of Jesus. And many events that transpired in Israel's history point to future fulfillment. But those who try to fit these and other such Scriptures exclusively into the very last days events are causing confusion. Understanding the eras to which these terms apply is essential to the study of eschatology. Otherwise we will find ourselves applying the wrong Scriptures to the times that yet lie ahead. For example, if we apply Scripture's use of "the last days" in every instance to mean the very last days when the Lord returns, we will erroneously look to the future for events that have already transpired, and the specific elements associated with those events will not be forthcoming. This will give a skewed misunderstanding of what yet lies ahead, and will create expectations of events that will not come to pass. This could severely hamper some brethren's faith.

If, on the other hand, we assign every mention of "the last days" to past history—as does preterism—we will get an equally skewed misunderstanding. In either case, we will be left unprepared for what will really happen. Unless we rightly divide the Word of Truth, understanding which events pertain to the past, and which pertain to the future, as well as which pertain to both, we will not comprehend the trials that await us. Nor will we be prepared for them. This is why the hermeneutic principle of "context" is essential to any study of eschatology.

We are to live godly in this world, expecting the Lord's return at the proper hour—that is, the hour the Father has in His hands, not the hour we *think* the Lord should return. There has occurred immense consternation and even loss of faith for many who believed they could predict the time of the Lord's return, and especially for those who followed their prognostications. And do not be mistaken; the time has been set by the Father from the beginning. There is no validity to the expression "if the Lord tarries" (or "delays") His coming:

> For just a little while, and He who shall come will come, and will not delay. (Heb 10:37)

Nor can we do anything to cause Him to return any the sooner. An unfortunate understanding of 2 Peter 3:12 has left some with the impression that we can "hasten" the Lord's return:

> ...looking for and hasting unto the coming of the day of God, wherein the heavens being on fire shall be dissolved, and the elements shall melt with fervent heat? (KJV)

Some modern English translations have changed the word "hasting" to "hastening," which is an error. The Greek *speudo* means to desire "haste"— to earnestly desire or look forward to.

Another vital rule of understanding prophecies that relate exclusively to Israel is to understand them in an unbroken line of continuity without interspersing human history. By this I mean that whatever transpires in the world not related to Israel (such as the "Time of the Gentiles") is not to be considered part of those prophecies exclusive to Israel. Therefore, if a prophecy exclusive to Israel relates two events that are separated by other events and/or time periods not germane to the prophecy, those two prophetic events may appear to immediately follow after each other when, in truth, they may be separated by centuries. To reiterate: prophetic history is not the same as human history.

An example of an element not germane to any prophecy related to Israel is "the Time of the Gentiles," which is not found in any prophetic Scriptures.

7

THE SECOND COMING

The subject of the Lord's Second Coming is essential to any eschatological study. The questions to be answered are: 1) Will Jesus return to the earth; 2) If so, will His return be physically, or is/was it spiritually; 3) what will transpire if/when He does return physically? These are critical questions to any study of eschatology.

WILL JESUS RETURN?

Let us first deal with the preterist idea that Jesus already "returned in glory" in A.D. 70, and that His return was manifested through the destruction of Jerusalem and the Jewish temple.

If, according to Daniel's prophecy, the sacrifices were taken away during the middle of the seventieth "seven," the Lord would not have returned until at least sometime in A.D. 73. But whether A.D. 70 or 73, most of the apostles would have still been alive. We should expect that they would have been taken up to meet the Lord. If not, we should expect that they would have recorded the Lord's return "in glory." Otherwise the canon of Scripture would be incomplete considering that the central theme of personal redemption rests on the resurrection and the Lord's Second Coming. How is it that the fulfillment of this central theme was not recorded by the apostles?

The Book of Revelation, written by the apostle John, places the resurrection and the Lord's return in the future. Preterists do not accept the generally recognized year of A.D. 96 for John writing the Revelation. They insist that it was written prior to A.D. 70, although they cannot say for certain when that would have been. For the sake of argument we will not use the Book of Revelation in considering whether or not the resurrection and the Lord's return are still future. Rather, we will point out that this same John, whose Gospel and three epistles were written around A.D. 90, makes no mention of the resurrection or the Lord's return having already occurred. He closes His Gospel with these words of Jesus to Peter:

"If I will that he waits until I come, what is that to you? Follow Me."

Then this saying went out among the brethren that that disciple would not die. Yet Jesus did not say to him, "He will not die," but, "If I will that he wait until I come, what is that to you?"

The disciple of whom John wrote was John himself, who lived well past A.D. 70 and wrote His Gospel around A.D. 90. Why did he qualify these words if he did indeed remain alive when the Lord came in A.D. 70? And why was he not taken to be with the Lord in A.D. 70 when the resurrection is alleged by preterists to have occurred?

There are no eye-witness accounts that attest to the resurrection or the Lord having come in A.D. 70 or any time since. There is no preterist "history" or even theory prior to the Jesuit Luis De Alcasar's 17th-century writing.

The central Scripture used by preterists to support their contention that Jesus has already returned is the Olivet Discourse in which Jesus was asked by His disciples, "Tell us, when shall these things be? And what shall be the sign of Your coming, and of the end of the age [*aion*]?"

Jesus warned of wars, rumors of wars, famines, pestilence, and earthquakes in diverse places. He warned of persecution and false prophets, as well as apostasy. He then addressed the abomination of desolation spoken of by Daniel. Finally, He said, "And this Gospel of the Kingdom shall be proclaimed in all the world as a witness to all nations. Then the end shall come."

Because of the abomination of desolation set up in the temple in A.D. 70, and other elements of Jesus' prophecy having been fulfilled, at least to some degree, preterists assume that the "end of the age" has already come. They couple these verses with Mark 13:30 which describes the Lord's Second Coming and relates His words, "Truly, I say to you that this generation [*genea*] shall not pass until all these things are done." Let us add also Mark 9:1: "And He said to them, 'Truly, I say to you that there are some of those who stand here, who will not taste of death till they have seen the Kingdom of God come with power.'"

Let us look at each of these:

Matthew 24:34 & Mark 13:30

The Greek word translated "generation" in both of these verses is *genea*, which can mean the period of time of a specific person's or people's lifetime. But it can also mean an age or time not specific to any particular person or people. One cannot be dogmatic to say that it must unequivocally mean the people living at that time. We are in the age when God is dealing with men's sins and calling out for Himself a people who will be sanctified for His use in this age and in the next. This age has not passed away. Now, it may be argued that we cannot be dogmatic that the word must mean the entire age prior to the New Heavens and New Earth, and that's fine for the sake of argument. But lacking any evidence that the Lord has returned, considering that all things continue as before, and that for the past 2,000 years "the Church" has largely been apostate, there is no evidence that the Lord is ruling from Heaven with a rod of iron. His judgment is not being realized.

Mark 9:1

This Scripture is a preterist favorite to "prove" that the Lord has already returned in glory:

> "Truly, I say to you that there are some of those standing here who will not taste of death till they have seen the Kingdom of God come with power."

There is nothing stated prior to this that would be similar to the warnings in Matthew 24 or in Mark 13. The prior verse, which ends chapter eight is, "Therefore, whoever is ashamed of Me and of My words in this adulterous and sinful generation, of him also shall the Son of Man be ashamed when He comes in the glory of His Father with the holy angels." Then follows 9:1: "And He said to them, 'Truly I say to you that there are some of those who stand here who will not taste of death until they have seen the Kingdom of God come with power.'" The following verses in chapter nine do not relate to these words.

It is assumed by preterists that 8:38 and 9:1, being connected by the Lord, is proof that some of those standing there would be alive when He returned. But let us look more closely at these two verses in their context.

First, He was not speaking of *His* coming with power (the Second Coming), but the Kingdom of God coming with power. Second, it was not unusual for the Lord to make a statement about one subject and then change the subject dramatically with His next words (at least as recorded in the Scriptures). This is a pattern in prophetic Scripture where several centuries of time are compressed into a few verses.

This is a critical truth, essential to understanding end-times prophecy. I will reiterate: **There is a difference between prophetic history and human history.** The events described in prophetic history do not always follow immediately upon one another, even when they seem unequivocally to do so as stated; they are detached from human history. We will see this in relation to the prophecies of Daniel and others as we progress.

Mark 8:38 followed upon the Lord encouraging His disciples to take up their cross and follow Him, contrasting them with those who would be ashamed of Him during this age.

There has been no evidence for the past 2,000 years that Jesus returned spiritually to rule the nations with a rod of iron, and certainly there is no evidence that He returned bodily. Nor did the apostles who wrote after A.D. 70 mention anything about the Lord having returned either bodily or spiritually, or about Him currently ruling from Heaven.

So what did Jesus mean when He said that some standing there would see the Kingdom of God come with power? The Kingdom of God came with power when the Lord was resurrected, and when the Holy Spirit fell on the believers during the following Pentecost. Recall the Lord's words when He met with His disciples after His resurrection:

> Therefore, when they came together they asked Him, saying, "Lord, will You again restore the kingdom to Israel now?"
>
> And He said to them, "It is not for you to know the times or the seasons which the Father has put in His own power. But **you shall receive power after the Holy Spirit has come upon you,** and you shall be My witnesses both in Jerusalem and in all Judea, and in Samaria, and to the uttermost part of the earth."
>
> And when He had said these things He was taken up while they looked, and a cloud received Him out of their sight. (Ac 1:6-8)

The power of the Kingdom of God of which Jesus spoke was the power of the Holy Spirit coming on those who believe in Jesus. It is a completely different context from His Second Coming.

What is most significant, however, are the verses that follow:

> And while they stared toward the heavens as He went up, look! Two men stood by them in white clothing, who also said, "You men

of Galilee, why do you stand gazing up into the heavens? This same Jesus, who is taken up from you into the heavens, shall so come in the same way as you have seen Him go into the heavens." (Ac 1:10-11)

HOW WILL JESUS RETURN?

This brings us to the question of whether Jesus' return, regardless when it would occur, would be physical or spiritual. The two men in white clothing were certainly angels or messengers of God. They stated clearly that the Lord's return would be in the same manner as He left. What manner was that?

The answer is clear:

The disciples saw Him rise into a cloud in the heavens (the sky) on His way to Heaven (the abode of God) to sit at the right hand of the Father. If the angels' words are to be believed, then Jesus must return in the same manner—physically in the clouds of the sky. This cannot be allegorized or spiritualized away. (One must wonder why believers in Jesus would not want to believe these clear words.)

There are three Scripture passages that describe the Lord's coming, and all three attest that He will come visibly and physically, not spiritually or in secret (read them very carefully):

Matthew 24:29-31:

"Immediately after the tribulation of those days the sun shall be darkened, and the moon shall not give her light, and the stars shall fall from the heavens, and the powers of the heavens shall be shaken. And then the sign of the Son of Man shall appear in the heavens, and then all the tribes of the earth will sorrow, and they will see the Son of Man coming in the clouds of the heavens with power and great glory. And He shall send His angels with a great sound of a trumpet, and they shall gather together His elect from the four winds—from one end of the heavens to the other."

Mark 13:24-27:

"But after that tribulation in those days, the sun shall be darkened, and the moon shall not give her light, and the stars of the heavens shall fall, and the powers that are in the heavens shall be shaken. And then they shall see the Son of Man coming in the clouds with great power and glory. And then He shall send His angels, and shall gather together His elect from the four winds—from the uttermost part of the earth to the uttermost part of the heavens."

Luke 21:20-27:

"And when you see Jerusalem encircled with armies, then know that its desolation is near. Then let those who are in Judea flee to the mountains, and let those who are in the midst of it get out, and do not let those who are in the country enter there. For these are the days of vengeance, so that all things that are written may be fulfilled.

"But woe to those who are with child, and to those who nurse in those days! For there shall be great distress in the land, and wrath upon this people. And they shall fall by the edge of the sword, and shall be led away captive into all nations, and Jerusalem shall be trodden down by the Gentiles until the Time of the Gentiles is ended.

"And there shall be signs in the sun, and in the moon, and in the stars, and distress of nations on the earth with perplexity—the sea and the waves roaring, men's hearts failing them for fear and for seeing those things that are coming on the earth. For the powers of the heavens shall be shaken. And then they shall see the Son of Man coming in a cloud with power and great glory.

Revelation 6:12-17:

And I saw when he had opened the sixth seal, and, look! There was a great earthquake! And the sun became black as sackcloth of hair, and the moon became like blood, and the stars of the heavens fell to the earth, even as a fig tree casts her unripe figs when she is shaken by a strong wind.

And the heavens departed like a scroll when it is rolled together, and every mountain and island were moved out of their places. And the kings of the earth, and the great men, and the rich men, and the chief captains, and the mighty men, and every slave, and every freeman, hid themselves in the dens and in the rocks of the mountains, and said to the mountains and rocks, "Fall on us and hide us from the face of Him who sits on the throne, and from the wrath of the Lamb, for the great day of His wrath has come, and who will be able to stand?"

It is very important to understand that Revelation 6:12-17 relates to these verses in Matthew, Mark and Luke. When has there been a time in history when all the tribes of the earth sorrowed when they saw the Son of Man coming in the clouds of the sky with power and great glory? These verses make it clear that His coming will be physically, and that all eyes will see

Him; it will not be spiritually in a manner that no one would see Him. Luke 21:24 makes it clear that the Lord will not return until the Time of the Gentiles has come to an end. The Time of the Gentiles is the current period during which Israel is blinded in part and God is calling out of all nations non-Israelites to be grafted into New Covenant Israel; this is the mystery of God that had been hidden from the foundation of the world:

> For brethren, I do not want you to be ignorant of this mystery lest you would be wise in your own conceits, that blindness in part has happened to Israel until the fullness of the Gentiles has come in. And so all Israel shall be saved, as it is written, "There shall come out of Zion the Deliverer, and He shall turn away ungodliness from Jacob, for this is My covenant with them, when I shall take away their sins."
>
> As concerning the Gospel, they are enemies for your sakes, but as touching the election, they are beloved for the Fathers' sake. For the gifts and calling of God are irrevocable. (Ro 11:25-29)

Preterism completely ignores these crucial Scriptures, not only in saying the Lord has already returned, but that He has abandoned Israel..

So we see that Jesus will not return until the Time of the Gentiles has come to an end, at which time He will turn to the salvation of all Israel living at that time. His Word states unequivocally that He has not abandoned Israel, but has allowed partial blindness to be on that nation in order that His grace would be extended to the Gentiles during this age.

Why was it necessary for Israel to be partially blinded in order for the Time of the Gentiles to be fully implemented? Couldn't the Lord simply allow Israel and the Gentiles to come into the Kingdom together?

There are two reasons: 1) the Jews among the early believers were prone to keep the Law for themselves, as well as force the Law onto the Gentiles. Even today we see how many so-called Messianic Jews gravitate to the Law and impose it on all who join their congregations. That had to be avoided; 2) the Gentiles would always be "second-class citizens, not only in the eyes of Jewish believers, but in their own eyes as well; 3) because the Jews rejected their Messiah, it was necessary that they be made jealous of His grace shed upon the Gentiles in order that they, too, might eventually believe.

WHEN WILL JESUS RETURN?

No one knows, and no one can know.

We've seen that the great tribulation on Israel of which Jesus spoke as recorded in Matthew 24 pertained to the destruction of Jerusalem in A.D. 70. The next event to follow is the Lord's return to gather His saints "from the uttermost part of the earth to the uttermost part of the heavens" (Mk 13:24-27). Jesus said that His people would be able to discern the time in general, giving the fig tree putting forth its leaves as an example of knowing when summer is near. But the example of the fig tree does not give us a set time. Nor is the fig tree representative of the modern state of Israel being established. (We'll address this in depth later.)

Jesus said that prior to His return the world would be as it was in the days of Noah and Lot. Luke's Gospel expands on Matthew's Gospel in that respect:

> "And as it was in the days of Noah, so it shall also be in the days of the Son of Man. They ate, they drank, they married wives, they were given in marriage, until the day that Noah entered into the ark, and the flood came and destroyed them all.

> "Likewise also, as it was in the days of Lot, they ate, they drank, they bought, they sold, they planted, they built. But the same day that Lot went out of Sodom it rained fire and brimstone from the heavens and destroyed them all." (Lk 17:26-29)

Just prior to this, the Lord said that no man knows the hour when all these things would be fulfilled and the Lord would return—not even the angels of Heaven—but the Father only.

The fate that befell Sodom will befall the entire world when the Lord returns. Evil abounded then, and it will abound again, only multiplied millions of times due to the increase in the world's population. Those evils will become so normal to humanity that the majority of people will accept them as a matter of course. Even now we see how sodomy, abortion, adultery and fornication are being championed in the media and endorsed by government in many ways. In the United States, many among the nominally Christian population, particularly among the young, support abortion and same-sex "marriage." As these evils continue to gain acceptance among more and more of the earth's populace, we should look for the Lord's return.

A warning: Do not listen to teachers who set dates for the Lord's return. Many Christians are being duped by such false teachers, and it seems as if there is always a market for them. It is no different than the false teachers who Jesus warned us would say, "Look! He is in the desert!" or "Look! He is in the secret chambers!"

Jesus warned us not to listen to them. Although evil will abound and world conditions will deteriorate greatly prior to His coming again, there will be no catastrophic event to warn that the Lord's return is imminent;

men will go about their daily business just as always, with no clue of the judgment about to come on them. Only true believers in Jesus will perceive that the Lord's return is near (1Th 5:4), although the actual day and hour will not be known:

> But you have no need that I write to you of the times and the seasons, brethren, for you yourselves know perfectly that the Day of the Lord comes like a thief in the night. For when they shall say, "Peace and safety," then sudden destruction comes on them as travail on a woman with child, and they shall not escape.
>
> But you, brethren, are not in darkness, that that day should overtake you like a thief. You are all the children of light, and the children of the day; we are not of the night, nor of darkness.
>
> Therefore let us not sleep as others do, but let us watch and be sober. (1Th 5:1-6)

Obviously, Paul did not experience the catching up of the living saints during his lifetime. Nor did any of the other apostles. History records that several died years after the Lord returned according to preterist reckoning. Are we to suppose that all those who died, including the apostles, were not worthy?

Although we cannot know the day or the hour of the Lord's return, there are two things that must transpire first:

> Now we beseech you, brethren, by the coming of our Lord Jesus Christ, and by our gathering together to Him, that you not be suddenly disturbed in mind, nor be troubled, either by spirit, or by word, or by letter as from us, that the Day of Christ is at hand. Let no man deceive you by any means, for that day shall not come until there first comes a falling away, and that man of sin is revealed—the son of perdition who opposes and exalts himself above all that is called God, or that is worshipped, so that he, as God, sits in the temple of God, showing himself that he is God. (2 Th 2:1-4)

The apostasy has continued since the first century, ebbing and flowing with resurgence of truth throughout the world. And there have been many anti-Christs or men of sin throughout history. But the greatest apostasy and the final man of sin must be revealed before the Lord returns (2Th 2:1-4).

Rather than trying to decipher Scripture to pinpoint the day of the Lord's return, let us be content that He is coming and that we will be with Him if we remain faithful.

WHAT WILL HAPPEN WHEN JESUS RETURNS?

To recap, there are a number of theories about what will transpire when Jesus returns. Some teachers say that He will come when the New Heavens and New Earth are established; there will be no interlude of time known as the Millennium between when He sets foot on the earth and when the cosmos is destroyed to make way for the new creation of God.

Others insist that He has already come, and that there is nothing for the future but the New Heaven and New Earth. Still others say that He will not come to the earth, but will gather His saints and take them immediately to Heaven, and from there He will rule over the nations with a rod of iron.

Still others teach that the Lord's Second Coming will be in two stages: First He will appear in the heavens to gather together His saints and will from there pour out His wrath on the remaining inhabitants of the earth; He will then return to the earth to establish His Millennial Kingdom. After the 1,000 years have expired God will melt the elements of the present creation and reform them into a new universe where sin will have no place.

We have seen that Matthew 24:29-31, Mark 13:24-27, and Revelation 6:12-17 tell of the same event—the Lord's Second Coming—in different ways.

Matthew 24:29-31 describes the sun being darkened, the moon not giving her light, the stars falling from the heavens, and the powers of the heavens being shaken. The Lord then appears like lightning shining from the east to the west, with power and great glory. All the tribes of the earth will sorrow when they see Him, and His angels will gather His chosen people from one end of the heavens to the other.

Mark 13:24-27 describes the sun being darkened, the moon not giving her light, the stars falling from the heavens, and the powers of the heavens being shaken. "Then they [mankind] will see the Son of Man coming in the clouds with great power and glory." Then He will send His angels to gather His chosen people from the farthest part of earth to the farthest part of the heavens.

Revelation 6:12-17 describes the same scenario. It adds that all mankind will call on the mountains and rocks to fall on them and to hide them from the wrath of the Lamb which is to come. Man will know that the Lord is about to pour out His wrath on the earth for its sins and for having persecuted His people.

Read all three of these scriptural passages together and you will see the broader picture. All three passages indicate that when the Lord appears it will be in His resurrected body so that all mankind will see Him and will be in fear of His wrath. Revelation places these events at the opening of the sixth seal in the book which only the Lion of the tribe of Judah (the Lamb of God) is found worthy to open (Rv 5:1-14).

Recall, also, Joel's prophecy:

"And it shall come to pass afterward, that I will pour out My Spirit on all flesh, and your sons and your daughters shall prophesy, your old men shall dream dreams, your young men shall see visions. And I will also pour out My Spirit on the servants and on the handmaids in those days, and I will show wonders in the heavens and in the earth: blood, and fire, and pillars of smoke. The sun shall be turned into darkness, and the moon into blood, before the great and the terrible Day of YHWH comes." (Joel 2:28-31)

Here is an example of prophetic history as opposed to human history: the day of Pentecost when the Holy Spirit was poured out on the disciples of Christ is separated by the Time of the Gentiles, at this point almost two millennia, from when the signs in the heavens heralding the Lord's return will be seen. Reading only Joel without the whole counsel of God's Word would easily leave people believing that all those events would transpire on the same "day." The reader would not understand that the "Day of YHWH" in this instance spans some two millennia, from Pentecost to the Lord's return.

We do not yet see the Lord on the earth, but still in the heavens.

Zechariah, however, describes what will occur when the Lord does return to the earth:

"Look! The Day of YHWH comes, and your spoil shall be divided in your midst, because I will gather all nations against Jerusalem to battle. And the city shall be taken, and the houses rifled, and the women ravished, and half of the city shall go forth into captivity, and the remnant of the people shall not be cut off from the city."

Then YHWH shall go forth and fight against those nations, as when He fought in the day of battle.

And in that day His feet shall stand on the Mount of Olives which is before Jerusalem on the east, and the Mount of Olives shall cleave in the middle thereof toward the east and toward the west, and there shall be a very great valley. And half of the mountain shall remove toward the north, and half of it toward the south.

And you shall flee to the valley of the mountains, for the valley of the mountains shall reach to Azal. Yes, you shall flee just as you fled from before the earthquake in the days of Uzziah king of Judah. And YHWH my God shall come (and all the saints with You).

> And it shall happen in that day, that the light shall not be clear, nor dark, but it shall be one day which shall be known to YHWH, not day, nor night. But it shall happen that at evening time it shall be light.
>
> And it shall be in that day, that living waters shall go out from Jerusalem, half of them toward the former sea, and half of them toward the hinder sea; it shall be in summer and in winter.
>
> And YHWH shall be king over all the earth. In that day there shall be one YHWH, and His name one.
>
> All the land shall be turned into a plain from Geba to Rimmon south of Jerusalem, and it shall be lifted up and inhabited in her place, from Benjamin's gate to the place of the first gate, to the corner gate, and from the tower of Hananeel to the king's winepresses.
>
> And men shall dwell in it, and there shall no longer be utter destruction, but Jerusalem shall be safely inhabited. (Zec 14:1-11)

This cannot be the destruction of Jerusalem in A.D. 70 because it describes a time when God will gather "all nations" against Jerusalem. Only Rome came against Jerusalem in A.D. 70. It also speaks of the Mount of Olives being split from east to west, of living water flowing from Jerusalem when Yahweh will be King over all the earth. Nothing in history or Scripture has ever transpired to fit this prophecy.

Some may argue that Rome had conquered the known world at that time, so, in a sense, Rome represented all the nations. But that would be a stretch at best. Besides, the armies of the Romans were not destroyed. The Lord did not deliver Jerusalem. Rather, Jerusalem was destroyed and the remnant of Israel were for the most part scattered throughout the nations. No peace came to Jerusalem from that battle, and Jerusalem has never been safely inhabited since that time.

The truth remains that the Mount of Olives is still intact. The language is too precise to be allegorical; it must be describing actual changes to the physical characteristics of the land.

This is clearly a messianic prophecy of the Lord's Second Coming, and it indicates that at that time Jerusalem will be attacked by all the nations united in a common cause.

8
THE PRESENT AGE

There are a number of Scriptures that some teachers have erroneously attributed to this present age, and specifically to the end of this age. These have to do largely with the Hebrew prophet Daniel's visions and encounters with heavenly beings who conveyed to him God's plan for the redemption of mankind in general, and Israel in particular, as well as the redemption of His entire creation.

I will remind the reader of what I said early on—that all prophecy in Scripture relates to the nation of Israel, particularly the prophecies given to and through the Hebrew prophets who wrote in the books that comprise the Tanakh—what most Christians commonly call "the Old Testament."

We will start with Daniel's interpretation of dreams experienced by Babylonia's King Nebuchadnezzar as found in chapter 2 of the Book of Daniel:

> And in the second year of the reign of Nebuchadnezzar, Nebuchadnezzar dreamed dreams by which his spirit was troubled, and his sleep left him. Then the king commanded to call the magicians, the astrologers, the sorcerers, and the Chaldeans, in order to show the king his dreams. So they came and stood before the king.
>
> And the king said to them, "I have dreamed a dream, and my spirit was troubled to know the dream."

Then the Chaldeans said to the king in Syriac, "O king, live forever! Tell your servants the dream, and we will show the interpretation."

The king answered and said to the Chaldeans, "The thing is gone from me. If you will not make known to me the dream with its interpretation, you shall be cut in pieces, and your houses shall be made a dunghill! But if you show the dream and its interpretation you will receive from me gifts and rewards and great honor. Therefore show me the dream and its interpretation!"

They answered again and said, "Let the king tell his servants the dream, and we will show the interpretation of it!"

The king answered and said, "I know for certain that you want to gain the time, because you see the thing has gone from me! But if you will not make known to me the dream, there is but one decree for you because you have prepared lying and corrupt words to speak to me till the time is changed! Therefore, tell me the dream, and I will know that you can show me its interpretation!"

The Chaldeans answered before the king and said, "There is not a man on earth that can show the king's matter! Therefore there is no king, lord, or ruler that asked such things of any magician, or astrologer, or Chaldean. And it is a rare thing that the king requires, and there is no one else who can show it to the king except the gods, whose dwelling is not with flesh!"

For this reason the king was angry and very furious, and commanded to destroy all the wise men of Babylon. And the decree went out that the wise men should be slain. And they sought Daniel and his fellows to be slain.

Then Daniel answered with counsel and wisdom to Arioch the captain of the king's guard that had gone out to slay the wise men of Babylon. He answered and said to Arioch the king's captain, "Why is the decree so hasty from the king?"

Then Arioch made the thing known to Daniel.

Then Daniel went in and asked of the king that he would give him time, and that he would show the king the interpretation.

Then Daniel went to his house and made the thing known to his companions, Hananiah, Mishael, and Azariah, that they would desire mercies of the God of Heaven concerning this secret so that Daniel and his fellows would not perish with the rest of the wise men of Babylon.

Then the secret was revealed to Daniel in a night vision. Then Daniel blessed the God of Heaven.

Daniel answered and said, "Blessed be the name of God forever and ever, for wisdom and might are His! And He changes the times and the seasons; He removes kings, and sets up kings; he gives wisdom to the wise, and knowledge to those who know understanding; He reveals the deep and secret things; He knows what is in the darkness, and the light dwells with Him. I thank You and praise You, O You God of my fathers, who has given me wisdom and power, and has made known to me now what we desired of You, for You have now made known to us the king's matter."

Therefore Daniel went in to Arioch, whom the king had appointed to destroy the wise men of Babylon. He went and said this to him: "Do not destroy the wise men of Babylon! Bring me in before the king and I will show the king the interpretation."

Then Arioch quickly brought Daniel in before the king and said this to him: "I have found a man from the captives of Judah who will make known to the king the interpretation."

The king answered and said to Daniel, whose name was Belteshazzar, "Are You able to make known to me the dream that I have seen, and its interpretation?"

Daniel answered in the presence of the king, and said, "The wise men, the astrologers, the magicians, the soothsayers, cannot show to the king the secret which the king has demanded. But there is a God in Heaven who reveals secrets, and makes known to the king Nebuchadnezzar what shall be in the latter days. Your dream and the visions of your head upon your bed, are these:

"As for you, O king, your thoughts came into your mind upon your bed, what would come to pass hereafter, and He who reveals secrets makes known to you what shall come to pass.

"But as for me, this secret is not revealed to me for any wisdom that I have more than anyone living, but that for their sakes the interpretation shall be made known to the king, and that you might know the thoughts of your heart.

"You, O king, saw, and, look, a great image! This great image, whose brightness was excellent, stood before you, and its form was fearsome. This image's head was of fine gold, his chest and his arms of silver, his belly and his thighs of brass, his legs of iron, his feet part of iron and part of clay.

"You looked until a stone was cut out without hands, which struck the image upon his feet that were of iron and clay, and broke them to pieces. Then the iron, the clay, the brass, the silver, and the gold was broken to pieces together, and became like the chaff of the summer threshing floors. And the wind carried them away so that no place was found for them. And the stone that struck the image became a great mountain and filled the whole earth. This is the dream, and we will tell its interpretation to the king.

"You, O king, are a king of kings, for the God of Heaven has given you a kingdom, power and strength, and glory. And wherever the children of men dwell, He has given into your hand the animals of the field and the fowls of the skies, and has made you ruler over them all. You are this head of gold.

"And after you there shall arise another kingdom inferior to you, and another third kingdom of brass which shall bear rule over all the earth. And the fourth kingdom shall be strong as iron, forasmuch as iron breaks in pieces and subdues all things. And like iron that breaks all these, it shall break in pieces and bruise.

"And whereas you saw the feet and toes, part of potters' clay, and part of iron, the kingdom shall be divided. But there shall be in it the strength of the iron, inasmuch as you saw the iron mixed with miry clay. And as the toes of the feet were part of iron, and part of clay, so the kingdom shall be partly strong, and partly broken. And whereas you saw iron mixed with miry clay, they shall mingle themselves with the seed of men, but they shall not adhere to one another, even as iron is not mixed with clay.

"And in the days of these kings the God of Heaven shall set up a Kingdom which shall never be destroyed. And the Kingdom shall not be left to other people, but it shall break in pieces and consume all these kingdoms, and it shall stand forever.

"Forasmuch as you saw that the stone was cut out of the mountain without hands, and that it broke in pieces the iron, the brass, the clay, the silver, and the gold, the great God has made known to the king what shall come to pass in the future. And the dream is certain, and its interpretation sure."

Then the king Nebuchadnezzar fell upon his face and gave homage to Daniel, and commanded that they should offer an oblation and sweet fragrances to him.

The king answered Daniel and said, "It is the truth that your God is a God of gods, and a Lord of kings, and a revealer of secrets, seeing you could reveal this secret."

Then the king made Daniel a great man, and gave him many great gifts, and made him ruler over the whole province of Babylon, and chief of the governors over all the wise men of Babylon.

Then Daniel requested of the king, and he set Shadrach, Meshach, and Abed-nego, over the affairs of the province of Babylon. But Daniel sat in the gate of the king.

At first glance this appears to have more to do with the world than with the nation of Israel. But we will see as we progress that all prophecy has from the beginning been centered on the Land of Promise given by God to Abraham and his natural descendants through Isaac and Jacob (Israel). History reveals the nations that succeeded Babylonia in their order, and each has fit the descriptions according to the quality of the elements within the image of Nebuchadnezzar's dream: Babylonia (The gold head suggests that Babylonia's culture and religion would form the basis for all others coming after it); Medo-Persia (The chest and arms of silver suggest wealth and strength, but not the wealth of Babylonia); Greece (the brass of which the belly and thighs are made is even more inferior, and nothing much is said about it other than it would rule over all the earth—that is, the known world which centered on the Promised Land. This was Alexander the Great's short-lived domain.); Rome (the iron legs connote great strength and military power. Rome was certainly known for these as with ruthlessness she ruled the nations for the longest period. The fourth kingdom, Rome, was divided between the east and the west, eventually to be conquered but remain dormant as its influences spread throughout the world.)

The final kingdom, represented by the feet and toes of iron and clay, is yet to rise; it will still be rooted in the Roman Empire, but will be mingled with the influences of other nations, particularly, it seems today, those which would adopt Islam as their religion. It will be divided and partly strong, having emerged from the Roman Empire [iron], and partly weak [the miry clay] because the people will not have a common heritage. This may well be a merged confederacy comprised of the West [Rome] and the Middle East [Islam] which mingles the strong and the weak into a homogenized supra-national government. However the final kingdom is formed, because iron and clay cannot mix sufficiently to hold together, and each nation will retain some semblance of its national identity, there will be constant conflict.

The great mountain that destroys the image is the Kingdom of Christ which will take over the nations on the Lord's return.

Here I would like to give space to an opposing view.

Some teach that the fourth kingdom, represented by the legs of iron, is the same as the feet and toes of iron and clay. This is based largely on the idea that because Babylon (the city to fall [Rv 18:2-10]) was ruled by the first three kingdoms, Babylonia, Persia and Greece, but not by Rome, then Rome does not fit into the equation. Therefore, Greece is the last world kingdom prior to the final world kingdom, and Rome has nothing to do with it.

I considered this, and dug deeper into the history of Babylon the city. It starts with the biblical prophecies of Babylon's eternal desolation:

> Look! I will stir up against them the Medes, who will not regard silver, and as for gold, they will not delight in it. Their bows also will dash the young men to pieces, and they will have no pity on the fruit of the womb; their eye shall not spare children.
>
> And Babylon, the glory of kingdoms, the beauty of the Chaldees' excellency, shall be as when God overthrew Sodom and Gomorrah. It shall never be inhabited; neither shall it be dwelt in from generation to generation; neither shall the Arabian pitch tent there; neither shall the shepherds make their fold there. But wild animals of the desert shall lie there, and their houses shall be full of howling creatures. And owls shall dwell there, and he-goats shall dance there. And the wild animals of the islands shall cry in their desolate houses, and serpents in their pleasant palaces. And her time is near to come, and her days shall not be prolonged. (Isa 13:17-22)

> Prepare against her the nations with the kings of the Medes, its captains, and all its rulers, and all the land of his dominion. And the land shall tremble and sorrow, for every purpose of YHWH shall be performed against Babylon, to make the land of Babylon a desolation without an inhabitant....
>
> Then you will say, "O YHWH, You have spoken against this place to cut it off, so that no one shall remain in it, neither man nor cattle, but that it shall be desolate forever."
>
> And it shall be, when you have made an end of reading this book, that you shall bind a stone to it, and cast it into the midst of Euphrates. And you shall say, "Thus shall Babylon sink, and shall not rise from the evil that I will bring upon her, and they shall be weary." Thus far are the words of Jeremiah. (Jer 51:28-64)

It is clear from these Scriptures that the prophecy of Babylon's eternal desolation would apply immediately after it was destroyed by the Medes and Persians. The Romans did conquer the land of Babylonia after defeating the Greeks, but all the Roman Trajan found were ruins of the ancient city.

From the time that the Medes and Persians destroyed the city of Babylon it has remained uninhabited—a wilderness. Its ruins were discovered and excavated in the early to mid-1800s, and in 1983 the late Iraqi dictator, Saddam Hussein, attempted to rebuild the city on top of the ruins. The U.S. invasion of Iraq put a stop to his grandiose plans to thwart God's Word, and today the city remains a ruin. Although it is a tourist attraction today, if Bible prophecy is true, then Babylon will never be rebuilt as a viable city.

Just because the Romans did not have control of the city doesn't mean the Roman Empire is not represented by the iron legs in Nebuchadnezzar's dream. Babylon was a ruin when Alexander conquered the Persians. He died in Babylonia (also sometimes called Babylon), but the city of Babylon was no more a viable conquest for the Greeks than it was for the Romans.

Another reason put forth for the idea that we are living in a Greek world is that the English language, deriving a large portion of its etymology from Greek, is the *lingua franca* of the earth.

So is the world today really a Greek world or a Roman world based on the etymology of English? Well, partly both, but mostly Roman. Western Civilization, whose influence over the entire earth is palpable, grew from out of the Roman Empire. Latin forms the basis for the language of all the significant elements of science, commerce and jurisprudence. The medical and other scientific communities communicate in Latin, as does the legal system. Virtually all mottos and slogans of governments and commerce are in Latin. And although university fraternities still use Greek for their names in honor of the origins of the university, virtually all mottos over university portals are in Latin.

Samplings of English words by various etymologists have demonstrated that Latin far outstrips Greek as their origins, with Germanic languages being second, and French (which derived from Latin) being third.

Using the *Online Etymology Dictionary*, my own random sampling for Latin vs. Greek origins (without regard to Germanic and French) came out to 79% Latin and 21% Greek. This surprised even me. I thought it would be about even. But English derives far more from Latin than from Greek. Rome took from Greece, true, but in terms of earthly nations succeeding each other, Rome remains the nation identified in Nebuchadnezzar's dream image as following after Greece.

Some believe that the fourth nation is not Rome but Islam. Yet Islam did not remove Greece; Rome did. There is little doubt, however, that Islam will be among the most formidable forces on earth from this point on. Yet the West still has the military and economic strength to continue as the world's foremost power. By my reckoning Islam and Western apostatized Christianity will be the major spiritual elements in the feet and toes of the final kingdom. Islam's aspiration is global conquest, which will further meld different elements of humanity into one homogenous group. Yet there is no denying that the vestiges of the Roman Empire still exist in Western Civilization, and that the Holy Roman Empire maintains much political and religious strength through the sovereign state of the Vatican. Rome was divided into ten kingdoms (the ten toes), and has maintained the greatest presence in the earth by way of its commerce, science, technology, arts, jurisprudence and military might among the Western nations.

Evidence of the fourth empire being Rome lies in Daniel 7:1-27. There we see that the fourth kingdom alone has the ten horns that represent ten rulers over the empire. Details that indicate this to be Rome (with the names of the rulers) are found in chapter eight (pp. 275-280).

Certainly Rome does indeed wield the greatest cultural influence over the West, and has spread throughout the world through Western colonization. All that remains is for the final Roman/Islamic Empire to come to fruition.

Now there is an extremely important point regarding this prophecy: all these major world powers have related to the Promised Land—and to Jerusalem in particular—in ways that other world empires have not. This is why they, and not other world powers, are found in Nebuchadnezzar's dream. We know about the dynasties of the East, particularly that of China, which have impacted world history; we also know of the empires of the Americas that existed thousands of years ago. Yet none of these are mentioned in Scripture. Nor is the United States of America—unarguably the greatest economic, political and military power ever seen on earth. Only those nations that have conquered, or will conquer, Jerusalem are mentioned in Nebuchadnezzar's dream.

Jerusalem has been the focal point of all empires that surround it from the four principle points of the compass, beginning with Egypt and ending with Rome. The final empire, which appears to be a homogenous empire comprised mainly of Western European and Middle Eastern nations (both of which comprised the ancient Roman Empire), has yet to come to full manifestation. At the time of this writing we are seeing only its beginnings.

9

JACOB'S TROUBLE

After the Body of Christ is caught up to meet the Lord in the air there will begin a time of great tribulation on the nation of Israel. This is not the same as the tribulation that will come on the saints under the anti-Christ, but will be the fulfillment of Daniel's seventieth seven—the second three-and-one-half year period of time that will close out the Lord's dealing with Israel.

After describing in the opening of the sixth seal the Lord's appearing to receive the Body of Christ to Himself (Rv 6:12-17), the Book of Revelation turns its attention to the nation of Israel and begins to address the time referred to in Jeremiah 30:7-9 as "Jacob's Trouble":

> "Alas! For that day is great, so that none is like it! It is the time of Jacob's Trouble, but he shall be saved out of it. For it shall come to pass in that day," says YHWH of Hosts, "that I will break his yoke from off your neck, and will burst your bonds, and strangers shall no longer enslave him. But they shall serve YHWH their God, and David their king, whom I will raise up to them."

This obviously speaks of the ultimate deliverance of Israel from her enemies, and foretells the resurrection of David to sit again on his throne in Jerusalem.

But what about the "great tribulation" spoken of by Jesus that befell Jerusalem in A.D. 70? Jesus said that there had never been a day like it, nor would there ever be again. How could Jesus and Jeremiah be describing the same thing if they are separated by so many centuries?

Again, prophetic history must be considered. The first three-and-one-half years of Jacob's Trouble occurred during the First Jewish-Roman War led by Vespasian and Titus, which lasted three-and-one-half years. (A more detailed account is found in chapter 13, "Understanding the Prophecies"— specifically pages 146-150); the second three-and-one-half years will be fulfilled under the coming anti-Christ. Each event marks one half of the seventieth seven of Daniel's prophecy; they are separated by the Time of the Gentiles. It is after the first half of Daniel's seventieth seven that Jesus said He would return immediately to gather His saints (Mt 24:29-31). The context in which He spoke was the destruction of the temple in which He stood at that time.

What about the word "immediately"? If He said He would come "immediately after the tribulation of those days" (the first half of Daniel's seventieth seven), must not the preterists be correct in saying He already returned, albeit spiritually?

Yet again, prophetic history comes into play. The Time of the Gentiles is never considered in Hebrew prophecy because it was still a mystery hidden in God, to be revealed only after the Lord's ascension and His pouring out of the Holy Spirit on all flesh, Jew and Gentile. So according to prophetic history, when the Time of the Gentiles has come to an end the Lord's return to gather His saints in the air will indeed be immediate to the closing of the first half of Daniel's seventieth seven. He will later set foot on the earth when He delivers Israel at the end of the second half of Daniel's seventieth "seven."

The Lord's Second Coming will be in two stages: first to gather His saints at the resurrection; second to set foot on the earth in the conquest of the nations and to establish His millennial reign. So His actual return to set foot on the earth is only one coming, not two.

His prophecy also has two stages: 1) the destruction of the temple in A.D. 70; 2) His return to deliver Israel at the end of the second half of Daniel's seventieth seven. The Lord's deliverance of Jerusalem will not be in a single day. Jacob's Trouble was suspended after A.D. 70, to be resumed at a later time. That coming time will be after the Body of Christ is caught up to meet the Lord, and prior to the Lord completing His deliverance of Israel:

"For, look! The days come," says YHWH, "that I will bring again from the captivity of My people Israel and Judah," says YHWH, "and I will cause them to return to the land that I gave to their fathers, and they shall possess it."

And these are the words that YHWH spoke concerning Israel and concerning Judah.

For YHWH says this: "We have heard a voice of trembling, of fear, and not of peace. You ask now, and see if a man bears a child. Why do I see every man with his hands on his loins like a woman in travail, and all faces are turned into paleness?

"Alas! For that day is great, so that none is like it; it is the time of Jacob's Trouble, but he shall be saved out of it. For it shall happen in that day," says YHWH of Hosts, "that I will break his yoke from off your neck and will burst your bonds, and aliens shall no longer enslave him." (Jer 30:3-8)

Israel was not saved out of the Roman siege, nor out of the Babylonian or Assyrian sieges. Yet this Scripture says that "in that day"—the day Israel is in the Promised Land again—God will no longer allow aliens to rule over His people. These verses are a prophecy for the future—a time when Israel will be in the Promised Land and threatened by her enemies.

Why is this time called "Jacob's Trouble" and not "Israel's Trouble"?

"Jacob" means "supplanter"—one who usurps the place of another. Jacob took Esau's birthright through trickery. When God changed Jacob's name to Israel He was calling him "Prince with God" or "Power with God."

When the nation of Israel is rebellious it is often called "Jacob" in Scripture, sometimes interchangeably with "Israel." When it is at peace with God and obedient it is primarily called "Israel," but also interchangeably with "Jacob." Israel has always been a mixture of obedience and rebellion; there have always been faithful Israelites within the nation even at its most rebellious, and unfaithful Israelites when the nation is most obedient. As it was in A.D. 70, in these last days Israel remains exceedingly rebellious. This most likely is why God calls their time of great tribulation, "Jacob's Trouble."

Scripture indicates that the second half of Jacob's Trouble will begin with the removal of the saints to meet the Lord in the air and the subsequent pouring out of God's wrath on the earth—particularly on the realm of the last-days anti-Christ. According to the Book of Revelation this remaining time of Jacob's Trouble will last three-and-one-half years, just as did the first half:

And there appeared a great wonder in the heavens: a woman clothed with the sun, and the moon under her feet, and on her head a crown of twelve stars. And being with child she cried out, travailing in birth, and in pain to be delivered.

And there appeared another wonder in the heavens, and look! A great red dragon having seven heads and ten horns, and seven crowns on his heads. And his tail drew the third part of the stars of the heavens and cast them to the earth. And the dragon stood before the woman who was ready to be delivered in order to devour her child as soon as it was born.

And she brought forth a man child who was to rule all nations with a rod of iron, and her child was caught up to God, and to His throne.

And the woman fled into the wilderness where she has a place prepared by God so that they should feed her there a thousand two hundred and sixty days [three-and-one-half years].

And there was war in Heaven. Michael and his angels fought against the dragon. And the dragon fought, and his angels, and did not prevail; neither was their place found any more in Heaven.

And the great dragon was cast out—that old serpent, called "the Devil," and "Satan," who deceives the whole world; he was cast out into the earth, and his angels were cast out with him.

And I heard in Heaven a loud voice saying, "Now has come salvation, and strength, and the Kingdom of our God, and the power of His Christ, for the accuser of our brethren is cast down, who accused them before our God day and night. And they overcame him by the blood of the Lamb, and by the word of their testimony, and they did not love their lives even unto the death.

"Therefore, rejoice you heavens, and you who dwell in them. Woe to those who inhabit the earth and the sea! For the Devil has come down to you having great wrath, because he knows that he has but a short time."

And when the dragon saw that he was cast to the earth he persecuted the woman who brought forth the man child. And two wings of a great eagle were given to the woman so that she might fly into the wilderness, into her place, where she is nourished for a time, and times, and half a time [three-and-one-half years] from the face of the serpent.

And the serpent cast out of his mouth water like a flood after the woman so that he might cause her to be carried away by the flood. And the earth helped the woman, and the earth opened her mouth and swallowed up the flood that the dragon cast out of his mouth.

And the dragon was angry with the woman, and went to make war with the remnant of her seed who keep the commandments of God, and have the testimony of Jesus Christ. (Rv 12:1-17)

Some believe the woman is "the Church," but this vision is for the time of Jacob's Trouble; the Body of Christ has already been caught up to meet the Lord in the air (Rv 6:12-17; Mt 24:29-31; Mk 13:24-27; Lk 12:24-28). Luke places the catching away of the saints in Christ at the end of the Time of the Gentiles (Lk 20:21-27).

Another reason to believe that the woman is Israel is the description of the remnant who keep the commandments of God and have the testimony of Jesus Christ. The Body of Christ today does not keep the commandments of God—the Mosaic Law. But the Jews who will live after the Body of Christ is taken out will keep those commandments, yet also have the testimony of Jesus Christ. They will believe in Him on seeing Him.

We don't yet know the particulars of this prophecy that relate how the earth will open and swallow the "flood" or armies of the anti-Christ acting under Satan's (the dragon's) direction. But the woman is Israel as described in Joseph's dream in Genesis 37:9-10:

And he dreamed yet another dream, and told it to his brothers, and said, "Look, I have dreamed another dream. And, look! The sun and the moon and the eleven stars made obeisance to me."

And he told it to his father, and to his brothers. And his father rebuked him, and said to him, "What is this dream that you have dreamed? Shall I and your mother and your brothers indeed come to bow down ourselves to you to the earth?"

Jacob interpreted Joseph's dream to mean that the sun (Jacob), the Moon (Rachel), and the eleven stars (Jacob's other sons) would one day bow before Joseph. This was fulfilled after Joseph was sold into slavery by his brothers, later to rise to become second only to Pharaoh in Egypt. A distinction is that in Joseph's dream there were eleven stars, whereas in John's revelation there are twelve stars, which would include Joseph. The woman was not in Joseph's dream because she (the nation) had not yet come into existence. In Revelation the woman represents the nation—not the man,

Israel—which was born as the twelve stars. Only women give birth, so Israel is represented by a woman, not a man.

Although there is a great difference between modern Israel in unbelief, and the coming kingdom of Israel under the Messiah, it was necessary that the modern state of Israel come into existence as a prelude to the Lord's return. It is not the fulfillment of the gathering of Israel into the Promised Land from out of the Diaspora; it is merely a prelude to that final event, but its birth as a nation is significant. Even before modern Israel was born, its enemies mobilized to destroy it. Vastly outnumbered and lacking support from any other nation, Israel was supernaturally helped by God to destroy her enemies' forces.

Considering the rule for prophetic history which allows for spans of time, might John have seen that event, then wrote of events to follow? Israel was about to be reborn in part when threatened with destruction.

Regardless whether or not the birth of Israel in 1948 was what John saw, the battle for the nation's survival has continued unabated since that time. It will culminate three-and-one-half years after the Lord appears in the sky to gather His elect from the earth at the resurrection.

During that time there will be huge numbers of conversions among the Jews after they have seen their Messiah:

"The burden of the Word of YHWH for Israel," says YHWH, who stretches out the heavens, and lays the foundation of the earth, and forms the spirit of man within him.

"Look! I will make Jerusalem a cup of trembling to all the people around when they shall be in the siege both against Judah and against Jerusalem. And in that day I will make Jerusalem a burdensome stone for all people. All who burden themselves with it shall be cut in pieces, although all the people of the earth are gathered together against it.

"In that day," says YHWH, "I will strike every horse with astonishment, and his rider with madness, and I will open My eyes upon the house of Judah, and will strike every horse of the people with blindness.

"And the governors of Judah shall say in their hearts, 'The inhabitants of Jerusalem shall be my strength in YHWH of Hosts,' their God.

"In that day I will make the governors of Judah like a hearth of fire among the wood, and like a torch of fire in a sheaf, and they shall devour all the people around them, on the right hand and on the left.

And Jerusalem shall be inhabited again in her own place, even in Jerusalem.

"YHWH shall also save the tents of Judah first, so that the glory of the house of David and the glory of the inhabitants of Jerusalem do not magnify themselves against Judah.

"In that day YHWH shall defend the inhabitants of Jerusalem, and he who is feeble among them in that day shall be like David, and the house of David shall be like God—like the angel of YHWH before them.

"And it shall happen in that day, that I will seek to destroy all the nations that come against Jerusalem.

"And I will pour upon the house of David, and upon the inhabitants of Jerusalem, the spirit of grace and of supplications, and they shall look upon Me whom they have pierced, and they shall mourn for Him like one mourns for his only son, and shall be in bitterness for Him, like one who is in bitterness for his firstborn.

"In that day there will be a great mourning in Jerusalem, like the mourning of Hadadrimmon in the valley of Megiddon. And the land shall mourn, every family apart; the family of the house of David apart, and their wives apart; the family of the house of Nathan apart, and their wives apart; the family of the house of Levi apart, and their wives apart; the family of Shimei apart, and their wives apart; all the families that remain, every family apart, and their wives apart." (Zec 12:1-14)

These verses are further proof that the Lord's return will not be in secret, but all mankind will see Him coming in the clouds. The Jews will look on Him whom they pierced, and they will mourn; they will return to keeping the commandments of God, and will add to that their testimony of Jesus as their Messiah. Israel's deliverance from this trial is also proof that this is yet future. Every previous siege against Jerusalem has resulted in that city's destruction, not in the destruction of those who came against her. In this final siege, Israel in particular will mourn for having rejected her Messiah for all the years since He first came to the earth as Jesus of Nazareth. But at the end of the three-and-one-half years they will also defend themselves at the last with the Lord's help.

It appears as if the Lord will return to deliver Israel at a time when Jerusalem is attacked by all the nations of the earth. But before He does, there will be Jacob's Trouble, the three-and-one-half years when Israel will suffer greatly. During that time there will be chosen by God 144,000

Israelites represented by the man child in John's revelation. The man child is made up of Israelites, not Gentiles. All believers in Jesus will have been caught up to meet Him prior to this as the Lord is seen coming in the clouds to pour out his wrath on the earth (Rv 6:12-17; Mt 24:29-31; Mk 13:24-27; Lk 12:24-28). What follows is this:

> And after these things I saw four angels standing on the four corners of the earth, holding the four winds of the earth, so that the wind should not blow on the earth, nor on the sea, nor on any tree.
>
> And I saw another angel ascending from the east, having the seal of the living God. And he cried out with a loud voice to the four angels to whom it was given to hurt the earth and the sea, saying, "Do not hurt the earth, or the sea, or the trees till we have sealed the servants of our God in their foreheads."
>
> And I heard the number of those who were sealed. And there were sealed a hundred and forty-four thousand of all the tribes of the children of Israel. (Rv 7:1-4)

These 144,000 are comprised of 12,000 from each of the twelve tribes of Israel, proving that they are true Israelites. There is no scriptural or historical evidence to suggest otherwise.

These 144,000 Israelites will be caught up to the Lord before they can be destroyed by the anti-Christ: "And she brought forth a man child who was to rule all nations with a rod of iron, and her child was caught up to God, and to His throne" (Rv 12:5).

Some believe, or at least question, if these two mentions of the 144,000 are referring to the same people, but there is no reason to suggest that they are speaking of two different companies of 144,000 souls.

Notice that all the promises of deliverance also speak of a time afterward in which Israel will dwell in the land safely after having been gathered from the nations. That time, commonly referred to as "The Millennium," has been called into question by many over the centuries. It is paramount to any eschatological study that the issue of the Millennium be addressed, simply because of its being central to the beliefs of many Christians. But before we address the Millennium, we must first study the Scriptures that relate to the Eternal Age, generally believed to encompass the New Heavens and the New Earth. Then we will see if there are other Scriptures that speak of an age other than the present age and the Eternal Age. And if so, what will it be like?

10

THE ETERNAL AGE

In contrast to this present age, Scripture reveals a future of eternal peace and joy in the presence of our Father God and His Son. What, exactly, is in store for us during that eternal state? To hear most preachers in the pulpits and in the Christian media tell it, the Eternal Age will be characterized by Christians living in Heaven, blissful and content, generally at rest and/or eternally praising God. But what does Scripture say?

THE NEW HEAVENS AND THE NEW EARTH

We are told that the Eternal Age will not be one of the spirit only, but of a new physical reality called "the New Heavens and the New Earth." Were the Scriptures to speak of a "New Heaven" alone, one might surmise that it would be addressing only the abode of God. But they speak of New Heavens (the starry realm) and a New Earth (the planet on which we live). These New Heavens and New Earth will be eternal:

"For, look! I create New Heavens and a New Earth, and the former shall not be remembered, nor come into mind." (Isa 65:17)

"For as the New Heavens and the New Earth, which I will make, shall remain before Me," says YHWH, so shall your seed and your name remain." (Isa 66:22)

Nevertheless, according to His promise we look for New Heavens and a New Earth, wherein dwells righteousness. (2Pe 3:13)

The Revelation given to John gives a bit more detail when he is allowed to see the Bride of Christ, the New Jerusalem, come to the earth from Heaven:

And I saw New Heavens and a New Earth, for the first heavens and the first earth were passed away, and there was no more sea.

And I, John, saw the holy city, New Jerusalem, coming down from God out of Heaven, prepared as a bride adorned for her husband. And I heard a great voice out of Heaven saying, "Look! The tabernacle of God is with men, and He will dwell with them, and they shall be His people, and God Himself shall be with them, and be their God.

And God shall wipe away all tears from their eyes, and there shall be no more death, nor sorrow, nor crying, nor shall there be any more pain, for the former things are passed away.

And He who sat on the throne said, "Look! I make all things new!"

And He said to me, "Write, for these words are true and faithful."

And He said to me, "It is done. I am Alpha and Omega, the Beginning and the End. To him who is thirsty I will give from the fountain of the water of life freely. He who overcomes shall inherit all things, and I will be his God, and he shall be My son." (Rv 21:1-7)

No more death, no more sorrow, no more crying, no more pain. Obviously the Eternal Age will not experience warfare or strife of any kind, but will be a time of peace and joy.

And if Heaven is to be our eternal abode, why then is there going to be a New Earth? That's just it; Heaven is not our eternal abode—the New Earth will be our eternal abode, and our Father God will move His tabernacle (His dwelling place) to the New Earth with the New Jerusalem—the heavenly city.

Why the need for the New Heavens and New Earth? Because the present creation has become corrupted through the sin of Satan and the pollution of mankind. The universe, as beautiful as it appears to man's eyes, is in a state of decay and chaos. When we look through our powerful telescopes we see evidence of Satan's fall: exploding stars, colliding galaxies, super novae, black holes. They are beautiful to behold from the distance of billions of light years, but they are like fireworks on a vastly grander scale. Fireworks rocket into the sky, explode, and fall in ashes into darkness. So, too, our universe is exploding and burning into ashes of darkness.

On a lesser scale we see the result of man's sins on the condition of the earth. Man's science and technology has contributed much to the destruction of our ecosystem. Pollution is destroying fragile life in our seas; forests are suffering from the effects of acid rain and other pollution spewed out by man's manufacturing processes. Plastics and atomic waste will be around for hundreds—even thousands—of years, clogging our ecosystem.

Am I some radical environmentalist fearful that mankind will destroy the planet? Of course not. Before that can happen the Lord will intervene. But were He not to intervene, then yes, it could happen. I have no affinity with radical environmentalist groups, yet there is a reason for me to point out these things. It is to bring understanding as to why it will be necessary for God to destroy utterly every aspect of the current creation and start anew. To accomplish this will take "fervent heat" of an intensity only God is capable of employing:

> But the present heavens and the earth are reserved by the same Word, held fast for fire for the day of judgment and the damnation of ungodly men.

> But, beloved, do not be ignorant of this one thing: that with the Lord one day is as a thousand years, and a thousand years as one day. The Lord is not slack concerning his promise (as some men count slackness) but is patient toward us, not willing that any would perish, but that all would come to repentance.

> But the Day of the Lord will come as a thief in the night, in which the heavens shall pass away with a great noise, and the elements shall melt with fervent heat, the earth also and the works that are in it shall be burned up.

> Seeing then that all these things shall be dissolved, what manner of persons ought you be in all holy conduct and godliness, looking for and eagerly awaiting the coming of the Day of God, wherein the heavens, being on fire, shall be dissolved, and the elements shall melt with fervent heat?

> Nevertheless, according to His promise we look for New Heavens and a New Earth wherein dwells righteousness.

> Therefore, beloved, seeing that you look for such things, be diligent so that you may be found by Him in peace, without spot, and blameless. And account that the patience of our Lord is salvation, even as our beloved brother Paul also, according to the wisdom given to him has written to you, as also in all his letters, speaking in them of these things—in which are some things hard to be understood— which they who are unlearned and unstable pervert, as they do also the other Scriptures, to their own destruction.

You, therefore, beloved, seeing you know these things before, beware lest you also, being led away with the error of the wicked, fall from your own steadfastness. But grow in grace and in the knowledge of our Lord and Savior Jesus Christ.

To him be glory both now and forever. Amen. (2Pe 7:18)

Thus we know that the elements will melt, and out of this the Lord will fashion New Heavens and a New Earth. The elements God created cannot be annihilated (except by Him); they are eternal. But they can be changed and re-formed into something new and better. It is this new and better earth that we look forward to—a New Earth to which God will move His abode from the present Heaven. And we will live in eternal peace.

Again: "God shall wipe away all tears from their eyes, and there shall be no more death, nor sorrow, nor crying, nor shall there be any more pain, for the former things are passed away."

If there are none of these, then there will be no warfare. Keep these things in mind as we consider now whether or not there will be an age interim to the present age and the Eternal Age. For if Scripture speaks of a time where there is still death, sorrow, and other unhappy circumstances, then it cannot be speaking of the Eternal Age. If it speaks of the Lord ruling with a rod of iron over the nations of the earth after the resurrection, it cannot be speaking of the present age. And there are far too many Scriptures that describe just such a time that does not fit into either the present age or the Eternal Age.

11
THE MILLENNIUM

When believers in Jesus speak of "the Millennium" they are referring to a one-thousand year period that will transpire between the present age and the Eternal Age of the New Heavens and New Earth. Even amillinnialists and postmillinialists use the word in their attempts to refute belief in it. The belief that the resurrection will occur prior to that literal 1,000-year reign is known as "premillenialism."

Just as the question of the Lord's Second Coming is essential to any eschatological study, so, too, is the subject of the Millennial Kingdom: 1) Will the Lord establish a Millennial Kingdom on the earth; 2) when will/did this transpire; 3) what form will the Kingdom take; 4) will Israel have a part in the Kingdom; 5) how long will the Kingdom last; 6) what will transpire during the Millennium?

We will address all these questions and more in this chapter.

The word "millennium" means "thousand." It refers to any 1,000-year time period. For example, the year 2001 marked the beginning of the third millennium A.D. Theologically, "Millennium" refers to the thousand-year reign of Jesus Christ on the earth as revealed in Revelation 20:1-7:

> And I saw an angel come down from Heaven, having the key of the abyss and a great chain in his hand. And he laid hold on the dragon—that old serpent, which is the Devil, and Satan—and bound

him for a thousand years, and cast him into the abyss, and shut him up, and set a seal on him so that he could no longer deceive the nations till the thousand years should be fulfilled. And after that he must be loosed a little season.

And I saw thrones, and they sat on them, and judgment was given to them. And I saw the souls of those who were beheaded for the witness of Jesus, and for the Word of God, and who had not worshipped the beast or his image, nor had received his mark on their foreheads, or on their hands. And they lived and reigned with Christ for a thousand years. But the rest of the dead did not live again until the thousand years were finished. This is the first resurrection.

Blessed and holy is he who has a part in the first resurrection; on such the second death has no power, but they shall be priests of God and of Christ, and shall reign with Him for a thousand years.

And when the thousand years are over, Satan shall be loosed out of his prison and shall go out to deceive the nations that are in the four quarters of the earth—Gog and Magog—to gather them together to battle, the number of whom is as the sand of the sea.

These Scriptures are dismissed by preterists who insist that the thousand years is allegorical, and that there is no such thing as a Millennial Age. Those who do take these Scriptures literally are generally premillennialists who say that the Lord will return to the earth prior to the Millennium. The two opposing views to premillennialism are amillennialism and postmillennialism.

Amillennialism teaches that evil will increase and that there will appear in the last-days a man known as the anti-Christ whom Jesus will destroy upon His return to the earth. But rather than establish a literal 1,000-year reign on the earth, Jesus will immediately renew the heavens and the earth. This is among the more popular millennial theories within the Reformed churches. With few exceptions amillenialists do not take the Bible literally where "apocalyptic" events are recorded (e.g., the Book of Revelation).

Postmillennialism posits that Jesus is reigning over the earth presently in order to fulfill the Great Commission, which they define as acceptance of the Gospel on a worldwide basis. The most well-known and most widely-read postmillenialist today is R.C. Sproul, founder and chairman of Ligonier Ministries. Sproul is unabashedly an adherent to Reformed Theology, and has dedicated his life to teaching that theological discipline. His eschatology is definitely postmillennial. Says Sproul:

Postmillennialists criticize amillennialists and premillennialists for their pessimism. This view, widespread in centuries past, is gaining adherents today and stresses the Gospel's power. Christ reigns from the throne of heaven to ensure the success of the Great Commission. Multitudes will trust Jesus and transform the world, producing a golden age of peace and justice. As in amillennialism, most think the Millennium symbolizes a long time span, after which Christ ushers in the eternal state. Postmillennialism's optimism encourages Christians to take dominion of the earth (Ge 1:28), while the other views may imply that applying the biblical worldview to society is not as important, thus focusing solely on rescuing people from a world where the Gospel will have no lasting impact. Scripture's underlying framework, the sure growth of God's kingdom, is the bedrock of biblical postmillennialism (Isa 2:1-4; Mt 13:31-33).[1]

Citing Isaiah 2:1-4 at Biblia.com, Sproul assumes that it speaks of the present age:

The word that Isaiah the son of Amoz saw concerning Judah and Jerusalem.

It shall come to pass in the latter days
THAT THE MOUNTAIN OF THE HOUSE OF THE LORD
shall be established as the highest of the mountains,
and shall be lifted up above the hills;
and all the nations shall flow to it,
and many peoples shall come, and say:
"Come, let us go up to the mountain of the LORD,
to the house of the God of Jacob,
that he may teach us his ways
and that we may walk in his paths."
For out of Zion shall go the law,
and the word of the LORD from Jerusalem.
He shall judge between the nations,
and shall decide disputes for many peoples;
and they shall beat their swords into plowshares,
and their spears into pruning hooks; nation shall not lift up sword against nation,
neither shall they learn war anymore. (ESV)

---

[1] R.C. Sproul, "The Millennium - Part II," www.ligonier.org/learn/devotionals/millennium-part-ii/

Contrary to Sproul's surmising, these verses do not refer to the present age but to the Millennial Kingdom. They are indicative of the rebirth of the kingdom of Israel because they are "concerning Judah and Jerusalem." Judah is the nation where Jerusalem and the temple were situated. It has not existed as a kingdom since it went into captivity to Babylonia. When the Jews returned from Babylonia they never regained their autonomy as a nation, and certainly not as a kingdom.

But neither postmillennialists nor amillennialists believe in a future Israelite kingdom. They believe that Israel has been abandoned by God and replaced by "the Church." But whether or not this prophecy is specifically for Judah in the future, for Sproul to cite Isaiah's prophecy "concerning Judah" to represent his "golden age" is irreconcilable with his eschatology.

Sproul's words sound good, but there is nothing in Scripture to suggest that the Gospel will ever be received by a sufficient number of people to effect the transformation to a "golden age of peace and justice." The many verses which speak of such a "golden age" (Sproul's term) refer rather to the Millennial Kingdom with Jesus reigning physically on the earth.

It is disingenuous for postmillennialists to insist, when scoffing at the idea of the Millennium, that the word "Millennium" is not in the Bible, yet think it's perfectly okay to use the term "golden age," which isn't in the Bible either. The idea of a "golden age" originated in Greek mythology and is today more of a New Age term for the dawning "Age of Aquarius."

A careful reading of the command of the Lord reveals that He merely commissioned His disciples to proclaim the Gospel throughout the world; there is nothing about converting the world to usher in a "golden age."

In truth, the Lord tells us of just the opposite at the end of this age:

"And as it was in the days of Noah, so it shall also be in the days of the Son of Man. They ate, they drank, they married wives, they were given in marriage, until the day that Noah entered into the ark, and the flood came and destroyed them all.

"Likewise also, as it was in the days of Lot, they ate, they drank, they bought, they sold, they planted, they built. But the same day that Lot went out of Sodom it rained fire and brimstone from the heavens, and destroyed them all.

"It will even be this way in the day when the Son of Man is revealed." (Lk 17:26-30)

So will Christianity conquer the world only to lose it before the Lord returns? What glory to God is there in that?

WILL THERE BE A MILLENNIUM?

There is only one book of Scripture that mentions a 1,000-year period when Jesus will reign on the earth. Revelation 20:1-7 is clear in that regard. Prior to that, Revelation 19 reveals the Lord coming to the earth with the armies of Heaven to battle against the anti-Christ and the false prophet:

And I saw Heaven opened, and, look! A white horse! And He who sat on him was called "Faithful" and "True," and in righteousness He judges and makes war.

His eyes were like a flame of fire, and on His head were many crowns, and He had a name written that no man knew but He Himself.

And he was clothed with a robe dipped in blood, and His name is called "The Word of God."

And the armies that were in Heaven followed Him on white horses, clothed in fine linen, white and clean.

And out of his mouth goes a sharp sword so that with it He would strike the nations. And He shall rule them with a rod of iron. And He treads the winepress of the fierceness and wrath of Almighty God.

And He has on His robe and on His thigh a name written: "KING OF KINGS, AND LORD OF LORDS."

And I saw an angel standing in the sun, and he cried out with a loud voice, saying to all the fowls that fly in the midst of the heavens, "Come and gather yourselves together to the supper of the great God so that you may eat the flesh of kings, and the flesh of captains, and the flesh of mighty men, and the flesh of horses, and of those who sit on them, and the flesh of all men, both free and bond, both small and great."

And I saw the beast, and the kings of the earth and their armies, gathered together to make war against Him who sat on the horse, and against His army.

And the beast was taken, and with him the false prophet who worked miracles before him, with which he deceived those who had received the mark of the beast, and those who worshipped his image. These both were cast alive into a lake of fire burning with brimstone.

And the remnant were slain with the sword by Him who sat on the horse, which sword proceeded out of His mouth. And all the fowls were filled with their flesh. (Rv 19:11-20)

The above describes the destruction of the anti-Christ (the beast) and his false prophet after they have conquered Jerusalem for a short time.

Immediately we read of the 1,000-year reign of Christ on the earth (Rv 20:1:7 above).

It is clear from these Scriptures that the following takes place: 1) The Lord returns with His armies; 2) The "beast" or anti-Christ will be cast into the lake of fire along with the false prophet who leads the people to take a mark identifying them as worshippers of the beast; 3) the remnant of the anti-Christ's army will be slain and cleansed from the land by the fowls of the air; 4) Satan will be bound for a thousand years so he can no longer deceive the nations; 5) the saints who suffer for the Lord and do not take the mark of the beast will live and reign with Him for a thousand years as priests of God and of Christ.

There is nothing in Scripture to pinpoint the date when the Millennial Kingdom will be established. All we know is that it will commence sometime soon after the anti-Christ and the false prophet are removed and Satan is bound in the bottomless pit. These events will occur when the Lord returns to the earth with His resurrected saints.

Is The Thousand Years Literal?

For some reason many Christians don't want to believe these clear words of Scripture. They choose to allegorize them and say that the thousand years is metaphorical. Preterists in particular claim that all apocalyptic references in Scripture are allegorical, but they offer no concrete interpretations of those alleged allegories. They don't deny that those references are biblical—that they are inspired by the Spirit of God. But in their estimation such Scriptures are beyond understanding.

Did God then give us His Word without the ability to understand it? Did the Holy Spirit inspire John to write the Revelation of Jesus Christ as a mere exercise in futility? Did the Holy Spirit inspire the ancient Hebrew prophets to write of future events in a manner that cannot be understood? Did they write about a future kingdom of Israel if, in truth, there will be no future kingdom of Israel?

Such a thought is ridiculous. Yet just as preterists insist that the reign of Jesus over the earth is not physical but spiritual from Heaven, they also insist that the thousand years is not literal but allegorical. After all, they reason, Peter said that "one day is with the Lord as a thousand years, and a thousand years as one day." Also, the Psalmist said, "For a thousand years is in Your sight but as yesterday when it is past, and as a watch in the night" (Ps 90:4). Therefore, they conclude, any mention of a thousand years cannot be literal.

This is totally illogical. To say that the thousand years mentioned in Revelation 20 is not literal based on those two Scriptures is to make a definitive statement based on conjecture. The principle is no different than a professed atheist saying there is no God. How can he know that? The most any man can say in refusing to believe in God is, "I am not convinced that God exists." So, too, the preterists who deny the Millennial Kingdom can say at best only that they are not convinced that the thousand years are literal. They cannot say unequivocally that they are not literal. Yet if they cannot be sure, what good are their teachings? But these people write and speak in such definite terms about it that their sense of logic is conspicuously absent.

Yes, in the Lord's sight, because He exists from eternity to eternity, the time span of a thousand years is like one day to Him. That does not justify teaching that the thousand years of Revelation 20 is of an indefinite period, or merely has a spiritual application which is impossible to define. To apply their rule based on Psalms 90:4 and 2 Peter 3:8 would require them to say that there is a literal Millennium, but it can last for only one day. After all, a thousand years is like one day, not like fifty years, or two weeks, etc.

If the Word of God says that Christ will reign with His saints over the earth for a thousand years, why do intelligent and sincere believers want to say it doesn't mean what it says? But, then, if it does mean what it says, the entire preterist premise falls apart, and that beloved theological system and its venerated teachers are found in error. Not many people are willing to admit they've been duped, or to negate decades of a dearly-held theological system.

Logic insists that if one wishes to use Psalms 90:4 and 2 Peter 3:8 to "prove" that the Millennium will not be a reality, and/or will not last a thousand years, by saying the thousand years represent one day, one must also apply every mention of one day in Scripture to mean a thousand years. Therefore, after Jesus called Simon to follow him, it would have been the following thousand years later that He would have called Philip (Jn 1:41-43). Such applications would be innumerable and, of course, ridiculous. One may not arbitrarily claim that the "thousand years" in Revelation 20 doesn't mean exactly that, any more than they can claim that "one day" doesn't mean exactly that.

The thousand years (Gr., *chilias etos*) must be taken literally. Satan will be bound in the bottomless pit; the beast and the false prophet will be cast in the lake of fire. All ungodly men will be purged from the earth, either at Armageddon or at the Judgment of the Nations (Mt 25:31-46). There will be only a relatively few men left to enter Christ's Millennial Kingdom (Mt 25:34). Redeemed Israel, having been saved upon seeing her Messiah will become the earth's chief nation, fulfilling Isaiah 2:2-4; Ezekiel 37:21-28; Zechariah 9:10; 14:9.

The context of Revelation 20 does not suggest anything other than a literal thousand years without allegorizing it, which is a scoundrel's way of avoiding the truth of God's Word. If the Lord Himself uses allegory such as in His parables, or if Scripture is clearly speaking allegorically, one may accept that. But Revelation 20 is not clearly allegorical. Therefore, it must be taken literally. God doesn't play games with His Word.

SCRIPTURES THAT SUPPORT THE MILLENNIAL AGE

We've seen what the present age is like, and what the Eternal Age will be like. Are there Scriptures that speak of a time that cannot fit into either of those two ages? Truth be told, there are so many that they cannot all be quoted without doubling the size of this book. We will look at a number of them, however, and see how they cannot possibly fit this present age or the Eternal Age; they must, therefore, be speaking of an interim age—the age we call the Millennium. We will start by addressing whether or not Israel will have a place in the Millennium.

Will Israel Have A Part In The Kingdom?

There are differing views of Israel for the latter days. The preterist says Israel is no longer a part of God's plan; she lost that privilege when she crucified her Messiah, leaving God's blessings and promises for "the Church." This is called "replacement theology," the idea that "the Church" has replaced Israel in God's eternal plan.

On the dispensationalist side, there are those who say that Israel will inherit an earthly kingdom but "the Church" will inherit a heavenly kingdom; "the Church" will remain in Heaven while the Lord rules over the earth from Jerusalem. This is because "the Church" is spiritual, but Israel is temporal.

This is partially true. The Body of Christ is spiritual, but the resurrection will be bodily; we will inherit new physical bodies that have celestial properties. Our bodies will be immortal, but they will be every bit as physical as Jesus' resurrected body in which he ate with His disciples.

Scripture is clear that the resurrected saints will inherit the Kingdom of God on earth as joint heirs with Christ, and that His faithful saints will reign with Him over the Millennial Kingdom (Rv 20:6). The restored kingdom of Israel will consist of mortal men and women ruled by resurrected saints, chief of whom will be David (Jer 30:9; Eze 34:23-25). So in that sense we may say that Israel is an earthly kingdom and the Body of Christ is a spiritual Kingdom. But both will be active on the earth during the Millennium. They will not be separated earth from Heaven:

> Blessed and holy is he who has a part in the first resurrection. On such the second death has no power, but they shall be priests of God and of Christ, and shall reign with Him a thousand years. (Rv 20:6)

That thousand-year reign with Him will be on earth over the nations, including Israel.

The Gathering of Israel

During the Millennium all mortal Israelites will be gathered by their Messiah into the land promised to Abraham for his natural descendants. Preterists quote Joshua 21:43 to argue that this was fulfilled when Israel took possession of the Promised Land, and therefore there will be no future kingdom for Israel:

> And YHWH gave to Israel all the land that He swore to give to their fathers, and they possessed it, and dwelt there. (Jo 21:43)

The preterists are correct in saying the promise was fulfilled when Israel took possession of the Promised Land, but they err by neglecting another prophecy. After Israel and Judah had been driven from that possession by the Assyrians and Babylonians respectively, Jeremiah wrote:

> YHWH, God of Israel, speaks this, saying, "Write in a book all the words that I have spoken to you. For, look, the days come" says YHWH, "that I will bring again the captivity of My people Israel and Judah," says YHWH, "and I will cause them to return to the land that I gave to their fathers, and they shall possess it." (Jer 30:2-3)

Notice that Jeremiah speaks specifically of Israel and Judah; this cannot mean "the Church" which is made of both Jew and Gentile as one new man in Christ, often referred to as "spiritual Israel" but never "spiritual Judah" or "spiritual Israel and Judah."

Clearly, God promised to restore all the land to Israel and Judah that they possessed prior to their captivity. That includes all the land as one possession because before Solomon died Israel and Judah were one nation. Therefore, the restoration will include the city of Jerusalem.

Jeremiah 30:2-3 is a *new* promise, made during Judah's captivity in Babylonia, to *restore* the natural descendants of Israel and Judah to their land. The new possession will be larger than the previous one, but it will encompass the borders occupied by Israel and Judah before their captivities.

This later promise has never been fulfilled. The kingdom of Judah has not existed since the beginning of the Babylonian Captivity, and Israel has never in this age returned to possess all the land promised to their fathers. Nor will they until the Lord returns to call them back.

Preterists fail to recognize that God's plan of redemption foresaw that Israel would reject her Messiah. Did God not know of it from the beginning? Of course He did. Yet He made these promises of a new Israelite kingdom anyway. God is not double-minded.

The Lord's answer to His disciples when they asked if He would at that time restore the kingdom to Israel should help us understand that, yes, the kingdom will be restored to Israel at a future date:

> "It is not for you to know the times or the seasons that the Father has put in His own power. But you shall receive power after the Holy Spirit has come upon you, and you shall be My witnesses both in Jerusalem and in all Judea, and in Samaria, and to the uttermost part of the earth." (Ac 1:7-8)

The Lord did not say, "What do you mean? The kingdom will never be restored to Israel. I have a plan for the Gentiles to inherit a spiritual kingdom along with a remnant from Israel. It's called 'the Church.'"

No, all He said was that it wasn't for them to know the times or the seasons over which the Father has power. He did not say that all the sayings of the prophets will never be realized because Israel would reject Him (which rejection He prophesied would happen). So to understand Israel's part in the Millennial Kingdom we must still rely on those prophecies.

Notice, especially, that the following Scriptures speak primarily of Israel being brought back into the Promised Land and living in peace under the reign of both Yahweh and the resurrected King David.

> "Therefore I will save My flock, and they shall no longer be a prey, and I will judge between cattle and cattle. And I will set up one shepherd over them, and he shall feed them—My servant David—he shall feed them, and he shall be their shepherd.
>
> "And I YHWH will be their God, and My servant David a prince among them. I YHWH have spoken it.
>
> "And I will make with them a covenant of peace, and will cause the hurtful creatures to leave the land, and they shall dwell safely in the wilderness, and sleep in the woods.

"And I will make them and the places around My hill a blessing, and I will cause the shower to come down in its season; there shall be showers of blessing.

"And the tree of the field shall yield her fruit, and the earth shall yield her increase, and they shall be safe in their land, and shall know that I am YHWH when I have broken the bands of their yoke and delivered them out of the hand of those who served themselves of them.

"And they shall no longer be a prey to the heathen, nor shall the animals of the land devour them, but they shall dwell safely, and no one shall make them afraid.

"And I will raise up for them a plant of renown, and they shall no longer be consumed with hunger in the land, nor bear the shame of the heathen anymore. Thus they shall know that I, YHWH their God, am with them, and that they, the house of Israel, are My people," says the Lord YHWH. (Eze 34:22-30)

The Lord YHWH says this: "Look! I will take the children of Israel from among the heathen where they have gone, and will gather them on every side and bring them into their own land. And I will make them one nation in the land on the mountains of Israel, and one king shall be king to them all. And they shall no longer be two nations, nor shall they be divided into two kingdoms anymore at all. Neither shall they defile themselves any longer with their idols, nor with their detestable things, nor with any of their transgressions, but I will save them out of all their dwelling places wherein they have sinned, and will cleanse them so that they shall be My people, and I will be their God.

"And My servant David shall be king over them, and they all shall have one shepherd; they shall also walk in My judgments, and observe My statutes, and do them.

"And they shall dwell in the land that I have given to My servant Jacob, wherein your fathers have dwelt. And they shall dwell therein, even they, and their children, and their children's children forever, and My servant David shall be their prince forever.

"Moreover I will make a covenant of peace with them; it shall be an everlasting covenant with them, and I will place them, and multiply them, and will set My sanctuary in the midst of them forever.

"My tabernacle shall also be with them. Yes, I will be their God, and they shall be My people. And the heathen shall know that I,

YHWH, sanctify Israel when My sanctuary shall be in the midst of them forever." (Eze 37:21-28)

"For it shall come to pass in that day," says YHWH of Hosts, "that I will break his yoke from off your neck, and will burst your bonds, and strangers shall no longer enslave him. But they shall serve YHWH their God, and David their king, whom I will raise up to them."

Thus YHWH says, "Look! I will bring again the captivity of Jacob's tents, and have mercy on his dwelling places, and the city shall be built on her own heap, and the palace shall remain after its manner.

"And out of them shall proceed thanksgiving and the voice of those who make merry. And I will multiply them, and they shall not be few; I will also glorify them, and they shall not be small. Their children also shall be as before, and their congregation shall be established before Me, and I will punish all who oppress them.

"And their nobles shall be from themselves, and their governor shall proceed from their midst, and I will cause him to draw near, and he shall approach to Me. For who is this that engaged his heart to approach Me?" says YHWH.

"And you shall be My people, and I will be your God."(Jer 30:8-22)

Hosea tells us that Israel will "seek YHWH their God, and David their king":

"For the children of Israel shall abide many days without a king, and without a prince, and without a sacrifice, and without an image, and without an ephod, and without teraphim. Afterward the children of Israel shall return and seek YHWH their God and David their king, and shall fear YHWH and His goodness in the latter days." (Hos 3:4-5)

Israel has abided many days without a king, without a prince, and without a sacrifice. David had been long dead when this was written. There is no reason to think other than literally when the Scriptures often speak of David reigning over Israel again. He will be resurrected and will sit on the throne of Israel as its prince (or king under the Messiah; the terms "prince" and "king" are often interchangeable in Scripture). The Lord will be King not only over Israel, but over the entire earth:

Why do the heathen rage, and the people imagine a vain thing?
The kings of the earth set themselves, and the rulers take counsel

together against YHWH, and against His anointed, saying, "Let us break their bands asunder, and cast away their cords from us."

He who sits in Heaven shall laugh; the Lord shall have them in derision. Then He shall speak to them in His anger, and trouble them in His wrath.

"Yet I have set My King upon My holy hill of Zion. I will declare the decree: 'YHWH has said to me, "You are My Son; this day I have begotten You. Ask of Me, and I shall give you the heathen for Your inheritance, and the uttermost parts of the earth for Your possession. You shall break them with a rod of iron; You shall dash them in pieces like a potter's vessel.'"

Now therefore, be wise, O you kings. Be instructed, you judges of the earth. Serve YHWH with fear, and rejoice with trembling. Kiss the Son, lest He be angry, and you perish from the way when His wrath is kindled even a little. Blessed are all those who put their trust in Him. (Ps 2:1-12)

So God will set His Son on Mount Zion to rule the nations with a rod of iron. In Ezekiel 43:1-7, the Lord speaks of the place of His throne and the soles of His feet dwelling in the midst of Israel forever. Thus He is affirming that He will be reigning over Israel and the whole world from Jerusalem during the Millennium.

It is clear from these prophecies that the resurrected David will be on the throne of the restored kingdom of Israel.

Some protest this idea, saying that "David" in these prophecies is really Jesus. But it doesn't say "the Lord" or "Jesus" will be king; it says David will be king. Why can't we accept the Word for what it says? Or do those who protest this not really believe in a physical resurrection? If the saints are to rule over the nations along with Christ, why would the resurrected David not be the ruler over Israel?

The question arises, "Didn't God promise David that Israel would never fail to have a man from his house on the throne?" If that is true, then it must be the Lord Jesus who would be on the throne of Israel because it's obvious that there hasn't been a man on the throne since Israel went into captivity to Babylonia. Therefore, Jesus has been on the throne of Israel while in Heaven.

But we must also acknowledge that there was no man on the throne from the time shortly after Israel went into the Babylonian Captivity until the Lord was born. And during His life He never ascended the throne. In the place of David's lineage the Herodians ruled Judea just prior to, during, and for a while after the Lord came the first time. The Herodians were not true Israelites, and certainly were not in the line of David. Their ancestry was not Jewish, but Idumaean—a people descended from Esau and forcibly converted to Judaism by the Hasmonean rulers in Palestine.

So did the Lord's promise to David fail?

No. Because as long as there was a kingdom of Israel (split into two kingdoms after Solomon) there was always a descendant of David on the throne in Jerusalem.

But the kingdom ceased to exist with the Babylonian Captivity. And it has not existed since that time. Therefore, all the prophecies relating to the coming kingdom of Israel and the Messiah's reign through David must yet be future. The prophecy has not failed, nor will it. When the kingdom is restored, David will be restored to the throne.

These Scriptures do not take away anything from the Lord. He will rule over David and Israel as well as over the nations of the world. If anything, this should give us greater confidence in our blessed hope: the resurrection of our bodies to eternal life and inheritance of the Kingdom of God.

When this was written David had been in the grave for centuries. These verses must be referring to the resurrected David, which means this time must be after the present age.

Of whom is God speaking but Israel gathered into their land out of the present Diaspora? These conditions certainly have not existed from the time Judah returned to the land for a brief time after the Babylonian Captivity. We also see that David will be brought back to rule over Israel along with Yahweh. So David will be the one shepherd over Israel (as opposed to the time when Israel had two kings—one over the northern kingdom of Israel and one over the southern kingdom of Judah). Israel will be joined as one nation with one king, David. Jesus (Yahweh of the Old Covenant) will rule over all the earth, and David will be king over Israel.

When has that ever happened? And how can it happen in the scenario that preterism offers, in which Jesus doesn't return to the earth until after "the Church" has taken rule over the nations, and then will immediately come the New Heavens and New Earth? Preterism discards all the Scriptures of Israel's return and of David and Yahweh (Jesus) reigning on earth together.

These Scriptures cannot be speaking of the Eternal Age, because they speak of God's judgment on any who afflict Israel. Who can afflict Israel during the Eternal Age?

Is Yahweh really Jesus? Is He not the Father in Heaven? Yahweh is the name of the Father, and it is the name of His Son, just as my name, Dager, is the name of my father. Consider these verses that speak of Yahweh coming back to earth:

Look! The Day of YHWH comes, and your spoil shall be divided in your midst! "For I will gather all nations against Jerusalem to battle, and the city shall be taken, and the houses rifled, and the women ravished, and half of the city shall go forth into captivity, and the residue of the people shall not be cut off from the city."

Then YHWH shall go forth and fight against those nations as when He fought in the day of battle. And in that day His feet shall stand on the Mount of Olives that is before Jerusalem on the east, and the Mount of Olives shall cleave in the midst thereof toward the east and toward the west, and there shall be a very great valley, and half of the mountain shall remove toward the north, and half of it toward the south.

And you shall flee to the valley of the mountains, for the valley of the mountains shall reach to Azal. Yes, you shall flee as you fled from before the earthquake in the days of Uzziah king of Judah. And YHWH My God shall come (and all the saints with You)!

And it shall come to pass in that day, that the light shall not be clear, nor dark. But it shall be one day that shall be known to YHWH, not day, nor night. But it shall happen that at evening time it shall be light. And it shall be in that day, that living waters shall go out from Jerusalem, half of them toward the former sea, and half of them toward the hinder sea. It shall be in summer and in winter.

And YHWH shall be king over all the earth. In that day there shall be one YHWH, and His name one.

All the land shall be turned as a plain from Geba to Rimmon south of Jerusalem, and it shall be lifted up, and inhabited in her place, from Benjamin's gate to the place of the first gate, to the corner gate, and from the tower of Hananeel to the king's winepresses.

And men shall dwell in it, and there shall no longer be utter destruction, but Jerusalem shall be safely inhabited. (Zec 14:1-11)

"But you be glad and rejoice forever in that which I create. For, look! I create Jerusalem a rejoicing, and her people a joy. And I will rejoice in Jerusalem, and enjoy My people, and the voice of weeping shall no longer be heard in her, nor the voice of crying.

"From then on there shall no longer be an infant of days, nor an old man that has not filled his days. For the child shall die a hundred years old, but the sinner being a hundred years old shall be accursed.

"And they shall build houses and inhabit them, and they shall plant vineyards and eat their fruit. They shall not build, and another inhabit; they shall not plant, and another eat. For the days of My people are as the days of a tree, and My chosen shall long enjoy the work of their hands.

"They shall not labor in vain, nor bring forth for trouble, for they are the seed of the blessed of YHWH, and their offspring with them.

"And it shall come to pass that before they call, I will answer, and while they are still speaking, I will hear.

"The wolf and the lamb shall feed together, and the lion shall eat straw like the bullock. And dust shall be the serpent's food. They shall not hurt or destroy in all My holy mountain," says YHWH. (Isa 65:18-25)

Do either of these Scriptures speak of the present age? No, because Yahweh (Jesus) will have returned to stand on the Mount of Olives to deliver Jerusalem from her enemies, but not until Jerusalem is first captured by anti-Christ.

Do they speak of the Eternal Age? No, because the heathen will still be on the earth and will eventually rebel against the Lord (Rv 20:1-10). Death will still be in effect, which means sin will still be in man's nature. Death is the last enemy to be destroyed (1 Co 15:26). So these Scriptures must be speaking of the present earth, not the New Earth, and of a future age, not the present age.

Whose feet will stand on the Mount of Olives? No one seriously believes it will be the Father, because He remains in Heaven until New Jerusalem comes down to the New Earth. But the New Earth will not have yet been created during the time of which these Scriptures speak.

Again, could these Scriptures be speaking of the present age? No, because they tell of Jerusalem and God's chosen people (Israel) dwelling safely and enjoying extremely long life in God's holy mountain (where Yahweh—Jesus Christ returned—will dwell). Wild animals will exist in peace on God's holy mountain (Zion), but not necessarily in other places. The preterist "golden age" cannot make such promises even if "the Church" were ruling over the nations.

These prophecies extend the blessings of the Millennial Age to God's people, Israel. It is not stated, but it is possible that those blessings will extend to non-Israelites who are faithful to the Lord during that time.

The Book of Ezekiel contains some of the most comprehensive prophecies of the restored kingdom of Israel. Unfortunately most teachers have misinterpreted them to apply to the present age. But there we find that the Israelites who have been scattered throughout the world will one day return when the Lord Himself calls for them.

Ezekiel was carried by the Spirit of God and set down in the middle of a valley full of dried bones. He was commanded by God to prophesy over the bones that they would come together and He would put flesh on them and cause them to live.

> Then He said to me, "Son of man, these bones are the whole house of Israel. 'Look,' they say, 'Our bones are dried, and our hope is lost; we are cut off for our parts.'
>
> "Therefore prophesy, and say to them, 'YHWH says this: "Look, O My people, I will open your graves and cause you to come up out of your graves, and bring you into the land of Israel. And you shall know that I am YHWH when I have opened your graves, O My people, and brought you up out of your graves, and shall put My Spirit in you, and you shall live, and I shall place you in your own land. Then you shall know that I, YHWH, have said it, and performed it," says YHWH.'" (Eze 37:11-14)

God opening the graves and bringing the people into the land speaks of the saints of Israel coming into the Promised Land after being resurrected. This indicates that the resurrected saints from among Israel will rule over the Promised Land with the Lord. They will rule over the mortal people of Israel who will be gathered from all the nations:

> And it shall come to pass in that day, that the Lord shall set His hand again the second time to recover the remnant of His people that shall be left, from Assyria, and from Egypt, and from Pathros, and from Cush, and from Elam, and from Shinar, and from Hamath, and from the islands of the sea. And He shall set up an ensign for the nations, and shall assemble the outcasts of Israel, and gather together the dispersed of Judah from the four corners of the earth. (Isa 11:11-12)

Here the prophecy regards mortal Israelites who will come back to their land from out of the nations during the Millennial Age.

"Look, the days come," says YHWH, "that the plowman will overtake the reaper, and the treader of grapes him who sows seed, and the mountains will drop sweet wine, and all the hills will melt.

"And I will bring again the captivity of My people of Israel, and they shall build the waste cities and inhabit them, and they shall plant vineyards, and drink their wine; they shall also make gardens, and eat their fruit.

"And I will plant them on their land, and they shall no longer be pulled up out of their land that I have given them," says YHWH your God. (Am 9:13-15)

There are myriad such Scriptures that speak of the Lord gathering from out of the nations all Israel to bring them into the Promised Land in perpetuity, never to be pulled out again. Others speak of the resurrected saints inhabiting the land. Certainly neither has yet occurred.

The dispersed of Judah cannot be construed as anyone other than the descendants of Abraham, Isaac and Jacob who would comprise the kingdom of Judah. These are not Gentiles or "the Church."

Therefore, the Lord YHWH says this: "Now I will bring again the captives of Jacob, and have mercy on the whole house of Israel, and will be jealous for My holy name, after they have borne their shame, and all their trespasses whereby they have trespassed against Me when they dwelt safely in their land and no one made them afraid—when I have brought them again from the people and gathered them out of their enemies' lands, and am sanctified in them in the sight of many nations. Then they will know that I am YHWH their God who caused them to be led into captivity among the heathen, but I have gathered them into their own land, and have left none of them there anymore. Neither will I hide My face from them anymore, for I have poured out My spirit upon the house of Israel," says the Lord YHWH. (Eze 39:25-29)

Again, this prophecy was given after Israel and Judah had gone into captivity. It does not pertain to the original occupation of the land or to the present modern state of Israel. It will be the kingdom of Israel restored to its fullness. The land will be brought back from the sword (the wars against Israel will have ceased), and the people will dwell safely.

WHAT WILL TRANSPIRE DURING THE MILLENNIUM?

There are many prophecies that describe the Millennium. Again, the most comprehensive are found in Ezekiel. Scripture reveals many things about the Millennium that will astound believers who have never read of them, or who have trusted teachers of end-times prophecy who have missed or purposely ignored those Scriptures. This is a fascinating study, well worth our investment of time.

Following are some of the prophecies that describe the Millennium:

And He shall judge among the nations, and shall rebuke many people. And they shall beat their swords into plowshares, and their spears into pruning hooks. Nation shall not lift up sword against nation, nor shall they learn war anymore. (Isa 2:4)

During the Millennium Jesus will sit on His throne in Jerusalem, and all the nations will bring tribute to Him (Zec 14:16-19 above).

And there shall come forth a rod out of the stem of Jesse, and a Branch shall grow out of his roots. And the spirit of YHWH shall rest upon Him—the spirit of wisdom and understanding; the spirit of counsel and might; the spirit of knowledge and of the fear of YHWH—and shall make Him of quick understanding in the fear of YHWH. And He shall not judge according to what His eyes see, or reprove according to what His ears hear. But with righteousness He shall vindicate the poor, and decide with equity for the humble of the earth, and He shall strike the earth with the rod of His mouth, and He shall slay the wicked with the breath of His lips. And righteousness shall be the belt around His waist, and faithfulness the belt of His loins.

The wolf shall also dwell with the lamb, and the leopard shall lie down with the kid, and the calf and the young lion and the fatling together—and a little child shall lead them.

And the cow and the bear shall feed; their young ones shall lie down together, and the lion shall eat straw like the ox.

And the nursing child shall play on the hole of the asp, and the weaned child shall put his hand on the vipers' den. They shall not hurt or destroy in all My holy mountain, for the earth shall be full of the knowledge of YHWH just as the waters cover the sea.

And in that day there shall be a root of Jesse, who shall stand as an ensign of the people. The Gentiles shall seek it, and His rest shall be glorious. (Isa 11:1-10)

All of this land will be ruled from Jerusalem by the resurrected David, and will be the headquarters for all the resurrected saints who will reign with Christ. For Jesus will also be on His throne in Jerusalem:

Again the word of YHWH of Hosts came to me, saying, "YHWH of Hosts says this: 'I was jealous for Zion with great jealousy, and I was jealous for her with great fury.'

"YHWH says this: 'I have returned to Zion and will dwell in the midst of Jerusalem, and Jerusalem shall be called a city of truth, and the mountain of YHWH of Hosts—the holy mountain.'

"YHWH of Hosts says this: 'There shall yet old men and old women dwell in the streets of Jerusalem, and every man with his staff in his hand for very age. And the streets of the city shall be full of boys and girls playing in its streets.'

"YHWH of Hosts says this: 'If it is marvelous in the eyes of the remnant of this people in these days, should it also be marvelous in My eyes?' says YHWH of Hosts.

"YHWH of Hosts says this: 'Look! I will save My people from the east country, and from the west country, and I will bring them, and they shall dwell in the midst of Jerusalem, and they shall be My people, and I will be their God, in truth and in righteousness.'

"YHWH of Hosts says this: 'Let your hands be strong, you who hear in these days these words by the mouth of the prophets, which were in the day that the foundation of the house of YHWH of Hosts was laid, that the temple might be built. For before these days there was no work for man, nor any work for animal; neither was there any peace to him who went out or came in, because of the affliction. For I set all men, everyone, against his neighbor. But now I will not be to the remnant of this people as in the former days,' says YHWH of Hosts. 'For the seed shall be prosperous; the vine shall give her fruit, and the ground shall give her increase, and the heavens shall give their dew. And I will cause the remnant of this people to possess all these things.

"'And it shall come to pass, that as you were a curse among the heathen, O house of Judah, and house of Israel, so I will save you, and you shall be a blessing. Do not fear, but let your hands be strong.'

"For YHWH of Hosts says this: 'As I thought to punish you when your fathers provoked Me to wrath,' says YHWH of Hosts, 'and I did not change my mind, so I have again thought in these days to do well to Jerusalem and to the house of Judah. Do not fear.'" (Zec 8:1-15)

So Zechariah 8:3 says God "will dwell in the midst of Jerusalem." The context is the Millennium, not this present age, and not any time past.

These millennial prophecies must relate to an age other than the present one because they have not been fulfilled, nor can they be fulfilled without the Lord present. One may say they are merely allegories, but who can say without question what the allegories represent? God doesn't speak in riddles; He speaks prophecy. If all the prophecies of the Millennial Age are merely allegory, then a huge portion of Scripture cannot be understood!

Occasionally God does use allegory in His Word, but He is careful to make clear what the allegory represents, just as Jesus explained His parables to His disciples. I would ask those who say all this is allegory, what does beating their swords into plowshares represent? The "peacekeeping" warfare of the United Nations Organization? Hardly. What does the wolf lying down with the lamb represent? What does it mean that a child will play with serpents and not be injured? What does it mean the nations will no longer learn war with one another? These prophecies must relate to a time when the Lord will rule over the nations with a rod of iron.

Yet Scripture also says that the heathen rage against the Lord, wanting to break His bands. This will occur at the end of the Millennium when Satan is loosed for a season to deceive the nations into thinking they can throw off the iron rule of the King in Jerusalem. During the Millennium many will be born who will not have known the world prior to the Lord's conquest. They will know only that they must pay tribute to the foreign King who rules them with a rod of iron, or suffer the consequences. They will have rebellion in their hearts but will be unable to give vent to that rebellion until Satan is released to deceive them into thinking they can set themselves free. Although the nations will not have learned war during the thousand years, they will still have warfare in their hearts. All it will take is the proper spark.

> And when the thousand years are over, Satan shall be set loose from his prison and will go out to deceive the nations that are in the four quarters of the earth—Gog and Magog—to gather them together to battle, the number of whom is as the sand of the sea.
>
> And they went up on the breadth of the earth and encircled the camp of the saints about, and the beloved city.
>
> And fire came down from God out of Heaven, and devoured them.

And the Devil that deceived them was cast into the lake of fire and brimstone where the beast and the false prophet are, and shall be tormented day and night forever and ever. (Rv 20:7-10)

What could be more clear? This is not allegory. The details are well defined and discernible to any honest heart. And those prophecies that speak of spears, bows and arrows, weapons and chariots made of wood for the earthly armies at the end of the Millennium give further evidence that man's military capabilities will have been decimated when the Lord first returns.

WHAT FORM WILL THE KINGDOM TAKE?

From among those who believe in the literal Millennial Kingdom there have come a number of different descriptions of what the Kingdom will look like. Most picture it as a time of peace, tranquility and prosperity for the whole earth. It is believed that there will be no wars, and that the nations will worship the Lord without reservation. In short, the Millennial Kingdom will be the long sought-after Utopia envisioned by virtually all religions and philosophies. But is this true?

It appears as if, at the beginning of the Millennium, Israel will be involved in its own deliverance from its enemies when the Lord will fight against the nations that gather against Jerusalem:

And this shall be the plague by which YHWH will strike all the people that have fought against Jerusalem: their flesh will consume away while they stand upon their feet, and their eyes will consume away in their holes, and their tongue will consume away in their mouth. And it shall happen in that day, that a great tumult from YHWH shall be among them, and everyone will lay hold on the hand of his neighbor, and his hand will rise up against the hand of his neighbor.

And Judah shall also fight at Jerusalem, and the wealth of all the heathen round about shall be gathered together, gold, and silver, and apparel, in great abundance. (Zec 14:12-14)

"In that day," says YHWH, "I will strike every horse with astonishment, and his rider with madness, and I will open My eyes upon the house of Judah, and will strike every horse of the people with blindness.

"And the governors of Judah will say in their hearts, 'The inhabitants of Jerusalem shall be my strength in YHWH of Hosts their God.'

"In that day I will make the governors of Judah like a hearth of fire among the wood, and like a torch of fire in a sheaf, and they shall devour all the people around them, on the right hand and on the left. And Jerusalem shall be inhabited again in her own place, even in Jerusalem." (Zec 12:4-6)

These Scriptures do not relate to any past events as evidenced by the context which clearly indicates a future final deliverance of Jerusalem by the Lord when He returns.

But what about the remainder of the 1,000 years after Jerusalem has been secured by the Lord? Will there then be the Utopian society wherein all mankind will revel in the blessings of the Lord?

Zechariah gave us a clue when he prophesied:

And it shall happen that everyone that is left of all the nations that came against Jerusalem shall go up from year to year to worship the King, YHWH of Hosts, and to keep the Feast of Tabernacles. And it shall be that whoever will not come up of all the families of the earth to Jerusalem to worship the King, YHWH of Hosts, no rain shall be on them.

And if the family of Egypt that has no rain does not go up, and does not come, there shall be the plague by which YHWH will strike the heathen that do not come up to keep the Feast of Tabernacles.

This shall be the punishment of Egypt, and the punishment of all nations that do not come up to keep the Feast of Tabernacles. (Zec 14:16-19)

Notice that Zechariah affirms that there will be heathen during the Millennial Age, indicating that outside of Israel the heathen will be allowed to continue in their paganism. But the nations that attacked Jerusalem will be required to keep the Feast of Tabernacles or suffer drought and plague. Such a scenario has never taken place; it must yet be future. It indicates that not everyone among the nations will be willing to worship the Lord, and certainly not at Jerusalem. But there is nothing to indicate that warfare will be engaged in by the nations, either among themselves or against the Lord at Jerusalem. Rather, the Lord will punish the nations that do not obey Him, by withholding rain. If that does not bring them into compliance He will send a plague on them.

Again, we know this is still in the future because the Gentiles were never commanded to go to Jerusalem to keep the Feast of Tabernacles, or to keep any of the Law. But the Millennium will be a time when mortal men will be ruled with a rod of iron and will have to pay tribute to Yahweh at Jerusalem. Justice will be meted out swiftly for all wrongdoers. There will be no plea bargaining for criminals; the Lord and His saints will judge righteously. It will be a time when the Lord Himself will demonstrate to the nations the manner in which they should have governed themselves.

So the Millennial Kingdom will not be a time of rest except from warfare. Men will still have to live in obedience to the Lord or suffer the consequences. This is why the Lord will rule with a rod of iron.

Nor will everyone worship the true God. Mention of the heathen indicates that the worship of false gods will continue even during the Millennium. This is affirmed by the prophet Micah:

> For all people will walk, everyone, in the name of his god, and we will walk in the name of YHWH our God forever and ever.
>
> "In that day," says YHWH, "I will assemble her [Israel] who limps, and I will gather her who is driven out, and her whom I have afflicted. And I will make her who limped a remnant, and her who was cast far off a strong nation, and YHWH shall reign over them in Mount Zion from now on, even forever." (Mic 4:5-7)

How does this reconcile with Zephaniah 2:11?:

> YHWH will be terrible to them, for He will emaciate all the gods of the earth, and men shall worship Him, everyone from his place, even all the isles of the heathen.

When the Lord returns He will indeed destroy everything that is detestable before Him. But as time goes by man's evil nature will cause him to eventually slide back into idolatry so that by the end of the Millennium mankind will be ready to rebel against the righteous King.

HOW EXTENSIVE WILL THE ISRAELITE KINGDOM BE?

Ezekiel, who also wrote during the Babylonian Captivity, outlined the borders for the return of Israel to the land in the last days (during the Millennium).

> "And this shall be the border of the land toward the north side: from the great sea, the way of Hethlon, as men go to Zedad, Hamath, Berothah, Sibraim, which is between the border of Damascus and the border of Hamath, Hazar-hatticon, which is by the coast of Hauran.
>
> And the border from the sea shall be Hazar-enan, the border of Damascus, and the north northward, and the border of Hamath. And this is the north side.

"And the east side you shall measure from Hauran, and from Damascus, and from Gilead, and from the land of Israel by Jordan, from the border to the east sea. And this is the east side.

"And the south side southward, from Tamar even to the waters of strife in Kadesh, the river to the great sea. And this is the south side southward.

"The west side also shall be the great sea from the border, till a man come over against Hamath. This is the west side.

"So shall you divide this land to yourselves according to the tribes of Israel.

"And it shall come to pass, that you shall divide it by lot for an inheritance to yourselves, and to the aliens that sojourn among you, which shall father children among you, and they shall be to you as born in the country among the children of Israel; they shall have inheritance with you among the tribes of Israel.

"And it shall come to pass, that in whatever tribe the alien sojourns, there you shall give him his inheritance," says the Lord YHWH. (Eze 47:15-23)

These ancient names are difficult to ascertain due to their obsolescence, But it appears as if the entire Arabian Peninsula and the northeastern shores of the African Continent (east from the Nile River) will comprise the kingdom of Israel during the Millennium.

The land is much more extensive than Israel possessed originally. Millennial Israel will extend from the Mediterranean Sea at Hethlon (near Tripoli, Lebanon) to the Euphrates River near Baghdad. The eastern border will be the Euphrates River to the Persian Gulf; there it will encompass the whole Arabian Peninsula from around the Gulf of Oman into the Arabian Sea. The southern border will be the southern coast of the Arabian Peninsula through the Gulf of Aden. The western border will be along either the West Bank or the East Bank of the Red Sea. At some point it will traverse west to the Nile River and will extend northward to the Mediterranean Sea.

It is obvious that millennial Israel will occupy much of the territory of those nations that have been its enemies during this present age. The irony of that should not be lost to those who protest Israel's expansion today. It is God who sets the borders of all the nations (Ps 74:17).

The portion of allotment to the tribes of Israel does not encompass this entire land mass; some of it will be meted out to non-Israelites who bear children in the land (Eze 47:22-23).

THE MILLENNIAL TEMPLE

During the Millennium, a third temple will be built by the Lord Jesus:

"Look! I will send My messenger, and He shall prepare the way before Me. And the Lord, whom you seek, shall suddenly come to His temple—the messenger of the covenant, in whom you delight. Look! He shall come!" says YHWH of Hosts.

But who may stand in the day of His coming? And who shall stand when He appears? For He is like a refiner's fire, and like fullers' soap, and He shall sit as a refiner and purifier of silver. And He shall purify the sons of Levi, and purge them like gold and silver, that they may offer to YHWH an offering in righteousness.

Then the offering of Judah and Jerusalem will be pleasant to YHWH as in the days of old, and as in former years. (Mal 3:1-4)

Malachi's prophecy was partially fulfilled when Jesus came to the temple to cleanse it. But His act of cleansing was not permanent, because Israel slid further into apostasy after crucifying Him. The ultimate fulfillment of this prophecy must take place during the Millennium.

Likewise, the prophesies of Ezekiel have to do with the Millennium, not the present age. The application of Ezekiel 40:1 all the way through 47:12 to an alleged temple to be built in present-day Israel is erroneous. According to Zechariah, the Word of YHWH said that Jesus will build the next temple:

"And speak to him, saying, 'This says YHWH of Hosts, saying, "See the man whose name is The Branch. And He shall grow up out of His place, and He shall build the temple of YHWH. He shall build the temple of YHWH, and He shall bear the glory, and shall sit and rule upon His throne. And He shall be a priest upon His throne, and the counsel of peace shall be between them both. And the crowns shall be to Helem, and to Tobijah, and to Jedaiah, and to Hen the son of Zephaniah, for a memorial in the temple of YHWH. And those who are far off [the distant future] shall come and build in the temple of YHWH, and you shall know that YHWH of Hosts has sent Me to you. And this shall come to pass if you will diligently obey the voice of YHWH your God."'" (Zec 6:12-15)

Ezekiel describes Messiah entering the temple through the eastern gate:

Afterward he brought me to the gate—the gate that looks toward the east. And, look! The glory of the God of Israel came from the way of the east, and His voice was like the noise of many waters, and the earth shined with His glory!

And it was according to the appearance of the vision that I saw—according to the vision that I saw when I came to destroy the city. And the visions were like the vision that I saw by the river Chebar, and I fell on my face.

And the glory of YHWH came into the house by the way of the gate whose prospect is toward the east.

So the Spirit took me up and brought me into the inner court and, look! The glory of YHWH filled the house! And I heard Him speaking to me out of the house, and the man stood by me. And he said to me, "Son of man, the place of My throne, and the place of the soles of My feet, where I will dwell in the midst of the children of Israel forever, and My holy name, shall the house of Israel no longer defile—neither they, nor their kings, by their whoredom, nor by the carcasses of their kings in their high places." (Eze 43:1-7)

This prophecy has not yet been fulfilled. Israel did defile the second temple, even up to the day it was destroyed. Jesus said that they had turned it into a den of thieves. And no doubt, the presence of YHWH departed when the veil was torn from top to bottom on the death of Jesus, the Messiah.

We know from Isaiah 11:1-5, which describes the Lord's Second Coming, that The Branch is the Lord Jesus. The crowns given to the four Israelites named indicates that these resurrected saints will be honored for their faithfulness to YHWH during their mortal lifetimes, just as the resurrected David will be honored with the throne of Israel. Those who are far off are the Israelites who will be gathered into the Promised Land from out of all the nations when the Lord Jesus returns.

These verses have been given a spiritual connotation by some who reject the idea of a literal temple being built by the Lord. They say the Body of Christ is the temple that Jesus would build, and He will rule from Heaven over His creation through that temple.

It is true that we are called the temple of God because God's Spirit dwells in us if we have saving faith in Jesus as our Redeemer. Also, the corporate Body of Christ may be considered the dwelling place of God. But in this case we are concerned with the physical temple to be built in Jerusalem by the Lord when He returns. The specific mention of the four Israelites, as well as the statement that the temple would be built by men "from far off" can have no reference to the Body of Christ. Jesus will build the temple by employing Israelites who have returned from the Diaspora.

Ezekiel, chapters 40 through 43 describe the Millennial Temple. This was written during the Babylonian Captivity, after the destruction of Solomon's temple and before the construction of Zerubbabel's temple. For this reason those who do not believe in the Millennial Kingdom, and/or do not believe in the restored kingdom of Israel, suggest that Ezekiel is describing Zerubbabel's temple. But the description of the Temple in Ezekiel does not match that of Zerubbabel's temple, which was later refurbished in the Hellenistic style by Herod the Great.

Also, there was a prophecy related to Ezekiel's Temple that has yet to be fulfilled:

> And He said to me, "Son of man, the place of My throne, and the place of the soles of My feet, where I will dwell in the midst of the children of Israel forever, and the house of Israel shall no longer defile My holy name—neither they nor their kings by their whoredom, nor by the carcasses of their kings in their high places." (Eze 43:7)

This cannot be said of Zerubbabel's temple (aka Herod's temple), which was defiled by the Jewish Zealots during the siege of Jerusalem by the Roman general Titus. These prophecies in Ezekiel of a coming temple must be for the future.

Nor can it be for this age. God will not sanction any temple built by men, nor will He dwell in it:

> "God, who made the world and all things in it, seeing that He is Lord of Heaven and earth, does not live in temples made with hands, nor is worshipped with men's hands as though He needed anything, seeing He gives to all, life, and breath, and all things, and has made from one blood all nations of men to dwell on all the face of the earth, and has determined the times before appointed, and the bounds of their habitation so that they should seek the Lord, if perhaps they might search for Him and find Him, though He is not far from every one of us." (Ac 14:24-27)

These words were spoken by the apostle Paul as he reasoned with the Greeks on Mars' Hill. They are for the present age, known as "the Time of the Gentiles." They were not for the time that the temple in Jerusalem functioned. That time ended with Jesus' death when the veil of the temple was torn and the Holy of Holies exposed. From that time until the Lord returns, God's presence will not dwell in temples made by the hands of men. But when the Lord returns He will build the Millennial Temple and will enter into it from the East Gate:

> Then he brought me back the way of the gate of the outward sanctuary which looks toward the east, and it was shut. Then YHWH said to me, "This gate shall be shut; it shall not be opened, and no man shall enter in by it because YHWH, the God of Israel, has entered in by it. Therefore it shall be shut. It is for the prince; the prince, He shall sit in it to eat bread before YHWH; He shall enter by the way of the porch of that gate, and shall go out by the way of the same." (Eze 44:1-3)

This prophecy can be fulfilled only by the Lord Jesus when He returns. According to Ezekiel 43:1 the prince is Jesus. Again, the terms "king" and "prince" are often interchangeable in Scripture.

The eastern gate to the city was sealed in 1541 by the Ottoman Sultan Suleiman the Magnificent. It has been suggested that he did this not only for defensive reasons, but in order to prevent fulfillment of the prophecy of Israel's Messiah entering through it. This is why a Muslim cemetery was built in front of the gate. Muslims erroneously think that Jewish priests are not permitted to enter cemeteries. Thus, in their thinking, Elijah, who would precede the Messiah, was a descendent of Aaron, and therefore would be a priest of Israel and unable to enter through the eastern gate.

Now, in view of all this, is it possible that men will build something they call the temple of God, even without God's sanction, prior to the Lord's return? Of course, anything is possible in that regard. But would God call it "the temple of God"? Not likely.

Yet I remain open to the possibility that such a structure could be built, and that the last-days anti-Christ might enter it to make his proclamation. But I wouldn't hold my breath waiting for it.

Reinstitution of Sacrifices

The instructions for the building of the Millennial Temple require that provision be made for sacrifices. No sacrifices today are of any merit because the blood of Jesus covers the sins of His people during this time. Those mortal Israelites who are brought into the Millennial Kingdom will have to offer sacrifices in order to demonstrate their obedience to God.

Do not be alarmed at this. These people will not have come to God through faith in Jesus Christ. They will believe only after they have seen Him return in the clouds.

After the Lord returns, those Israelites who would not believe until they were forced to do so by what they will see (the Lord returning in the clouds) will not have had faith in the blood of Christ to cleanse them prior to this. They will have missed that opportunity. Now they will have to offer sacrifices in the Millennial Temple with the understanding that they represent the Lord's sacrifice, not in foresight, but in hindsight. But it is still the blood of Christ that cleanses from all sin.

Some will dispute this. But remember that the temple of which Ezekiel speaks is a future temple commissioned by God Himself. This is not Solomon's temple, or Zerubbabel's (Herod's) temple. Both were destroyed. Additionally, this is said to be the temple where The Branch, Jesus, will sit on His throne (Zec 6:12-15). This temple has never been built.

Even if it were a temple built prior to the establishment of the Millennial Kingdom (which it is not), these are God's commands for sacrifices; they cannot be ignored. That it is a yet future temple is supported by the fact that no previous temples have been built to the specifications revealed to Ezekiel. More important, the Messiah never entered into any previous temple in this manner:

And, look! The glory of the God of Israel came from the way of the east, and His voice was like a noise of many waters! And the earth shined with his glory! (Eze 43:2)

The reinstitution of the sacrifices, the observance of God's feasts, new moons, Sabbaths, and all that pertained to ancient Israel will be a testimony to the nations that Israel (in this case, mortal men, not the resurrected) belongs to God. For another shock to the system, consider that circumcision of the flesh will once again be an ordinance of God:

And YHWH said to me, "Son of man, mark well, and see with your eyes, and hear with your ears, all that I say to you concerning all the ordinances of the house of YHWH, and all of its laws, and mark well the entering in of the house, with every going out of the sanctuary.

"And You shall say to the rebellious—to the house of Israel—'The Lord YHWH says this: "O you house of Israel, let it suffice you of all your abominations, in that you have brought into My sanctuary aliens, uncircumcised in heart, and uncircumcised in flesh, to be in My sanctuary, to pollute it—even My house—when you offer My bread, the fat and the blood, and they have broken My covenant because of all your abominations. And you have not kept the charge of My holy things, but you have set keepers of My charge in My sanctuary for yourselves.""'

The Lord YHWH says this: "No alien, of any alien that is among the children of Israel—uncircumcised in heart, or uncircumcised in flesh—shall enter into My sanctuary." (Eze 44:5-9)

This is still in the context of the Millennial Temple. The reason for the reinstitution of the Law is that the Israelites (as well as the Gentiles) who enter into the Millennial Kingdom will be considered rebellious because they did not come to God through the Messiah when they had the chance before entering into the Kingdom. They were idolatrous, many involved in New Age and other philosophies today, even atheism and agnosticism. Yet there evidently will be a remnant among Israel from the descendants of Zadok who will not have been idolatrous, and will bear the honor of ministering to God:

"And the Levites that went far away from Me when Israel went astray—who went astray from Me after their idols—they shall bear their iniquity. Yet they shall be ministers in My sanctuary, having charge at the gates of the house and ministering to the house. They shall slay the burnt offering and the sacrifice for the people, and they shall stand before them to minister to them.

"Because they ministered to them before their idols and caused the house of Israel to fall into iniquity, therefore I have lifted up My hand against them," says the Lord YHWH, "and they shall bear their iniquity. And they shall not come near Me to do the office of a priest to Me, nor come near any of My holy things in the most holy place. But they shall bear their shame and their abominations which they have committed.

"But I will make them keepers of the charge of the house for all its service, and for all that shall be done therein. But the priests, the Levites—the sons of Zadok that kept charge of My sanctuary when the children of Israel went astray from Me—they shall come near Me to minister to Me, and they shall stand before Me to offer to Me the fat and the blood," says the Lord God. "They shall enter into My sanctuary and they shall come near My table to minister to Me, and they shall keep My ordinance." (Eze 44:10-16)

Scripture and history record that Zadok was high priest in Solomon's temple (the first temple), and that the high priesthood continued in his lineage through the second-temple era. That portion of Ezekiel's prophecy was partially fulfilled in the second temple. But there are many prophecies that have partial fulfillment in types and shadows of ancient Israel. The priesthood of Zadok began with Solomon, continued through the second-temple era, and will be reinstated with the Millennial Temple.

Only God knows the hearts of these people; it will be up to Him to determine who fits where. It is not up to us to question how all these things will take place; we know only that they will. Let us take God at His Word and not try to fit Scripture to theological presuppositions.

As we've seen, the Millennial Temple will never be defiled. The Gentiles, as well as the Jewish Zealots, did defile the last temple, and this rule was never imposed on the priests in that temple where all Levites acted as priests. Only the Levites from the lineage of Zadok will be allowed to draw near to God to offer the sacrifices in the Millennial Temple.

The idea of the sacrifices being reinstituted has caused some consternation among the detractors of the Millennium, and even among many who believe in the coming Millennial Age. They insist that there can no longer be any sacrifices because Jesus was the ultimate sacrifice. To suggest that God will require sacrifices in the future is to deny the blood of Jesus. Yet in view of Ezekiel's references to sacrifices in the Millennial Temple (e.g., Eze 44:10-16, etc.), we must believe Scripture even when it seems to be contradictory or contrary to what we understand. There are many mysteries that God has not yet revealed, most of which are reserved for our understanding after the resurrection.

Let us consider a few truths:

1) The sacrifice that Jesus offered was not for Israel only, but for the whole world (1Jn 2:2). During this Time of the Gentiles the Lord has left off dealing with Israel as a nation and a kingdom. Presently He is gathering to Himself a new man made from two—Jew and Gentile. Temple sacrifices pertain only to Israel as a kingdom and nation;

2) Those who receive Jesus must do so by faith, not by sight. Even when He was among the Jews, performing great signs and wonders, they did not believe in Him. Nor have most men, Jew or Gentile, believed in Him throughout this present age. When He appears in the sky the Jews will see Him and they will mourn because they will recognize their Messiah. From that time on there will be no faith without sight. The Jews will be forced to acknowledge the Messiah and to worship Him. They will have to prove their faith by offering the sacrifices commanded by God, just as the Gentiles will have to prove their faith and obedience by bringing their gifts to the King in Jerusalem during the Feast of Tabernacles;

3) The sacrifices will still point to the redemptive work of Christ, but they will not be offered as types or shadows of the perfect sacrifice of a coming Messiah. They will be a commemoration of what He did on the cross, looking backward, not forward;

4) Who are we to challenge God's Word on this or any other issue? If He says the sacrifices will be reinstituted, then it is not ours to question why.

There is far too much scriptural evidence for a Millennial Temple and the sacrifices that will be offered there, to dismiss them as allegory or to suggest that the Lord has annulled them. Let us take God's Word for what it clearly says, and not try to make it fit into any theological presuppositions.

The Ark of the Covenant

The Ark of the Covenant will not be in the Millennial Temple because the Lord Himself will dwell there:

"And it shall come to pass, when you are multiplied and increased in the land in those days," says YHWH, "they shall no longer say, 'The Ark of the Covenant of YHWH,' nor shall it come to mind. Neither shall they remember it; neither shall they visit it; neither shall that be done anymore. At that time they shall call Jerusalem the throne of YHWH, and all the nations shall be gathered into it, to the name of YHWH, to Jerusalem. Neither shall they walk anymore after the imagination of their evil heart." (Jer 3:16-17)

The present-day search for the Ark of the Covenant will never bear fruit. There are many rumors that the Ark has been found, but no proof of such claims exists. Much has been made of the assertion that a cleric in Ethiopia guards the Ark of the Covenant in a building into which no man is permitted to enter. But that is nothing more than an empty claim. Because no one can enter the building, no one can verify that the Ark is there. But Scripture gives us a more sure word as to its whereabouts:

And the temple of God was opened in Heaven, and there was seen in His temple the Ark of His Covenant. And there were lightning, and voices, and thundering, and an earthquake, and great hail. (Rv 11:19)

Christians who are looking with anticipation for the rebuilding of the temple and the discovery of the Ark of the Covenant are wasting their time. The Ark of the Covenant is in Heaven; it is no longer on the earth.

It is posited by some that the Ark in which Aaron placed his staff, the manna, and the tablets of the Law was merely a copy of the Ark that is in

Heaven. Some say that this Ark in Heaven is the original which was the pattern for the one Moses constructed. There is no scriptural evidence to support this idea. There was only one Ark of the Covenant known to John and spoken of elsewhere in Scripture. And there was only one staff of Aaron that was in the Ark, as well as one set of stone tablets upon which Moses wrote the Ten Commandments. Yet even if the Ark mentioned in John's Revelation is different from the one Moses built, that does not negate the truth that God will not honor any temple made by men today.

The reason the belief is held that the Ark John saw is not the one Moses built is that men do not want to give up the idea that they will one day see the temple rebuilt before the Lord returns. The Ark of the Covenant was under the mercy seat, upon which the blood of the sacrifices was sprinkled. Without the Ark of the Covenant no legitimate sacrifices can be offered in any temple that might be built today. Thus, no legitimate temple can be built. It is possible that the Ark was taken to Heaven to assure this.

Either way, God would not call an illegitimate temple constructed by unbelievers, "the temple of God."

But doesn't Scripture say that the anti-Christ will stand in the temple proclaiming that he is God?

Not exactly. We will be addressing that issue, based on 2 Thessalonians 3:4, as we progress.

ALL NATIONS WILL WORSHIP THE LORD

Although it will be necessary for Israel to vanquish her enemies and take absolute control of the Promised Land, eventually all nations will come to worship the Lord, at least outwardly, for part of the Millennial Age. The Lord will destroy all false gods within the Promised Land and put down all His enemies, requiring that YHWH alone be worshipped:

"Go and proclaim these words toward the north and say, 'Return, you backsliding Israel,' says YHWH, 'and I will not cause My anger to fall on you, for I am merciful,' says YHWH, 'and I will not keep anger forever.

"'Only acknowledge your iniquity, that you have transgressed against YHWH your God, and have scattered your ways to the aliens under every green tree, and you have not obeyed My voice,' says YHWH.

"'Turn, O backsliding children,' says YHWH, 'for I am married to you, and I will take you one from a city, and two from a family, and I will bring you to Zion, and I will give you shepherds according to My heart, who shall feed you with knowledge and understanding.

"'And it shall happen, when you are multiplied and increased in the land in those days,' says YHWH, 'they shall no longer say, "The Ark of the Covenant of YHWH," nor shall it come to mind, nor shall they remember it, nor shall they visit it, nor shall that be done anymore.

"'At that time they shall call Jerusalem the throne of YHWH, and all the nations shall be gathered to it—to the name of YHWH—to Jerusalem. Nor shall they walk any longer after the imagination of their evil heart.

"'In those days the house of Judah shall walk with the house of Israel, and they shall come together out of the land of the north to the land that I have given for an inheritance to your fathers.'" (Jer 3:12-18)

Never since the days of Solomon have Israel and Judah walked together. And the Ark of the Covenant was important to the last temple. These prophecies cannot have been fulfilled in the past, nor will they be fulfilled until the Lord returns to gather all Israel and Judah back into the Promised Land. At that time all the nations of the earth will gather in the name of YHWH during the Feast of Tabernacles.

The Psalmist has issued these prophecies:

The humble shall eat and be satisfied. Those who seek YHWH shall praise Him; Your heart shall live forever.

All the ends of the world shall remember and turn to YHWH, and all the families of the nations shall worship before You. For the Kingdom is YHWH's, and He is the governor among the nations. (Ps 22:26-28)

All nations whom You have made shall come and worship before You, O Lord, and shall glorify Your name. (Ps 86:9)

When the Psalmist said, "The humble shall eat and be satisfied," he was stating a prelude to Psalms 37:11: "The humble shall inherit the earth and shall delight themselves in the abundance of peace."

Isaiah echoed this sentiment:

The humble shall also increase their joy in YHWH, and the poor among men shall rejoice in the Holy One of Israel. (Isa 29:19)

In what have come to be known as "the Beatitudes," Jesus said, "Blessed are the humble, for they shall inherit the earth" (Mt 5:5).

None of these prophecies have been realized. And coupled with other Scriptures that speak of the Lord ruling from Jerusalem over the whole earth, we understand that they will not be realized until He returns bodily to the earth as He promised.

At that time, Paul's iteration of Isaiah's prophecy (Isa 45:23) will be fulfilled:

> For it is written, "'As I live,' says the Lord, 'every knee shall bow to Me, and every tongue shall confess to God.'" (Ro 14:11)

> Therefore, God has also highly exalted Him and given Him a name that is above every name, so that at the name of Jesus every knee should bow, of things in Heaven and things in earth, and things under the earth, and that every tongue should confess that "Jesus Christ is Lord" to the glory of God the Father. (Php 2:9-11)

Yet although all knees must bow, and all tongues must confess that Jesus Christ is Lord, it doesn't necessarily mean that the hearts of all men will be changed. Human nature will never change; all men are born in sin and are rebellious in heart. At the end of the Millennial Age their rebelliousness will be fully manifested.

THE FINAL REBELLION

During the Millennial Age men will not have the power to express their rebelliousness. When Scripture says that the Lord will rule the nations with a rod of iron, they are acknowledging that truth. A rod of iron would not be necessary were men changed to holiness in their nature without the new birth through faith in Christ.

Any hint of rebellion will be dealt with swiftly and justly. That is what is meant by ruling with a rod of iron. There will be no plea bargains for lawbreakers; there will be no pandering to sin. Justice will be meted according to the Law without respect of persons. Even the threat that the nations will receive no rain if they do not obey the Lord, and the more severe penalties if the nations persist in their refusal to do so, is proof that such rebellion will be entertained by men.

Further proof is that at the end of the Millennial Age Satan will be freed to deceive the nations into gathering against the King in Jerusalem in a final attempt to dethrone Him:

And when the thousand years are over, Satan shall be freed from his prison and shall go out to deceive the nations that are in the four quarters of the earth—Gog and Magog—to gather them together to battle, the number of whom is as the sand of the sea.

And they went up on the breadth of the earth, and encircled the camp of the saints about, and the beloved city.

And fire came down from God out of Heaven and devoured them.

And the Devil who deceived them was cast into the lake of fire and brimstone where the beast and the false prophet are, and shall be tormented day and night forever and ever. (Rv 20:7-10)

Satan will not be cast into the lake of fire earlier when the anti-Christ and the false prophet are cast in, which will be at the beginning of the Millennial Age. Satan's ultimate doom will come at the end of the Millennial Age. That will be after the final rebellion before the Lord renews the heavens and the earth.

The truth is that even with righteousness prevailing throughout the Millennial Age, mankind will largely want to rebel against the Lord. They will resent the righteous rule of swift justice and enforced compliance to the Law of God. They will consider the Lord and His saints hindrances to their "human potential," their "self-determination," and their "personal freedom" which are so precious to man. But until Satan is freed they will be powerless to do anything but acquiesce or suffer the consequences of their sins.

Gog and Magog

We read in Revelation 20:7 above, that certain peoples identified as Gog and Magog will be brought against the Lord in Jerusalem at the end of the Millennium.

As incredible as this seems, why should it surprise us? As we consider the very last days of the Millennium we see that there will be many nations who will be deceived to think they can come against Jerusalem to war against the King and the inhabitants of the city (Rv 20:7-9).

But does the prophecy not say, "neither shall they learn war any more" (Isa 2:4; Mic 4:3)?

This prophecy has to do with nation lifting up sword against nation. There will be no more wars between nations. The final battle against Jerusalem will be all the nations united against the King of the earth. Revelation 20:8 speaks of Gog and Magog leading the nations that are deceived by Satan to attempt an overthrow of the "repressive" Kingdom into which they have had to bring their tribute for the past one-thousand years.

Ezekiel also mentions the rebellion led by Gog and Magog:

And the word of YHWH came to me, saying, "Son of man, set your face against Gog, the land of Magog, the chief prince of Meshech and Tubal, and prophesy against him, and say, 'The Lord YHWH says this: "Look! I am against you, O Gog, the chief prince of Meshech and Tubal, and I will turn you back, and put hooks into your jaws, and I will bring you forth, and all your army, horses and horsemen, all of them clothed with all sorts of armor, even a great company with bucklers and shields, all of them handling swords: Persia, Ethiopia, and Libya with them; all of them with shield and helmet. Gomer, and all his bands; the house of Togarmah of the north quarters, and all his bands, and many people with you.

""Be prepared, and prepare for yourself, you, and all your company that are assembled to you, and be a guard to them.

""After many days you shall be visited. In the latter years you shall come into the land that is brought back from the sword and is gathered out of many people, against the mountains of Israel which have always been waste, but it is brought forth out of the nations, and they shall dwell safely all of them.

""You shall ascend and come like a storm; you shall be like a cloud to cover the land, you, and all your armies, and many people with you."

"'The Lord YHWH says this: "It shall also come to pass that at the same time, things will come into your mind, and you will think an evil thought, and you will say, 'I will go up to the land of unwalled villages; I will go to those who are at rest, who dwell safely, all of them dwelling without walls, and having neither bars nor gates, to take a spoil, and to take a prey,' to turn your hand upon the desolate places that are now inhabited, and upon the people that are gathered out of the nations, which have gotten cattle and goods, that dwell in the midst of the land.'"

""Sheba, and Dedan, and the merchants of Tarshish, with all its young lions, shall say to you, 'Have you come to take a spoil? Have you gathered your company to take a prey—to carry away silver and gold, to take away cattle and goods, to take a great spoil?'"

"'Therefore, son of man, prophesy and say to Gog, "The Lord YHWH says this: 'In that day when My people of Israel dwell safely, will you not know it? And you will come from your place out of the north parts, you and many people with you, all of them riding on horses, a great company, and a mighty army. And you will come up against My people of Israel like a cloud to cover the land; it shall be in the latter days, and I will bring you against My land so that the heathen may know Me, when I shall be sanctified in you, O Gog, before their eyes.'

""'The Lord YHWH says this: 'Are you he of whom I have spoken in old time by My servants the prophets of Israel who prophesied in those days many years that I would bring you against them?'

""'And it shall come to pass at the same time when Gog shall come against the land of Israel," says the lord YHWH, "that My fury shall come up in My face. For I have spoken in My jealousy and in the fire of My wrath, surely in that day there shall be a great shaking in the land of Israel so that the fishes of the sea, and the fowls of the heavens, and the beasts of the field, and all creeping things that creep upon the earth, and all the men that are upon the face of the earth, shall shake at My presence, and the mountains shall be thrown down, and the steep places shall fall, and every wall shall fall to the ground. And I will call for a sword against him throughout all My mountains," says the Lord YHWH. "Every man's sword shall be against his brother. And I will plead against him with pestilence and with blood, and I will rain upon him, and upon his bands, and upon the many people that are with him, an overflowing rain, and great hailstones, fire, and brimstone. Thus will I magnify Myself, and sanctify Myself, and I will be known in the eyes of many nations, and they shall know that I am YHWH."

"'Therefore, you son of man, prophesy against Gog, and say, "The Lord YHWH says this: 'Look! I am against you, O Gog, the chief prince of Meshech and Tubal, and I will turn you back, and leave but the sixth part of you, and will cause you to come up from the north parts, and will bring you upon the mountains of Israel. And I will strike your bow out of your left hand, and will cause your arrows to fall out of your right hand. You shall fall upon the mountains of Israel, you, and all your bands, and the people that are with you. I will give you to the ravenous birds of every sort, and to the beasts of the field to be devoured. You shall fall upon the open field, for I have spoken it,' says the Lord YHWH.

""And I will send a fire on Magog, and among those who dwell carelessly in the isles, and they shall know that I am YHWH. So I will make my holy name known in the midst of My people Israel, and I will not let them pollute My holy name any longer, and the heathen shall know that I am YHWH, the Holy One in Israel.'"

"Look! It has come, and it is done," says the Lord YHWH. "This is the day of which I have spoken.

"And those who dwell in the cities of Israel shall go forth, and shall set on fire and burn the weapons, both the shields and the bucklers, the bows and the arrows, and the hand staves, and the spears, and they shall burn them with fire for seven years, so that they shall take no wood out of the field, nor cut down any out of the forests. For they shall burn the weapons with fire, and they shall spoil those that spoiled them, and rob those that robbed them," says the Lord YHWH.

"And it shall come to pass in that day, that I will give to Gog a place there of graves in Israel, the valley of the passengers on the east of the sea, and it shall stop the noses of the passengers, and they shall bury Gog and all his multitude there, and they shall call it 'The Valley of Hamon-gog.'

"And for seven months the house of Israel shall be burying them so that they may cleanse the land. Yes, all the people of the land shall bury them, and it shall be to them a renowned day that I shall be glorified," says the Lord YHWH.

"And they shall sever out men of continual employment, passing through the land with the passengers to bury those that remain upon the face of the earth, to cleanse it. After the end of seven months they shall search, and the passengers that pass through the land, when any sees a man's bone, then he shall set up a sign by it, till the buriers have buried it in the valley of Hamon-gog.

"And also, the name of the city shall be Hamonah. Thus shall they cleanse the land.

"And, you son of man, the Lord YHWH says this: 'Speak to every feathered fowl, and to every beast of the field: "Assemble yourselves, and come! Gather yourselves on every side to My sacrifice that I sacrifice for you—a great sacrifice upon the mountains of Israel—that you may eat flesh, and drink blood. You shall eat the flesh of the mighty, and drink the blood of the princes of the earth, of rams, of lambs, and of goats, of bullocks, all of them fatlings of Bashan. And you shall eat fat till you are full, and drink blood till you are drunk, of My sacrifice which I have sacrificed for you. Thus you shall be filled at My table with horses and chariots, with mighty men, and with all men of war,'" says the Lord YHWH.

"And I will set My glory among the heathen, and all the heathen shall see My judgment that I have executed, and My hand that I have laid upon them. So the house of Israel shall know that I am YHWH their God from that day and forward. And the heathen shall know that the house of Israel went into captivity for their iniquity. Because they trespassed against Me, therefore I hid My face from them and gave them into the hand of their enemies so they all fell by the sword. According to their uncleanness and according to their transgressions have I done to them, and hid My face from them." (Eze 38-39)

It is popularly taught that these verses refer to a time when Gog and Magog, believed to be Russia and her allies from the north, will invade Israel during the present age. But we cannot separate these verses from Revelation 20:7-10. These are the only places in Scripture where Gog and Magog are mentioned together seeking to destroy Jerusalem, particularly at a time when Israel is dwelling safely after returning to their land. Israel has never dwelt safely in her land, certainly not in this present age. This attack by Gog and Magog will occur when Israel is dwelling safely without walls. Modern Israel continues to expand its construction of walls for defense. They will need those walls until the Lord returns, so this prophecy cannot be for this age; it must be for the future Millennial Age.

Notice also that the weapons of warfare will be burned as firewood for seven years. Few modern weapons can be used for firewood. This indicates that when the Lord returns to establish His reign for the thousand years all weapons of war will be destroyed and/or converted to peaceful use (Isa 2:4; Mic 4:3). The Lord's enemies will be using primitive weapons—bows and arrows—which can be easily burned after they are defeated.

This, coupled with the fact that Israel will have been gathered out of all nations into the land, is further proof that Gog and Magog will attack Jerusalem at the end of the Millennium, and not before.

If we think of the Millennium as anything, it must be as the Kingdom of God on earth. Currently the Kingdom of God on earth is manifested through the Holy Spirit working in those who are obedient to the Word of

God through faith in Jesus Christ. But when the Lord returns, the Kingdom of God will be fully manifested through His kingship.

12

THE KINGDOM OF GOD ON EARTH

The central aspect of Jesus' teachings was the Kingdom of God (Mt, "Kingdom of Heaven"). Everything, including personal salvation, He linked to the Kingdom of God. He never proclaimed the Gospel of personal salvation apart from the Kingdom of God. At the start of His ministry Jesus came into Galilee proclaiming the Gospel of the Kingdom of God, and saying, "The time is fulfilled, and the Kingdom of God is at hand! Repent, and believe the Gospel!" (Mk 1:14-15)

When He sent out the twelve apostles He charged them to proclaim the same message that He and John the Baptist had proclaimed:

Jesus sent these twelve out and commanded them, saying, "Do not go the way of the Gentiles, and do not enter into any city of the Samaritans. But rather, go to the lost sheep of the house of Israel. And as you go, preach, saying, 'The Kingdom of Heaven is near!'" (Mt 10:5-7)

Throughout His ministry Jesus focused entirely on the Kingdom of God, relating how righteousness is the basis for entering into it. In the Beatitudes He said:

"Blessed are those who are persecuted for the sake of righteousness, for theirs is the Kingdom of Heaven." (Mt 5:10)

In this same message He said, "I say to you, that unless your righteousness exceeds the righteousness of the scribes and Pharisees, you shall in no case enter into the Kingdom of Heaven." (Mt 5:20)

Righteousness is imputed through Christ. But living righteously is equated with doing the will of the Father:

"Not everyone who says to Me, 'Lord, Lord,' shall enter into the Kingdom of Heaven; but he who does the will of My Father who is in Heaven. Many will say to Me in that day, 'Lord, Lord, have we not prophesied in Your name, and in Your name have cast out devils, and in Your name done many wonderful works?' And then I will say to them, 'I never knew you; depart from Me, you who work wickedness.'" (Mt 7:21-23)

Righteousness is also equated with humility:

At the same time, the disciples came to Jesus, saying, "Who is the greatest in the Kingdom of Heaven?"

And Jesus called a little child to Himself, and set him in the midst of them, and said, "Truly I say to you, unless you are converted and become like little children, you shall not enter into the Kingdom of Heaven. Therefore, whoever will humble himself as this little child, the same is greatest in the Kingdom of Heaven." (Mt 18:1-4)

There is no mention of the Kingdom of Heaven by that name in all the writings of the Hebrew prophets, although Daniel 7:27 alludes to it:

And the kingdom and dominion, and the greatness of the kingdom under the whole heaven, shall be given to the people of the saints of the most High, whose kingdom is an everlasting kingdom , and all dominions shall serve and obey him.

As far as we know from Scripture, the first time the Israelites ever heard of the Kingdom of Heaven was when John the Baptist spoke of it, and Jesus expounded on it. The only kingdom from God to which the prophets refer is the kingdom of Israel. But the kingdom of Israel is not the Kingdom of Heaven to which Jesus referred.

That's not to say they never heard of the Kingdom of Heaven; we don't know for sure. But it is not found anywhere in Scripture prior to the writing of the Gospels.

Notice that some Scriptures refer to "the Kingdom of God," whereas others refer to "the Kingdom of Heaven." Is there a difference?

THE KINGDOM OF HEAVEN/THE KINGDOM OF GOD

Throughout the writings of the apostles there are two terms used interchangeably: "The Kingdom of God" and "The Kingdom of Heaven." There is a popular teaching that the Kingdom of Heaven is not the same as the Kingdom of God. It states that the Kingdom of Heaven is an earthly kingdom and the Kingdom of God is a heavenly kingdom, that the Kingdom of God encompasses the Kingdom of Heaven, but they are not one and the same.

Yet I believe the two terms are synonymous for a few reasons:

Matthew is the only Gospel writer who uses the term "Kingdom of Heaven." All other Gospel writers use the term "Kingdom of God" exclusively, as does the apostle Paul. If there were a difference, why do all the other writers not mention the Kingdom of Heaven? Certainly it should be important enough to merit their attention. And Matthew also uses the term "Kingdom of God," but on only a few occasions, one of which equates the two:

> Then Jesus said to His disciples, "Truly, I say to you that a rich man shall enter into the Kingdom of Heaven with difficulty. And again, I say to you it is easier for a camel to go through the eye of a needle than for a rich man to enter into the Kingdom of God." (Mt 19:23-24)

There are a number of corresponding Scriptures in the synoptic Gospels where Matthew uses "the Kingdom of Heaven" and the others use "the Kingdom of God." For one example read Mt 13:31-33; Mk 4:30-32; Lk 13:18-21. Matthew likens the Kingdom of Heaven to a grain of mustard seed which grows to become a great tree, and to leaven which a woman hid in her flour until the whole lump was leavened. Luke relates the same two parables under the same circumstances, while Mark relates only the parable of the mustard seed under the same circumstances.

In response to their question why He spoke in parables, Matthew 13:11 has Jesus telling His disciples that it is given to them to know the mysteries of the Kingdom of Heaven; Luke 8:10 has Jesus telling them it is given to them to know the mysteries of the Kingdom of God.

In Matthew 3:1-2 John the Baptist heralds the Kingdom of Heaven, while in Mark 1:14-15 he heralds the Kingdom of God.

The Kingdom of God/Heaven is both a spiritual and an earthly kingdom. All who are in Christ are in the Kingdom of God/Heaven even while we are on the earth. Yet the Kingdom is ruled from Heaven and includes the Heavenly realm:

Blessed be the God and Father of our Lord Jesus Christ, who has blessed us with all spiritual blessings in heavenly places in Christ. (Eph 1:3)

But God, who is rich in mercy for His great love wherein He loved us even when we were dead in sins, has made us alive together with Christ (by grace you are saved) and has raised us up together and made us sit together in heavenly places in Christ Jesus so that in the ages to come he might show the exceeding riches of His grace in His kindness toward us through Christ Jesus. (Eph 2:4-7)

This grace is given to me, who am less than the least of all saints, so that I should preach among the Gentiles the unsearchable riches of Christ, and to make all men see what is the fellowship of the mystery, which from the beginning of the world has been hid in God who created all things by Jesus Christ, with the intent that now to the principalities and powers in heavenly places might be known by the called out, the manifold wisdom of God according to the eternal purpose which he purposed in Christ Jesus our Lord in whom we have boldness and access with confidence by the faith in Him. (Eph 3:8-12)

So we are on the earth physically, but we are in the Kingdom of God spiritually.

THE KINGDOM OF CHRIST

Scripture does reveal a purely earthly kingdom:

...giving thanks to the Father, who has made us able to be partakers of the inheritance of the saints in light, who has delivered us from the power of darkness, and has translated us into the **Kingdom of His dear Son** in whom we have redemption through His blood—the forgiveness of sins. (Col 1:12-14)

For this you know: that no whoremonger, nor unclean person, nor covetous man, who is an idolater, has any inheritance in the **Kingdom of Christ** and of God. (Eph 5:5)

The Kingdom of Christ is the earthly Kingdom that will be fully manifested during the Millennium. When it says "the Kingdom of Christ and of God" it is not speaking of the same Kingdom, but of two Kingdoms—the Kingdom of Christ, the present-through-Millennial Kingdom, and the Kingdom of God, which is eternal. The Kingdom of Christ will one day give way to the Kingdom of God:

But now Christ has risen from the dead and become the first fruits of those who slept. For because death came by man, the resurrection of the dead also came by man. For as in Adam all die, even so in Christ all shall be made alive. But every man in his own order: Christ the first fruits, afterward those who are Christ's at His coming.

Then will come the end when He will have delivered up the Kingdom to God, the Father, when He shall have put down all rule and all authority and power.

For He must reign till He has put all enemies under His feet. The last enemy that shall be destroyed is death. For He has put all things under His feet. But when He says all things are put under Him, it is clear that He who put all things under Him is excepted.

And when all things shall be subjected to Him, then the Son Himself shall also be subject to Him who put all things under Him so that God may be all-in-all. (1Co 15:20-28)

If the Kingdom of Christ and the Kingdom of God were the same, then Christ would not have to "deliver the Kingdom to God (the Father)." The Father already rules over the Kingdom of God. This is further proof that the Millennial Kingdom of Christ will be a reality.

Presently the eternal Kingdom of God and the Kingdom of Christ/His dear Son are operating concurrently and will do so until the end of the Millennium, after which the Lord Jesus will deliver the Kingdom to the Father.

In the Millennial Kingdom of Christ, the political kingdom of Israel will be realized, not only in the reign of Christ, but in the reign of David.

When Jesus entered Jerusalem to shouts of "Hosanna!" the people voiced their expectation of the return of David's kingdom:

And those who went ahead, and those who followed, cried out, saying, "Hosanna! Blessed is He who comes in the name of the Lord! Blessed be the kingdom of our father David, that comes in the name of the Lord! Hosanna in the highest!" (Mk 11:9-10)

The Lord did not command His disciples to silence the crowd or to correct them. He accepted their praises along with the blessing of the Davidic kingdom. Moreover, He must have known that they would be doing and saying these things. This is why He had His disciples get the donkey for Him to ride. He knew He was going to be recognized as the Messiah who would bring again the kingdom to Israel.

Also, when His disciples asked Him if He would at that time restore the kingdom to Israel He did not correct them, but merely told them that it was not for them to know the time the Father has in His own power (Ac 1:6-7).

To summarize: The Kingdom of Christ is not the Kingdom of God, but the Kingdom of Christ is contained within the Kingdom of God and will continue to operate concurrently with the Kingdom of God until the close of the Millennial Age. The Kingdom of Christ is spiritual during this "Time of the Gentiles," and it will be manifested physically during the Millennium.

I use the terms "the Kingdom of God" and "the Kingdom of Heaven" interchangeably.

CHARACTERISTICS OF THE KINGDOM OF GOD

Because the Kingdom of God is operative on the earth it is subject to earthly problems here.

"And from the days of John the Baptist until now the Kingdom of Heaven is pressed upon, and the energetic grasp for it." (Mt 11:12)

This does not mean that people are eagerly pressing to get into the Kingdom of God, as some say. Show me anywhere that has ever taken place. People have to be persuaded to enter into the Kingdom of God; they have to be persuaded to live righteously in Christ by faith in order to do so. I believe this Scripture means that aggressive people seek to take control within the Kingdom of God. This is why Jesus warned of false teachers and wolves in sheep's clothing. The evidence throughout the centuries points to ungodly men who have taken authority over God's people.

This is also why, in His parables, Jesus spoke of good and evil existing together in the Kingdom of God. As He explained the mysteries of the Kingdom He spoke in earthly terms, not heavenly terms. He did not relate the Kingdom to the eternal, spiritual realm as often as He did the present earthly realm. He said the Kingdom of God is like:

- a man who sowed good seed but his enemy sowed weeds among the wheat (Mt 12:24-30);
- the unforgiving servant (Mt 18:23-35);
- the workers who complained about their wages (Mt 20:1-16);
- the invited guests to a prince's wedding killing the king's servants (Mt 22:2-14).

Jesus gave many other examples where good and evil operate side-by-side within the Kingdom of God on earth. This explains what Jesus meant when He answered the Pharisees:

And when it was demanded of Him by the Pharisees, when the Kingdom of God would come, He answered them and said, "The Kingdom of God does not come with observation. Neither will they say, 'Look here!' or, 'Look there!' For, look! The Kingdom of God is within you." (Lk 17:20-21)

This has been used by preterists as a "proof text" to deny the reality of the Millennial Kingdom. But Jesus was speaking to them in present terms, not the future. Evil men reside within the Kingdom of God, and in that sense the Kingdom of God is within all men for the present. While they are in the Kingdom, the Kingdom is in them, and in their midst. In truth, it will remain so until the end of the Millennial Age. But the time will come when evil is cast out of the Kingdom of God forever.

This does not mean that the Kingdom of God is limited to the earth; God's Kingdom is spiritual as well as physical. But the Lord's parables emphasize the earthly, material aspects of the Kingdom which, if heeded, will result in the inheritance of the Kingdom of God on earth for those who are faithful servants of the Lord. Those who do not receive Christ or heed His words will not inherit the Kingdom of God on earth. They will remain in their graves until the White Throne Judgment spoken of in Revelation:

And I saw a great white throne, and Him who sat on it from whose face the earth and the heavens fled away, and there was found no place for them.

And I saw the dead, small and great, stand before God. And the books were opened. And another book was opened, which is the Book of Life.

And the dead were judged out of those things which were written in the books, according to their works.

And the sea gave up the dead that were in it; and Death and Hades delivered up the dead that were in them. And they were judged every man according to their works.

And Death and Hades were cast into the lake of fire. This is the second death.

And whoever was not found written in the Book of Life was cast into the lake of fire. (Rv 20:11-15)

The books other than the Book of Life are not named, but it may be surmised that these are the books of Death—the second death that will be the lot of all who lived evil lives, whether or not they called themselves by the Lord's name.

Accordingly, when we consider the Lord's parables that speak of His servants who commit evil acts without repentance, we should understand that all men are God's servants, whether or not they acknowledge that truth. He called the pagan kings Nebuchadnezzar and Cyrus His servants, so all men ultimately serve His purposes even as they oppose Him.

However, there are those who consider themselves the Lord's servants but who do not live accordingly. They live contrary to His Word; they do not overcome the evil in this life but love the world more than the Kingdom of God. They engage in evil acts and fight against the saints of God who try to bring correction to bear in the Body of Christ. These are nominal Christians who will not inherit the Millennial Kingdom on earth. They may or may not survive the White throne Judgment; only the Lord will decide, and we cannot be dogmatic about any person's eternal fate.

We do know this: some people whose names are written in the Book of Life could have their names blotted out:

> "He who overcomes, the same shall be clothed in white garments, and I will not blot out his name from the Book of Life, but I will confess his name before My Father, and before His angels." (Rv 3:5)

If it were not possible to have one's name blotted out of the Book of Life, the Lord would not have mentioned it.

This should be a sobering wake-up call to all of us. Will we be found faithful to the Lord? Will we enter into the Millennial Kingdom of Christ and be safe from the possibility of suffering the second death? If we don't believe in that Kingdom, can we inherit it?

I'm not saying that those who do not believe in the literal Millennial Kingdom will not inherit it, or at least enter into it (either as resurrected or mortal). I'm asking the rhetorical question as a means to hopefully get them to rethink their preterist or other position that denies that the Millennial Kingdom as a reality. We'll leave the final answers to the Lord.

Concerning overcomers inheriting the Millennial Kingdom, I believe there is a lot of misunderstanding. Some think that it means certain saints will become perfected and sinless while in their mortal flesh, which is unscriptural. I believe Scripture gives us an idea of what it means to be an "overcomer" in Revelation 12:11—the saints overcome the accusations of Satan by the blood of the Lamb, and by the word of our testimony—our faith in Jesus Christ lived out through our lives which we do not love above Him. Overcoming is not living a perfect life; it is not being sinless; it is not even our works for Christ. It is our state of being in Him.

We can see the wisdom of God in the first resurrection to rule and reign with Christ on earth during that time. It will be a reward for faithful service in this life; it will be (or should be) an incentive for His people to live faithfully; it will be a testimony to men and angels, both faithful and fallen, of His righteous and just dealing with all mankind.

13
UNDERSTANDING THE PROPHECIES

As we consider certain Scriptures vital to last-days prophecies, we will see where they fit into the overall eschatological picture. Two of the most important are those which concern Nebuchadnezzar's dream and Daniel's vision.

NEBUCHADNEZZAR'S DREAM

Most of the prophecies dealing with events yet future were penned by Daniel and Ezekiel. Isaiah, Jeremiah, Micah, Joel, and others also spoke of those events, but not to the same degree. Daniel's interpretation of Nebuchadnezzar's dream, and Daniel's own vision, are especially crucial to understanding what the future holds. But we must not assume that every detail in Daniel's vision is yet future. Many details of the prophecies have already been fulfilled in history.

For example, when Daniel interpreted Nebuchadnezzar's dream he described several kingdoms that would follow upon each other. (Daniel 2:28-45) Only the major kingdoms that would conquer Jerusalem over the centuries are addressed in that prophecy.

The Kingdom of Heaven will destroy not only the present world system, but all world systems upon which it is based, originally Babylon. We know from history the identity of all the earthly kingdoms in this prophecy. The stone cut out of the mountain without hands is the Kingdom of God, which will rule over all kingdoms on the earth during the Millennium:

And the seventh angel sounded, and there were great voices in Heaven, saying, "The kingdoms of this world have become the kingdoms of our Lord, and of His Christ; and He shall reign forever and ever." (Rv 11:15).

Blessed and holy is he who has a part in the first resurrection; on such the second death has no power, but they shall be priests of God and of Christ, and shall reign with Him for a thousand years. (Rv 20:6)

DANIEL'S VISION

God gave Daniel a vision that revealed Israel's future. As we read through this prophecy we must keep in mind some important scriptural truths:

- There are principalities or "princes" who rule over the nations (Da 10:20; Eph 6:12);
- The prophecy spans many centuries, as proven through history;
- All scriptural prophecies are pertinent to Israel, not to the world at large;
- All directions of the compass relate to Jerusalem;
- The kingdom of the north is Syria;
- The kingdom of the south is Egypt;
- The kings of the north and of the south are not merely different men at different times who take the thrones of their predecessors; they are also spiritual principalities over the kingdoms addressed.

An example of this last truth is that the king of the north (Syria) in 11:6 is Antiochus, whereas the king of the north in 11:7 is Seleucus II. The various kings are not delineated because the kings are not merely the human rulers, but the spiritual princes over the lands. Thus, "he" at the beginning is the same as "he" at the end, even though the human agents change.

When I say that all scriptural prophecies are pertinent to Israel, I mean that we cannot force other nations into the prophecy if they are not directly involved with Israel. The times, including multiple centuries, that do not relate to Israel are also not found in the prophecies. Such is the "Time of the Gentiles," which is a distinct period in history when God is calling out a remnant from among the nations besides Israel (although many Israelites are also included).

Where possible I will intersperse the names of the human principals involved.

It is important that we take this lengthy path because many of these prophecies, while having already been fulfilled, have been erroneously interpreted by some teachers to be about the future anti-Christ. Thus, the historical references are interspersed.

Daniel 10:12–12:13, relate the vision given Daniel by God while by the river Euphrates at Hiddekel.

10:12–11:2: Then He said to me, "Do not fear, Daniel, for from the first day that you set your heart to understand and to humble yourself before your God, your words were heard, and I have come because of your words. But the prince of the kingdom of Persia withstood me twenty-one days. But, look! Michael, one of the chief princes, came to help Me, and I remained there with the kings of Persia.

Now I have come to make you understand what shall befall your people [Israel] in the latter days, for the vision is yet for many days...."

Then He said, "Do you know why I come to you? And now I will return to fight with the prince of Persia, and when I have gone forth, look, the prince of Greece shall come. But I will show you that which is noted in the Scripture of truth, and there is no one who holds with me in these things but Michael your prince. Also, I, in the first year of Darius the Mede, even I, stood to confirm and to strengthen him. And now I will show you the truth. Look, there shall yet stand up three kings in Persia and the fourth shall be far richer than they all, and by his strength through his riches he will stir up all against the realm of Greece."

These three kings came after Cyrus who gave the commandment to rebuild Jerusalem, which begins the prophecy; the three kings who followed Cyrus were Cambyses, Bardiya and Darius I. The fourth king was Xerxes I who took over his father, Darius's campaign against the Greeks. It was Xerxes I who led the Persian army against the small force of 300 Spartans at Thermopylae.

11:3-4: And a mighty king will stand up, who shall rule with great dominion and do according to his will. And when he stands up, his kingdom shall be broken, and shall be divided toward the four winds of the heavens, and not to his posterity, nor according to his dominion which he ruled. For his kingdom shall be plucked up, even for others beside those."

The mighty king was Alexander the Great of Greece. Alexander's kingdom would be parceled out to the four kings who came up in his place. These were Ptolemy in Egypt to the south; Antigonus in Asia to the north; Seleucus over both Syria and Babylon to the north and east respectively; and Cassander in Macedonia to the west.

11:5-35: "And the king of the south [Ptolemy Lagidae of Egypt] and one of his princes [Seleucus I of Syria] shall be strong, and he shall be strong above him, and have dominion; his dominion shall be a great dominion. And in the end of years they shall join themselves together, for the daughter of the king of the south [Ptolemy's daughter Berenice] shall come to the king of the north [Antiochus of Syria] to make an agreement. But she shall not retain the power of the arm, neither shall he stand, nor his arm. But she shall be given up, and those who brought her, and he who fathered her, and he who strengthened her in these times.

"But out of a branch of her roots, one [Berenice's brother, Ptolemy III] shall stand up in his estate who shall come with an army and shall enter into the fortress of the king of the north [Seleucus II], and shall deal against them, and shall prevail, and shall also carry captives into Egypt—their gods, with their princes, and with their precious vessels of silver and of gold—and he shall continue more years than the king of the north.

"So the king of the south [Ptolemy III of Egypt] shall come into his [Seleucus II's] kingdom, and shall return into his own land. But his [Seleucus II's] sons [Ceraunus and Antiochus III ("the Great")] shall be stirred up, and shall assemble a multitude of great forces. And one [Antiochus the Great] shall certainly come and overflow [through Jerusalem], and pass through. Then he shall return and be stirred up, even to his fortress.

"And the king of the south [Ptolemy III] shall be moved with anger, and shall come forth and fight with him—with the king of the north with a great multitude—but the multitude shall be given into his hand. And when he has taken away the multitude, his heart shall be lifted up, and he shall cast down many ten thousands. But he shall not be strengthened by it. For the king of the north shall return and shall establish a multitude greater than the former, and shall certainly come after certain years with a great army and with many riches. And in those times many shall stand up against the king of the south. And the robbers of your people [traitorous Jews who joined Ptolemy but later rebelled and joined Syria] shall exalt themselves to establish the vision [to liberate Judea]; but they shall fall.

"So the king of the north shall come and erect a rampart and take the most fenced cities, and the power of the south shall not withstand, nor his chosen people, nor shall there be any strength to withstand. But he who comes against him shall do according to his own will, and no one shall stand before him. And he shall stand in the glorious land [Judea], which shall be consumed by his hand.

"He will also set his face to enter [into Egypt] with the strength of his whole kingdom, and upright ones with him; he will do this, and he will give him [Ptolemy III through a peace treaty] the daughter of women [Cleopatra], corrupting her [Antiochus hoped Cleopatra would betray Ptolemy], but she will not stand on his [her father's] side, neither be for him.

After this he will turn his face toward the isles, and shall take many. But a prince for his own behalf [the Roman Consul] shall cause the reproach offered by him to cease. Without his own reproach he shall cause it to turn upon him. [Antiochus' plans to defeat Rome were turned on him and he was defeated.]

"Then he [Antiochus] will turn his face toward the fort of his own land [Syria]: but he shall stumble and fall, and not be found. Then in his place will stand up a raiser of taxes [Seleucus IV] in the glory of the kingdom, but within a few days he shall be destroyed, neither in anger, nor in battle. [He was poisoned for political reasons.]

"And in his place will stand up a vile person [Antiochus IV "Epiphanes"], to whom they will not give the honor of the kingdom. But he will come in peaceably, and obtain the kingdom by flatteries. And with the power of a flood they shall be conquered before him, and shall be broken, yes, also the prince of the covenant [Onias, the high priest in Jerusalem]. And after the covenant made with him he will work deceitfully, for he will come up, and will become strong with few people. He will enter peacefully upon the richest places of the province, and he will do that which his fathers have not done, nor his fathers' fathers: he will scatter the prey, and spoil, and riches among them. Yes, and he will weave his devices against the strongholds for a time.

"And he will stir up his power and his courage against the king of the south with a great army. And the king of the south will be stirred up to battle with a very great and mighty army, but he will not stand, for they will weave devices against him. Yes, they who feed from the portion of his food will destroy him, and his army will overflow, and many will fall down slain.

"And both these kings' hearts will be to do mischief, and they will speak lies at one table. But it shall not prosper, for the end shall still be at the appointed time.

"Then he will return into his land with great riches, and his heart will be against the holy covenant [Antiochus persecuted the Jews, perceiving them to be against him], and he will do exploits and return to his own land. At the time appointed he shall return and come toward the south, but it shall not be as the former, or as the latter, because the ships of Chittim [Roman Cyprus] shall come against him. Therefore he will be dejected and return, and have anger against the holy covenant [Antiochus desecrated the temple and stole the holy implements, slaying 40,000 Jews in the process]. So will he do: he will return and have an understanding with those who forsake the holy covenant. [Antiochus installed the unfaithful Jew, Menelaus, as high priest. He was of the tribe of Benjamin, not Levi, so was not qualified to be high priest.]

And support will stand on his side, and they will pollute the sanctuary of strength, and will take away the daily sacrifice. [In response to an uprising that exiled Menelaus, Antiochus retook Jerusalem and proceeded to pollute the altar with broth made of swine's blood, then dedicated the temple to the Greek god Zeus.] And they will place the abomination that makes desolate [he later slew a pig on the altar].

"And by flattery he will corrupt such as do wickedly against the covenant. But the people that know their God shall be strong and do exploits [thus began the war of the Maccabees]. And those who understand among the people will instruct many, yet they shall fall by the sword, and by flame, by captivity, and by spoil, for many days.

"Now when they fall, they will be aided with a little help, but many will embrace them with flatteries. [The Maccabees were of little help, and were ultimately defeated. However, they were able to retake Jerusalem for a time. They cleansed and rededicated the temple some three years after it had been desecrated.

"And some of those with understanding [believers] shall fall, to try them, and to purge, and to make them white, even to the time of the end, because it is still for an appointed time."

These verses are cited by some dispensationalists to relate to a last-days anti-Christ. But this is past history which refers to the Maccabean revolt. However, Antiochus IV was certainly a type of the last-days anti-Christ.

At this point, having addressed "the time of the end," the vision jumps ahead in time, ignoring for the most part "the Time of the Gentiles." Remember, this entire prophecy is for Daniel's people, Israel as a nation. Thus it is written as a continuous history uninterrupted by the Time of the Gentiles. Daniel continues:

11:36: "And the king shall do according to his will; and he will exalt himself, and magnify himself above every god, and will speak marvelous things against the God of gods, and shall prosper until the indignation is accomplished, for that which is determined shall be done."

The Roman Empire, though broken into ten kingdoms, will remain the world's dominant power until the end of this present age when the final kingdom, represented by the feet and toes of iron and clay, rises up. I believe this final kingdom involves the Ottoman Empire, but it has been subdued for a season until the time is right for it to come to full fruition through the unification of Europe with the Middle East nations. This will be the mingling of iron (the remnants of the Roman Empire) with clay (the Muslim nations).

It is here that Israel's history again enters during the Time of the Gentiles because the Ottomans captured Jerusalem. But for the most part the prophecy relates to future events just prior to the Lord's return.

We currently live in a Greco-Roman world, the English language being the dominant tongue among the nations. English stems from both Greek and Latin. But Greece was defeated by Rome which became the final empire to conquer Jerusalem during the time relevant to Daniel's prophecy. The Ottoman Empire conquered Jerusalem for a season, but that fell within the Time of the Gentiles, not during the time of Israel's temple. So although the Greek culture still has some influence in the world, as far as prophecy regarding Jerusalem is concerned Rome is the dominant, last-days empire which has been sublimated until the Time of the Gentiles comes to a close. At that time the last-days anti-Christ will bring together the nations that comprised the old Roman Empire (Europe, the Middle East and North Africa) into a new confederacy that will again threaten Jerusalem.

It appears as if Daniel places all the leaders of the Roman Empire under one umbrella, spanning the time from the empire's original conquests to the future. Again, it also appears as if the last-days anti-Christ will be a leader within a new confederation comprised of territories from the old Roman Empire. Thus we see him as he establishes a foothold in Jerusalem during later times (not the very last days) that will lay the groundwork for the final kingdom represented by the feet and toes made of iron and clay.

11:37-45: Neither shall he regard the god [*elohiym*: "gods"] of his fathers, nor the desire of women, nor regard any god, for he shall magnify himself above all. But in his estate he will honor the god of forces, and he will honor a god whom his fathers did not know with gold, and silver, and with precious stones, and pleasant things.

"He will do this in the most strongholds with a strange god whom he shall acknowledge and increase with glory. And he shall cause them to rule over many, and will divide the land for gain.

"And at the time of the end the king of the south [Egypt] will push at him, and the king of the north [Syria] shall come against him like a whirlwind—with chariots, and with horsemen, and with many ships—and he will enter into the countries, and will overflow and pass over.

"He will also enter into the glorious land, and many countries will be overthrown, but these will escape out of his hand: Edom, and Moab, and the chief of the children of Ammon [present-day Jordan]. He will stretch forth his hand also upon the countries, and the land of Egypt shall not escape. But he shall have power over the treasures of gold and of silver, and over all the precious things of Egypt, and the Libyans and the Ethiopians shall be at his steps.

"But news out of the east and out of the north will trouble him. Therefore he will go forth with great fury to destroy, and to utterly slay many. And he will plant the tabernacles of his palace between the seas in the glorious holy mountain [Zion]. Yet he shall come to his end, and No one shall help him."

These verses are also assumed by dispensationalists to refer to a last-days anti-Christ. I believe they describe the sixteenth-century rise of the Ottoman Empire under Caliph Osman Ibn Affan, which has left its mark on much of the old Roman Empire including parts of Western Europe, the Middle East and North Africa. The "king" is the spiritual principality of this empire, embodied in the religion of Islam. The Ottoman Empire at one time advanced as far as France, and had a strong foothold in Spain until driven out. The empire was characterized by accomplishments in art, architecture, science and mathematics (primarily by using the genius of the captured nations). Islam's holy sites are decorated with great splendor and wealth.

Today the Ottoman Empire has ceased to exist officially, but its Islamic influences remain. Jerusalem was taken by the Ottomans and remained in Muslim possession until the six-day war of 1967 when the modern state of Israel took control of the city. Today, one of Islam's most holy sites—the "tabernacle" called the Dome of the Rock—sits on the ancient temple mount (Zion), which is between the Mediterranean Sea and the Dead Sea. Caliph Osman Ibn Affan did indeed "plant the tabernacles of his palace between the seas in the glorious holy mountain."

But what about Edom, Moab and Ammon escaping out of his hand? Every map shows the Ottoman Empire controlling the entire Middle East. On the nation of Jordan's Web site we read:

> The four centuries of Ottoman rule (1516-1918 CE) were a period of general stagnation in Jordan. The Ottomans were primarily interested in Jordan in terms of its importance to the pilgrimage route to Mecca al-Mukarrama. They built a series of square fortresses—at Qasr al-Dab'a, Qasr Qatraneh, and Qal'at Hasa—to protect pilgrims from the desert tribes and to provide them with sources of food and water. However, the Ottoman administration was weak and could not effectively control the Bedouin tribes. Over the course of Ottoman rule, many towns and villages were abandoned, agriculture declined, and families and tribes moved frequently from one village to another. The Bedouins, however, remained masters of the desert, continuing to live much as they had for hundreds of years.[1]

So the influence of the Ottoman Empire in Edom, Moab and Ammon was relatively minor, and the people were never really conquered.

I see good reason to believe that the last-days anti-Christ will be a Muslim, possibly a Turk, for several reasons:

- Muslims worship Allah, a god (as redefined by Islam) their ancestors did not know. The original Allah was the god of war (a god of forces—or fortifications) of the pagan Arabs in Mecca. He was redefined by Islam as the only god. Not regarding the desire of women does not necessarily mean anti-Christ will be a sodomite as some teach. Muslims regard women as chattel;

---

[1] Kinghussein.gov.jo/his_ottoman.html.

- Islam is the greatest enemy of both Jews and Christians;
- Turkey is the land of Gog and Magog, which will attack Jerusalem at the end of the Millennium;
- The city of Pergamos on the island of Cyprus is said in Revelation 2:13 to be the place where the "seat of Satan" is. The Republic of Cyprus, which joined the European Union in 2004, is a Eurasian country in the Eastern Mediterranean. But Pergamos is actually controlled by the Turkish Republic of Northern Cyprus which was established as a separate state after years of dispute between Greek Cypriots and Turkish Cypriots. Revelation 13:2 says that Satan will give his seat to the anti-Christ. The Greek word for "seat" is *thronos*, from which we get the word "throne." By implication, it also means "power."
- Constantine moved the capital of the Roman Empire from Rome to Constantinople in Turkey. Today the city is called Istanbul, and is the nation's largest city.
- Turkey was the capital of the Ottoman Empire and unites the Islamic lands with the "Christian" lands of Western Europe. It is considered both European and Asian;
- Turkey is a "moderate" Islamic nation, which finds favor with the West, and could be a major factor in uniting both (the feet and toes of iron and clay).

I realize all of this flies in the face of most theories which say that the anti-Christ will be either a Christian or a Jew because he would have to be accepted as the Messiah. But there is nothing in Scripture to suggest that he will be a messiah figure to either the Jews or to Christians. In view of the Vatican's interfaith ecumenism, what better coalition for an anti-Christ union could there be than Islam and Roman Catholicism? The late Pope John Paul II stated that Islam's Allah is the same God worshipped by Christians. Today many leaders among Protestants and even Evangelicals are making the same statement.

John Paul II's successor, Benedict XVI, visited the Blue Mosque in Istanbul, Turkey, facing toward Mecca and bowing in prayer to the "one Lord of heaven and earth, merciful father of all mankind." He also predicted that Turkey "will be a bridge of friendship and collaboration between East and West."

The idea that Allah is the same God worshipped by Christians is one of the accepted maxims of the interfaith ecumenical movement. Many nominal Christians believe this lie and are seeking unity with Islam. Heads of state have for years been holding ecumenical religious services with Muslims, Jews and Christians. Under the name of "Chrislam," many Christian churches have been holding joint religious services with Muslims.

The anti-Christ's kingdom will be religious at its roots. Islam controls a large portion of the old Roman Empire to the east, and Roman Catholicism is still the preeminent religion of Western Europe. With the Church of England making noise that it seeks reunification with Rome, as does Lutheranism and the Eastern Orthodox religions, there is little standing in the way of a Roman-Ottoman religio-political union. Prince Charles, who may one day as England's king be the head of the Church of England, has stated that he does not want to be known as the defender of *the* faith, but as the defender of faith—all faith, including Islam. He has many ties to Islam even now.

Islam is the fastest growing religion in the world. Since the September 11, 2001 attacks on the World Trade Center and the Pentagon, who has been made the victim by the government and the media? Islam.

We are constantly fed the lie that Islam is a religion of peace, and that we can coexist with it. Christian pastors of varied institutions are increasingly having Muslim imams ("holy men") in their pulpits extolling their beliefs and denying Jesus as the Son of God to the applause of their Christian audiences. Their false religious creeds are not even challenged by these pastors who, by their silence, deny Jesus Christ as the only way to God.

With all the propaganda in favor of Islam since the 9/11 attacks, more people are looking into the religion of Islam and are adopting it in place of Christianity. As well, favor toward Islam among the American populous since the attack has risen considerably.

Co-existence may be possible in the United States, but the Gospel is forbidden to be proclaimed in Islamic nations no matter how much they seek unity with the West. Overall, Christians and Jews have suffered more under Roman Catholicism and Islam than under any other ideology.

When we consider the outcome to date of the Arab Spring uprisings we must conclude that fundamentalist Islam is taking over virtually all major Islamic countries. As a result, Christians and Jews are undergoing persecution far beyond anything that transpired under the despotic yet somewhat secular governments that have been overthrown.

These are very good reasons to rethink the "accepted wisdom" about who might be the anti-Christ.

We continue with Daniel's prophecy:

12:1: "And at that time [the very last days] Michael, the great prince who stands for the children of your people, shall stand up, and there shall be a time of trouble such as never was since there was a nation [Israel] even to that same time. And at that time your people shall be delivered, everyone who shall be found written in the book [Israelite believers in Jesus Christ]."

This coincides with Revelation 12:7-17:

And there was war in Heaven. Michael and his angels fought against the dragon. And the dragon fought, and his angels, and did not prevail; neither was their place found any more in Heaven.

And the great dragon was cast out—that old serpent, called "the Devil," and "Satan," who deceives the whole world; he was cast out into the earth, and his angels were cast out with him.

And I heard a loud voice in Heaven saying, "Now has come salvation, and strength, and the Kingdom of our God, and the power of His Christ, for the accuser of our brethren is cast down, who accused them before our God day and night. And they overcame him by the blood of the Lamb, and by the word of their testimony, and they loved not their lives unto the death.

"Therefore rejoice, you heavens, and you who dwell in them. Woe to the inhabitants of the earth and of the sea! For the Devil has come down to you, having great wrath, because he knows that he has but a short time."

And when the dragon saw that he was cast to the earth he persecuted the woman who brought forth the man child. And two wings of a great eagle were given to the woman so that she might fly into the wilderness, into her place, where she is nourished for a time, and times, and half a time, from the face of the serpent.

And the serpent cast out of his mouth water like a flood after the woman so that he might cause her to be carried away by the flood. And the earth helped the woman, and the earth opened her mouth and swallowed up the flood that the dragon cast out of his mouth.

And the dragon was angry with the woman, and went to make war with the remnant of her seed who keep the commandments of God, and have the testimony of Jesus Christ.

The Roman Catholic Church maintains that the woman who brought forth the man child represents Mary as the "Mother of God" who brought forth Jesus. But this is a future prophecy; it has nothing to do with Mary bearing Jesus. The man child is described in Revelation as a company of 144,000 Israelites who will be sealed against the Lord's judgment during the time of Jacob's Trouble (Rv 7:4).

Nor are these 144,000 Gentiles. They come forth when Michael stands up for Israel (Da 12:1; Rv 12:7).

Back to Daniel's prophecy:

12:2-10: "And many of those who sleep in the dust of the earth shall awake, some to everlasting life [the first resurrection], and some to shame and everlasting contempt [the second resurrection, which will take place at the end of the Millennium].

"And those who are wise shall shine like the brightness of the heavens, and those who turn many to righteousness like the stars forever and ever.

"But you, O Daniel, hide the words and seal the book to the time of the end. Many shall run back and forth, and knowledge shall be increased [This is a description of today's world]."

Then I, Daniel, saw, and, look! There stood two others, one on this side of the bank of the river, and the other on that side of the bank of the river. And one said to the man dressed in linen who was upon the waters of the river, "How long shall it be to the end of these wonders?"

And I heard the man dressed in linen who was upon the waters of the river, when he held up his right hand and his left hand to Heaven, and swore by Him who lives forever, that it shall be for a time, times, and a half [3-1/2 years; Satan will persecute Israel who will be driven into the wilderness for this time period (Rv 12:14)]. And when he will have accomplished to scatter the power of the holy people, all these things shall be finished."

And I heard, but I did not understand. Then I said, "O my Lord, what will be the end of these things?"

And he said, "Be on your way, Daniel, for the words are closed up and sealed till the time of the end [The Time of the Gentiles—the mystery of God—was hidden from Daniel, to be revealed later]. Many shall be purified and made white, and tested, but the wicked will do wickedly, and none of the wicked shall understand. But the wise shall understand."

Daniel then speaks of a second abomination that makes desolate which differs from that performed by Antiochus Epiphanes:

12:11: "And from the time that the daily sacrifice shall be taken away and the abomination that makes desolate set up, there shall be a thousand two hundred and ninety days."

This 1,290 days is the three-and-one-half years between the time the sacrifice was taken away with the abomination of desolation set up in A.D. 70, and the completion of all things (the Lord's return to bring all Israel back to the Promised Land). Those three-and-one-half years have been put on hold until the Time of the Gentiles is completed, just as the first three-and-one-half years were on hold during the time from the Lord's crucifixion until Vespasian began his campaign against the Jews in A.D. 67.

There is also an interlude in history that is not stated here. To understand, we must go back to Daniel 9:24-27:

"Seventy sevens [seventy periods of seven-years (490 years)] are determined upon your people and upon your holy city [Jerusalem] to finish the transgression, and to make an end of sins, and to make reconciliation for iniquity, and to bring in everlasting righteousness, and to seal up the vision and prophecy, and to anoint the most Holy." [Jesus will fulfill all this when He comes at the end of the seventy sevens. Only sixty-nine sevens were completed on His death.]

"Therefore, know and understand that from the going forth of the commandment to restore and to build Jerusalem, until the Messiah the Prince, shall be seven sevens, and sixty-two sevens [69 seven-year periods = 69 x 7, or 483 years, when Jesus entered Jerusalem to the cries of "Hosannah!"—the week of His death].

The street shall be built again, and the wall, even in troublous times" [Nehemiah's task led to the building of the second temple].

"And after the sixty-two sevens Messiah shall be cut off [killed], but not for himself [Jesus died for our sins, not for His own sins; He was sinless]. And the people of the prince that shall come [the Roman army under Vespasian, followed by Titus] shall destroy the city and the sanctuary, and its end shall be with a flood. And until the end of the war desolations are determined. And he will confirm the covenant with many for one seven [during the seventieth seven] and in the middle of the seven he will cause the sacrifice and the oblation to cease, and for the overspreading of abominations he will make it desolate, even until the consummation, and that which is determined shall be poured upon the desolate."

Some say that Jesus is the one who confirmed the New Covenant three-and-one-half-years after He began His ministry; at the end of His ministry He brought the prophecy to a close with His death that took away the need for animal sacrifices.

But this cannot be, because Daniel's prophecy said the Messiah would be killed after seven sevens plus sixty-two sevens (sixty-nine sevens). Yet the prince to come would cause the sacrifice and oblation to cease "in the middle of the [seventieth] seven"), not at the end of sixty-nine sevens. Thus, the sacrifices would be taken away three-and-one-half years after Messiah's death.

Jesus was killed at the end of sixty-nine sevens, leaving one seven-year period before the determination upon Israel and Jerusalem would be finished.

The context of these verses is the destruction of the temple by the Romans, not Jesus' crucifixion. The destruction of the temple completed the first half of the seventieth seven. Obviously this half-seven did not follow immediately after the sixty-ninth seven. God gave Israel some forty years to receive her Messiah before cutting off the sacrifices. So there was an interlude of time between the Messiah being killed and the sacrifices ceasing. None of the prophecies relating to the Lord's Second Coming have been fulfilled as yet, but there remains to be completed only one-half seven, not a full seven years.

Preterists say that the entire prophecy unfolded in an unbroken chain of events; there cannot be any lapse in time due to the immediacy of the language. But they ignore the forty-year lapse from the time of Jesus' death (the end of the sixty-ninth seven) to the destruction of the temple and the taking away of the sacrifices (the middle of the seventieth seven). If there was indeed such a lapse in time, then why, especially in view of the revelation of God's mystery (the Time of the Gentiles), could there not be a lapse in time to complete the seventieth seven?

On the other hand, it is commonly taught by dispensationalists that the entire seventieth seven remains. They believe that at the beginning of that period the anti-Christ will make a peace pact (the covenant) with Israel which is supposed to last seven years, but in the middle of that seven years anti-Christ will break his covenant and will attack Israel. Then the Lord will return to save Israel.

There are a number of problems with this. Where it is translated in the English "for one seven," the word "for" was added by the translators; it is not in the Hebrew. Also, the phrase "And he shall confirm" is taken from a single word, *gabar*, which means "to be strong," by implication, "to prevail, act insolently." The Hebrew word translated "many" is *rab*, meaning abundant in quantity, size, age, number, rank, or quality. The Hebrew could more properly be translated, "Many will be insolent against the covenant one seven," or during one seven.

Nor does it really say that the coming prince would cause the sacrifice and oblation to cease. It merely says the sacrifice and oblation would cease.

The Zealots themselves acted insolently against the Covenant, and caused the sacrifices and oblations to cease even before Titus destroyed the temple. Yet let us assume the traditional understanding that the coming prince would do all these things.

This is based on a misunderstanding of what Daniel is saying.

"The covenant" is the covenant between God and Israel. Some translations say, "a covenant," but there is no article—definite or indefinite—in this verse. The Hebrew *beriyth* is translated variously as "a covenant," "My covenant" and, when referring to the Mosaic Covenant, "the covenant." The only covenant known to Daniel was the Mosaic Covenant.

If the traditional understanding is true, how was the Mosaic Covenant confirmed, and by whom?

In A.D. 66, the Great Revolt began with the Jews of the Judea Province opposing the influence of Greek religion. The conflict escalated into anti-tax protests and attacks against Roman citizens. When the Roman garrison was overrun by Jewish rebels the Roman officials fled Jerusalem into Galilee.

In February, A.D. 67, Nero commanded the Roman general Vespasian to suppress the uprising. When he first approached Judea to bring it into subjection to Rome he assured the people that if they surrendered peacefully he would honor their religious traditions and would protect their temple sacrifices. Thus he confirmed, or promised to protect, the Mosaic Covenant. Upon Nero's death, Vespasian was compelled to return to Rome and eventually was named emperor. His son, Titus, took up Vespasian's cause and offered the same peace terms, but the Jewish Zealots were decimating their own people and were profaning the temple. They were committing unspeakable acts against God and against His people. Titus began his final campaign against Jerusalem in March, A.D. 70, after three-and-one-half years of battles in cities leading to Jerusalem that went at times in favor of the Zealots, and other times in favor of the Romans. When Titus took the holy city, the temple was destroyed contrary to Titus' wishes, but not until after the Zealots themselves had caused the sacrifices to cease by polluting the sanctuary with the blood of the slain and driving the priests from the temple. The destruction of the temple occurred in September, A.D. 70, three-and-one-half years after Vespasian began his campaign and initially confirmed the Mosaic Covenant with peace terms.

When Daniel says, "He will confirm the covenant for one seven," it doesn't mean a seven-year peace treaty will be signed, but that during the "one seven" that remained, the Covenant would be confirmed by the prince (Vespasian, and later, Titus) who would come. Had the Jews surrendered peacefully, the people would have been free to practice their religion, though required to submit to Rome and to pay taxes to support the empire.

Or perhaps some would look less favorably on Vespasian and Titus. Were they, then, the ones to act insolently against the Covenant?

In any case, whether consulting history in relation to the traditional translation of Daniel's prophecy, or looking more closely at the Hebrew words, it is obvious that it refers to the destruction of the temple in A.D. 70.

Yet what about the setting up of the abomination that causes desolation, which is generally believed by dispensationalists to be the setting up of an idol in a last-days temple in modern Israel?

After the final assault which began in the spring of A.D. 70 and ended in September, the abomination of desolation was set up when the Roman legions made sacrifices to their standards in the temple court. John Donahue, professor of ancient history at College of William and Mary, states:

> Beset by violent factional strife and internal discord, Jerusalem was a stubborn obstacle to the Roman pacification of Judea. Built on two hills and surrounded by walls, the city's fortifications were formidable. With four legions under his command, Titus began an assault on the city in spring, A.D. 70. In less than four weeks, his forces had breached the walls of the so-called New City, or suburb of Bezetha. Only the inner city and the Temple itself remained to be taken. A siege wall was quickly built around the city, and the circumvallation had the desired effect of increasing starvation. By August, the outer Temple court had been reached and, in the ensuing attack, the Temple was burned to the ground and all captives butchered. Titus was hailed as *imperator* by his troops. In a final desecration to the Temple, sacrifice was made to the Roman standards in the Temple court.[1]

The Roman standards were talismans that bore the images of animals, or gods or goddesses, such as Neptune or Minerva. These mascots were invoked for success in their military campaigns. This was the abomination of desolation spoken of by Daniel the prophet, and alluded to by Jesus in Matthew 24:15-16:

[1] John Donahue, "Titus Flavius Vespasianus (A.D. 79-81)," *De Imperatoribus Romanus*, (College of William and Mary).

"Therefore, when you see the abomination of desolation spoken of by Daniel the prophet established in the holy place (whoever reads, let him understand), then let those who are in Judea flee into the mountains."

Thus, the taking away of the sacrifices and the setting up of the abomination of desolation in A.D. 70 ended the first three-and-one-half years of Daniel's seventieth seven. The next three-and-one-half years will occur at the end of the Time of the Gentiles when Israel is driven into the wilderness under anti-Christ after he causes the Gentiles to tread Jerusalem underfoot.

"Blessed is he who waits and comes to the thousand three hundred and thirty-five days." (Da 12:12)

Why is he blessed who comes to the three-and-one-half years? These are they who will see the Lord's return, not to gather His saints, which will already have been resurrected and translated, but to set foot on the earth and establish His Millennial Kingdom.

"But you go your way till the end, for you shall rest, and stand in your place [resurrected] at the end of the days." Da 12:13)

There were two instances when an abomination that desolates the temple was set up. The first abomination was by the hand of Antiochus Epiphanes around 167 B.C.; the second took place in A.D. 70 when the temple was destroyed and the Romans made sacrifices to their idols. It is this latter abomination to which Jesus referred as recorded in Matthew 24:15 and Mark 13:14. There will be no third abomination of desolation because there will be no new temple until the one built by the Lord.

But didn't Jesus relate the abomination of desolation "spoken of by Daniel" to the time of His return? Let us look at Matthew 24:

And Jesus went out, and left the temple. And His disciples came to him in order to show him the buildings of the temple.

And Jesus said to them, "Do you not see all these things? Truly, I say to you, there shall not be left here one stone upon another that shall not be thrown down.

And as He sat on the Mount of Olives, the disciples came to Him privately, saying, "Tell us, when shall these things be? And what shall be the sign of Your coming, and of the end of this age?" (Mt 24:1-3)

The disciples asked Jesus a three-part question: When shall these things (the destruction of the temple) be? What shall be the sign of Your coming? What shall be the sign of the end of the present age?

They evidently thought all these events would transpire at the same time. But keep in mind that Jesus was speaking of the destruction of the temple in which He stood at the time. His prophecy concerned the nation of Israel without considering the "Time of the Gentiles," just as do all the Hebrew prophecies. However, before speaking of the destruction of the temple, He began by answering the question about the signs of the end of this present age:

And Jesus answered and said to them, "Be careful that no man deceives you, for many will come in My name, saying that I am Christ, and shall deceive many. And you will hear of wars and rumors of wars. See that you are not frightened, for all these things must come to pass.

"But the end is not yet. For nation shall rise against nation, and kingdom against kingdom. And there shall be famines, and pestilences, and earthquakes, in diverse places. All these are the beginning of sorrows.

"Then they will deliver you up to be persecuted, and will kill you, and you will be hated by all nations for My name's sake.

"And then many will be enticed to fall away, and will betray one another, and will hate one another.

"And many false prophets will rise, and will deceive many. And because iniquity will abound, the love of many will grow cold. But he who will endure to the end, the same shall be saved.

"And this Gospel of the Kingdom shall be proclaimed in all the world as a witness to all nations, and then the end shall come." (Mt 24:4-14)

This first portion of Jesus' answer deals with future prophecies regarding the world system and its persecution of His disciples. Much of it has transpired throughout the centuries. The reference to "he who will endure to the end, the same shall be saved," is similar to His admonitions to the seven assemblies in Asia as recorded in the Book of Revelation. This prophecy spans the Time of the Gentiles, and leads into the Lord's prophecy regarding the destruction of the temple, and the rest that relate to Israel as a nation. His next words answer the question about when "these things" (the destruction of the temple) would take place:

"Therefore, when you see the abomination of desolation, spoken of by Daniel the prophet, established in the holy place (whoever reads, let him understand), then let those who are in Judea flee into the mountains. Let him who is on the housetop not come down to take anything out of his house, neither let him who is in the field return back to take his clothes. "And woe to those who are with child, and to those who nurse in those days!

"But pray that your escape will not be in the winter, or on the Sabbath day. For then shall be great tribulation, such as was not since the beginning of the world to this time, no, nor ever shall be. And except those days should be shortened, no flesh would be saved. But for the elect's sake those days shall be shortened." (Mt 24:15-22)

This portion of Jesus' prophecy has been completed. Else why would He urge them to pray that their flight not be on the Sabbath?

In modern Israel, except for the most devout religious Jews, the Sabbath is not a hindrance to anything. It certainly isn't a hindrance to survival and warfare. This was a warning to His disciples of the destruction to come upon Jerusalem in their time.

The great tribulation of which Jesus spoke had to do with Israel's tribulation during the siege of Jerusalem from A.D. 66 to A.D. 70. One who reads the accounts of historians—particularly that of Josephus—will be made very aware of the truth of this prophecy relating to that time. It was so awful that women were killing and eating their children in order to survive. What greater tribulation can a nation suffer than that?

The most difficult portion of the Olivet Discourse is verse 29:

"Immediately after the tribulation of those days the sun shall be darkened, and the moon shall not give her light, and the stars shall fall from the heavens, and the powers of the heavens shall be shaken. And then there shall appear the sign of the Son of Man in the heavens, and then all the tribes of the earth shall mourn, and they shall see the Son of Man coming in the clouds of the sky with power and great glory." (Mt 24:29-30)

No one has ever seen the Lord return in the clouds of the sky. Yet He said, "Immediately after the tribulation of those days (the days of Jerusalem's destruction in A.D. 70)" all people would see Him return.

The Greek word translated "immediately" is *eutheos*, meaning "at once," or "soon." This would seem to lend credence to the preterist claim that the

Lord must already have returned. But remember that prophecies exclusive to Israel do not address events or time periods not exclusive to Israel. We know from several Scriptures that we are living in a period called "the Time of the Gentiles"—an interlude between the Lord's dealing with Israel at His first coming, and His dealing with Israel at His Second Coming. So in those terms, if we remove the Time of the Gentiles, there is no interlude between Matthew 24:22 and 24:29. Prophetically, they are immediate to each other.

Some might question this as a valid way of interpreting Matthew 24. But this is exactly why Israel failed to recognize her Messiah when He came the first time. They read their messianic prophecies as a continuous, unbroken sequence of events. Thus, they did not realize that their Messiah had to come first to suffer and die for the sins of the world, and then make a way for the Gentiles to enter into the Kingdom of God, then return a second time to rule over the nations and reestablish the nation of Israel.

It is not unreasonable to apply the same rule of interpretation to the prophecies regarding Israel as Jesus spoke them then, and as the apostle Matthew recorded them—particularly when we see that Jesus' prophecy of appearing in the sky, visible to all the nations, has not been fulfilled.

While most prophesy teachers focus on Matthew 24, they largely neglect the sequence of events as revealed in the Gospel of Luke. Answering the same question as to when the end would come, Jesus said:

"And when you see Jerusalem encircled with armies, then know that the desolation of it is near. Then let those who are in Judea flee to the mountains, and let those who are in the midst of it get out, and do not let those who are in the country enter there. For these are the days of vengeance, so that all things that are written may be fulfilled.

"But woe to those who are with child, and to those who nurse in those days! For there shall be great distress in the land, and wrath upon this people. And they shall fall by the edge of the sword, and shall be led away captive into all nations, and Jerusalem shall be trodden down by the Gentiles until the Time of the Gentiles is fulfilled." (Lk 21:20-24)

The Lord is saying that with the destruction of Jerusalem and the temple (in A.D. 70) there would follow a dispersion of the people into all the nations, setting in motion the Time of the Gentiles, which has lasted to this present day. Then, after the Time of the Gentiles:

"And there shall be signs in the sun, and in the moon, and in the stars, and distress of nations upon the earth with perplexity—the sea and the waves roaring, men's hearts failing them for fear and for seeing those things that are coming on the earth. For the powers of the heavens shall be shaken. And then they shall see the Son of Man coming in a cloud with power and great glory." (Lk 21:25-27)

Neither Matthew nor Mark mention the Time of the Gentiles. This has caused many to overlook this vital aspect of last-days prophecy. The Lord will not return until The man of sin is revealed and there occurs a great apostasy just before the Time of the Gentiles has come to an end with the resurrection of the dead in Christ.

We continue with Jesus' answer to His disciples as recorded in Matthew:

And He shall send His angels with a great sound of a trumpet, and they shall gather together his elect from the four winds—from one end of the heavens to the other." (Mt 24:31)

The trumpet heralding the Lord's return to gather His saints will be the last trumpet sounded, which will bring to an end the mystery of God:

And the Angel that I saw stand upon the sea and upon the earth lifted up His hand to Heaven, and swore by Him who lives forever and ever, who created the heavens and the things that are in it, and the earth and the things that are in it, and the sea and the things that are in it, that there should be no more time left, but in the days of the voice of the seventh angel, when he shall begin to sound, the mystery of God should be finished, as He has declared to His servants the prophets. (Rv 10:5-7)

What is the mystery of God? There are many Scriptures that allude to the "mystery of God," but the following three reveal what it is:

Now to Him who has the power to establish you according to my Gospel and the proclaiming of Jesus Christ according to the revelation of the mystery which was kept secret since the world began. (Ro 16:25)

I am made a minister according to the stewardship from God that is given to me for you, to fulfill the Word of God—the mystery that has been hidden from ages and from generations, but now is revealed to His saints to whom God would make known among the Gentiles what are the riches of the glory of this mystery, which is in you, Christ the hope of glory. (Col 1:25-27)

...having made known to us the mystery of His will, according to His good pleasure which He has purposed in Himself: that in the dispensation of the fullness of time He might gather together into one, all things in Christ, both that are in Heaven and that are on earth, even in Him in whom also we have obtained an inheritance, being predestined according to the purpose of Him who works all things after the counsel of His own will, that we who first trusted in Christ should be to the praise of His glory. (Eph 1:9-12)

As stated earlier, the mystery of God, hidden from the foundation of the world, is the grafting of the Gentiles into New Covenant Israel, making of two men, Jew and Gentile, one new man in Christ; the mystery of God continues during the Time of the Gentiles which will come to a close upon the resurrection and the catching up of the living saints to meet the Lord in the air.

Notice the parallel between Ephesians 1:10 ("that in the dispensation of the fullness of time He might gather together into one, all things in Christ, both that are in Heaven and that are on earth") and Mark 13:27:

And then He shall send His angels, and shall gather together His elect from the four winds—from the uttermost part of the earth to the uttermost part of Heaven.

When the seventh angel sounds, the mystery of God—the Time of the Gentiles—will end. This is the last trump, when the resurrection occurs:

Look, I show you a mystery: not all of us shall sleep, but we all shall be changed in a moment, in the twinkling of an eye at the last trump. For the trumpet shall sound, and the dead shall be raised incorruptible, and we shall be changed. For this corruptible must put on incorruption, and this mortal must put on immortality. (1Co 15:51-53)

The seventh, or last, angel prepares to sound his trumpet (Rv 10:7) after the events that have transpired during the first six trumpet judgments. This means that the Body of Christ will still be on the earth during those six judgments. The tribulation upon the saints will come from the world, but God's wrath will be upon the world for its rebellion against Him and the persecution of His saints.

The reference to the last trump that heralds the Lord's appearing has been largely ignored or explained away by pre-tribulation teachers who say the last trump in 1 Corinthians 51:52 is not the same as the last or seventh trumpet in Revelation 10:7. But there is no explanation given to reasonably come to that conclusion. Nor is there any reason given other than the assumption that this would negate the idea of the pre-tribulation rapture. However, there is nowhere in Scripture where any sequence of heavenly trumpets is found other than in Revelation 8:2–10:7. Why would Paul write of "the last trump" if there is no reference point to which we may relate?

We must understand, however, that the last trumpet sounding is not a single event, but the heralding of the events to unfold, which will take some time. Nor does the last trumpet immediately usher in the New Heavens and New Earth which preterists teach will occur simultaneously with the Lord's return. It is the time for the resurrection, which will precede the catching up of the living saints, both events preceding God's final judgment on anti-Christ's kingdom and His dealing with Israel during the last half of Daniel's seventieth seven. After that happens the Lord will return to set foot on the earth and establish His reign for one thousand years.

When Jesus said He would return "immediately" after the tribulation of those days (Mt 24:29), He was relating to Israel's history without regard to the Time of the Gentiles. He has not yet come back in the clouds to take His people out of the earth. This leap through time, as I've said, is a common prophetic method in dealing with Israel as a nation. I will again remind the reader that prophetic history is not the same as human history.

When Jesus spoke of coming desolation He must have been speaking of the desecration of the temple in which He stood, because that was the context of the questions asked of Him. He could not have been referring to Antiochus Epiphanes because his desecration of the temple had already taken place. Nor was he speaking of some future temple to be built prior to His return. There is no scriptural prophecy of a future temple apart from the Millennial Temple which Jesus will build as described in Ezekiel 41:1–45:7.

The idea that some future third temple will be built in the Zionist state of Israel, and that the future anti-Christ will set up in it the abomination of desolation, is the result of misunderstanding this and other Scriptures that relate to the second temple. There can be no legitimate temple built before Jesus returns; God will not sanction any sacrifices as long as faith in Jesus is the only means of salvation. Thus, He would never call a man-made temple "the temple of God" (2Th 2:4).

There is no reason to think that Daniel would have understood this to mean there would be two more temples built. He was given no word that would cause him to think of anything other than the desecration of the second temple. There is also no reason to think that God would establish any legitimate temple in the future during the Time of the Gentiles. The only temple prophesied is the Millennial Temple that will be built by the Lord when He returns (Eze 41:1–45:7).

14

THE TIME OF THE GENTILES

S cripture speaks of a period in Israel's history known as "the Time of the Gentiles." Among Bible scholars there are two understandings of what constitutes "the Time of the Gentiles." Some say the Time of the Gentiles began with Nebuchadnezzar's capture of Jerusalem and the subsequent removing of the Jews from their homeland to Babylonia; it will end with the Lord's return. Others say the Time of the Gentiles began with the destruction of the temple in A.D. 70 when the Jews were dispersed from their homeland for the last time, and it will last until the Lord returns.

The former rightly points out that since the Babylonian Captivity Jerusalem has been occupied by a number of succeeding empires.

The latter is also a viable interpretation in that there is no mention of the Time of the Gentiles anywhere in the writings of the prophets, and the first mention of it is by Jesus in relation to the destruction of the temple:

"And when you see Jerusalem encircled with armies, then know that its desolation is near. Then let those who are in Judea flee to the mountains, and let those who are in the midst of it get out, and do not let those who are in the country enter there. For these are the days of vengeance, so that all things that are written may be fulfilled.

"But woe to those who are with child, and to those who nurse in those days! For there shall be great distress in the land, and wrath upon this people. And they shall fall by the edge of the sword, and shall be led away captive into all nations, and Jerusalem shall be trodden down by the Gentiles until the Time of the Gentiles is fulfilled." (Lk 21:20-24)

Paul is the only other person to allude to "the Time of the Gentiles," but he refers to it as "the fullness of the Gentiles":

For I do not want, brethren, that you should be ignorant of this mystery lest you would be wise in your own conceits, that blindness in part has happened to Israel until the fullness of the Gentiles has come in. (Ro 11:25)

There is a difference, however. The fullness of the Gentiles most likely refers to all the Gentiles who will come to Christ during the Time of the Gentiles. In other words, the Time of the Gentiles will end with the last Gentile coming to Christ. For this reason I lean toward the latter understanding of the Time of the Gentiles, particularly when there is no definitive reference to it in the writings of Israel's prophets.

But rather than be dogmatic about it, I'll just say that for purposes of this study, references to the Time of the Gentiles will be in line with the Lord's prophecy regarding Jerusalem being trodden down by the Gentiles after the Jews were led away captive into all nations with the destruction of the temple in A.D. 70. It is not only a Time of the Gentiles to occupy Jerusalem, but spiritually for many Gentiles to be brought into the Kingdom of God.

During this Time of the Gentiles, natural Israel has been blinded in part as the Gospel is being proclaimed to all nations so that those who believe in Jesus as their Savior and Lord will be grafted into New Covenant Israel:

For I speak to you Gentiles (inasmuch as I am the apostle of the Gentiles, I magnify my office) if by any means I may provoke to emulation those who are my flesh, and might save some of them. For if their being casting away is the reconciling of the world, what shall the receiving of them be, but life from the dead?

For if the first fruits are holy, the lump is also holy. And if the root is holy, so are the branches. And if some of the branches are broken off, and you, being a wild olive tree, were grafted in among them, and with them partake of the root and fatness of the olive tree, do not boast against the branches. But if you boast, you do not bear the root, but the root you.

You will say then, "The branches were broken off so that I might be grafted in."

Well, they were broken off because of unbelief, and you stand by faith. Do not be proud, but fear. Because if God did not spare the natural branches, beware lest He also not spare you. (Ro 11:13-21)

The New Covenant, which God made with Judah and Israel (Jer 31:31; Heb 8:8), has not been nullified. It was not made with "the Church," but with the nation of Israel (which includes Judah). It was ratified through the blood of Jesus (Heb 12:24), and by God's grace the Gentiles who believe in Him are grafted into faithful Israel identified with that New Covenant. Now there is no longer Jew or Gentile, but we are one in Christ.

From the late first century to the present, boasting against Israel has characterized much of Christianity. The early so-called Church Fathers boasted against Israel; the Roman Catholic Church which emanated from those men's teachings has boasted against Israel; Protestantism has boasted against Israel. Today it is characteristic of preterism to boast against Israel. All such boasting displays ignorance of God's purpose and plan for Israel in the future.

The Body of Christ is unique in history; it is God's mystery hidden from eternity wherein the two—Jew and Gentile—would be joined into one new man (Eph 2:15). Yet God is not done with Israel. For after He takes the "new men" into Heaven in the resurrection and the catching up of the saints alive at that time, He will again deal with Israel for three-and-one-half years, purifying her through terrible ordeals under the anti-Christ.

All prophecies of the very last days that were written by Israel's prophets center on the nation of Israel. The Time of the Gentiles to be given the Gospel is an interlude separate from Israel's prophetic history (Daniel's seventy sevens). It will last until the resurrection when the Lord Jesus will appear in the clouds to gather His saints to Himself.

While there are prophecies that allude to the blessings of Israel upon the nations, the Time of the Gentiles is not clearly stated. Thus, many prophecies seem to jump these two millennia when, in God's dealing with Israel, the events are described in a consecutive timeline. We see this in the prophecy of Joel where God's Spirit is poured out on all flesh with no hint of time passing before the signs of "the notable Day of YHWH." This must be kept in mind as we look at all end-times prophecies, especially where we see terms that indicate immediacy between events.

It is because God has presented His prophecies in this way that Israel missed the identity of Jesus as its Messiah. They focused on the Scriptures that spoke of Him as a triumphant King, but failed to see that He must first suffer as the propitiation for man's sins. Some Scriptures presented Him as both suffering and triumphant, without regard to the centuries that must pass between.

The reason for the seeming immediacy in God's last-days prophecies is that they deal with Jerusalem, not taking into account the interlude of the Time of the Gentiles. Israel's history is presented by Israel's prophets as a seamless stream of events. Thus, all prophetic history centers on Israel, and particularly on Jerusalem. This is why there is no mention of the United States or other modern states that have not, or will not, conquer Jerusalem.

God has not abandoned Israel. At the end of the Time of the Gentiles (however it is defined)—when the resurrection occurs and the Body of Christ is caught up to meet the Lord in the air—the last chapter in God's dealing with the nation of Israel (the last half of Daniel's seventieth seven) will begin.

Paul warns Timothy that apostasy will increase during the Time of the Gentiles, and especially toward the end of this age, known also as "the last days":

This know also, that in the last days perilous times shall come... (2Ti 3:1-14)

It is significant that Paul places "the last days" in the future, while Peter placed "the last days" in his present time at Pentecost. Yet Peter also speaks of a future apostasy as a phenomenon of "the last days" which, in context, means the end of the present "Time of the Gentiles":

Knowing this first, that there shall come in the last days scoffers, walking after their own lusts and saying, "Where is the promise of his coming? For since the fathers fell asleep all things continue as they were from the beginning of the creation." (2Pe 3:3-4)

As Christians see events transpire that they assume should have taken place after the Lord returns, they will begin to doubt His return. Already preterist eschatology has gained many adherents, especially since some sensationalistic speculations on the timing of the Lord's return by certain dispensationalists failed to materialize. The more time passes, the more people will question, "Where is the promise of His coming?"

But then, did the Lord not say, "Therefore, you be ready also, because the Son of Man comes at an hour when you think not" (Lk 12:40)?

15
GREAT TRIBULATION

There has been much written about a coming "Great Tribulation" period which is believed to be a seven-year term during which the anti-Christ will reign over the nations. This seven-year period is gleaned from the seventy sevens of the prophecy given to Daniel, which we've covered in prior chapters. Those who believe in this coming seven-year Great Tribulation assert that the anti-Christ (believed by many to be the Russian premier) will make a seven-year peace pact with the modern state of Israel, and halfway through the seven years will break the pact and attack Israel.

As stated earlier, those who believe the Body of Christ will be taken out prior to this seven-year period are called "pre-tribulationists." Those who believe the Body of Christ will be taken out when the peace-pact is broken are "mid-tribulationists." And those who believe the Body of Christ will have to endure the entire seven-year "Great Tribulation" are post-tribulationists."

Most preterists, of course, do not believe anything future prophesied in Scripture, including a "Great Tribulation" will occur, because they believe all prophecy has been fulfilled with the exception of the New Heavens and New Earth. There are some preterists who believe there will be a time of great tribulation under a future anti-Christ, but these are not preterists in the purest sense. They blend Reformed theology with some dispensationalism, with the greater emphasis on Reformed theology.

Obviously, not all of these theories can be correct. Surely the Scriptures give some clarity to the issue of "Great Tribulation."

There are three passages that speak of "great tribulation." None use the definite article "the," but speak only of "great tribulation." "<u>The</u> Great Tribulation" is a fabrication based on the misconception that it refers to Daniel's seventieth seven and/or a seven-year peace pact between anti-Christ and Zionist Israel. The first mention relates Jesus' words to His disciples who asked Him when the things of which He spoke would occur:

> And as He sat on the Mount of Olives, the disciples came to Him privately, saying, "Tell us, when shall these things be? And what will be the sign of Your coming, and of the end of this age?" (Mt 24:3)

Jesus' answer to this three-part inquiry concluded with these words:

> "Therefore, when you see the abomination of desolation, spoken of by Daniel the prophet, established in the holy place (whoever reads, let him understand), then let those who are in Judea flee into the mountains. Let him who is on the housetop not come down to take anything out of his house, nor let him who is in the field return back to take his clothes. "And woe to those who are with child, and to those who nurse in those days!
>
> "But pray that your escape will not be in the winter, or on the Sabbath day. For then shall be great tribulation, such as was not since the beginning of the world to this time, no, nor ever shall be. And except those days should be shortened, no flesh would be saved. But for the elect's sake those days shall be shortened." (Mt 24:15-22)

Luke relates the same scenario, but with slightly different words, and without using the term "great tribulation." He finishes with these words:

> "And when you see Jerusalem encircled with armies, then know that its desolation is near. Then let those who are in Judea flee to the mountains, and let those who are in the midst of it get out, and do not let those who are in the country enter there. For these are the days of vengeance, so that all things that are written may be fulfilled.
>
> "But woe to those who are with child, and to those who nurse in those days! For there shall be great distress in the land, and wrath upon this people. And they shall fall by the edge of the sword, and shall be led away captive into all nations, and Jerusalem shall be trodden down by the Gentiles until the Time of the Gentiles is fulfilled.

"And there shall be signs in the sun, and in the moon, and in the stars, and distress of nations upon the earth with perplexity—the sea and the waves roaring, men's hearts failing them for fear and for seeing those things that are coming on the earth. For the powers of the heavens shall be shaken. And then they shall see the Son of Man coming in a cloud with power and great glory. (Lk 21:20-27)

When we combine Matthew 24:1-31 and Luke 21:7-27 we see that the great tribulation of which Jesus spoke would precede the current Diaspora and the Time of the Gentiles, which time we are currently in.

But He also said that immediately after the tribulation of those days He would be seen in the sky and would gather His saints (the resurrection and Rapture).

Revelation 6:12-17 describes this scenario at the opening of the sixth seal, just prior to the Lord's judgment on the earth.

We know from Romans 11:25 that Israel will be blinded until the Time of the Gentiles is completed, after which they will see Him whom they pierced and they will mourn (Zec 12:10; Jn 19:37). The Jews did not mourn for Him when they pierced Him; that mourning must yet be future.

How will they see Him? When He appears in the sky to gather together His elect (Mt 24:1-31; Mk 13:3-33; Lk 21:7-27; Rv 6:12-17).

Jesus was prophesying of the coming destruction of the temple in which they stood, which destruction occurred in A.D. 70. That was the completion of the first three-and-one-half years of Daniel's seventieth seven.

So although the idea of "The Great Tribulation" is taken from the Lord's reference in Matthew 24, we've seen that that great tribulation is in relation to the destruction of the temple in A.D. 70, after which Jesus said He would return "immediately." That great tribulation is the tribulation suffered by the Jews under the Roman siege that lasted three-and-one-half years.

However, Revelation 7:14 points to certain saints who have come out of "great tribulation":

After this I saw, and, look! A great multitude, which no man could number, of all nations, and tribes, and people, and languages, stood before the throne and before the Lamb, clothed with white robes, and palms in their hands, and cried with a loud voice, saying, "Salvation to our God who sits on the throne, and to the Lamb!"

And all the angels stood around the throne and around the elders and the four creatures, and fell on their faces before the throne and worshipped God, saying, "Amen! Blessing, and glory, and wisdom, and thanksgiving, and honor, and power, and might, be to our God forever and ever. Amen."

And one of the elders answered, saying to me, "Who are these who are arrayed in white robes, and from where did they come?"

And I said to him, "Sir, you know."

And he said to me, "These are they who came out of great tribulation and have washed their robes and made them white in the blood of the Lamb. Therefore they are before the throne of God, and serve Him day and night in His temple. And He who sits on the throne shall dwell among them. They shall hunger no longer, nor thirst anymore, neither shall the sun nor any heat light on them, for the Lamb who is in the midst of the throne shall feed them and shall lead them to living fountains of waters, and God shall wipe away all tears from their eyes." (Rv 7:9-17)

The great tribulation of which Jesus warned in Matthew 24 was upon the Jews in Jerusalem. His warning was to His disciples so they would discern the coming destruction upon the city and the temple.

The people who come out of great tribulation as stated in Revelation 7:9-17 are not Jews only, and not those in Jerusalem only, but come from out of every nation; they are Jewish and Gentile believers in Christ.

Prophetically, Jesus will return "immediately" after the tribulation upon Jerusalem in A.D. 70 because the Time of the Gentiles is not considered in His prophecy. Prophetically, it is as if the Time of the Gentiles never occurs, even though it is of such great importance to the Gentiles who come to Christ during that time.

In any case, Revelation 7:9-17 makes it clear that the Body of Christ will go through a time of great tribulation upon the whole earth, which is yet to come.

This company of believers from all nations are Jews and Gentiles combined. This is not speaking of a seven-year "Great Tribulation period" upon Israel. The scene occurs immediately after the world sees the Lord appear in the skies, and knows His judgment is about to fall:

And I saw when he had opened the sixth seal, and, look! There was a great earthquake. And the sun became black as sackcloth of hair, and the moon became like blood, and the stars of the heavens fell to the earth, even as a fig tree casts her unripe figs, when she is shaken by a strong wind. [cf., Mt 24:29-31 (after the tribulation); Mk

13:24-27 (after the tribulation); Lk 21:24-27 (when the Time of the Gentiles is completed)]

And the heavens departed like a scroll when it is rolled together, and every mountain and island were moved out of their places. And the kings of the earth, and the great men, and the rich men, and the chief captains, and the mighty men, and every slave, and every freeman, hid themselves in the dens and in the rocks of the mountains, and said to the mountains and rocks, "Fall on us and hide us from the face of Him who sits on the throne, and from the wrath of the Lamb, for the great day of His wrath has come, and who will be able to stand?" (Rv 6:12-17)

It is clear that the Body of Christ will be removed from the earth at the end of a period of great tribulation upon the whole earth, which coincides with the culmination of the Time of the Gentiles. This is the only reference to "great tribulation" that occurs toward the very last days. Neither it, nor any of the other references to "great tribulation" is preceded by the definite article "the." We don't know how long this time of "great tribulation" referred to in Revelation will last. But it is directed primarily at believers in Christ, not at Israel. Jacob's Trouble will resume (the first half ended in A.D. 70) after "great tribulation" upon the whole earth. The Body of Christ will suffer under the anti-Christ during that time of great tribulation.

This is how we will know the anti-Christ—how he will be revealed prior to the Lord coming to receive His saints. His warfare will be against God's people. His warfare against Israel as God's people will come after the saints are resurrected and caught up to be with the Lord with those alive and changed into immortality at the time.

Now, those who do not believe the Body of Christ will go through this great tribulation period, will surely point to Rv 3:10:

"Because you have kept the word of My patience, I also will keep you from the hour of temptation which shall come upon all the world, to test those who live on the earth." (Rv 3:10)

This is commonly thought to mean that the Lord will not allow Christians to be tested during "the Great Tribulation"; He will keep us from it by removing us from the world before it begins. But this is reading into this verse something it doesn't say. This interpretation ignores the context and assumes that this refers to a period of great tribulation upon the whole earth. Careful study reveals something different.

The Greek words for "world" and "earth" respectively in this verse are *oikoumene* and *ge*.

The first, *oikoumene*, merely means "land." It could refer to the whole earth, a region of the earth, or, at that time, the known world—the Roman Empire.

The second, *ge*, generally refers to a region, or the people who occupy a region. It could also refer to a country.

These are different from the Greek word most often used to mean the entire world, which is *kosmos*. *Kosmos* is found in Matthew 4:8:

> Again, the Devil took Him into an exceedingly high mountain and showed Him the kingdoms of the world (*kosmos*) and their glory.

It is obvious that the whole world is being spoken of here. *Kosmos* is also used by John the Revelator to refer to the entire world:

> All who live in the earth (*ge*; region) whose names are not written in the Book of Life of the Lamb slain from the foundation of the world (*kosmos*) shall worship him. (Rv 8:3)

Consistency dictates that, had John meant the entire world in verse 3:10, he would have used *kosmos* rather than *oikoumene* and *ge*.

We see then that the promise in Revelation 3:10 to keep God's people from the testing to come upon the region was a specific promise for a specific time to a specific people. It was to the assembly in Philadelphia during the first-century persecution of Christians within the Roman Empire. It has nothing to do with a future worldwide period of great tribulation.

"But why," some would ask, "would God make those He loves go through such a terrible time of testing? Does He not love us? Is our righteousness in Christ not sufficient for us to escape such a trial?

Such escapist thinking is largely the result of false teachings that suggest God wants all of His children to be healthy, wealthy and without care. Although this may be the ultimate desire of our heavenly Father, the truth remains that as long as we are in this sinful flesh it is necessary that we not be so without care in this world that we suffer in our relationship with Him.

His Word tells us many things contrary to the "health and wealth gospel" that permeates much of the Christian media. The word-faith and positive-confession teachings have done more to destroy faith in the true God than instill genuine faith that allows for suffering without failing in our relationship with Him.

The word-faith teachers like to emphasize Hebrews 11 as evidence that true faith brings riches and great power in this world. But their focus is only on verses 1 through 35a. They avoid the rest of the chapter:

... and others were tortured, not accepting deliverance, so that they might obtain a better resurrection.

And others had trials of cruel mocking and scourging, yes, moreover of bonds and imprisonment. They were stoned, they were sawn asunder, were tempted, were slain with the sword; they wandered about in sheepskins and goatskins. Being destitute, afflicted, tormented, they (of whom the world was not worthy) wandered in deserts, and in mountains, and in dens and caves of the earth.

And all these witnesses for faith did not receive the promise, God having provided some better thing for us so that without us they would not be made perfect. (Heb 11:35b-40)

Jesus warns us that in this world we would have tribulation. But He also urges us to be of good cheer because He has overcome the world (Jn 16:33).

The reason believers in Christ must suffer in varying degrees while in this world is to bring us to the place of death within ourselves. Our flesh fights against this; we don't want to give up the pleasures of this life. So we listen to those who tell us we can have it all; that godliness is evidenced by the gain we achieve in this life.

Jesus told His disciples:

"If anyone will come after Me, let him deny himself, and take up his cross and follow me. For whoever will save his life shall lose it, and whoever will lose his life for My sake shall find it." (Mt 16:24-25)

The writer of Hebrews said:

And you have forgotten the exhortation that speaks to you as to children, "My son, do not despise the chastening of the Lord, or faint when you are rebuked by Him, for whom the Lord loves He chastens, and scourges every son whom He receives."

If you endure chastening, God deals with you as with sons, for what son is he whom the father does not chasten? (Heb 12:5-7)

The sufferings of this life are for the purpose of bringing us into conformity to the image of Christ (Ro 8:29).

All this is true for us as individuals. However, the Lord also has a plan for bringing the corporate Body of Christ into a place of purification. Christ loves His called-out people and gave Himself for us "So that He may sanctify and cleanse it with the washing of water by the Word; that he may present it to Himself, a glorious called-out people, not having spot, or wrinkle, or any such thing, so that it would be holy and without blemish" (Eph 5:25-27).

Throughout the two millennia since Christ first came, His corporate Body has been full of spots, wrinkles and blemishes of all sorts. These imperfections are the result of friendship with the world. Even though there are true believers in the churches today, the churches are more worldly than they have ever been. And there is nothing that will cause separation from the world more than persecution from the world.

It's like a child who is warned not to pet a strange dog, but won't listen. He continues to disobey his parents' commands, thinking that the dog is his friend. Until the day the dog bites him severely enough that he realizes he can no longer be a friend to it. Now he is forced to separate.

Our heavenly Father has warned us repeatedly in His Word not to be friends with the world. Friendship with the world is enmity against God (Jas 4:4) So, too, is the carnal mind enmity against God (Ro 8:7). But Christians are so carnal in their minds that they continue to love the world and things in the world. They will not separate themselves from the world until the world bites them severely enough that they have no choice. They will either fall entirely into line with the world's philosophies and pleasures, or they will separate themselves, choosing God out of love.

Not all Christians will choose God; most will choose the world. We are witnessing this today as the churches and Christian institutions of learning increasingly adopt the world's philosophies, thinking they can be melded with God's Word into something better than His Word alone.

These are the spots and wrinkles of which the Lord wishes to purge us as a corporate Body. They are the reason Jude exhorts us to earnestly contend for the faith:

> Beloved, when I gave all diligence to write to you of the common salvation, it was necessary for me to write to you and exhort you that you should earnestly contend for the faith which was once delivered to the saints. For there are certain men who have crept in stealthily, who were long ago ordained for this condemnation—ungodly men, turning the grace of our God into lasciviousness and denying the only Lord God, and our Lord Jesus Christ. Therefore I will remind you,

though you once knew this, how the Lord, having saved the people out of the land of Egypt, afterward destroyed those who did not believe.

And the angels which did not keep their principality, but left their own habitation, He has reserved in everlasting chains under darkness for the judgment of the great day, even as Sodom and Gomorrah, and the cities around them in the same way, giving themselves over to fornication and going after strange flesh, are set forth as an example, suffering the vengeance of eternal fire.

Likewise also, these filthy dreamers defile the flesh, despise authority, and blaspheme the Glory.

Yet Michael the archangel, when contending with the Devil, disputing about the body of Moses, dared not bring against him a railing accusation, but said, "The Lord rebuke you."

But these revile those things of which they know nothing. But they corrupt themselves in those things they know naturally, as brute beasts.

Woe to them! For they have gone the way of Cain, and have run greedily after the error of Balaam for reward, and perished in the disobedience of Korah.

These are spots in your feasts of charity when they eat with you, feeding themselves without fear. They are clouds without water, carried around by winds; trees whose fruit withers; without fruit; twice dead; plucked up by the roots; raging waves of the sea foaming out their own shame; wandering stars to whom the blackness of darkness is reserved forever.

And Enoch also, the seventh from Adam, prophesied of these, saying, "Look! The Lord comes with ten thousand of his saints to execute judgment on all, and to convince all that are ungodly among them of all their ungodly deeds which they have ungodly committed, and of all their hard words which ungodly sinners have spoken against Him.

These are murmurers, complainers, walking after their own lusts, and their mouths speak great swelling words, having men's persons in admiration because of advantage.

But, beloved, you remember the words that were spoken before by the apostles of our Lord Jesus Christ, how they told you there would be mockers in the last time who would walk after their own ungodly lusts. These are they who separate themselves, sensual, not having the Spirit.

But you, beloved, building yourselves up on your most holy faith, praying in the Holy Spirit, keep yourselves in the love of God, looking for the mercy of our Lord Jesus Christ unto eternal life.

And on some have compassion, making a difference, and others save with fear, pulling them out of the fire, hating even the garment spotted by the flesh.

Now to Him who is able to keep you from falling, **and to present you faultless** before the presence of His glory with exceeding joy, to the only wise God, our Savior, be glory and majesty, dominion and power, both now and forever. Amen. (Jude 3-25)

This, then, is the reason there must be a time of great tribulation that will affect the relationship God's people have with the world. He must present to Himself a company of believers that is without spot or wrinkle, or any such thing.

This doesn't mean we will be sinless, perfected people; it means our hearts will be given so totally to God that we will have no love left for the world. A certain group of those who overcome the world and gather apart from false brethren (the spots in our feasts) will be the company without spot or wrinkle, or any such thing, that Jesus presents to Himself.

His purpose is to present to Himself an *ecclesia* without spot or wrinkle—the corporate Body of Christ, not individuals as sinless and perfected while mortal.

Rather than fear the tribulation that must come upon us, we should embrace it as a blessing from our heavenly Father as a means to bring us closer to Him and to prepare us for a more perfect resurrection.

16

ESCHATOLOGICAL ERRORS
DISPENSATIONALISM

There are many teachings related to eschatology which, if truly measured against what God's Word clearly teaches, are found to be in error. At the risk of offending some beloved brethren and teachers of the Word whom I admire apart from their eschatological understanding, I ask only that those who hold those understandings reconsider their position no matter where it falls along the eschatological spectrum.

This is not an exposé; there is no need to address by name those who espouse these teachings, many of whom are faithful brethren. It is merely an attempt to bring reason and truth to the use of certain Scriptures that have been adapted to fit certain eschatological biases.

There will be those who cite their favorite teachers to counter what is said herein. I ask those who disagree with what they read to cite only Scripture that clearly disproves what they read. By all means, test this writing as you should test all writings of men. There is no claim to infallibility on my part. But please understand that the intent of this writing is not to point you to men, but to God's Word. Test all things, therefore, by God's Word.

Above all things, we must strive for honesty, being willing to admit when our understanding has been shown to be faulty. In doing so, we are obliged to show that if a Scripture does not clearly state something, we have other Scriptures that explain it reasonably. At least we should confirm that the circumstance of the particular passage is consistent with Scriptures that are clear in their meaning elsewhere. There must be clarity in the Scripture passage or, at the least, sufficient evidence from the rest of Scripture to support what one says that passage means.

If this is not understandable at this point, I believe it will become so as examples are put forth.

Error #1: Modern Zionist Israel is the fulfillment of the prophecies regarding the gathering of Israel from out of the nations. Therefore, this generation of people will see the Lord's return.

Focusing on the words "this generation," the generally accepted teaching on these verses among pre-trib proponents is this:

> Jesus was speaking about the generation living during the time prophesied. Thus, when Israel (the fig tree) begins to sprout, we will know that the Rapture is about to take place. Israel became a nation in 1948; within one generation from that time—forty years after Israel became a nation—the Rapture should occur.

Answer: This is based on a faulty understanding of the fig tree in Matthew 24:29-35:

> "Immediately after the tribulation of those days the sun shall be darkened, and the moon shall not give her light, and the stars shall fall from the heavens, and the powers of the heavens shall be shaken. And then the sign of the Son of Man shall appear in the heavens, and then all the tribes of the earth will sorrow, and they shall see the Son of Man coming in the clouds of the heavens with power and great glory. And He shall send His angels with a great sound of a trumpet, and they shall gather together his elect from the four winds—from one end of the heavens to the other.
>
> "Now learn a parable of the fig tree: When its branch is still tender and puts forth leaves, you know that summer is near. So likewise, you, when you shall see all these things, know that it is near, even at the doors. Truly I say to you, this age shall not pass till all these things are fulfilled. The heavens and earth shall pass away, but My words shall not pass away."

Jesus said that this age (*genea*) would not pass until all these things are fulfilled. But because the Greek word *genea* is translated "generation" in virtually all English translations, it is assumed that Jesus was speaking of a generation of men (approximately forty years). Skeptics use this to say Jesus erred because He must have been speaking of His own generation. Some also use this translation to insist that Jesus already returned in the Spirit during His own generation; therefore He will not be coming back to establish His Millennial Kingdom.

When Israel became a nation in 1948, this teaching caused many to offer dates when the Lord would return. Some said it would—or could well be—by 1981. Others made a big deal of 1988, selling thousands of books that purported to support that premise.

Some have said they misjudged the timing; Israel "put forth its leaves" when it took control of the Old City of Jerusalem in 1967. They reset the end of the "generation" to as late as 2007. Yet the Lord has not returned as of the writing of this book.

There are a couple of things wrong with this teaching:

Nowhere in Scripture does the fig tree represent Israel. If one wishes to make the fig tree Israel, then the symbolism must also be applied to the grape vine, the pomegranate tree, the apple tree, the palm tree, and "all the trees of the field" mentioned in Joel 1:12. The only tree clearly used in the Bible to represent Israel is the olive tree (Ro 11:17-24). The olive branches in Zechariah 4:11 and Revelation 11:4 represent two Israelite prophets—branches from the olive tree.

Also, the "generation" in Matthew 24 is not necessarily a forty-year period or any other specific time period. Any application of the Greek word *genea* to mean a specific time period is erroneous. It literally means an age or era within time. *Genea* may also mean a tribe descended from a common ancestor—a "clan," "race," or "kind."

It is also possible that *genea* may refer to all the people living at a given time, such as the generation with which God was grieved because they would not enter into the Promised Land under Moses (Heb 3:10). Because God caused them to wander in the wilderness for forty years, some err in assuming that a generation is forty years.

Considering history and Scripture in total, what Jesus was saying is that this "age"—the time of the present world system—would not end until all the prophecies related to its close were fulfilled. His admonition was to discern the signs of the time when He will return, just as we would discern the coming of spring when the fig tree (or any tree) puts forth its leaves.

Error #2: The anti-Christ will be shot in the head, die, and rise to life again. Some say he will rise again in three days to counterfeit the resurrection of Jesus.

Answer: This error is based on a misunderstanding of Revelation 13:1-4:

> And I stood on the sand of the sea, and saw a beast rise up out of the sea, having seven heads and ten horns, and on his horns ten crowns, and on his heads the name of blasphemy. And the beast that I saw was like a leopard, and his feet were like the feet of a bear, and his mouth like the mouth of a lion. And the dragon gave him his power, and his seat, and great authority.
>
> And I saw one of his heads as if it were wounded to death. And his deadly wound was healed, and all the world wondered after the beast.

This beast, Satan's anti-Christ kingdom has seven heads (vs. 1)—the nations (heads) that have conquered Jerusalem. One of his heads (plural) is wounded to death. How many heads does a man have?

Obviously, the symbolism is not that of a man who is wounded in the head and dies (or almost dies), but of a nation. Specifically, it is one of seven nations (Rv 12:3; 13:1; 17:3-9); it was seemingly destroyed and will be revived in the last days. (We will go into this in greater detail in our study on the Book of Revelation.)

Those who think they will recognize anti-Christ by his being shot in the head won't have a clue when he does appear. This error has given rise to speculation that John F. Kennedy will one day rise from the dead to reign as the anti-Christ.

Errors #3 & #4: A third temple will be built in Jerusalem before the Lord returns, and the "abomination of desolation" is the last-days anti-Christ standing in the third temple, claiming to be God.

Answer: This is based on 2 Thessalonians 2:3-4:

> Let no man deceive you by any means, for that day shall not come until there first comes an apostasy, and that man of sin is revealed—the son of perdition who opposes and exalts himself above all that is called God, or that is worshipped, so that, as God, he sits in the temple of God, showing himself that he is God.

It is also based on the belief that the temple referred to in Daniel and Ezekiel is a third temple to be built by modern Israel before the Lord returns. The word translated "temple" in 2 Thessalonians 4 is the Greek *naos*. There are two Greek words used for "temple": *naos* and *hieron*. *Hieron* always refers to the specific Jewish temple structure or any part of it. Some Greek experts (e.g., *Vine's* and *Thayer's*) say that *naos* refers to the inner sanctuary. The more authoritative Bauer's *A Greek-English Lexicon of the New Testament and other early Christian Literature* offers examples where *naos* may refer to anything from the inner sanctuary to the general environs of the temple site, as well as the believer's body as the dwelling place of God. This is why Jesus spoke of His body as the temple (*naos*) as recorded in John 2:21. Paul used the word *naos* in every instance where he spoke of the temple of the body, but used *hieron* only one time, and that was in reference to the physical temple at Jerusalem (1Co 9:13). By using *naos* in 2 Thessalonians 2:4, consistency dictates that he was not speaking of the physical temple building at Jerusalem, but the general temple environs that still exist today.

There is no clear teaching that the future anti-Christ will sit in the sanctuary of a future temple. He may stand in the temple environs that still exist, but there is nothing to prove that another temple will be built. If it has any future reference left—if there was meant a double-application of the Lord's prophecy—it does not necessarily mean that there will be another temple built prior to the Millennium.

The site of the holy place is still on the temple mount, although exposed to the world. Archaeological research has determined the site of the holy place, which was quite large, to be under, or just north of, Islam's Dome of the Rock. If there is to be another abomination of desolation standing in the holy place it could well be on the site where the holy place stood; there anti-Christ may stand in the Dome of the Rock which sits in the temple environs, declaring himself to be God and gloating over having driven the Jews out of Jerusalem.

There is no scriptural proof that there will be a temple built before the Lord returns. The temple in Daniel is that built by Zerubbabel, and the temple in Ezekiel is clearly the Millennial Temple. There can be no "temple of God"—which implies sanction by God—as long as Jesus is the means of salvation to this present age. Men might erect something they call the temple of God, which many are proposing, but it will not be God's temple, and He will not dwell in it or visit it to honor any sacrifices presented there.

Error #5: The "falling away" in 2 Thessalonians 2:3 is really the Rapture, and so it will occur before the anti-Christ is revealed.

Answer: This is taught by convoluting of the words "falling away":

Let no man deceive you by any means: for that day shall not come, except there comes a falling away [*apostasia*] first, and that man of sin be revealed, the son of perdition.

It's really a stretch to make this error work. The Greek *apostasia* means to fall away from a position held, particularly a position of belief. The only other use of the word is by Luke in Acts 21:21 where Paul was told that it was reported he had taught all the Jews among the Gentiles to forsake (*apostasian*) Moses.

The proponents of this error insist that, in the case of 2 Thessalonians 2:3, *apostasia* means a separation, which must mean the Rapture, because Christians can't be here when anti-Christ comes. This circular reasoning is totally unreasonable and unsupported by Scripture. *Apostasia* is nowhere used in the context of a sudden grabbing or snatching away. This argument is a classic example of twisting God's Word to fit an eschatological presupposition, in this case, the pre-tribulation Rapture theory.

Error #6: "He who now letteth" (holds back) in 2 Thessalonians 2:7 (KJV) is the Holy Spirit who will be taken out of the world with "the Church" at the Rapture before anti-Christ is revealed.

Let's look at this entire passage in the KJV, which is the primary source for this error:

Now we beseech you, brethren, by the coming of our Lord Jesus Christ, and by our gathering together unto him,

That ye be not soon shaken in mind, or be troubled, neither by spirit, nor by word, nor by letter as from us, as that the Day of Christ is at hand.

Let no man deceive you by any means: for that day shall not come, except there come a falling away first, and that man of sin be revealed, the son of perdition;

Who opposeth and exalteth himself above all that is called God, or that is worshipped; so that he as God sitteth in the temple of God, shewing himself that he is God.

Remember ye not, that, when I was yet with you, I told you these things?

And now ye know what withholdeth that he might be revealed in his time.

For the mystery of iniquity doth already work: only he who now letteth will let, until he be taken out of the way.

And then shall that Wicked be revealed, whom the Lord shall consume with the spirit of his mouth, and shall destroy with the brightness of his coming: (2Th 2:1-8 KJV)

The error is stated thusly:

The Holy Spirit, indwelling the Body of Christ, is holding back the revealing of the man of sin. Therefore, when the Rapture takes place the Holy Spirit will be removed from the earth with the saints. Others say it is the preserving influence of "the Church" that is holding back the anti-Christ. In either case, only after the Rapture can the man of sin be revealed.

Answer: Now, as we have just shown, the apostasy and the revealing of the man of sin must come *before* the gathering together to Jesus. Therefore the Rapture cannot occur both before and after the anti-Christ is revealed.

First, the Holy Spirit is never taken off the earth. No Scripture anywhere suggests this. There will be people saved—particularly Israelites—who will be indwelt by the Holy Spirit. His presence will enable them to resist the mark of the beast; certainly no man can be holy through effort of the flesh alone. And the Body of Christ is certainly not in any position to hold back the anti-Christ. It has too inflated a view of its own spirituality. If anything, the apostate condition of most churches today has created a situation where even true believers are being persuaded away from biblical understanding. The Emergent Church Movement is strong among evangelical churches, moving them toward unity with the Vatican; charismania becomes more pronounced every year; liberal theology is finding its way into evangelical churches through the World-Christian Movement. As well, Chrislam is gaining great inroads into the churches through major proponents of interfaith cooperation such as Rick Warren, whose P.E.A.C.E. plan seeks social and economic justice as well as world peace.

Satan has a deception for every taste. If believers can't discern these deceptions how will they discern the ultimate deception until it is too late? The price to be paid will be one's faith or one's life.

No, "the Church" is in no position to restrain the anti-Christ.

So what does it mean when it says (in the KJV), "only he who now letteth will let, until he be taken out of the way"?

The Greek translated "who now letteth will let until he be taken out of the way" is *ho katecho arti heos ginomai ek mesos.* Literally, "he who restrains at present until out of [the] midst he be."

Some say the literal translation is "only the restraining just now until out of [the] midst it [or he] comes."

The operative word is *ginomai,* from the same root as the word *genesis,* which connotes coming into being. It does not mean "taken out of the way." He, or it, will come when he who holds it back releases it to come.

Nowhere does it say "He" is the Holy Spirit who will be taken "out of the earth." The problem has been the assumption that both "he"s are the same. But the second "he" or "it" is the fullness of the mystery of iniquity that is already at work:

> Little children, it is the last time. And as you have heard that anti-Christ will come, even now there are many anti-Christs, whereby we know that it is the last time. (1Jn 2:18)

Consider again 2 Thessalonians 2:7 properly translated:

> For the mystery of iniquity already works, only now holding fast until coming forth.

It is important that Paul states the mystery of iniquity is already at work prior to speaking of "he who letteth." There are two ways to look at this verse. The first is that the one restraining the coming of the mystery of iniquity or lawlessness is the Lord. The second is that the one restraining is another principality.

Looking at the first consideration, the first "He" may well be the Lord, who is restraining the second "he" from coming out of the midst of the nations or people to assume authority. In other words, the Lord is now holding back the revealing of the anti-Christ until the proper time for the anti-Christ to come out of the midst of his people.

The second consideration has some merit as well. It suggests that something or someone is hindering something else from coming into place. Scripture gives an example in the Book of Daniel where the Angel of the Lord had to fight the prince of Persia in order that the prince of Greece could come (Da 10:1-20). The prince of Persia was a spiritual power that controlled the major world system while Persia was dominant. He had to be taken out of the way in order for the prince of Greece to come. Every principality of every age has had to be taken out of the way for the succeeding principality to arise.

When Rome disintegrated it was divided among ten generals. Their rule lasted but a short time before the Barbarians overthrew the ancient Roman Empire, seemingly for good. Over the centuries there have risen a number of world powers: Spain, Portugal, France, Russia, Germany, Britain, the United States. All the world powers since ancient Rome came out of the Roman Empire—the British Empire being the most dominant until the United States of America arose. Now it appears as if the United States is losing its dominance and the European powers are combining to assert their previous power, but this time in concert. As well, there is arising a union of Asian nations—the "kings of the East" (Rv 16:12). The final world power will most likely be a combined Roman/Ottoman Empire (mixing iron and clay).

In order for the anti-Christ to be revealed, the prince of the present world order must be taken out of the way. But he is resisting—restraining what must eventually be revealed.

Why these principalities resist is not stated, but it may be that once they have served their purpose they are consigned to the bottomless pit to await their eventual destruction. It is possible that the spiritual principality over the present world system is holding back Apollyon, who will strengthen the anti-Christ in his dominion, as we see from Revelation 9:1–11:7.

Some insist that Satan's kingdom is not divided, based on Jesus' words in Matthew 12:26 and Luke 11:17. But Satan's kingdom will not stand. The Lord was addressing Satan's work in men. But the evidence of Daniel suggests that Satan's higher minions still seek their own power.

In any case, the "he" is not the Holy Spirit in the believers, but either the Lord restraining the anti-Christ until the proper time, or a satanic principality that does not want to make way for the final principality. When he is removed by the Lord and His angels, the anti-Christ will be revealed. In either case, it is the Lord who removes, not the one to be removed.

Error #7: John being called up to Heaven in Revelation 4:1 represents the pre-tribulation Rapture.

> After this I saw, and, look! A door was opened in Heaven. And the first voice that I heard was as it were that of a trumpet speaking with me, which said, "Come up here, and I will show you things which must be after this. "

Answer: This is pure conjecture, also based on circular reasoning that, because "the Church" is no longer mentioned after the letters to the seven assemblies are dictated, then it must have been raptured before anything else in the Book of Revelation occurs. Thus, John's ascending into Heaven represents the Rapture of the saints in general.

This is another example of trying to make Scripture fit a presupposition. It is first assumed that the Rapture must occur prior to all the judgments and tribulations delineated in the following chapters, so it is convenient to assume that John's ascension must represent the Rapture. But that's not what it says. John merely recorded his experience of being taken up to Heaven to witness the Day of the Lord (not "the Lord's Day"), and to receive knowledge of the things that must take place after his time.

Error #8: Matthew 24:40-41 is a description of the Rapture:

"Then two will be in the field; the one shall be taken, and the other left. Two women will be grinding at the mill; the one shall be taken, and the other left."

Answer: This is a description of God's judgment, not the Rapture. The context of these verses is the return of the Lord, so it is easy to see how the belief that this represents the Rapture might arise. However, these verses have to do with judgment as we see when put in context:

"But as the days of Noah were, so also shall be the coming of the Son of Man. For as in the days that were before the flood they were eating and drinking, marrying and giving in marriage until the day that Noah entered into the ark, and did not know until the flood came and took them all away. So also the coming of the Son of Man shall be.

"Then two will be in the field; the one shall be taken, and the other left. Two women will be grinding at the mill; the one shall be taken, and the other left.

"Watch therefore, because you do not know what hour your Lord will come. (Mt 24:37-43)

Just as the flood took away the ungodly, so too, when the Lord appears, some will be taken away to destruction. This does not negate the idea of the Rapture. But it is because of sloppy exegesis in this and other areas, that the detractors of the Rapture have been able to convince many that even the concept of the Rapture is a myth. There are sufficient Scriptures to prove the Rapture; we need not manufacture "proofs."

Error #9: Israel will be attacked, which will be the battle of Armageddon, prompting the Lord to return and rescue Israel. This is a misunderstanding of Zechariah 12:1-11:

"The burden of the word of YHWH for Israel," says YHWH, who stretches out the heavens, and lays the foundation of the earth, and forms the spirit of man within him:

"Look! I will make Jerusalem a cup of trembling to all the people around when they shall be in the siege both against Judah and against Jerusalem. And in that day I will make Jerusalem a burdensome stone for all people. All who burden themselves with it shall be cut in pieces, although all the people of the earth are gathered together against it.

"In that day," says YHWH, "I will strike every horse with astonishment, and his rider with madness, and I will open My eyes upon the house of Judah, and will strike every horse of the people with blindness.

"And the governors of Judah shall say in their hearts, 'The inhabitants of Jerusalem shall be my strength in YHWH of Hosts their God.'

"In that day I will make the governors of Judah like a hearth of fire among the wood, and like a torch of fire in a sheaf, and they shall devour all the people around them, on the right hand and on the left. And Jerusalem shall be inhabited again in her own place, even in Jerusalem."

YHWH shall also save the tents of Judah first, so that the glory of the house of David and the glory of the inhabitants of Jerusalem do not magnify themselves against Judah.

In that day YHWH shall defend the inhabitants of Jerusalem, and he who is feeble among them in that day shall be like David, and the house of David shall be like God—like the angel of YHWH before them.

"And it shall happen in that day, that I will seek to destroy all the nations that come against Jerusalem.

"And I will pour upon the house of David, and upon the inhabitants of Jerusalem, the spirit of grace and of supplications, and they shall look upon Me whom they have pierced, and they shall mourn for Him like one mourns for his only son, and shall be in bitterness for Him, like one who is in bitterness for his firstborn.

"In that day there will be a great mourning in Jerusalem, like the mourning of Hadadrimmon in the valley of Megiddon."

Answer: Verse 10 places this prophecy in the future: they will look upon Jesus (YHWH saying "upon Me") whom they have pierced. This is at the time when the nations will gather against Jerusalem in the very last days—the time of Jacob's Trouble when Israel is driven into the wilderness for three-and-one-half years (Rv 12:14).

While it appears as if the Lord is going to destroy anti-Christ before anti-Christ takes Jerusalem, it doesn't actually say that. Israel will be in the wilderness for three-and-one-half years while Jerusalem will be trodden underfoot by the nations under anti-Christ:

And when the dragon saw that he was cast to the earth he persecuted the woman [Israel] which brought forth the man child. And two wings of a great eagle were given to the woman so that she may fly into the wilderness, into her place, where she is nourished for a time, and times, and half a time, from the face of the serpent.

And the serpent cast out of his mouth water as a flood after the woman so that he might cause her to be carried away by the flood. And the earth helped the woman, and the earth opened her mouth and swallowed up the flood which the dragon cast out of his mouth. And the dragon was infuriated with the woman and went to make war with the remnant of her seed who keep the commandments of God and have the testimony of Jesus Christ. (Rv 12:13-17)

When the Lord returns for His people the unbelieving of Israel will see Him and will mourn; they will realize they have rejected their Messiah. But it will be too late. They will have been abandoned by all other nations and will be driven into the wilderness by anti-Christ's forces. God will protect a remnant of Israel, and anti-Christ will not be able to harm them. This will infuriate him. But he will be able to reach many of those who have turned to Jesus in faith, and will persecute them.

After the three-and-one-half years (the last half of Daniel's seventieth seven) the Lord will return to the earth and will deliver Jerusalem into the hands of His people once and for all.

It appears as if, even though seeing the Lord in the clouds receiving His people, most Israelites will not understand enough to be counted among those "who keep the commandments of God and have the testimony of Jesus Christ." Yet they will be protected by the Lord so they can enter into the Millennial Kingdom.

Error #10: Russia will attack Israel at any moment, and will be destroyed by the Lord on His return. This error is based on Ezekiel 38:2–39:7:

"Son of man, set your face against Gog—the land of Magog, the chief prince of Meshech and Tubal—and prophesy against him, and say, 'The Lord YHWH says this: "Look, I am against you, O Gog, the chief prince of Meshech and Tubal, and I will turn you back and put hooks into your jaws. And I will bring you forth—and all your army, horses and horsemen, all of them clothed with all sorts of armor—a great company with bucklers and shields, all of them handling swords: Persia, Ethiopia, and Libya with them, all of them with shield and helmet, Gomer, and all his bands; the house of Togarmah of the north quarters, and all his bands, and many people with you.

"You be prepared, and you prepare for yourself and all your company that are assembled to you, and you be a guard to them.

"After many days you shall be visited; in the latter years you shall come into the land that is brought back from the sword and is gathered out of many people, against the mountains of Israel which have always been waste but is brought forth out of the nations, and they shall dwell safely all of them.

"You shall ascend and come like a storm; you shall be like a cloud to cover the land, you and all your bands, and many people with you.'"

"The Lord YHWH says this": 'It shall also come to pass that at the same time things will come into your mind, and you will think an evil thought. And you will say, "I will go up to the land of unwalled villages; I will go to those who are at rest, who dwell safely, all of them dwelling without walls, and having neither bars nor gates, to take a spoil and to take a prey." To turn your hand upon the desolate places that are now inhabited, and upon the people that are gathered out of the nations, which have gotten cattle and goods, that dwell in the midst of the land. Sheba, and Dedan, and the merchants of Tarshish, with all of its young lions, will say to you, "Have you come to take a spoil? Have you gathered your company to take a prey—to carry away silver and gold, to take away cattle and goods, to take a great spoil?"'"

"Therefore, son of man, prophesy and say to Gog, 'The Lord YHWH says this: "In that day when My people of Israel dwell safely, will you not know it? And you shall come from your place out of the north parts, you, and many people with you, all of them riding upon

184 The Day of Yahweh

horses—a great company, and a mighty army—and you shall come up against My people of Israel as a cloud to cover the land. It shall be in the latter days, and I will bring you against My land so that the heathen may know Me, when I shall be sanctified in you before their eyes, O Gog....'

"Therefore, you son of man, prophesy against Gog, and say, 'The Lord YHWH says this: "Look! I am against you, O Gog, the chief prince of Meshech and Tubal, and I will turn you back and leave but the sixth part of you, and will cause you to come up from the north parts, and will bring you upon the mountains of Israel. And I will strike your bow out of your left hand, and will cause your arrows to fall out of your right hand.

""You shall fall on the mountains of Israel, you, and all your bands, and the people that are with you. I will give you to the ravenous birds of every sort, and to the beasts of the field to be eaten. You shall fall upon the open field. For I have spoken it," says the Lord YHWH. "And I will send a fire on Magog, and among those who dwell carelessly in the isles, and they shall know that I am YHWH.

""So I will make My holy name known in the midst of My people Israel, and I will not let them pollute My holy name anymore. And the heathen shall know that I am YHWH, the Holy One in Israel.""'

The myth goes something like this:

Russia is the country to the north that opposes Israel today. It is (or was, as the Soviet Union) the only other major world power with any military strength capable of amassing sufficient might against Israel. It will ally itself with the other nations that surround Israel and will attack the Holy Land. At that time, the Lord will return to rescue Israel and will destroy Russia.

Answer: This is linked to Error #9, but it adds to it by attempting to identify the anti-Christ's kingdom as Russia. It makes for good reading, but it's not true. The chief prince is Gog from the land of Magog, he is not the Russian premier. Magog was a son of Japheth (Ge 10:1-5). His brothers were Meshech, Tubal, Gomer, Javan and Madai. Togarmah was a son of Gomer; Tarshish was a son of Javan.

All of these sons of Japheth settled in what is today Turkey. Gog and Magog descended from Japheth, the father of the Turks. Both lived in the land of Magog.

Some say Gomer settled in Russia. But that is immaterial. The mention of all these tribes tells us that "Gog and Magog" is Turkey, not Russia. Gog, not Gomer, is the chief prince or leader. Turkey lies directly north of Israel, and despite its relatively moderate stance toward Israel for some time, it is turning more and more against Israel. It is a leading Muslim nation, having been the seat of the Ottoman Empire, and is the land bridge between Europe and the Middle East.

Regardless of these truths, the description of Gog and Magog attacking Jerusalem indicates that this is not the battle of Armageddon that will take place upon the Lord's return. Ezekiel 38 and 39 are millennial prophecies. They describe the battle at the end of the Millennium when Israel is dwelling safely, not because of a peace pact with the anti-Christ, but because the Lord's rule over the earth will be secure. Only after Satan is released from the bottomless pit will the nations be deceived to think they can overthrow the rule of Jesus Christ (Rv 20:7-15). Gog and Magog will be the instruments by which Satan will deceive the other nations to think they can once again establish "democracy" on the earth.

Again, this battle must not be confused with Armageddon, which will be anti-Christ mustering all the nations to battle the Lord when He returns with His resurrected saints to the earth (Rv 16:12-16). Present-day Palestine, which encompasses Jerusalem, will be the site of the battle of Armageddon. But Armageddon is not World War III, pitting nation against nation, which has been a fanciful portrayal by some. Neither is it anti-Christ's armies fighting against Israel, the United States, and/or China. It is anti-Christ's armies mustering to battle the Lord when He descends from Heaven to the earth. The nations will have suffered God's wrath from the time of His first appearing to gather His saints, until the end of the second three-and-one-half years of Daniel's seventieth seven when He will set His feet on the earth. They will be in fear of the Lord's further judgment when He sets foot on the earth, and will think their superior weapons can defeat Him and His angels and saints.

*   *   *

There are a number of other errors found within dispensational eschatology, but these should suffice to at least cause some rethinking on the part of honest seekers of truth.

17

ESCHATOLOGICAL ERRORS

PRETERISM

As stated earlier, preterists believe that all prophecy related to the end times has been fulfilled with the exception of the New Heavens and New Earth, which will take place upon the Lord's return. They insist that He already returned "in glory" in A.D. 70 with the destruction of the Jewish temple. Preterism rests almost entirely on an erroneous assumption based on the perceived immediacy of the language used in some prophecies. For example, Jesus saying He would come "immediately" after the tribulation of those days of "great tribulation" during which the temple would be destroyed. We will look at this and other seemingly convincing "proof texts" of preterism to see if any of them are viable. We will consult the New King James Version of the Bible (NKJV) or the New American Standard Bible (NAS) because these are popular versions among Reformed theologians.

Error #1: Jesus returned with the destruction of the temple in A.D. 70.
Answer: According to the prophecy given to Daniel, the sacrifices would be cut off in the middle of the seventieth seven. So when the temple was destroyed and the sacrifices cut off in A.D. 70, it was in the middle of the seventieth seven. The Lord would not return for another three-and-one-half

years according to the prophecy. So even if He did return "in glory" it would not have been in September, A.D. 70, but in March, A.D. 74. According to Luke 21:24 and Romans 11:25-27, Jerusalem will be controlled by the Gentiles until the Lord returns at the end of the Times of the Gentiles, which time we are currently in. Therefore, as I've stated throughout this writing, the second half of Daniel's seventieth seven is still in the future. In any case, there is no mention of the Lord's return in any form within any of the Gospels or epistles written after those dates.

Error #2: Preterists say that Jesus spoke about the Kingdom of God coming in His day; therefore, there is no future Kingdom of God on earth. This is based on several verses briefly cited below:

"The Kingdom of Heaven is at hand" (Mt 3:2);

"Who warned you to flee from the wrath about to come?" (Mt 3:7);

"The axe is already laid at the root of the trees" (Mt 3:10; Lk 3:9);

"The Kingdom of Heaven is at hand" (Mt 4:17; 10:7);

"The age about to come" (Mt 12:32);

"The Kingdom of God is at hand" (Mk 1:15);

"His winnowing fork is in His hand" (Lk 3:17);

"The Kingdom of God has come near [to you]" (Lk 10:9; 11).

Answer: There is no argument that the Lord was speaking of His first coming through which the Kingdom of God came to Israel. But He was not addressing His Second Coming. The Kingdom of God was manifested through the signs and wonders He performed. The Kingdom of God has more than one manifestation; it first came to the earth through the creation, then through Adam and all the godly men and women who served the Lord through the ages. They all manifested the Kingdom of God to some degree. But when the Lord Jesus came He manifested the Kingdom of God fully in the Spirit. This does not rule out His coming again physically to manifest the Kingdom of God over all the nations through His rule with a rod of iron.

There are other more difficult Scriptures that preterism offers, but those cited above have no bearing on the truth of the Lord's future return for His saints and His Millennial Kingdom.

Error #3: Preterism assumes that replacement theology is behind a number of Scriptures that address the loss of standing for the Jews. For example, speaking to the priests, scribes and elders, Jesus warned them through the parable of the owner of the vineyard that they would lose their inheritance: "He will come and destroy the vine-growers, and will give the vineyard to others" (Mt 21:40-45; Mk 12:1-11; Lk 20:15-19).

Answer: The Lord was indeed warning the religious leaders and elders that they would not enjoy the fruits of the Kingdom. But there is nothing in these verses to say that His final judgment would happen in their lifetimes. He also said to them, "And I say to you that many will come from east and west, and sit down with Abraham, Isaac, and Jacob in the kingdom of heaven. But the sons of the kingdom will be cast out into outer darkness. There will be weeping and gnashing of teeth" (Mt 8:11-13 NKJV).

This is a promise for the future kingdom of Israel when Abraham, Isaac and Jacob have been resurrected. They have not yet sat down in the Kingdom of Heaven with all the saints. So these verses do not establish replacement theology, nor do they refute the coming Millennial Kingdom.

Error #4: Preterists say that because Jesus gave many indications that the end was about to come upon those with whom He spoke, there is nothing left to come. It is assumed that because the Lord spoke of judgment upon those who opposed Him, that judgment would be the final one for them:

Answer: Speaking to Caiaphas and the whole Sanhedrin, Jesus said, "You shall see the Son of Man sitting at the right hand of Power, and coming on the clouds of the heavens." (Mt 26:64; Mk 14:62; Lk 22:69)

The operative word translated in Matthew and Mark as "you shall see" is a form of *optanomai*, which doesn't state who will see. It merely means that the Lord will be seen, or will allow Himself to be seen, "sitting at the right hand of power and coming on the clouds of the heavens." It has been assumed by preterists that the Lord was telling the Sanhedrin and Caiaphas that they personally would see this, but there is no scriptural or historical evidence that they ever did see it. Finally, if "you shall see" is a correct understanding, there is also the possibility that the Lord was speaking generically, "you" being all the Jews at the time He would return. Remember, even He didn't know the time of His return, so it would have been presumptuous to say definitely that Caiaphas and those with him would witness His return. There is just nothing conclusive to be drawn from this account which would support the preterist position. We must look elsewhere for that.

Error #5: There are a number of preterist proof texts that point to imminency through the use of the words "about to," "soon," "immediately," etc. A few such verses are these:

"The Son of Man is about to come in the glory of His Father with His angels; and will then recompense every man according to his deeds" (Mt 16:27);

"There is about to be a resurrection of both the righteous and the wicked" (Ac 24:25);

"I solemnly charge you in the presence of God and of Christ Jesus, who is about to judge the living and the dead" (2Ti 4:1);

"For yet in a very little while, He who is coming will come, and will not delay" (Heb 10:37).

Answer: All of these are true statements relative to the prophetic history of Israel. Within the prophetic timeline that the Lord established for the nation of Israel, particularly the kingdom of Israel, all prophecy follows in quick succession. But, again, we must remind the reader that Israel's prophetic history is not the same as world history. The interim known as the Time of the Gentiles has interrupted the prophetic timeline for the nation of Israel until the fullness of the Gentiles has been completed. So, yes, these prophecies were "immediate" to Israel's prophetic timeline, but not to world history.

Error #6: Preterists also take liberty with several verses, removing them from their context in order to "prove" their theory. One in particular they cite to assert that God's final judgment has come upon Israel is Luke 21:21:

"These are the days of vengeance, in order that all things that are written may be fulfilled."

Answer: The context is the destruction of the temple in A.D. 70, which preterists would agree. But they would say it is all past history. However, this verse leads into the following judgment upon Israel: "And they will fall by the edge of the sword, and be led away captive into all nations. And Jerusalem will be trampled by Gentiles until the times of the Gentiles are fulfilled (Lk 21:24 NKJV).

What happens when the Time of the Gentiles is fulfilled? Then the Lord will return:

"For I do not desire, brethren, that you should be ignorant of this mystery, lest you should be wise in your own opinion, that blindness in part has happened to Israel until the fullness of the Gentiles has come in. And so all Israel will be saved, as it is written:

"The Deliverer will come out of Zion,
"And He will turn away ungodliness from Jacob;
"For this is My covenant with them,
"When I take away their sins." (Ro 11:25-27 NKJV)

The Deliverer (Jesus) will come out of Zion when the Time of the Gentiles is completed, which time we are presently in. This is yet future.

Error #7: Preterists believe that certain Scriptures that address the people spoken to are evidence that the Lord would come in their lifetime. A few follow:

1) "This generation will not pass away until all these things take place" (Mt 24:34).

Answer: At the risk of being redundant (I warned you), I will iterate what I said in a previous chapter:

The Greek word translated "generation" in both of these verses is *genea*, which can mean the period of time of a specific person's or people's lifetime. But it can also mean an age or time not specific to any particular person or people. One cannot be dogmatic to say that it must unequivocally mean the people living at that time. We are in the age when God is dealing with men's sins and calling out for Himself a people who will be sanctified for His use in this age and in the next. This age has not passed away. Now, it may be argued that we cannot be dogmatic that the word must mean the entire age prior to the New Heavens and New Earth, and that's fine for the sake of argument. But lacking any evidence that the Lord has returned, considering that all things continue as before, and that for the past 2,000 years "the Church" has largely been apostate, there is no evidence that the Lord is ruling from Heaven with a rod of iron. His judgment is not being realized.

2) "Assuredly, I say to you, there are some standing here who shall not taste death till they see the Son of Man coming in His kingdom" (Mt 16:27-28).

Answer: In order to avoid too much redundancy, I will refer the reader back to pages 48-49, and just say that the Lord came in His Kingdom when He was resurrected.

3) And He said to them, "Assuredly, I say to you that there are some standing here who will not taste death till they see the Kingdom of God present with power" (Mk 9:1).

Answer: I address this earlier as well, on pages 48-49. The Kingdom of God came with power at Pentecost.

Error #8: The "catching up" in 1 Thessalonians 4:16-17 will not occur until the Lord actually descends to the earth.

For the Lord Himself shall descend from Heaven with a shout—with the voice of the archangel, and with the trump of God—and the dead in Christ shall rise first. Then we who are alive and remain shall be caught up together with them in the clouds to meet the Lord in the air, and so shall we ever be with the Lord.

This error is stated thusly:

The Greek word *apantesis* (translated "meet" in 1Th 4:17) has the connotation of meeting someone at a particular point while that someone continues on his way. It is the same idea as that found in Acts 28:15 where the brethren from Rome came to meet Paul at the Appii forum and the three taverns, and then continued with him to Rome. They did not meet Paul and return with him whence he came. Therefore, the idea of a Rapture to be with the Lord while He pours out His wrath upon the earth is erroneous.

Answer: *Apantesis* does not carry the automatic meaning of meeting and continuing in a journey. It is a noun, which is better understood as "a meeting." The saints will be caught up to "a meeting" with the Lord. Just because that word is used of the meeting between Paul and the brethren at Appii does not mean it must always be understood in that fashion. Also, there's no reason to think that, along the way, Paul and the brethren didn't tarry awhile.

There are two Greek words translated "meet" (as an encounter) in the Scriptures: *apantesis* and *sunantesis*. *Apantesis* is found in Matthew 25:6 where the virgins go out to meet the bridegroom, in Acts 28:15 where Paul meets the brethren at Appii, and in 1 Thessalonians 4:17 where the saints are caught up to meet the Lord in the air. Based on these, the proponents of this error insist the meaning is an immediate return with the Lord.

What they omit is the fact that Matthew uses *sunantesis* as a synonym in 25:1 where the virgins are told to go meet the bridegroom, demonstrating that there is no real difference between the two words. We could say they went to "meet" the Lord or "encounter" the Lord. Same thing.

There is insufficient evidence offered in this myth to offset the many Scriptures we've cited that prove otherwise.

Error # 9: Preterism states that Jesus' prophecy that the Gospel would be proclaimed throughout the whole world (Mt 24:14), then the end would come, has been fulfilled. They cite Romans 10:18 and Acts 17:6:

> But what does it say ? "The word is near you, in your mouth and in your heart"—that is, the word of faith which we are preaching,
> So faith comes from hearing, and hearing by the word of Christ. But I say, surely they have never heard, have they? Indeed they have; "Their voice has gone out into all the earth, and their words to the ends of the world." (Ro 10:17-18 NAS)

> But the Jews, becoming jealous and taking along some wicked men from the market place, formed a mob and set the city in an uproar; and attacking the house of Jason and some brethren before the city authorities, shouting, "These men who have upset the world have come here also." (Ac 17:5-6 NAS)

Answer: The problem is in the English translation to the word "world." Romans 10:18 should read, "Their voice has gone out into all the region (Gr: *ge*), and their words to the ends of the land (Gr. *oikoumene*). Acts 17:6 should read, "These men who have upset the land (Gr: *oikoumene*) have come here also." These words are in contrast to the Greek *kosmos*, which means the whole of the earth.

But to be honest, the Lord said in Matthew 24:14: "This gospel of the kingdom shall be preached in the whole world (Gr: *oikoumene*) as a testimony to all the nations, and then the end will come" (NAS). Jesus did not say that the Gospel would be proclaimed throughout the whole world.

So are preterists technically correct because the Lord said the Gospel would be proclaimed throughout the whole land, and, in fact, it was proclaimed throughout the whole land, thus the end should have come already?

No, because today the Gospel has been proclaimed throughout the whole world, it had to be the Lord's intent. Yet when the statements were made as recorded in Romans and Acts, the Gospel had not gone to the whole world. It hadn't yet made it to the Americas, Australia, New Zealand, the darkest parts of Africa or Asia.

The preterist argument is at best inconclusive; it does not prove anything one way or the other, nor are preterism's detractors proven correct.

There are other preterist proof texts, but most are stretches at best, and none conclusively prove the preterist position. When all Scripture prophecy is taken together, preterism falls apart.

17

AN ESCHATOLOGY TIMELINE

The following timeline is based on clearly stated Scriptures, particularly those in the books of Daniel, Ezekiel and Revelation. Admittedly, there is future fulfillment of prophecies which will not be understood until revealed by the Lord through circumstances that line up with heretofore sealed prophecy:

> "But you, O Daniel, close up the words and seal the book to the time of the end. Many will run back and forth, and knowledge will be increased." (Da 12:4)

> And when the seven thunders had uttered their voices, I was about to write. And I heard a voice from Heaven saying to me, "Seal up those things that the seven thunders uttered, and do not write them." (Rv 10:4)

As I have stated throughout this writing, all prophecy pertains to the nation of Israel in general, and Jerusalem in particular. The central prophecy on which all others rest in regard to the last days is that given to Daniel in which seventy seven-year periods are addressed:

> "Seventy sevens are determined upon your people and upon your holy city, to finish the transgression, and to make an end of sins, and

to make reconciliation for iniquity, and to bring in everlasting righteousness, and to seal up the vision and prophecy, and to anoint the most Holy.

"Know therefore and understand, that from the going forth of the commandment to restore and to build Jerusalem until Messiah the Prince shall be seven sevens, and sixty-two sevens. The street shall be built again, and the wall, even in troublous times.

"And after the sixty-two sevens Messiah shall be cut off, but not for Himself. And the people of the prince that will come will destroy the city and the sanctuary, and its end shall be with a flood, and until the end of the war desolations are determined.

"And he shall confirm the covenant with many for one seven. And in the midst of the seven he will cause the sacrifice and the oblation to cease. And for the overspreading of abominations he will make it desolate until the end is decided for the desolate." (Da 9:24-27)

I reiterate that the timeline for prophetic history is not the same as that for human history. This is reflected in the accompanying chart at the end of this chapter, which intersperses two gaps in Israel's prophetic history.

The first gap is that of some forty years that transpired between the time Messiah was killed at the end of the sixty-ninth seven of Daniel's prophecy, and the beginning of the first three-and-one-half years of the seventieth seven with the approach to Jerusalem by Vespasian in February of A.D. 67. At that time Vespasian offered peace terms to Jerusalem if the Jews would submit to Rome's authority and pay tribute, in which case he would honor (confirm) the covenant and allow the Jews to worship YHWH without interference.

The second gap in the timeline of Israel's prophetic history is the present Time of the Gentiles during which all who receive Israel's Messiah as their Savior are grafted into Israel under the New Covenant that Jesus made with the houses of Israel and Judah (Jer 31:31; Heb 8:8):

This prophecy was fulfilled in Jesus Christ. The New Covenant in the blood of Christ Jesus is that which He made with the houses of Israel and Judah, and into which all who have faith in Him may enter.

The Lord did not make His New Covenant with something called "the Church," but all promises of redemption are found in His New Covenant with Israel and Judah. Because Christianity rejected this truth and claimed that "the Church" is a company of blessed people apart from Israel, its understanding of end-times prophecy has been faulty. It doesn't see the Time of the Gentiles as an interruption in the prophetic timeline for Israel, but sees it either as the end-all of prophecy (preterism), or as distinct from Israel altogether (dispensationalism).

Now, I should clarify that we are not grafted into national Israel, but New Covenant Israel of faith (or, as some call it, "spiritual Israel"). Our inheritance is not earthly Jerusalem, which will be for national Israel during the Millennium. Our inheritance is in the New Jerusalem, the Bride of Christ which will descend from Heaven to the earth at the end of the Millennium.

It is my hope that our readers will see and understand this vital truth in order to not be deceived and thus miss the true signs of the Lord's return.

*   *   *

The timeline for prophecy concerning Israel, the appearance of Messiah, and the end of this age is as follows:

Daniel's 1 through 7 sevens (49 years): The temple is commissioned and construction begun on it and on the walls of Jerusalem;

Daniel's 8 through 69 sevens (434 years; 483 years total): Messiah enters Jerusalem and the temple, then is killed;

God allows the sacrifices to remain for some 40 years while the Gospel is being proclaimed to the Jews;

February, A.D. 67: Daniel's seventieth seven begins with Vespasian's approach to Jerusalem with peace terms and the promise to honor the Covenant if the city would pay tribute to the Roman emperor.

September, A.D. 70: Half-way through Daniel's seventieth seven, the sacrifices were taken away as prophesied, the temple was destroyed, the Jews were again dispersed among the nations, and the Time of the Gentiles began (Lk 21:20-27);

The Time of the Gentiles continues until this present time, some 2,000 years;

Believers in Christ look for His return, but must first wait for the man of sin to be revealed (2Th 2:3);

Unknown date: Anti-Christ (most likely a Muslim leader) will appear and will be recognized by God's true servants;

Unknown date: Anti-Christ will form a coalition comprised of Western nations and Muslim states;

Unknown date: Anti-Christ will form an alliance with a religious leader, either another Muslim or from Western Christianity, most likely the latter;

Unknown date and duration: A time of great tribulation will be on the whole earth, or at least on the regions ruled by the anti-Christ. Christians and Jews will be persecuted;

Unknown date and duration: All the world, or at least the regions under the anti-Christ's dominion will see the mark of the beast instituted;

Unknown date: The Lord will appear in the skies and the next stage of the first resurrection will occur. Those believers in Christ who are alive at the time will be changed into immortality and will be gathered with the resurrected to meet the Lord in the air. After this, the anti-Christ will come against Jerusalem and will succeed in once again driving the Jews from the city into the wilderness where they will be protected for the next three-and-one-half years. The second half of Daniel's seventieth seven will commence. God's judgment will bring devastation to the anti-Christ's kingdom through natural and supernatural calamities;

At the end of Daniel's seventieth seven (490 prophetic years): The Lord will return to the earth with His saints to take the kingdoms of this world for Himself. Satan will be bound in the bottomless pit for 1,000 years;

For one thousand years: The Lord will rule with a rod of iron along with His saints. His headquarters will be in Jerusalem;

At the end of the thousand years: Satan will be set loose; Gog and Magog will form armies from all the nations to come against Jerusalem as she dwells peacefully;

The Lord will destroy the armies; a period of cleansing for the land will take place;

The second resurrection will occur. All who were not in the first resurrection will be judged according to their works and will either enter into Eternity in the New Earth or be cast into the lake of fire;

Unknown date and duration: At a time determined by the Father, the present cosmos will be destroyed and remade to usher in the Eternal Age with New Heavens and a New Earth;

New Jerusalem will descend from Heaven to the New Earth and the Father will dwell with His people through all eternity.

*   *   *

Admittedly, this timeline is sketchy, simply because it would take all of Scripture to detail every stage, and many things are not yet revealed.

The chart on the following page will help the reader understand prophetic history as it relates to world history.

TIMELINE OF PROPHETIC HISTORY AS OPPOSED TO HUMAN HISTORY (NOT TO SCALE)

Daniel's seventy sevens delineated with black band, interrupted by the Time for the Gentiles (delineated in grey) to be grafted into the New Covenant Jesus made with Israel and Judah according to Jeremiah 31:31 and Hebrews 8:8.

The Time for the Gentiles is the Mystery of God hidden throughout the ages, and is thus not part of the prophetic history of Israel.

New Heaven & New Earth (Eternity Future)

2nd Resurrection - Final Battle - Gog & Magog
Eternal Age Begins - Great White Throne Judgment; New Heavens & New Earth
Satan is Loosed

Undetermined time for cleansing of the Land

The Millennium (1,000 Years)
Christ reigns on earth with His saints

During 2nd half of 70th seven, tribulation on Israel (Jacob's Trouble), when anti-Christ will drive the Jews into the wilderness for 3-½ years. Mark of the Beast will be instituted.

Satan is bound
Messiah sets foot on earth - Destroys Anti-Christ
Resurrection/Rapture - End of Time for Gentiles
Tribulation on nations
Messiah returns
Anti-Christ is revealed
Aug., AD 70 - Titus destroys temple
Feb., AD 67 - Vespasian offers peace, affirms covenant with Jews
Messiah comes; brings New Covenant with Israel & Judah; is killed

2nd half 70th seven
The Time for the Gentiles
Mystery of God (Approx. 2,000 yrs.)
1st half 70th seven
Forty Year Gap
Sixty-two sevens (434 Years)
Sixty-nine sevens (483 Years)
Seven sevens
Daniel's Seventy sevens (490 prophetic years total)

Decree to build temple
Construction of temple

PART II
A STUDY ON THE BOOK OF REVELATION

PREFACE

The Book of Revelation must be the focal point of any study on eschatology as the most comprehensive prophecy of the very last days. It is the final compilation and expanding of all previous eschatological prophecies given by the Lord in the writings of both the prophets and the apostles. All eschatological references in Scripture point to the revelations the Lord Jesus gave to the apostle John as recorded in this book.

Traditionally, the Book of Revelation has been called "The Book of the Revelation of Jesus Christ to Saint John," or "Revelation" for short. However, contained within this revelation are a series of revelations, many details of which are reiterated in more than one of the revelations. For example, certain events pertaining to the very last days of this age are described in differing detail through more than one revelation. This is important for proper understanding.

We must also keep in mind that the prophecies of the Book of Revelation center primarily on Jerusalem. We cannot apply them to other portions of the world such as the United States.

The author of the Book of Revelation identifies himself merely as "John," and states that he was on the island of Patmos when he received his first vision. As a result, the author of Revelation is sometimes referred to as John of Patmos.

For centuries Bible scholars have accepted the time for the writing of the Book of Revelation as sometime just prior to the end of the first century—A.D. However, modern disputations have arisen over when it was written. Historically, dating to the second century, it was accepted that the book was written by John the apostle while in exile during the reign of the Roman emperor Domitian, around A.D. 81-96. However, the second-century Syriac version places John's exile during the reign of Nero, around A.D. 54-68. Historians have for the most part accepted the later date until recently. The earlier date was first proposed in modern times by liberal theologian John Robinson in his book, *Redating the New Testament* (1976), although he did attribute it to John the apostle.

According to Irenaeus, Polycarp, having been a student of John, attributes the later dating to the Book of Revelation. Which dating one accepts might determine one's eschatology. Conversely, one's eschatology might determine which dating one accepts. Preterism agrees with Robinson that it was written prior to the destruction of the temple in A.D. 70, thus positing that all its prophecies have been fulfilled, and that the seven heads of the "beast" in chapter 17 represent the succession of Roman emperors from Caligula (reigned A.D. 37-41) to Vespasian (reigned A.D. 69-79).

In view of our examination of the history of Rome in relation to Jerusalem and the prophecy of Daniel 7:23-24 coupled with Revelation 12:3, I believe in this case that the preterists are correct, although the first emperor would have been Julius Caesar who was the first Roman emperor and whose reign began shortly after Pompey conquered Jerusalem.

Even so, as we'll see in our study, many of Revelation's prophecies have no historical record of fulfillment. We are still looking to the future for their unfolding.

The following chapters will be a study on the Book of Revelation, parsing every verse.

All eschatological references in the writings of both the prophets and the apostles, point to the Revelation the Lord Jesus gave to the apostle John, as recorded in this book. "The Revelation of Jesus Christ" complements all of the other Scriptures that He has given to us in the writings of the prophets and the apostles.

Quotes from the Book of Revelation will be in bold type for easier reference as the study progresses.

Quotes from other portions of Scripture will be in normal type face.

1

JOHN ON THE DAY OF THE LORD

This book is the revelation that God (the Father) gave to Jesus in order to show believers in Christ things that were yet in the future. The Father gave it to Jesus, who gave it to His messenger, who gave it to John, who bears record of everything he was shown.

REV. 1:1-2:
The Revelation of Jesus Christ, which God gave to Him, to show to His servants things which must shortly come to pass, and He sent and signified it by His messenger [Gr., *angelos*] to His servant John, who bore record of the Word of God, and of the testimony of Jesus Christ, and of all things that he saw.

One area of dispute that has arisen from these opening verses centers on the words "which must shortly come to pass." Because of the word "shortly," it has been determined by some that all of the events revealed to John must have already taken place. It is insisted that "shortly means shortly; it doesn't mean a period of two thousand years." This is the premise of the preterist approach to eschatology: all things have already transpired; there are no (or few) prophecies that are yet future; even the Lord's return has taken place, and we are currently living in the Millennium (or even the New Heavens and New Earth). Preterists believe that Jesus returned spiritually at the end of the Old Covenant period which ended with the destruction of the temple in A.D. 70, and that He is now ruling the nations from Heaven. The reason the world is still in such terrible shape is because "the Church" has failed in its responsibility to infuse the Gospel into every culture. Once that is accomplished, "the Church" will rule the nations under the spiritual headship of Jesus.

This is the philosophy of Christian Reconstructionism, a form of dominion theology which states that Christians must take control over the nations and impose the Old Covenant penal sanctions in society. (For an in-depth analysis of dominion theology, see *Vengeance Is Ours: The Church In Dominion*, Sword Publishers.)

It would seem as if the understanding is correct that the events of the Book of Revelation were to take place shortly after the vision was given to John. However, the same Holy Spirit who inspired John to write these words also inspired the other authors of Scripture. The KJV translates *tacheos* (from the same root as *tachos*) in 1 Timothy 5:22 as "suddenly," which gives a different meaning to the word. In 1 Thessalonians 5:2 and 2 Peter 3:10 we read that the Day of the Lord will come like a thief in the night—that is, without warning. The idea is that He will return "suddenly" or "quickly."

We find the same word in Luke 18:7-8, translated "speedily" where the Lord, speaking of God avenging His people says: "And shall God not avenge His own elect who cry out day and night to Him, though He bear long with them? I tell you that He will avenge them speedily. Nevertheless when the Son of Man comes, will He find faith on the earth?"

Has God yet avenged His people? If we substitute "suddenly" for "speedily" we have a better understanding. God's vengeance will be meted out when the Lord returns:

> And to you who are troubled, rest with us when the Lord Jesus shall be revealed from Heaven with His mighty angels in flaming fire, taking vengeance on those who do not know God, and who do not obey the Gospel of our Lord Jesus Christ—who shall be punished with everlasting destruction from the presence of the Lord and from the glory of His power when He shall come to be glorified in His saints and to be admired by all those who believe in that day (because our testimony among you was believed). (2Th 1:7-10)

God's vengeance on the enemies of His people is yet future, to be meted out when Jesus returns with His angels and saints (Jude 1:14). That has not yet occurred.

Nor does "speedily," or "shortly" always mean imminence in man's terms. God speaks from His own terms.

> But, beloved, do not be ignorant of this one thing: that with the Lord one day is as a thousand years, and a thousand years as one day. (2Pe 3:8)

As we've said throughout this book, prophetic history is different from human history. As we review the events of the Book of Revelation we will see that some of the prophecies, but not all, were indeed imminent to John's time. We will also see that "the last days" relating to the Lord's coming began with His first coming and will culminate in His Second Coming.

It is generally accepted that John penned the Book of Revelation around A.D. 96. By that time Jerusalem had been sacked, the temple destroyed, and Israel dispersed among the nations. If this is true, we cannot place all of the events of Revelation back in time. At least some must have been forward from the turn of the second century onward. This must be kept in mind as we analyze the many prophecies of this book.

Now, those who believe that John received these revelations prior to A.D. 70 interpret all of them within the time frame of the temple that existed at that time. We needn't get into a dispute over this. There are no historical precedents that indicate all of these prophecies were fulfilled at that time.

1:3:
Blessed is he who reads, and those who hear the words of this prophecy, and keep those things that are written in it, for the time is at hand.

"He who reads" is the messenger to the assembly; "those who hear" are the people within the assembly.

There is a special blessing afforded those who do not merely read or hear this prophecy, but keep the things that are written. To read or hear entails more than putting one's eyes to the page or inclining one's ears to the ether; it involves one's understanding and believing what one reads or hears. One cannot believe without first understanding.

To "keep the things written" means to be partakers of the prophecy. Those who live in obedience to the commands of the book while living through the events that are prophesied will receive special blessings or favor from God, which will allow them to endure and overcome the hardships that lie ahead. This is why Jesus says to His called-out assemblies, "He who has an ear, let him hear what the Spirit says...." (Rv 2:1–3:22). Those who hear and obey will receive the blessings; those who do not hear and obey will be judged unfaithful.

1:4-6:

John to the seven assemblies that are in Asia: Grace be to you, and peace, from He who is, and who was, and who is to come, and from the seven spirits that are before His throne, and from Jesus Christ, who is the faithful witness, and the first begotten of the dead, and the prince of the kings of the earth, to Him who loved us, and washed us from our sins in His own blood, and has made us kings and priests to God and His Father. To Him be glory and dominion forever and ever. Amen.

John is writing to seven assemblies of believers in Asia Minor, specifically in the area of present-day Turkey. This does not mean that these words are for only these seven, for God has deigned to grant to us, who are far off from them in time, the words which will apply in the very last days. However, there are aspects of these messages that do apply specifically to these seven assemblies (things which must shortly come to pass), and which must be kept in that context lest we misapply them to others, including ourselves today.

These seven autonomous assemblies of God's called-out people (His *ecclesia*) are singled out for special prophecies which apply individually to each. Yet while they are individually addressed, they are meant to be read to all the assemblies, and they carry the same promises to those who overcome within all the assemblies.

The Lord's salutation was one of grace and peace, a manner in which He addresses His beloved, whether to commend them or to warn of His displeasure.

The phrase, "from He who is, and who was, and who is to come," refers to the eternal nature of God. That this is the Father Yahweh rather than Jesus is suggested by the separate greeting, "and from Jesus Christ." However, as we will see in verse 11, John hears a voice saying, "I am Alpha and Omega, the First and the Last." John turns and sees that the voice is that of Jesus: "I am He who lives, and was dead, and, look! I am alive forever." Jesus refers to Himself as "Alpha and Omega, the beginning and the ending who is, and who was, and who is to come, the Almighty" (Rv 1:8), so this term also applies to Jesus as the one "who is" (the resurrected Jesus); "who was" (referring to Jesus' time on earth before His death and resurrection); and "who is to come" (Jesus will again return to the earth), while revealing that He is Yahweh, the

Word of God who came forth from the Father—who is also called Yahweh—of the same nature and essence. This is as far as this mystery of God's nature can go; to try to press further would intrude into the very nature of God, which man cannot do.

These seven spirits before the throne of God go throughout the whole earth, emanating from the Lamb of God (Rv 5:6). Does God have seven spirits? The four mentions of "the seven spirits of God" in Revelation (1:4; 3:1; 4:5; 5:6), are the only references in all of Scripture. However, the angel of Yahweh showed Zechariah a vision in which stood a gold candlestick having seven lamps, with two olives trees on either side of it. The interpretation of the seven lamps is found in Zechariah 4:9 as "the eyes of YHWH, which run back and forth through the whole earth."

Scripture throughout speaks of only one Holy Spirit. So we know that the "seven Spirits of God" spoken of here are not the Holy Spirit. But because they emanate from the Lamb of God's throne, and are sent throughout the whole earth, it would seem that they represent the omniscience of God in some manner.

Verse 6 tells us that Jesus has made us kings and priests to God and His Father. Kings are rulers. We are told that those in Christ who overcome the trials and tribulations of this world will one day rule and reign over the nations with a rod of iron (Rv 8:26-29).

Priests minister sacrifices and bring offerings before God. Believers in Christ need no priests other than our High Priest, Jesus. However, the lost do need men who act in the role of priests to pray for them, to show them the way to God, and to offer to them the opportunity to enter into the sacrifice that Jesus provided for their sins. All true believers in Christ are priests in the respect that we lead the lost to Jesus Christ, who is the only mediator between God and men.

1:7:
Look! He comes with clouds, and every eye shall see Him, and they also who pierced Him, and all nations of the earth shall wail because of Him! Even so, Amen!

This is the first mention of the Lord's return in the Book of Revelation. It speaks of Jesus returning in the clouds in the same manner in which He left after His resurrection (Ac 1:9-11). We are told that when He returns every eye will see Him. Those who pierced Him are the Jews. This verse by itself makes no distinction between the Lord coming to catch up His saints and His return to the earth, but we are told that all the nations of the earth will wail, or be in fear, when they see Him coming. They will know that His judgment is coming with Him. Revelation 6:15-16 describes men of all rank calling on the mountains and rocks to fall on them and hide them from the face of the Lamb (Jesus), sitting on His throne, and from His wrath.

This refers to His coming to take His saints, which is an event distinct from His returning to set His feet on the earth.

1:8:
"I am Alpha and Omega, the beginning and the ending," says the Lord who is, and who was, and who is to come—the Almighty.

Here we see the same expression, "who is, and who was, and who is to come," applied to the Almighty. The Almighty is Yahweh of the prophets' writings. As noted above, Jesus also refers to Himself as "Alpha and Omega" as recorded in Rv 22:13-16. Jesus, then, as the Word of God who created all things (Jn 1:1-14), is Yahweh of the prophets' writings. Isaiah 9:6 describes the nature of Jesus:

> For a child is born to us; a son is given to us, and the government shall be on His shoulder, and His name shall be called Wonderful, Counselor, The Mighty God, The Everlasting Father, The Prince of Peace.

1:9:
I John, who also am your brother and companion in tribulation and in the Kingdom and endurance of Jesus Christ, was in the isle that is called Patmos for the Word of God and for the testimony of Jesus Christ.

John assures the seven assemblies that He is their brother in Christ, and that he is also suffering tribulation as they were. To be in the Kingdom and endurance of Jesus Christ meant that John and the assemblies were counted within the Kingdom of Christ, and were enduring under the tribulation appointed them.

John had been exiled to the island of Patmos—a Turkish island in the Aegean Sea—because of His testimony for the Word of God and Jesus Christ. This was the manner in which he was persecuted. There is nothing to identify this John with the apostle John, but early Christian tradition assumed this to be so. Certainly this John wrote with the authority of an apostle, and his revelations have thus far proven true.

Now begins the series of revelations "of things that must shortly come to pass."

JOHN WITH JESUS ON THE DAY OF THE LORD
1:10-11:

I was in the spirit on the Day of the Lord, and heard behind me a great voice, as of a trumpet, saying, "I am Alpha and Omega, the first and the last," and, "What you see, write in a book and send it to the seven assemblies that are in Asia—to Ephesus, and to Smyrna, and to Pergamos, and to Thyatira, and to Sardis, and to Philadelphia, and to Laodicea."

English translations invariably say, "I was in the spirit on the Lord's day," leading most commentators to say that John was in a trance on a Sunday, which they believe to be "the Lord's Day." Both assumptions are at best, questionable; at worst, erroneous.

John's experience is not the same as a trance or dream; these are stated elsewhere in Scripture where they occur (e.g., Ge 37:5-9; Mt 1:20; etc.). If John was in a trance, there is nothing else in the Book of Revelation to suggest it. Rather, he was visited by the Lord Himself, and by His angels, or messengers.

At the risk of offending many good brethren, it is necessary to say that the idea that "the Lord's Day" means Sunday, or the "first day of the week" is based on the erroneous Roman Catholic assumption that Jesus was buried on a Friday and rose on the next Sunday morning. This would be contrary to the Lord's teaching that, as Jonah was in the belly of the whale for three days and three nights, so He would be in the heart of the earth for three days and three nights. The Lord did not rise on any morning; He was buried during the evening of 14 Nisan, and He rose during the evening of 17 Nisan. The women came to the tomb on the morning of the first day of the week, but the Lord had already risen. Therefore, He had to have risen on the evening of the previous Sabbath. For a thorough debunking of the Friday-Sunday myth see Media Spotlight's *Facts & Fallacies of the Resurrection*.

The possessive, "Lord's day" could as easily be translated "Day of the Lord," which would indicate that John's revelation concerns the last days. In other words, John was transported in his spirit to the Day of the Lord by entrance into the heavenly realm.

Whatever direction he was facing, he heard behind him a great, loud voice, identifying the speaker as being Alpha and Omega. What the speaker was about to reveal, He wanted John to write in a book which was to be sent to the seven assemblies. The entire book (singular) was to be sent to the seven assemblies. Thus, the prophecies specifically given to each assembly were to be shared with all the other assemblies. For example, what was written to the assembly at Ephesus was also to be read to the assemblies in Smyrna, Pergamos, Thyatira, Sardis, Philadelphia and Laodicea. Thus, each prophecy had an individual application, but it also applied to all the assemblies. This is why, after each prophecy to the individual assemblies, we find that these were what the Spirit was saying to the "assemblies" (plural).

1:12-16:

And I turned to see the voice that spoke with me. And being turned, I saw seven golden candlesticks, and in the midst of the seven candlesticks one like the Son of Man, clothed with a garment down to the foot, and belted about the waist with a golden belt.

His head and His hair were white like wool—as white as snow—and His eyes were like a flame of fire, and His feet like fine brass as if they burned in a furnace, and His voice like the sound of many waters.

And He had in His right hand seven stars, and out of His mouth went a sharp two-edged sword. And His countenance was like the sun shining in its strength.

Upon turning, John sees Jesus as Alpha and Omega. The seven golden candlesticks represent the seven assemblies to which Jesus was dictating the writing. In the midst of the seven assemblies stands the Son of Man (the term Jesus ascribed to Himself when He walked the earth). But here we see Him in His glorified state after His resurrection. He wears a garment that covers his entire body, with a belt made of gold—probably spun gold. The awesomeness of His appearance is symbolic. Not to be dogmatic, but I believe His white hair denotes wisdom and age; eyes like fire denotes omniscience—the ability to see and judge all things; the voice as the sound of many waters means that He thundered, or spoke loudly—with authority; the feet of brass speak of skin that is golden-tanned in color. His entire skin, not just His feet, were this color.

The Lord's glorified body is remarkably different from the body He had when He walked the earth. This does not mean that His resurrected body, in which He appeared to His disciples, is not the same body. Inasmuch as He appeared and disappeared at will, ate food, and invited Thomas to put his fingers into the wounds in His hands, we can be sure that His resurrected body is the same body that was in the tomb. But there appears to be a difference either in manifestation or in the glorification process which allows for a more magnificent presence. Some try to speak dogmatically that the resurrected body is not physical but spiritual (whatever that means), or it is a different body than the one possessed during this age, or some other reasoning. We cannot be dogmatic about this; it is one of the mysteries that will be revealed to us when we know Him fully after our own resurrection:

> For now we see through an obscure glass, but at that time, face to face. Presently I know in part, but at that time I shall know, even as I am also known. (1Co 13:12)

Let us not concern ourselves with how God will reconstruct those who have gone to dust, or who have been blown to bits. He will do what He will do in the manner in which He chooses to do it. Our faith is in the bodily resurrection of Jesus as the first-fruits of the redemption of His creation. It is also in looking forward to the day of our own resurrection when we will be glorified like Him.

I won't argue the point of whether certain prophets as recorded in their writings saw a "theophany," a physical representation of a spirit being, or whether the Word of God had a physical, celestial body prior to coming to earth. That question cannot be resolved even by the claim that "God is Spirit." Spirit has substance; our finite minds cannot comprehend the nature of God beyond what He has revealed to us. Let us not be dogmatic about His appearance or lack thereof. We do know that His resurrected body is flesh and bones, and that He can eat, sit, be touched, and walk among men, among other things. The two-edged sword that proceeds from His mouth is the Word of God:

> For the Word of God is alive, and powerful, and sharper than any two-edged sword, piercing even to the dividing apart of soul and spirit, and of the joints and marrow, and is a discerner of the thoughts and intents of the heart. (Heb 4:12)

The Word of God is not just the Scriptures, but everything that God truly speaks. For us, today, however, the Scriptures are our sole authority for all truth relative to our beliefs and practices. They cut to the very heart of men's thoughts and intents.

The Lord's eyes of flame discern all things about all men. Nothing is hidden from Him. Even when we try to fool ourselves (which is common practice in trying to justify sin) we cannot fool Him.

His countenance, as the sun in its strength, speaks of holiness and purity—the brightest of white—under which nothing impure can stand.

1:17-19:

And when I saw Him I fell at His feet as dead. And he laid his right hand on me, saying to me, "Do not fear. I am the First and the Last. I am He who lives, and was dead, and, look, I am alive forevermore, amen, and have the keys of Hades and of Death.

"Write the things that you have seen, and the things that are, and the things that shall be hereafter."

These verses confirm further that John was seeing Jesus in His resurrected body. By saying that He had the keys to Death and Hades (Greek: *Hades*—the underworld where all spirits of the righteous were kept, separated by a great chasm from the unrighteous [Lk 16:19-31] prior to the resurrection), Jesus was telling John not to fear, because He had the power of the resurrection in His hands.

We should digress slightly to address a misconception that has led many Christians into areas of spiritual activity based on an erroneous understanding of Matthew 16:18:

"And I say also to you, that you are Peter, and on this rock I will build my called out people, and the gates of Hades shall not prevail against it."

It is commonly taught among proponents of today's "spiritual warfare" deception that we are commanded to storm the gates of "Hell" and defeat Satan through such things as prayer walking, rebuking Satan, commanding demonic principalities to leave cities, and other nonsense which is nowhere supported in Scripture.

Jesus did not mean that the Body of Christ is to attack the gates of "Hell," or more properly, Hades, erroneously supposed to be Satan's headquarters where he and his demons are in control of punishing the ungodly. This is more Greek myth than spiritual truth. Satan does not control Hades; God controls Hades. Satan is the prince of the power of the air (Eph 2:2). He is not torturing lost souls in "Hell."

When Jesus said that the gates of Hades would not prevail against His *ecclesia*, He was saying that the gates of Hades would not be able to prevent the resurrection of the saints. (See our Media Spotlight special reports *Deliverance: Demonization and the Christian*, and *Does Hell Exist; Is it Eternal?*)

Jesus instructed John to write what he had seen, and the things that are (current events in the lives of the assemblies), and the things that shall be hereafter (future prophecies). He then explains the mystery of the vision John had just seen:

1:20:

"The mystery of the seven stars that you saw in My right hand, and the seven golden candlesticks: the seven stars are the messengers of the seven assemblies: and the seven candlesticks that you saw are the seven assemblies."

We see that the seven candlesticks are the seven assemblies of believers in Asia Minor to whom the Lord will speak in the following chapter. Jesus held in His right hand the seven stars (angels, or messengers) of the seven assemblies.

Questions have arisen whether these messengers are men or angels. The word used is *angelos*, which, in most of the writings of the apostles, refers to spirit beings.

The Gereek word *angelos* means "messengers," which may be either men or angels. This word is employed some sixty times in this book, and in most cases it refers to spirit beings. Yet as we read the messages to the *angelos* of the assemblies, we see that they are being spoken to as one would speak to a man. At that time there were few individual copies of the Scriptures (what Christians call "the Old Testament") available to everyone as there are today. The Scriptures were read in the assembly by an appointed reader—most likely an elder in the assembly. This does not mean that the messengers are "pastors" in the modern sense of the word. The modern concept of pastoral clergy was unknown and came about later as an outgrowth of Roman Catholicism. However, in the assemblies there were elders who were entrusted with spiritual ministry to the saints. There were in some assemblies, elders who acted as apostles in planting the assemblies and overseeing them until they came to maturity, at which time they appointed other elders. In the letters to the assemblies that follow, it is most likely that the "angels" are those elders—messengers—assigned to read the letters. As we read through these messages we will see that the messengers are apostles or elders within the assemblies. They hold special positions.

2
LETTERS TO SEVEN ASSEMBLIES

The seven assemblies in Asia Minor are to receive certain messages that address those things that are both pleasing and displeasing to the Lord. Jesus dictates to John the letters he is to send to the messengers of the seven assemblies, beginning with the assembly in Ephesus.

THE LETTER TO EPHESUS
REV. 2:1-7:

"To the messenger of the assembly of Ephesus write: 'These things says He who holds the seven stars in His right hand, who walks in the midst of the seven golden candlesticks: "I know your works, and your labor, and your patience, and how you cannot bear those who are evil. And you have tested those who say they are apostles, and are not, and have found them liars, and have borne, and have patience, and for My name's sake have worked and have not weakened. Nevertheless I have somewhat against you because you have left your first love.

""'Therefore, remember from where you have fallen, and repent and do the first works, or else I will come to you quickly, and will remove your candlestick out of its place, unless you repent.

""'But this you have: that you hate the deeds of the Nicolaitans, which I also hate.'"

"He who has an ear, let him hear what the Spirit says to the assemblies. To him who overcomes I will give to eat from the tree of life that is in the midst of the Paradise of God."

The messenger had tested those who said they were apostles, and exposed them as false brethren within the assembly. Yet in spite of these good traits, he had failed in leaving His first love. His first love is the Lord Himself. By leaving the Lord, it is implied that he had fallen into some sin that was hindering His relationship to God. He was warned that unless he repented of his sin the Lord would remove the assembly from his influence; he would lose his ministry. That the assembly can be removed from the messenger indicates that this word is to the messenger primarily, but certainly to the assembly as well, since it was to be read to the entire assembly which would share in the sin by tolerating it.

The warning was that this judgment was imminent. Yet the messenger was commended because he hated the deeds of the Nicolaitans—those who would impose a priesthood, or clergy, which the Lord hates. (Is it not incongruous that today virtually all churches operate on the Nicolaitan principle of clergy-laity distinction?)

That this same message is for all assemblies at all times is stated in verse seven: "He who has an ear, let him hear what the Spirit says to the assemblies" (plural). This is a warning to all believers who are caught in sin—particularly those in leadership within the assemblies, and more particularly those who function on the clergy-laity principle. All who overcome will be given the tree of life in the midst of God's paradise.

THE LETTER TO SMYRNA
2:8-11:

"And to the messenger of the assembly in Smyrna write: 'These things says the First and the Last, who was dead, and is alive: "I know your works, and tribulation, and poverty (but you are rich), and I know the blasphemy of those who say they are Jews, and are not, but are the synagogue of Satan.

"'Fear none of those things that you will suffer. Look, the Devil will cast some of you into prison so that you may be tested, and you will have tribulation for ten days. You be faithful unto death, and I will give you a crown of life.'

"He who has an ear, let him hear what the Spirit says to the assemblies. He who overcomes shall not be hurt by the second death."

The messenger at Smyrna is told that the assembly had no serious faults. It was in tribulation and poverty, but was rich in the things of God. It was under persecution by unfaithful Jews who had rejected their Messiah. Thus, He likened them to the synagogue of Satan—religious but evil men who masqueraded as God's elect while striving to kill God's true elect.

In spite of their purity, the believers at Smyrna were warned that God would allow Satan to cast some into prison to test them. Those who remained faithful would be put to death, but would inherit a crown of life.

What does this say of the word-faith prosperity message? Many erroneously assume that tribulation comes upon believers because of sin or lack of faith. In truth, God purifies and perfects His saints through tribulation and testing:

> "I have said these things to you so that in Me you may have peace. In the world you have tribulation, but be of good courage; I have overcome the world." (Jn 16:33)

> And when they [the apostles] had proclaimed the Gospel to that city, and had taught many, they returned again to Lystra, and to Iconium, and Antioch, confirming the souls of the disciples and exhorting them to continue in the faith, and that we must enter into the Kingdom of God through much tribulation. (Ac 14:21-22)

> And not only so, but we glory in tribulations also, knowing that tribulation works patience, and patience, experience, and experience, hope. And hope does not make us ashamed because the love of God is shed abroad in our hearts by the Holy Spirit who is given to us. (Ro 5:3-5)

> Yet let us suffer for doing good, not for doing evil (1Pe 3:17).

Again, this message is for all the assemblies, and we, today, can learn from this word: he who overcomes by sacrificing his life will not be hurt by the second death, which will be in the lake of fire (Rv 20:14).

THE LETTER TO PERGAMOS
12-17:

"And to the messenger of the assembly in Pergamos write: 'These things says He who has the sharp sword with two edges: "I know your works, and where you live—where Satan's seat is—and you hold My name fast and have not denied My faith, even in those days in which Antipas was My faithful martyr who was slain among you where Satan dwells.

""""But I have a few things against you because you have there those who hold the doctrine of Balaam who taught Balak to cast a stumbling block before the children of Israel, to eat things sacrificed to idols, and to commit fornication. You also have those who hold the doctrine of the Nicolaitans, which thing I hate.

""""Repent, or else I will come to you quickly, and will fight against them with the sword of My mouth."'

"He who has an ear, let him hear what the Spirit says to the assemblies. To him who overcomes I will give to eat from the hidden manna, and will give him a white stone, and in the stone a new name written which no man knows except he who receives it."

The assembly in Pergamos was in the midst of Satan's territory. What this means is debated among scholars. Some believe Pergamum was the center of emperor worship in the Roman Empire; others believe the center of paganism had moved from Babylon to Pergamum. But if Satan's seat is where paganism rules, then it is all over the world. This must have a more specific meaning.

We see in Revelation 13:2 that Satan gives his seat and authority to the beast that is to come. The seat represents dominion, as a throne. Satan's throne was in Pergamum; it was from there that he sought to destroy the works of God and institute his own reign over the earth.

Pergamum was an ancient Greek city in Mysia located 27 km from the Aegean Sea. Pergamum became the capital of a flourishing Hellenistic kingdom and one of the principal centers of Hellenistic civilization.

In Roman times it was the site of the temples to Athena, Hera and Demeter, and the great altar of Zeus.

In the face of the evil around them, the believers at Pergamum held fast to the name of Jesus and did not deny the faith, even when Antipas was martyred in their midst. His death did not cause them to faint.

Yet they tolerated in their midst some who held the doctrine of Balaam, which allowed for fornication and eating things sacrificed to idols. They also had among them some who held the doctrine of the Nicolaitans. They were to repent, either by bringing these false brethren to repentance, or by removing them from their midst. Jesus does not say that He will fight against the assembly in total, but that He will come and fight against the false brethren with the Word of God. This would expose the sin of the entire assembly in tolerating these evils.

And, again, this message is for all the assemblies, lest any others tolerate the same evils. Those who overcome by removing themselves from the evil will be given hidden manna, and a white stone with a new name.

The hidden manna was that which was placed by Aaron in the Ark of the Covenant. It was hidden from sight and kept for God without corruption, to which the rest of the manna was subject. This would imply a special consecration upon the believer who overcomes: he will never see corruption, but will be hidden in God. The white stone may have several meanings. Normally, when we see the word "stone," we think of a rock. But a stone may be precious, like diamonds. Whiteness represents holiness. The purest diamonds are crystal clear, without blemish. Jesus said that He would sanctify and cleanse His people with the washing of water by the Word:

> ...so that He might present it to Himself a glorious assembly, not having spot, or wrinkle, or any such thing, but that it would be holy and without blemish. (Eph 5:27)

This stone, then, is a holy stone, wherein the name of he who overcomes by separating himself from evil will be engraved. This will be a new name known only to the person who overcomes. Perhaps, just as Cephas was renamed Peter by Jesus, those who overcome will be called by special traits that they possessed which glorified God.

THE LETTER TO THYATIRA
2:18-29:

"And to the messenger of the assembly in Thyatira write: 'These things says the Son of God, who has His eyes like a flame of fire, and His feet are like fine brass: "I know your works, and charity, and service, and faith, and your patience, and your works—and the last to be more than the first. Notwithstanding, I have a few things against you because you allow that woman Jezebel, who calls herself a prophetess, to teach and to seduce My servants to commit fornication and to eat things sacrificed to idols. And I gave her room to repent of her fornication, and she did not repent.

""Look! I will cast her and those who commit adultery with her into a bed, into great tribulation, unless they repent of their deeds.

""And I will kill her children with death, and all the assemblies shall know that I am He who searches the reins and hearts, and I will give to every one of you according to your works.

""'"But to you I say, and to the rest in Thyatira, as many as do not have this doctrine, and who have not known the depths of Satan, as they say, I will put no other burden on you. But hold tight to that which you already have until I come.

""'"And he who overcomes and keeps My works to the end, to him I will give power over the nations, and he shall rule them with a rod of iron; they shall be broken to bits like the vessels of a potter, even as I received from My Father. And I will give him the Morning Star.'"

"He who has an ear, let him hear what the Spirit says to the assemblies."

The believers at Thyatira were increasingly diligent in service (the last more than the first). Yet the messenger of Thyatira had allowed a Jezebel—an evil, power-hungry woman—to teach the assembly. In so doing, she led the assembly into fornication and sacrificing to idols.

The same sins as those enumerated to the assembly at Pergamum are found here: fornication and eating things sacrificed to idols. The Lord gave this Jezebel time to repent—probably by bringing His warning to her through some human agent—but she remained steadfast in her sins.

He warns that He will cast her into great suffering with those who follow her teachings unless they repent. Jezebel was either this woman's real name or a euphemism for a rebellious woman, named so after the Zidonian wife of Ahab. Her children were not necessarily by physical birth, but spiritual birth.

All the assemblies will know that God sees all their deeds, and that He will reward all according to those deeds.

Jesus tells the messenger that He will put no other burden on him or on those in the assembly that remain faithful.

Those who remain faithful to the end will be given power to rule the nations with a rod of iron. This means they will reign during the Millennium when Christ has returned and is ruling over all the nations. It is difficult to see how any true believer in Jesus could miss the reality of the Millennial Kingdom in view of this and so many other Scriptures that attest to it.

The morning star is Jesus:

"I, Jesus, have sent My angel to testify to you these things in the assemblies. I am the root and the offspring of David, and the bright and morning star." (Rv 22:16)

We will belong to Him, and He will belong to us.

THE LETTER TO SARDIS
3:1-6:

"And to the messenger of the assembly in Sardis write: 'These things says He who has the seven Spirits of God, and the seven stars: "I know your works, that you have a name that you live, and are dead. Be watchful, and strengthen the things that remain that are ready to die, for I have not found your works perfect before God.

""""Remember therefore how you have received and heard, and hold tight and repent. If therefore you will not watch, I will come upon you like a thief, and you shall not know what hour I will come upon you.

""""You have a few names even in Sardis who have not defiled their garments, and they shall walk with Me in white, for they are worthy.

""""He who overcomes, the same shall be clothed in white garments, and I will not blot out his name out of the Book of Life, but I will confess his name before My Father, and before His angels.'"

"He who has an ear, let him hear what the Spirit says to the assemblies."

The assembly at Sardis had a reputation that it was alive, yet it was dead.

It is often said that the assembly at Laodicea is a good representation of the condition of the churches today. The assembly at Sardis is even more representative of today's churches. With much fanfare they espouse feel-good teachings that are really perversions of God's Word.

They are called "alive" when, in truth, they are dead—fraught with false doctrine, with demonic and fleshly expressions which are attributed to the Holy Spirit, and with a self-serving, prideful spirit.

But just as in today's churches, in Sardis there were a few things of truth that remained. It was necessary for the assembly to strengthen those things that were on the verge of dying because its works were not pure before God. He calls the assembly to repentance and to remember the truths it had received, and to hold fast to them. Otherwise He would come upon the assembly unexpectedly (like a thief) and destroy it. This means He would judge it for its sins. It does not mean the assembly would remain until He returns again.

In spite of the assembly's sins, there were a few who had kept themselves pure. They will be in the resurrection because they are worthy; they will not have their names blotted out of the Book of Life, but Jesus will confess their names before the Father and His angels.

THE LETTER TO PHILADELPHIA
7-13:

"And to the messenger of the assembly in Philadelphia write: 'These things says He who is holy, He who is true, He who has the key of David, He who opens, and no man shuts, and shuts, and no man opens: "I know your works. Look, I have set before you an open door, and no man can shut it, because you have a little strength and have kept My word, and have not denied My name.

""Look, I will make them of the synagogue of Satan—who say they are Jews, and are not, but lie—look, I will make them to come and worship before your feet, and to know that I have loved you.

""Because you have kept the word of My endurance, I will also keep you from the hour of testing which shall come upon all the world to test those who dwell upon the earth.

""Look! I come quickly! Hold tight that which you have, so that no man takes your crown.

""Him who overcomes I will make a pillar in the temple of My God, and he shall no longer go out. And I will write upon him the name of My God and the name of the city of My God, which is New Jerusalem that comes down out of Heaven from My God, and I will write upon him My new name."'

"He who has an ear, let him hear what the Spirit says to the assemblies."

Here, Jesus introduces a new phrase, "the key of David." David represents the kingdom of Israel on earth. He will be resurrected to reign over Israel when the Lord returns (Jer 30:8-9; Hos 3:5). The key represents Jesus' authority over the kingdom of Israel as well as over the Kingdom of Heaven on earth. No man can open or shut the way into the Kingdom. That is for the Lord alone.

The Lord is telling the assembly that He has opened to them the way into the Kingdom because of their works, and that they have little strength, yet they have kept His Word and have not denied His name. He promises to make the unfaithful Jews come and bow before these saints they have been persecuting.

Because the saints at Philadelphia had kept His word and had endurance, they will be kept from the hour of testing which will try all men's souls. It was the lot of the early believers to face such persecution. It has been so throughout the centuries in some places, and it will be so at the end of this age prior to the Lord's coming to take His people out of the earth.

The popular pre-trib teaching that this verse means "the Church" will not go through the Great Tribulation is in error. This interpretation ignores the context of a letter to a specific assembly. It assumes that this refers to the period of great tribulation upon the whole earth. Careful study reveals something different.

As stated earlier, the Greek words for "world" and "earth" respectively in this verse are *oikoumene* and *ge*.

The first, *oikoumene*, merely means "land." It could refer to the whole earth, a region of the earth, or at that time the known world—the Roman Empire. The second, *ge*, generally refers to a region, or the people who occupy a region. It could also refer to a country.

These are different from the Greek word most often used to mean the entire world, which is *kosmos*.

Consistency dictates that, had John meant the entire world in verse 3:10, he would have used *kosmos* rather than *oikoumene* and *ge*.

We see then that the promise in Revelation 3:10 to keep God's people from the testing to come upon the region was a specific promise for a specific time to a specific people. It was to the assembly in Philadelphia during the first-century persecution of Christians within the Roman Empire. It has nothing to do with a future worldwide period of great tribulation.

The Lord further warns the brethren to hold fast and not let anyone steal their crown of life through deceit, leading them away from Christ.

Those who overcome will be pillars in the Millennial Temple. They will be important to the temple service, and will be in the New Jerusalem. They will bear the name of Yahweh and the new name given by Jesus.

This is for all who overcome from among all the assemblies.

THE LETTER TO LAODICEA
14-22:

"And to the messenger of the assembly of the Laodiceans write: 'These things says the Amen, the faithful and true witness, the beginning of the creation of God: "I know your works, that you are neither cold nor hot. I would that you were cold or hot. So then, because you are lukewarm, and neither cold nor hot, I will spew you out of My mouth.

""Because you say, 'I am rich, and increased with goods, and have need of nothing,' and do not know that you are wretched, and miserable, and poor, and blind, and naked, I counsel you to buy from Me gold tried in the fire so that you may be rich, and white garments so that you may be clothed and that the shame of your nakedness does not show. And anoint your eyes with eye salve so that you may see.

""As many as I love, I rebuke and chasten. Therefore, be zealous and repent.

""Look! I stand at the door and knock. If any man hears My voice and opens the door I will come in to him and will dine with him, and he with me.

""To him who overcomes I will grant to sit with Me in My throne, even as I also overcame and am set down with my Father in His throne."'

"He who has an ear, let him hear what the Spirit says to the assemblies."

It is assumed by many that the seven assemblies represent some sort of "seven ages" of the universal "Church." The last "church," Laodicea, represents some final "Church Age." But there is nothing in all of history or Scripture to substantiate this myth. To those who believe this, tell us, if you can, what were the signs of the other alleged "Church Ages"?

This teaching is peculiar to the western churches because they see what they perceive to be "the Church" as rich in material wealth, but poor spiritually. This may be true, but it doesn't mean that Laodicea represents a final "Church Age."

Take this teaching to anywhere else in the world and see how it plays among believers in Christ. One of the problems with the western churches is that they see themselves as the center of God's spiritual universe. The vast majority of true believers are found in other countries, many living under extreme conditions of persecution and deprivation of material goods.

So before we begin this portion, let us put aside the notion that Laodicea represents some final "Church Age."

Jesus describes Himself as "the beginning of the creation of God." The Watchtower Society (Jehovah's Witnesses) says this means Jesus is not God in the flesh, but a created being—the first created angel who was given a special anointing. Specifically, they believe He is the Archangel Michael.

The word "beginning" in the Greek is *arche*, which may carry one of two meanings: 1) first in rank, or primary in principality and rule; 2) first in order of occurrence. Jesus is the ruler of the creation of God, the Word of God by whom all things were made (Jn 1:1-14). Thus, the first meaning would apply, and there is nothing in Scripture to suggest that Jesus is Michael.

It isn't clear whether it was the messenger of Laodicea himself, or the assembly, that was neither cold nor hot.

In any case, we may reasonably assume that if the messenger was lukewarm, the assembly was lukewarm as well, meaning that it had no real passion for the things of God, but it held to them as a form of religion. For this reason, Jesus threatened to spew it out of His mouth—to reject it and have nothing to do with it. This is a terrible judgment.

It may be asked why He would treat the lukewarm with more contempt than He would the cold. Perhaps because those who are cold toward God have a passion for other things. But they have a passion nonetheless. Often that passion can be turned toward God. The lukewarm are generally apathetic; they have no passion for anything; they are dead, period.

It is because of the wealth of Laodicea that the assembly thought it was rich while, in truth, it was poor, blind, naked, and all the other things charged against it. Thus, it had to buy gold tried in the fire, which means it would have to endure hardship to test its faith. If it overcame, it would be rich and pure, and spiritually sound. The crucible of tribulation would be the Lord's means of chastening the assembly He still loved. Those who repent would be saved and would overcome to sit with Him on His throne.

At this point we leave the things that are, in order to enter into the things "which must be hereafter." A popular myth has it that, because "the Church" is no longer mentioned in the Book of Revelation past this point, it means it has been raptured; therefore, everything from chapter four onward has nothing to do with "the Church." This myth is based on the previously addressed myth that the letters to the seven assemblies represent seven stages in the so-called Church Age. But there is nothing in history or in Scripture to support either myth. Those who promote this teaching rely most on the description of Laodicea as the last-days "Church." But, as we said, that is peculiarly American and, in some cases western European in concept.

So, too, is another popular myth which says that John being taken to Heaven in the spirit represents the Rapture of "the Church," further establishing the idea that the end of chapter three is the Rapture, which separates the rest of the Book of Revelation.

We will see as we progress that, in truth, the Body of Christ will be on the earth through much of what is to be revealed to John.

To all of us Jesus says, "He who has an ear, let him hear what the Spirit says."

3

JOHN'S REVELATION OF HEAVEN

The first portion of John's revelation from the Lord had to do with recording the Lord's words of warning and encouragement to the seven assemblies in Asia Minor. Those words addressed "the things that are." To receive a series of revelations regarding "the things which must be hereafter," John is taken up to Heaven in the spirit. Before he receives the first in the series of revelations, he encounters the heavenly scene before God's throne.

REV. 4:1:
After this I saw, and, look! A door was opened in Heaven. And the first voice that I heard was as it were that of a trumpet speaking with me, which said, "Come up here, and I will show you things which must be after this."

Because John is told, "Come up here," some proponents of the pre-tribulation rapture theory insist that this means the Rapture occurs before the events that follow. This is a stretch of the imagination. It is a classic example of twisting Scripture to fit a theological presupposition, and present it in a dogmatic fashion at that. There is nothing to indicate that John's being called into Heaven to receive the revelations has anything to do with the Rapture.

4:2:
And immediately I was in the spirit, and, look, a throne was
set in Heaven, and one sat on the throne.

Again, being "in the spirit" is not the same as being in a trance.
Evidently, John's spirit was in Heaven while his body may have remained
on the earth. He saw God's throne in Heaven, and God the Father sitting
on the throne. A similar thing happened to someone Paul knew:

> Over fourteen years ago I knew a man in Christ (whether in the
> body, I cannot tell, or whether out of the body, I cannot tell. God
> knows), such a one caught up to the Third Heaven. And I knew such
> a man, (whether in the body, or out of the body, I cannot tell. God
> knows), how he was caught up into Paradise and heard inexpressible
> words that it is not lawful for a man to speak. (2Co 12:2-4)

Some say this was Paul himself, but I doubt it because he says
immediately after, that he would boast about such a man, but he would not
boast about himself except in his shortcomings.

The Third Heaven refers to the place of God's throne. There are three
heavens mentioned in Scripture: 1) the firmament above the earth—the
earth's atmosphere; 2) interstellar and intergalactic space; 3) God's abode.
No one knows the exact location of Heaven, but that it is a celestial, physical
place is commonly found in Scripture. We know that Jesus ascended into
Heaven in His resurrected body, so it is not some other "dimension" on
earth. In pronouncing judgment on Lucifer, Isaiah gives a clue that at least
one entrance into Heaven is in the north (from the vantage point of earth):

> For you have said in your heart, "I will ascend into Heaven; I
> will exalt my throne above the stars of God; I will also sit on the mount
> of the congregation, in the sides of the north! I will ascend above the
> heights of the clouds; I will be like the most High!" (Isa 14:13-14)

Now, before we become embroiled in an argument over this issue, let's
remember that the earth is in orbit around the sun, which orbits the Milky
Way galaxy, which traverses its own circle within a cluster of galaxies that
are spinning throughout the universe. The allusion to the sides of the north
may or may not be taken literally without hindering one's walk with Christ.
An interesting fact is that the northern sky is visible from virtually every
inhabited spot on earth except the extreme southern latitudes. Looking at
a globe we see that the vast majority of land mass is northward from the
Tropic of Capricorn. There is very limited habitation southward from there.

We are told that when Jesus returns in the sky every eye will see Him. Could He be coming from the north?

A popular hymn says, "Keep your eye on the eastern sky" in reference to His coming. But why? Only because Jesus said that His coming would be sudden, just as the lightning comes out of the east and flashes even to the west (Mt 24:27). But this is a comparison to the sky-filling characteristics of lightning; it is not a dogmatic statement that He will come from the east.

I've said all this as an interesting sidelight—another digression to hopefully inspire the reader to search out the wonders of God's Word. Wherever Heaven is, that is where Jesus is at the right hand of the Father. John describes the scene around His throne:

4:3:

And He who sat was to look upon like a jasper and a sardinian stone, and around the throne there was a rainbow that looked like an emerald.

This is a vivid description of God's brightness shining as a light with its multi-faceted colors revealed. We can't make any more of this than what is stated. Attempts to spiritualize the sight and explain the colors and the gems represented fail for lack of biblical precedence.

We know that no mortal can look upon the face of God and live (Ex 33:20). God's glory is such that mortal men would die from the brightness. How, then, did John see these things? He was in the spirit; his body was on earth. Whatever the case, John was a witness to this heavenly scene.

4:4:

And around the throne were twenty-four seats, and on the seats I saw twenty-four elders sitting, clothed in white garments, and they had on their heads crowns of gold.

Surrounding the throne of God are twenty-four lesser thrones on which are seated twenty-four elders clothed in white raiment, which represents the purity of the saints. Crowns of gold represent the rule and authority which is promised to the redeemed.

Who are these elders? Revelation 5:9-10 indicates that they are redeemed men from out of all the nations:

And they sang a new song, saying, "You are worthy to take the book and to open its seals, for you were slain, and have redeemed us to God by Your blood out of every kindred, and language, and people, and nation, and have made us kings and priests to our God, and we shall reign on the earth."

Some modern translations render this verse differently, in a manner that causes some to suggest they are angels:

> And they sang a new song, saying, "Worthy are You to take the book and to break its seals; for You were slain, and purchased for God with Your blood men from every tribe and tongue and people and nation.
>
> "You have made them to be a kingdom and priests to our God; and they will reign upon the earth." (Rev. 5:9-10 NAS)

For a detailed explication of why I believe these are redeemed men and not angels, see Appendix B.

The number twenty-four has caused some to suggest that these could be the twelve patriarchs of Israel and the original twelve apostles. But Revelation 5:9 reveals them to be redeemed from all the nations, not just Israel. Exactly who these twenty-four elders are is not stated.

4:5:
And out of the throne proceeded lightning and thundering and voices. And there were seven lamps of fire burning before the throne, which are the seven Spirits of God.

Lightning, thundering and voices represent the power of God—in this case, His power of judgment. The seven lamps of fire are said to be the seven Spirits of God, which were first mentioned in 1:4.

4:6-8:
And before the throne there was a sea of glass like crystal, and in the midst of the throne, and around the throne, were four beings full of eyes in front and in back.

And the first living being was like a lion, and the second being like a calf, and the third being had a face like a man, and the fourth being was like a flying eagle.

And each of the four beings had six wings about him, and they were full of eyes within. And they do not rest day and night, saying, "Holy, holy, holy, Lord God Almighty, who was, and is, and is to come."

The crystal sea is not as water, but a pavement like that of crystal or glass before the throne. The four "beasts," as stated in some translations of

Scripture, are not beasts (an unfortunate translation), but living beings (*zoa*) or angels such as those who appeared to Ezekiel:

> And I looked, and saw a whirlwind come out of the north—a great cloud, and a fire folding in on itself. And a brightness was about it, and out of its midst as the color of amber, out of the midst of the fire.

> Also out of its midst came the likeness of four living beings. And this was their appearance: they had the likeness of a man. And each one had four faces, and each one had four wings.

> And their feet were straight feet, and the soles of their feet were like the sole of a calf's foot, and they sparkled like the color of polished brass.

> And they had the hands of a man under their wings on their four sides; and the four had their faces and their wings.

> Their wings were joined one to another; they did not turn when they went; each one went straight forward.

> As for the likeness of their faces, the four had the face of a man and the face of a lion on the right side; and the four had the face of an ox on the left side; the four also had the face of an eagle.

> Thus were their faces. And their wings were stretched upward—two wings of each one were joined to one another, and two covered their bodies....

> And the likeness of the firmament upon the heads of the living being was like the color of the terrible crystal, stretched forth over their heads above.

> And under the firmament were their wings, straight, the one toward the other; everyone had two, which covered their bodies on this side, and every one had two, which covered on that side.

> And when they went, I heard the noise of their wings, like the noise of great waters, as the voice of the Almighty, the voice of speech, as the noise of an army. When they stood, they let down their wings.

> And there was a voice from the firmament that was over their heads when they stood and had let down their wings.

> And above the firmament that was over their heads was the likeness of a throne, as the appearance of a sapphire stone, and upon the likeness of the throne was the likeness as the appearance of a man above upon at.

> And I saw as the color of amber, as the appearance of fire around within it—from the appearance of his loins even upward, and from

the appearance of his loins downward—I saw as it were the appearance of fire, and it had brightness round about.

As the appearance of the bow that is in the cloud in the day of rain, so was the appearance of the brightness round about. This was the appearance of the likeness of the glory of YHWH. And when I saw it I fell upon my face, and I heard a voice of one who spoke. (Eze 1:4-28)

Ezekiel saw the same things John saw, but from the vantage point of the earth. John stood above the crystal sea, whereas Ezekiel saw the crystal sea as a firmament above the four living beings. The translations between the description of Ezekiel and that of John are not clear whether each living being has four faces, or the description is that of four living beings with four different faces. The latter would seem to be more likely, which is how John's encounter is stated.

4:9-11:

And when those beings give glory and honor and thanks to Him who sat on the throne, who lives forever and ever, the twenty-four elders fall down before Him who sat on the throne, and worship Him who lives forever and ever, and cast their crowns before the throne, saying, "You are worthy, O Lord, to receive glory and honor and power, for you have created all things, and for your pleasure they are and were created."

The twenty-four elders demonstrate that their authority is surrendered to the authority of the Lord. They affirm that the One on the throne is "Lord" who has created all things, and for His pleasure they were created.

REV. 5:1-4:

And I saw in the right hand of Him who sat on the throne a book written within and on the backside, sealed with seven seals. And I saw a strong angel proclaiming with a loud voice, "Who is worthy to open the book, and to loosen its seals?"

And no man in Heaven or in earth, or under the earth, was able to open the book or to look at it. And I wept much because no man was found worthy to open and to read the book, or to look at it.

The book with seven seals is the revelation of "things which must be hereafter" (Rv 1:19). Each chapter of the book is sealed. No man is worthy to open the book or to look within it. This caused John to weep at the unworthiness of man to know the things of God except God reveal them to us.

5:5-6:
And one of the elders said to me, "Do not weep. Look! The Lion of the tribe of Judah, the Root of David, has prevailed to open the book and to loosen its seven seals."

And I saw, and, look! In the midst of the throne and of the four creatures, and in the midst of the elders, stood a Lamb as if it had been slain, having seven horns and seven eyes, which are the seven Spirits of God sent forth into all the earth.

It is obvious from the description of the Lamb that this is Jesus who was slain for our sins, and who is called "the Lion of the tribe of Judah," and "the Lamb of God." The elder tells John to look at the Lion of the tribe of Judah. Yet when John looks at Jesus he does not see a lion, but a lamb. This speaks of Jesus appearing in two roles: 1) as the ruler of Judah and Israel; 2) as the sacrifice for all men's sins regardless of the nation into which they were born.

The lion and the lamb are diametrically opposite in character: one strong, fierce and destructive; the other weak, meek, and humble. One devours; the other is devoured. These describe the characteristics of Jesus who came first as the Lamb of God to die for the sins of the world, and who will come again as the Lion of the tribe of Judah to bring vengeance upon God's enemies.

Again there is reference to the seven Spirits of God. Here we see that they are represented by the seven horns and seven eyes of the Lamb of God. This may be another way of saying that within Jesus dwells the fullness of divinity bodily (Col 2:9).

5:7-10:
And He came and took the book out of the right hand of Him who sat on the throne.

And when He had taken the book, the four beings and twenty-four elders fell down before the Lamb, every one of them having harps and golden vials full of aromas, which are the prayers of saints.

And they sang a new song, saying, "You are worthy to take the book and to open its seals, for you were slain, and have redeemed us to God by Your blood out of every kindred, and language, and people, and nation, and have made us kings and priests to our God, and we shall reign on the earth!"

The Lamb (Jesus) takes the book out of the Father's hand, whereupon the four beings fall before the Lamb and worship Him. The twenty-four elders present to Him the prayers of the saints, and praise Him for redeeming them out of every kindred, tongue and people and nation. This description of redemption indicates that the twenty-four elders are not the twelve patriarchs of Israel and the twelve original apostles, but are twenty-four men who represent the redeemed from all the nations.

Although the Scriptures are silent on the actual identity of these elders, the fact that they call out to the Lamb that He has made them kings and priests, and that they will reign on the earth, proves that they are redeemed men and not angelic beings. (Again, some modern English versions read differently, but see Appendix B for my reasoning that these are men and not angels.)

5:11-14:

And I looked, and I heard the voice of many angels around the throne and the creatures and the elders. And their number was ten thousand times ten thousand, and thousands of thousands, saying with a loud voice, "Worthy is the Lamb who was slain, to receive power, and riches, and wisdom, and strength, and honor, and glory, and blessing!"

And every creature that is in Heaven, and on the earth, and under the earth, and such as are in the sea, and all that are in them, I heard saying, "Blessing, and honor, and glory, and power be to Him who sits on the throne, and to the Lamb, forever and ever!"

And the four creatures said, "Amen!"

And the twenty-four elders fell down and worshipped Him who lives forever and ever.

All the heavenly host join in to worship the Lord Jesus. These, in turn, are joined by the entire creation in worshiping the Lamb.

That all creation worships the Lamb is evidence that He is the Word of God—God incarnate—who is worthy of worship. No man, angel or other living being is ever counted worthy of worship in God's Word. And God says He will share His glory with no one (Isa 42:8).

These scenes are a prelude to the Lord opening the seals of the book which reveal events that were to follow in human history—particularly Israel's history.

4

THE FIRST REVELATION

Now begins a series of ten revelations the Lord gave to John, describing the events that will transpire leading up to the Lord's Second Coming, the Millennial Kingdom, and the New Heavens and New Earth. Some of the events in these ten revelations overlap from one revelation to another. This is critical to understanding the prophecies.

REV. 6:1-2:

And I looked when the Lamb opened one of the seals, and I heard as it were the noise of thunder, one of the four beings saying, "Come and see."

And I saw, and look! A white horse! And He who sat on him had a bow, and a crown was given to Him and He went forth conquering, and to conquer.

One of the four beings revealed to John the events of the first aspect of God's judgment: a man on a white horse with a bow (warfare), and a crown (authority; power). This man would accomplish great conquests. Some insist that this is Jesus coming to conquer the earth. Some say that Jesus has already conquered the nations; the calamities that follow are His judgments that took place on Jerusalem in A.D. 70.

Others say that this is the anti-Christ, and that is a reasonable assumption. However, it is just as viable to say that Jesus is at the head of judgment which will come in the form of the following horsemen. He will conquer the earth through their actions. More likely, the red horse carries an angel who will bring warfare. The verses that follow indicate that these calamities are worldwide, not just local to Jerusalem. They also speak to the many wars, famines and pestilences that have plagued the earth to increasingly greater degree in the past two millennia. As we progress we will see that these are relevant to the end of this present age.

63-4:

And when He had opened the second seal I heard the second being say, "Come and see."

And there went out another horse that was red, and power was given to him who sat on it to take peace from the earth, and that they should kill one another. And a great sword was given to him.

Another of the living beings reveals the events of the second aspect of God's judgment: a being on a red horse, representing warfare throughout the earth. A great sword speaks of tremendous destruction, bloody in nature.

6:5-6:

And when he had opened the third seal I heard the third being say, "Come and see." And I saw, and look! A black horse! And he who sat on him had a pair of balances in his hand. And I heard a voice in the midst of the four beings say, "A measure of wheat for a denarius, and three measures of barley for a denarius, and see that you do not hurt the oil and the wine."

The "measures" addressed here are of uncertain dry volume. One "measure" is believed to have been equal to about one liter of dry volume. A denarius was a Roman coin which generally represented a day's wages. Thus, the rider on the black horse represents famine and economic distress. These would be the consequences of the wars revealed in the first two seals. Commentators have suggested that the command to not hurt the oil and wine are evidence that the wealthy will not be affected by the economic chaos, because oil and wine were considered staples of only the wealthy at the time John wrote.

In Scripture, oil and wine were important elements to the temple sacrifices and offerings of the Jews. Oil and wine were also used as remedies for injuries, and are often associated with blessings from God. They were not as essential to sustaining life as were wheat and barley, but the command to not hurt, or do wrong to the oil and wine could mean that the luxuries of the wealthy will not be harmed. History has certainly proven that the greatest suffering in any calamity falls on the poor first and foremost.

6:7-8:

And when He had opened the fourth seal I heard the voice of the fourth being say, "Come and see."

And I saw, and look! A pale horse! And his name that sat on him was Death, and Hades followed with him. And power was given to them over the fourth part of the earth to kill with sword, and with hunger, and with death, and with the animals of the earth.

The rider on the pale horse is Death. Hades following may indicate that there are actually five horses. Death leads the unredeemed to Hades, the place of departed souls who have not died in Christ. Both Death and Hades are given power to kill a quarter of the earth's population with additional war, famine, pestilence and animals. The kind of animals, whether domesticated or wild, is not stated, but during famines it has happened that even domesticated animals have turned on their masters.

As these first four seals are opened, each of the four beings in turn beckons John to look on the scene presented. This gives cohesiveness to the four scenes which speak of destruction on the earth in varying forms.

6:9-11:

And when He had opened the fifth seal I saw under the altar the souls of those who were slain for the Word of God and for the testimony that they held.

And they cried with a loud voice, saying, "How long, O Lord, holy and true, do You not judge and avenge our blood on those who dwell on the earth?"

And white robes were given to every one of them, and they were told that they should rest yet for a little season until their fellow servants also and their brethren, that would be killed as they were, would be fulfilled.

These are the martyrs for the testimony of Jesus, killed by anti-Christ for their faith. They are told to wait until other believers who are destined for martyrdom must be killed.

The claim is often made that these are not today's saints, but "tribulation saints"—those who are left behind when Jesus comes to take His

"Church" out of the world in the Rapture. But this is not clearly stated; it must be read into the text to support that theological presupposition. Let us reserve judgment on this until we have read further.

6:12-17:
And I saw when He had opened the sixth seal, and, look! There was a great earthquake! And the sun became black as sackcloth of hair, and the moon became like blood, and the stars of the heavens fell to the earth, even as a fig tree casts her unripe figs when she is shaken by a strong wind.

And the heavens departed like a scroll when it is rolled together, and every mountain and island were moved out of their places. And the kings of the earth, and the great men, and the rich men, and the chief captains, and the mighty men, and every slave, and every freeman, hid themselves in the dens and in the rocks of the mountains, and said to the mountains and rocks, "Fall on us and hide us from the face of Him who sits on the throne, and from the wrath of the Lamb, for the great day of His wrath has come, and who will be able to stand?"

The sixth seal heralds the wrath of God about to be poured upon an unbelieving world. The description of the sun being darkened, the moon turning to blood, and the stars being cast to the earth, as well as the other dramatic scenes, represent the Day of Yahweh, which, in different times and places, meant God's visitation with judgment. Israel had its "Day of Yahweh" when it went into captivity to Assyria. Judah had its "Day of Yahweh" when it went into captivity to Babylonia. Egypt, Assyria and Babylonia each had their "Day of Yahweh" when they were judged. This particular Day of Yahweh is God's wrath poured upon the anti-Christ's kingdom. The sixth seal reveals the Lord (the Lamb) in Heaven about to bring destruction. Thus, everyone will see Him, and they will wail for fright (Rv 1:7). This is actually the Lord coming for His saints as revealed in the following Scriptures:

"But after that tribulation in those days, the sun shall be darkened, and the moon shall not give her light, and the stars of the heavens shall fall, and the powers that are in the heavens shall be shaken. And then they shall see the Son of Man coming in the clouds with great power and glory. And then He shall send His angels, and shall gather together His elect from the four winds—from the uttermost part of the earth to the uttermost part of Heaven." (Mk 13:24-27)

"Immediately after the tribulation of those days the sun shall be darkened, and the moon shall not give her light, and the stars shall fall from the heavens, and the powers of the heavens shall be shaken. And then the sign of the Son of Man shall appear in the heavens, and then all the tribes of the earth will sorrow, and they shall see the Son of Man coming in the clouds of the heavens with power and great glory. And He shall send His angels with a great sound of a trumpet, and they shall gather together his elect from the four winds—from one end of the heavens to the other." (Mt 24:29-31)

The language of both Matthew and Mark indicate that the Lord's return would occur immediately after the tribulation of which He spoke. Preterists believe He was speaking of the tribulation to come upon Jerusalem in A.D. 70. Dispensationalists believe He was speaking of a last-days "Great Tribulation" period of seven years.

In this case the preterists are correct, but not entirely. With the first half of Daniel's seventieth seven completed in A.D. 70, the Lord's coming would be "immediately" after that time in *prophetic history*. I reiterate: prophetic history is not the same as human history. Prophetically, A.D. 70 marked the halfway point in great tribulation upon Jerusalem; when the Lord returns, then prophetically it will be "immediately" after the tribulation upon Jerusalem in A.D. 70. Lacking understanding of prophetic history as opposed to human history, preterists are incorrect in assuming that the Lord returned in A.D. 70. They are at a loss to reasonably explain what happened to the last half of Daniel's seventieth seven. The Lord's return is yet future.

Dispensationalists err in thinking there is coming a seven-year period of "great tribulation" upon the earth and/or Israel, during which (halfway through) anti-Christ will break a supposed treaty with Israel and launch his attacks against the nation.

When Jesus said He would return "immediately" after the tribulation of those days (the first half of Daniel's seventieth "seven"—the destruction of the temple) He was speaking prophetically. His return would not be immediate in human history but in prophetic history (see the Timeline Chart on page 199). His return in this instance will be to gather His saints in the air at the resurrection, not to set His feet on the earth. That will take place after the Battle of Armageddon when He defeats the anti-Christ's armies as they surround Jerusalem at the end of Daniel's seventieth seven.

But there will also be a time of tribulation on the earth under the anti-Christ. However one understands the idea of a "Great Tribulation," His return is yet future, and the Body of Christ will be on the earth during a time of tribulation yet to come on the whole earth.

Immediately after that tribulation on the whole earth at the end of the Time for the Gentiles, and prior to the second half of Daniel's seventieth seven and Jacob's Trouble, the Lord will return for His elect and gather them from the four corners of the earth, and from Heaven. They will be prepared to return with Him to establish His Kingdom on the earth.

The world will see the Lord coming in clouds to receive His people (Mt 24:30; Mk 13:26; Rv 20:16). When the world sees this awesome event, people of every station of life will mourn and shake with fear because they will know that His wrath is about to be poured upon them, "for the great day of his wrath has come, and who will be able to stand?" (Rv 6:17).

These verses (Rv 6:12-17) describe the resurrection, after which all the saints will be caught up to meet the Lord.

The Resurrection

When we speak of the Lord's Second Coming, we must realize that there are events attached to His actual return to set His feet on the earth, but which either precede or follow upon His return. Preceding His return to set foot on the earth will be His appearing in the clouds to gather together His elect from the earth and Heaven:

> But I would not have you be ignorant, brethren, concerning those who are asleep, so that you do not sorrow as others who have no hope. For if we believe that Jesus died and rose again, even so those also who sleep in Jesus, God will bring with Him.
>
> For this we say to you by the word of the Lord: that we who are alive and remain until the coming of the Lord shall not go before those who are asleep. For the Lord Himself shall descend from Heaven with a shout, with the voice of the archangel, and with the trump of God, and the dead in Christ shall rise first. Then we who are alive and remain shall be caught up together with them in the clouds to meet the Lord in the air, and so shall we ever be with the Lord.
>
> Therefore comfort one another with these words. (1Th 4:13-18)

As mentioned in our study on eschatology, the Greek, *harpazo*, (caught up) implies a sudden snatching up or taking away. The word "rapture" carries more of a connotation of spiritual ecstasy, which is how the verse has been viewed by those who do not believe in a literal catching up of the saints.

While so much focus has been on the Rapture, that event is really an addendum to the resurrection of the saints. The catching up follows immediately upon the resurrection of those who are asleep in Christ at the time of His appearing. The catching up is part of the resurrection. All who are asleep in Christ will be raised to life first, then those who are alive at that time will be caught up with them. Paul reminds us of the validity of the resurrection of Jesus, and the truth that those who are in Him will also be resurrected. Those who are alive at the time will be changed from corruptible to incorruptible:

> Look, I show you a mystery: not all of us shall sleep, but we all shall be changed in a moment, in the blinking of an eye at the last trump. For the trumpet shall sound, and the dead shall be raised incorruptible, and we shall be changed. For this corruptible must put on incorruption, and this mortal must put on immortality.
>
> So when this corruptible shall have put on incorruption, and this mortal shall have put on immortality, then the saying shall be brought to pass that is written, "Death is swallowed up in victory. O death, where is your sting? O grave, where is your victory?"
>
> The sting of death is sin, and the strength of sin is the Law. But thanks be to God, who gives us the victory through our Lord Jesus Christ.
>
> Therefore, my beloved brethren, you be steadfast, unmovable, always increasing in the work of the Lord, inasmuch as you know that your labor in the Lord is not in vain. (1 Co 15:51-58)

These words to the Corinthians from Paul iterate what he stated in different words to the assembly at Thessalonica.

Some say the seals are not chronological in order, so the saints revealed in the fifth seal must be "tribulation saints," not "the Church" which they believe is worthy to escape all these things.

Firstly, why should we think these are not chronological events? If they are not in chronological order, then in what order should they be placed? There is nothing to suggest otherwise. To insist on this is to make the Scriptures fit the theological biases of a pre-tribulation secret rapture theory.

Secondly, no one is really worthy to escape.

But, it is argued, does the Lord not say that we are not appointed to wrath? Yes, He does. But what is the context of that promise?

> But you have no need that I write to you of the times and the seasons, brethren, for you yourselves know perfectly that the Day of the Lord so comes as a thief in the night. For when they shall say,

"Peace and safety," then sudden destruction comes upon them like travail upon a woman with child, and they shall not escape.

But you, brethren, are not in darkness, that that day should overtake you as a thief. You are all the children of light, and the children of the day; we are not of the night, nor of darkness.

Therefore let us not sleep as others do, but let us watch and be sober. For they who sleep, sleep in the night, and they who are drunk are drunk in the night. But let us, who are of the day, be sober, putting on the breastplate of faith and love, and for a helmet, the hope of salvation. For God has not appointed us to wrath, but to obtain salvation by our Lord Jesus Christ who died for us so that, whether we wake or sleep, we should live together with Him.

Therefore comfort yourselves together, and edify one another, even as also you do. (1Th 5:1-11)

These verses are taken by the pre-trib theorists to mean that "the Church" will not be on the earth during a supposed "Great Tribulation," particularly since they deal with the Lord's coming again. But Paul is warning the brethren not to be unprepared for the things that will come upon that generation. The wrath of which he speaks is not any great tribulation, but the wrath of God upon the lost—condemnation as opposed to salvation. Nowhere are we guaranteed that we will not endure tribulation. Whether during that terrible time we are awake (are alive) or sleep (are dead), we will live together with the Lord.

In any case, even during the tribulation on the whole earth under anti-Christ, God is capable of preserving His saints from destruction. But He will allow many to taste death at the hands of the anti-Christ.

And why should we fear, considering that it carries with it a better resurrection:

And what more shall I say? For the time would fail me to tell of Gideon, and of Barak, and of Samson, and of Jephthae; of David also, and Samuel, and of the prophets who through faith subdued kingdoms, worked righteousness, obtained promises, stopped the mouths of lions, quenched the violence of fire, escaped the edge of the sword, out of weakness were made strong, grew brave in fight, turned to flight the armies of the aliens.

Women received their dead raised to life again, and others were tortured, not accepting deliverance, so that they might obtain a better resurrection. (Heb 11:32-35)

A better resurrection speaks of greater rewards.

There are more convincing Scriptures, but we will address them as we come to them.

REV. 7:1-8:

And after these things I saw four angels standing on the four corners of the earth, holding the four winds of the earth so that the wind could not blow on the earth, or on the sea, or on any tree.

And I saw another angel ascending from the east, having the seal of the living God, and he cried with a loud voice to the four angels to whom it was given to hurt the earth and the sea, saying, "Do not hurt the earth, nor the sea, nor the trees, till we have sealed the servants of our God in their foreheads."

And I heard the number of those who were sealed, and there were sealed one hundred and forty-four thousand of all the tribes of the children of Israel.

Of the tribe of Judah were sealed twelve thousand. Of the tribe of Reuben were sealed twelve thousand. Of the tribe of Gad were sealed twelve thousand. Of the tribe of Asher were sealed twelve thousand. Of the tribe of Naphtali were sealed twelve thousand. Of the tribe of Manasseh were sealed twelve thousand. Of the tribe of Simeon were sealed twelve thousand. Of the tribe of Levi were sealed twelve thousand. Of the tribe of Issachar were sealed twelve thousand. Of the tribe of Zebulon were sealed twelve thousand. Of the tribe of Joseph were sealed twelve thousand. Of the tribe of Benjamin were sealed twelve thousand.

"After these things" or after the sixth seal had been opened, and, consequently, before the seventh seal is opened, John sees four angels holding back God's judgments until they have sealed God's servants in their foreheads. This is a seal of protection against the wrath of God to come. It is also a sign of their special consecration. An example of this is found in Ezekiel 9:1-7:

He cried also in my ears with a loud voice, saying, "Cause those who have charge over the city to draw near, every man with his destroying weapon in his hand."

And, look! Six men came from the way of the higher gate, which lies toward the north, and every man a slaughter weapon in his hand. And one man among them was clothed with linen, with a writer's inkhorn by his side, and they went in and stood beside the brass altar.

And the glory of the God of Israel went up from the cherub, on which He was, to the threshold of the house. And He called to the man clothed with linen, who had the writer's inkhorn by his side. And YHWH said to him, "Go through the midst of the city, through the midst of Jerusalem, and set a mark on the foreheads of the men who sigh and who cry out because of all the abominations that are done in the its midst."

And to the others He said in my hearing, "You go after him through the city, and strike. Do not let your eye spare, nor have pity. Slay utterly old and young, both maids, and little children, and women. But do not come near any man on whom is the mark. And begin at My sanctuary."

Then they began at the old men who were in front of the house.

And He said to them, "Defile the house, and fill the courts with the slain! Go forth!"

And they went forth and slew in the city.

The 144,000 revealed in Revelation 7:1-8 are true Israelites of the flesh (12,000 from each tribe named) who will have turned to the Lord Jesus when they see Him coming in the clouds. But they will not have been in the company of the redeemed to escape the time of God's wrath. God's mark on their foreheads is a contrast to the mark of the anti-Christ that the false prophet will cause to be placed on all people. They will also be protected from the effects of God's wrath.

7:9-17:

After this I saw, and, look! A great multitude which no man could number, of all nations, and tribes, and people, and languages, stood before the throne and before the Lamb, clothed with white robes, and palms in their hands, and cried with a loud voice, saying, "Salvation to our God who sits on the throne, and to the Lamb."

And all the angels stood around the throne and around the elders and the four beings, and fell on their faces before the throne and worshipped God, saying, "Amen! Blessing, and glory, and wisdom, and thanksgiving, and honor, and power, and might be to our God forever and ever. Amen."

And one of the elders answered, saying to me, "Who are these who are arrayed in white robes, and from where did they come?"

And I said to him, "Sir, you know."

And he said to me, "These are they who came out of great tribulation and have washed their robes and made them white in the blood of the Lamb. Therefore they are before the throne of God, and serve Him day and night in His temple. And He who sits on the throne shall dwell among them. They shall hunger no longer, nor thirst anymore, neither shall the sun nor any heat light on them, for the Lamb who is in the midst of the throne shall feed them and shall lead them to living fountains of waters, and God shall wipe away all tears from their eyes."

Here we see the saints in the first resurrection who have been slain or survived during the time of great tribulation on the whole earth (not on Israel). They are not present on the earth when God pours His wrath on the nations of the anti-Christ. These saints come from all nations, kindreds, people and languages, which means they were saved during the Time of the Gentiles.

The Time of the Gentiles will close with the resurrection of the dead in Christ and the transformation of the saints living at the time. From that point on, God will reestablish His covenant with Israel and will preserve the true Israelites who resist the anti-Christ's kingdom, although the Jews will be driven out of Jerusalem for three-and-one-half years—the second half of Daniel's seventieth seven. How the nations will fare during this time we will see as we progress.

SUMMARY OF THE FIRST REVELATION

The First Revelation spans the period from the appearance of anti-Christ to the saints appearing in Heaven after the resurrection and the Rapture. It begins with the Lord opening six seals of a book only He can open.

The First Seal: Anti-Christ goes out to conquer those God places in his hands;

The Second Seal: Warfare increases, probably between the kingdom of the anti-Christ and the rest of the nations that escape his dominion;

The Third Seal: Famine results from worldwide warfare;

The Fourth Seal: Death enlarges Hades with untold numbers of people worldwide who will die from pestilence, war, famine, and wild animals;

The Fifth Seal: The souls of the saints martyred for their faith during that period of worldwide great tribulation cry out for God's justice;

The Sixth Seal: Terrible events in the heavens herald the resurrection and the Lord coming to receive His saints (the Rapture), and mankind calling on the earth to hide them from His wrath which is to come. Before God pours His wrath on the kingdom of the anti-Christ, He seals 144,000 true Israelites to preserve them against God's wrath. They will eventually be caught up to Him (Rv 12:5), while a remnant of Israel flees into the wilderness.

The Seventh Seal: The heralding of seven trumpet judgments begins the second revelation which overlaps the first revelation, giving in greater detail the events that will transpire under the aforementioned six seals.

5
THE SECOND REVELATION

The seventh seal reveals through seven trumpet judgments the time of great tribulation to come upon the earth (not merely Israel) under the anti-Christ (revealed in the opening of the first seal). Each trumpet is given to a particular angel to sound. These and other events appear to occur throughout the entire earth. However, it is possible that many are confined to the land and sea proximate to anti-Christ's kingdom which is regional, at least at first.

REV. 8:1-6:

And when He had opened the seventh seal there was silence in Heaven about the space of half an hour. And I saw the seven angels that stood before God, and seven trumpets were given to them.

And another angel, having a golden censer, came and stood at the altar. And much incense was given to him so that he could offer it with the prayers of all saints on the golden altar which was before the throne. And the smoke of the incense, which came with the prayers of the saints, ascended out of the angel's hand before God.

And the angel took the censer and filled it with fire from the altar and cast it into the earth, and there were voices, and thunder, and lightning, and an earthquake. And the seven angels who had the seven trumpets prepared themselves to sound.

We are not told why there is silence in Heaven for one hour, but there is a pause between the first and second revelations to John. The first revelation ended with the resurrection of the saints. The second revelation describes God's trumpet judgments on the anti-Christ's kingdom prior to the resurrection of the saints which will occur at the last trump.

Before the trumpets begin to sound, an angel fills his censer with incense and offers it to God with the prayers of the saints. This indicates God hearing His saints' prayers for retribution on their enemies who have persecuted them under the anti-Christ, and have resisted God's grace (Rv 6:9-11). After offering the incense to God, the angel casts the censer to the earth, indicating that God is about to answer the prayers of His saints.

8:7:

The first angel sounded, and there followed hail and fire mingled with blood, and they were cast upon the earth, and the third part of trees was burnt up, and all green grass was burnt up.

This indicates a great drought brought by supernatural means so that one-third of every living plant is burned up. No doubt fires will play a large part in this judgment. Men will be unable to prevent the great fire storms that will result from a prolonged and supernaturally created drought.

8:8-9:

And the second angel sounded, and as it were a great mountain burning with fire was cast into the sea, and the third part of the sea became blood, and the third part of the creatures that were in the sea and had life, died, and the third part of the ships were destroyed.

This mountain is possibly a great meteor that strikes the sea (salt water) and causes one-third of all life on the sea, including life aboard the ships at sea, to be destroyed. Such a meteor strike would wreak havoc with the weather as well. If this is not a meteor, then it may be metaphor for something else which has not yet been revealed.

8:10-11:

And the third angel sounded, and there fell a great star from the heavens, burning like a lamp, and it fell upon the third part of the rivers and upon the fountains of waters. And the name of the star is called Wormwood. And the third part of the waters became wormwood, and many men died from the waters because they were made bitter.

This star might be an angel named Wormwood. It cannot be a meteor because it selectively poisons one-third of the earth's rivers (fresh water). Men will die from the poisoned water, and no doubt from thirst as well. Just as Pharaoh, a type of anti-Christ, hardened his heart against God's judgments, so the last-days anti-Christ will harden his heart, as will his devotees, bringing further judgments.

8:12-13:

And the fourth angel sounded, and the third part of the sun was struck, and the third part of the moon, and the third part of the stars, so that the third part of them was darkened, and the day shone not for a third part of it; and the night likewise.

And I looked, and heard an angel flying through the midst of Heaven [or "the heavens"?], saying with a loud voice, "Woe, woe, woe, to the inhabitants of the earth because of the other voices of the trumpet of the three angels that are yet to sound!"

Some say these plagues are the result of man's pollution of the planet. But Scripture indicates they are directly attributable to God. They are administered through the spirit realm. The earth's weather will be drastically altered. With a third of its light gone, the sun will not give enough warmth to grow food, plants and trees to sustain much life. On top of all this, an angel flies through Heaven (or the heavens—the skies) promising even greater woes upon the inhabitants of the earth than what they have already suffered.

9:1-4:

And the fifth angel sounded, and I saw a star fall from Heaven to the earth, and the key of the bottomless pit was given to him. And he opened the bottomless pit, and there arose a smoke out of the pit, like the smoke of a great furnace, and the sun and the air were darkened because of the smoke from the pit.

And out of the smoke there came locusts upon the earth, and power was given to them, as the scorpions of the earth have power. And it was commanded them that they should not hurt the grass of the earth, nor any green thing, nor any tree, but only those men who do not have the seal of God in their foreheads.

The star falling from Heaven is an angel holding the key to the bottomless pit. Scripture in several places refers to God's angels as stars (Jdg 5:20; Job 38:7; Da 8:10; Rv 12:4). That this star is clearly an angel suggests that the stars that fall in the previous trumpet judgments are also angels.

9:5-12:
And it was given to them that they should not kill them, but that they should be tormented five months. And their torment was like the torment of a scorpion when he strikes a man.

And in those days men shall seek death, and shall not find it, and shall desire to die, and death shall flee from them.

And the shapes of the locusts were like to horses prepared for battle, and on their heads were as it were crowns like gold, and their faces were as the faces of men. And they had hair like the hair of women, and their teeth were like the teeth of lions. And they had breastplates, as it were breastplates of iron, and the sound of their wings was like the sound of chariots of many horses running to battle. And they had tails like scorpions, and there were stings in their tails, and their power was to hurt men five months.

And they had a king over them, who is the angel of the abyss, whose name in the Hebrew language is Abaddon, but in the Greek language he has his name Apollyon.

One woe is past, and, look! There come two more woes afterward!

The reason the last three trumpets are separated in severity from the first four is that the great tribulation has been revealed through nature and/or the acts of men up to this point. The fifth trumpet heralds tribulation from demonic sources, which will be far more terrifying.

This angel responding to the fifth trumpet opens the bottomless pit, out of which come demonic forces likened to locusts—that is, so great in number that with the smoke of the pit they blot out the sun. The "locusts" are demonic forces or fallen angels that are presently bound, but will be turned loose upon the earth to wreak destruction. They are fierce in their countenance, strong to do battle, and they have authority to hurt men for five months, so much so that men will seek death yet will not be able to find it.

A fanciful speculation put forth by certain teachers is that this is John's way of describing helicopters engaged in warfare. It is said that helicopters might have looked like locusts to John and he had no way of relating what they were other than in terms familiar to him. One teacher strongly implies that the smoke from the bottomless pit is from the burning oil wells set afire in Kuwait by Saddam Hussein's forces. Because one newspaper referred to Hussein as "the Destroyer," this teacher believes that we are currently in the time of the fifth trumpet judgment.

However, if these are helicopters the question arises why they are unable to kill anyone for five months, but are able only to torment them. No, these are by their description some sort of demonic beings. But they appear to conduct themselves in a manner similar to that of locusts as they swarm over the land. And yet they are told not to hurt the grass, the trees, or any vegetation. This is one of those things that may be understood only at the time it occurs.

The king over these forces, Abaddon, or Apollyon, is their chief fallen angel. There is nothing to suggest this is Satan. Satan has not been bound in the bottomless pit, but up to this time has been the prince of the power of the air (Eph 2:2), and the prince of this world system (Jn 12:31).

8:13-21:

And the sixth angel sounded, and I heard a voice from the four horns of the golden altar that is before God, saying to the sixth angel who had the trumpet, "Loose the four angels who are bound in the great river Euphrates."

And loosed were the four angels who were prepared for an hour, and a day, and a month, and a year, in order to slay the third part of men.

And the number of the army of the horsemen were two hundred million, and I heard the number of them.

And thus I saw the horses in the vision, and those who sat on them, having breastplates of fire, and of jacinth, and brimstone. And the heads of the horses were like the heads of lions, and out of their mouths issued fire and smoke and brimstone.

By these three was the third part of men killed: by the fire, and by the smoke, and by the brimstone, that issued out of their mouths.

For their power is in their mouth, and in their tails, for their tails were like serpents, and had heads, and with them they do hurt.

And the rest of the men who were not killed by these plagues still did not repent of the works of their hands, that they should not worship devils and idols of gold, and silver, and brass, and stone, and of wood—which neither can see, nor hear, nor walk. Neither did they repent of their murders, or of their sorceries, or of their fornication, or of their thefts.

It's very likely that this scene represents a cataclysmic warfare, not against Israel, but throughout the whole world. The four angels that are bound in the great river Euphrates are being kept for a specific purpose at a specific hour. One third of men had already been slain by the previous judgments. Either one third more of the original number of men at the time of judgment will be killed, or one third of the remnant will be killed when they are slain by the warfare loosed upon them by these four angels.

The horsemen seem to appear out of nowhere. But if we return to the first four seals we see the four horsemen described there. These are the four angels that bring war, famine, pestilence and death. The number of the four horsemen's army is 200 million strong, indicating that virtually every nation will be involved in this war. Some say the 200 million horsemen will be the Chinese army that will be able to approach Israel through the dried-up Euphrates River. Others suggest that China will ally itself with the United States against the anti-Christ. All this is pure speculation. It has not yet been revealed who or what the 200 million horsemen represent. They are not the locusts, but they are linked to the four angels that are presently bound in the Euphrates River. That the angels are bound indicates that they are fallen angels, and that the 200 million horsemen will do their bidding. Beyond that, we cannot speculate. This, too, is sealed till the end.

Regardless what this army is, we learn that in spite of God's palpable judgment, men will refuse to repent, thus validating the justness of God's judgment.

REV. 10:1-6:

And I saw another mighty angel come down from Heaven, clothed with a cloud, and a rainbow was on his head, and his face was as it were the sun, and his feet like pillars of fire. And he had in his hand a little book open, and he set his right foot on the sea, and his left foot on the earth, and cried out with a loud voice as when a lion roars. And when he had cried out, seven thunders uttered their voices.

And when the seven thunders had uttered their voices, I was about to write, and I heard a voice from Heaven saying to me, "Seal up those things that the seven thunders uttered, and do not write them."

And the angel that I saw stand on the sea and on the earth lifted up his hand to Heaven, and swore by Him who lives forever and ever, who created the heavens and the things that are in it, and the earth and the things that are in it, and the sea and the things that are in it, that there should be no more time left.

The sixth trumpet heralds the last of the judgments from God coinciding with the opening of the six seals. Just as at the end of the sixth seal and the opening of the seventh seal we see the Lord return for His saints at the end of the Time of the Gentiles, so at the end of the sixth trumpet we see the end of the Time of the Gentiles. From his description this angel from Heaven is not one of the seven angels bearing trumpets. He is sent directly from the throne of God to proclaim certain mysteries which John is about to write until told not to do so. He then reveals that time has run out for proclaiming the Gospel during this Time of the Gentiles.

The King James language ("there should be time no longer") has left some to think that this means the concept of time comes to an end, and "eternity" is about to be ushered in, where there is no time. But that is not what it means. As long as the creation remains—which it will for eternity after being renovated through fire—there will be time. This passage means that time has run out for the present age—the Time of the Gentiles (however it is defined)—which we shall see in the next verse.

10:7:

But in the days of the voice of the seventh angel, when he shall begin to sound, the mystery of God will be finished, as He has declared to His servants the prophets.

As stated earlier, the mystery of God is the Gospel of Jesus Christ, making of Jew and Gentile one new man in Christ, who will inherit the Kingdom of God:

> Now to Him who has the power to establish you according to my Gospel and the proclaiming of Jesus Christ according to the revelation of the mystery which was kept secret since the world began. (Ro 16:25)

> I am made a minister according to the stewardship from God that is given to me for you, to fulfill the word of God—the mystery that has been hidden from ages and from generations, but now is revealed to His saints to whom God would make known among the Gentiles what are the riches of the glory of this mystery, which is in you, Christ the hope of glory. (Col 1:25-27)

> ...having made known to us the mystery of His will, according to His good pleasure which He has purposed in Himself: that in the dispensation of the fullness of times He might gather together into one, all things in Christ—that are both in Heaven and on earth—in

Him in whom we have also obtained an inheritance, being predestined according to the purpose of Him who works all things after the counsel of His own will, that we who first trusted in Christ should be to the praise of His glory. (Eph 1:9-12)

Notice the parallel between Ephesians 1:10 "that in the dispensation of the fullness of times He might gather together into one, all things in Christ, both that are in Heaven, and that are on earth"—and Mark 13:27:

And then He shall send His angels, and shall gather together His elect from the four winds—from the uttermost part of the earth to the uttermost part of Heaven.

When the seventh angel sounds, the mystery of God (the Time of the Gentiles to be brought into the Kingdom of God—when God has made of two men one new man in Christ Jesus) will be completed. This occurs upon the resurrection of the dead in Christ and the catching up of the saints alive at the time. This is the blast of the last trumpet:

Look, I show you a mystery: not all of us shall sleep, but we all shall be changed in a moment, in the blinking of an eye at the last trump. For the trumpet shall sound, and the dead shall be raised incorruptible, and we shall be changed. For this corruptible must put on incorruption, and this mortal must put on immortality. (1Co 15:51-53)

The reference to the last trumpet which heralds the resurrection and the catching up of the living saints has been largely ignored or explained away by some pre-tribulation rapture teachers. They say that the last trump in 1 Corinthians 51:52 is not the same as the last or seventh trumpet blast in Revelation 10:7. But there is no reason given other than the assumption that this would negate the theory of the pre-tribulation rapture. However, there is nowhere in Scripture where any sequence of heavenly trumpets is found other than in Revelation 8:2–10:7. Why would Paul speak of "the last trump," if there is no reference point for us to relate it to? The only reference to any sequential sounding of heavenly trumpets available to us is that of Revelation 8:2–10:7.

Nor does the last trump immediately usher in the New Heaven and New Earth, which preterists teach will occur simultaneously with the resurrection. It is the time of the resurrection, which will precede the catching up of the living saints, both of which events will precede God's final judgment upon anti-Christ's kingdom. That judgment will coincide with the second three-and-one-half years of Daniel's seventieth seven. Anti-Christ, under Satan's command, will fight against God's judgment by turning his wrath against Israel. After His judgment of the anti-Christ, the Lord will return to establish His thousand-year reign on the earth.

To understand this it would be helpful to superimpose upon each other the first and second revelations. Both the first and second revelations describe in different manners the indeterminate length of time of great tribulation on the earth under the anti-Christ (as opposed to the three-and-one-half years of tribulation on Israel under the anti-Christ); both reveal the Lord's return for His saints at the end of that tribulation period on the earth which will herald the last half of Daniel's seventieth seven. The second revelation adds the last trumpet which heralds Jesus' gathering of the saints.

Most teachers of end-time prophecy miss this truth because they don't separate these distinct "tribulations." Dispensationalists are looking only for a distinct seven-year tribulation period upon Israel. Preterists aren't looking for anything except, in some cases, worsening conditions in the world before "the Church" eventually takes over. Both have misled believers to think that nothing of any real negative consequence will befall the Body of Christ, which will leave many both spiritually and temporally vulnerable.

SUMMARY OF THE SECOND REVELATION

The First Trumpet: Destruction of the earth through fire;

The Second Trumpet: Destruction of one-third of all life through a possible meteor strike;

The Third Trumpet: Poisoning of the fresh water supplies;

The Fourth Trumpet: Portions of the heavens blotted out, possibly bringing chaotic changes in the climate;

The Fifth Trumpet: Demons and/or fallen angels are released from the bottomless pit to torment men for five months;

The Sixth Trumpet: Worldwide war is unleashed;

The Seventh Trumpet: The mystery of God—the Time of the Gentiles and the proclaiming of the Gospel to the nations—comes to an end. This is the time when the saints are caught up to meet the Lord in the air before His final judgment on anti-Christ's kingdom, after which He comes back to the earth. The period of time that passes from when the seventh angel begins to sound his trumpet and the final blast upon his trumpet is not revealed.

6

THE THIRD REVELATION

The third revelation deals with the great tribulation upon Israel under anti-Christ's persecution, and details God's judgments on anti-Christ's kingdom through His two witnesses. It begins by the Lord telling John to eat the book that reveals His judgments:

REV. 10:8-11:

And the voice that I heard from Heaven spoke to me again, and said, "Go and take the little book that is open in the hand of the angel who stands on the sea and on the earth."

And I went to the angel, and said to him, "Give me the little book."

And he said to me, "Take it, and eat it up, and it will make your stomach upset, but it will be in your mouth sweet as honey."

And I took the little book out of the angel's hand, and ate it up, and it was in my mouth sweet as honey. And as soon as I had eaten it, my stomach was upset.

And he said to me, "You must prophesy again before many peoples, and nations, and languages, and kings."

The little book, which is sweet in the mouth but bitter to the stomach, appears to be the Word of God that John must bring before all the earth through the remainder of the revelations. It is a judgment upon the world for its evil:

"Woe to those who call evil good, and good evil—that put darkness for light, and light for darkness—that put bitter for sweet, and sweet for bitter!" (Isa 5:20)

The prophecy (the sweetness of God's Word) before the nations will convict of sin and speak judgment (bitterness) for turning what is good to evil, and turning what is evil to good.

REV. 11:1-4:

And there was given to me a reed like a rod, and the angel stood, saying, "Rise, and measure the temple of God, and the altar, and those who worship therein. But leave out the court that is outside the temple, and do not measure it, because it is given to the Gentiles.

"And they shall tread underfoot the holy city for forty-two months. And I will give power to My two witnesses, and they shall prophesy a thousand two hundred and sixty days, clothed in sackcloth. These are the two olive trees, and the two candlesticks, standing before the God of the earth."

Which temple is this? If John wrote prior to A.D. 70, it may reasonably be assumed that this is Zerubbabel's temple which was destroyed then. If he wrote later than that, then this is either a new temple to be built in Jerusalem before the Lord returns, or it is the Millennial Temple. The reason for measuring the temple is not stated, but the measuring recalls the vision of Ezekiel in which a heavenly being measures the Millennial Temple (Eze 40:1–42:20).

The court outside the temple is for the Gentiles. Every temple had an outer court for the Gentiles who came to worship the true God, as will the Millennial Temple (Eze 40:31).

Does this mean that the Gentiles will tread underfoot a new temple for three-and-one-half years?

No. Whichever temple this is, whether the one destroyed in A.D. 70 or the Millennial Temple, it doesn't necessarily follow that it will be trod underfoot by the Gentiles.

The Greek texts were void of paragraphs and punctuation. The manner in which the verse is structured in English gives the impression that the Gentiles in the outer court are the same as those who tread underfoot the holy city. However, we are told that the Gentiles will tread upon the city (not a temple) for three-and-one-half years.

Why do I not see this as a temple to be constructed in Israel before the Lord returns? Because Zionist Israel is anti-Christ. It is an enemy of God because it rejects His Son and persecutes His saints. There is no way God would honor with His presence anything built by an apostate Judaism. It will not be until the Lord returns in the clouds and those (the Jews) who pierced Him see Him, that they will believe and be converted. And there is no way Christian Jews led by God's Spirit would rebuild the temple; they know that they are the temple of God. They also know that during this age there is no legitimacy to a temple; Christ died once for all, there is no more sacrifice for sin (Heb 10:10-18). Until the Time of the Gentiles comes to an end, there will be no temple in Jerusalem sanctioned by God.

But again, it is possible that something the Jews might call a temple may be built, but it will not be a legitimate temple to house the presence of Yahweh. More likely, however, the measuring of the temple is parenthetical, and the Gentiles treading underfoot the city belongs as a lead-in to verse three:

> And they shall tread underfoot the holy city for forty-two months. And I will give power to My two witnesses, and they shall prophesy a thousand two hundred and sixty days, clothed in sackcloth.

The statement that the Gentiles will tread underfoot the holy city for forty-two months, during which the two witnesses will prophesy, means that this will be during the second half of Daniel's seventieth seven; the two witnesses did not appear during the siege of A.D. 70.

While the Gentiles are treading underfoot the holy city, Jerusalem (not a temple), God's two witnesses will come to prophesy during that same period of time. They are described as the two olive trees and the two candlesticks standing before the God of the earth. These are first seen in the Book of Zechariah:

> And the angel that spoke with me came again, and awakened me as a man who is wakened out of his sleep, and said to me, "What do you see?"
>
> And I said, "I have seen, and look! A candlestick all of gold, with a bowl on top of it, and its seven lamps on it, and seven pipes to the seven lamps, which are on the top of it, and two olive trees by it, one on the right side of the bowl, and the other on the its left side."
>
> So I answered and spoke to the angel who spoke with me, saying, "What are these, my lord?"

Then the angel who spoke with me answered and said to me, "Do you not know what these are?"

And I said, "No, my lord."

Then he answered and spoke to me, saying, "This is the word of YHWH to Zerubbabel, saying, 'Not by might, nor by power, but by My Spirit,' says YHWH of Hosts."....

Then I answered and said to him, "What are these two olive trees on the right side of the candlestick and on its left side?"

And I answered again, and said to him, "What are these two olive branches which through the two golden pipes empty the golden oil out of themselves?"

And he answered me and said, "Do you not know what these are?"

And I said, "No, my lord."

Then he said, "These are the two anointed ones who stand by YHWH of the whole earth." (Zec 4:1-14)

The olive tree represents Israel. There is much speculation about who these men are. We know from Scripture that there are two men who did not taste death, but were taken to Heaven alive: Enoch and Elijah. Jesus said that Elijah would come, and also that he had come in the person of John the Baptist. Not that Elijah was reincarnated, but that John the Baptist came in the spirit of Elijah proclaiming the coming of the Lord. The true Elijah will come again prior to the Lord's return to the earth.

Zechariah wrote his prophecy around the middle of the sixth century B.C. Elijah was already in Heaven, having been taken sometime during the ninth century B.C. Enoch, of course, had been taken many centuries earlier (Ge 5:24). These two are most likely the olive trees that Zechariah saw standing beside YHWH.

These verses indicate that God is now dealing with Israel after the Time of the Gentiles has come to an end with the resurrection and catching up of the saints to be with the Lord.

11:5:

"And if any man will hurt them, fire proceeds out of their mouth and devours their enemies. And if any man will hurt them he must be killed in this manner."

Recall Zechariah 4:6, cited above: "Not by might, nor by power, but by My Spirit." This is how the two witnesses will destroy God's enemies. This is not literal fire, but the power of God's Word. Fire is associated with judgment. Believers are baptized with water and with God's Spirit; the ungodly are baptized with fire (Lk 3:16-17). Those who oppose these two witnesses will be baptized with fire by the witnesses' words, dying in the same manner Ananias and Saphira were slain (Ac 5:1-10).

11:6-8:

"These have power to shut the heavens so that it does not rain in the days of their prophecy, and have power over waters to turn them to blood, and to strike the earth with all plagues as often as they will.

"And when they shall have finished their testimony, the beast that ascends out of the abyss shall make war against them, and shall overcome them, and kill them. And their dead bodies shall lie in the street of the great city, which spiritually is called 'Sodom' and 'Egypt,' where also our Lord was crucified.

After three-and-one-half years the two witnesses will be put to death by Apollyon, perhaps through some human agency. Elijah and Enoch will eventually taste of death.

The great city is Jerusalem. The reason it is spiritually called Sodom and Egypt is because it has been unfaithful to God who had chosen to place His temple and His presence there. It is where Jesus was crucified.

11:9-10:

"And those of the people and tribes and languages and nations will see their dead bodies three-and-a-half days, and will not allow their dead bodies to be put in graves. And they who dwell on the earth will rejoice over them and make merry, and will send gifts to one another because these two prophets tormented those who dwelt on the earth."

When this prophecy was written, it was impossible for the nations to see what would transpire in Jerusalem. Even if the news of it went out, it would have taken weeks and even months to reach some parts of the world. It is only with the increase in knowledge that has brought mass communications and satellite television coverage that such a scenario is even possible.

The people will rejoice because the plagues brought by the two witnesses will be ended. Or so they will think.

11:11:

And after three-and-a-half days the spirit of life from God entered into them, and they stood on their feet, and great fear fell on those who saw them. And they heard a loud voice from Heaven saying to them, "Come up here!" And they ascended up to Heaven in a cloud, and their enemies saw them.

Rising from the dead after three-and-a-half days must convince the people that God is at work. Their bodies would have begun decomposing, proving them to be dead.

That these men could be killed means that they had never died previously. That they had stood before the throne of God in Heaven means that they had been taken to Heaven bodily without seeing death. Thus, the idea that these two are Enoch and Elijah is all the more strengthened.

11:13-14:

And the same hour there was a great earthquake, and the tenth part of the city fell, and in the earthquake seven thousand men were slain, and the remnant were frightened and gave glory to the God of Heaven.

The second woe is past, and, look! The third woe comes quickly!

One tenth of Jerusalem will be leveled by this earthquake, killing seven thousand. This will cause the remnant to give glory to God. Whether or not this means they had a life-changing repentance is not stated. We know that even God's enemies have given Him glory when they could not stand before Him (1Sa 6:5).

Next, we are told of the Lord's return to the earth to rule over the nations.

11:15:

And the seventh angel sounded, and there were great voices in Heaven, saying, "The kingdoms of this world have become the kingdoms of our Lord, and of His Christ; and He shall reign forever and ever!"

Again the seventh angel sounds. At the first blast of the seventh trumpet the Lord appears to gather His saints to Heaven. At the second blast of the seventh trumpet the Lord returns to the earth with His saints, and will establish His one-thousand year (millennial) reign over all the nations.

The significance of the seventh, or last, trump is paralleled in Joshua 6:16:

And it came to pass at the seventh time, when the priests blew with the trumpets, Joshua said to the people, "Shout! for YHWH has given you the city!"

The seventh trumpet was the end of Israel's siege against Jericho, which allowed them to inherit the Promised Land. Likewise, the seventh, or last, trumpet will herald God's siege against the anti-Christ's kingdom, and will make the way open for the saints to inherit the earth.

Confusion has abounded among "prophecy experts" because they think that the "last trump" is one blast of the seventh trumpet when, in truth, there are two blasts of the seventh trumpet. It's still the same trumpet, sounded twice.

When the seventh angel **begins to sound**, the resurrection will occur (Rv 10:7). This same angel sounds again when the Lord comes to the earth (Rv 11:15). A period of time (the three-and-one-half years of Daniel's seventieth seven) will pass between the two blasts of the last trumpet. This time period will see the last woe of destruction upon anti-Christ's kingdom.

11:16-18:
And the twenty-four elders who sat before God on their thrones, fell on their faces and worshipped God, saying, "We give You thanks, O Lord God Almighty, who is, and was, and is to come, because You have taken to Yourself Your great power, and have reigned! And the nations were angry, and Your wrath has come, and the time of the dead that they should be judged, and that You should give rewards to Your servants the prophets, and to the saints, and those who fear Your name, small and great, and should destroy those who destroy the earth!"

This is the time for judging the dead in Christ who will be given rewards. The rest of the dead will be judged in the second resurrection which will come after the Millennium (Rv 20:5). These verses address the reward of judging and ruling the nations during the Millennium, given to the saints.

11:19:
And the temple of God was opened in Heaven, and there was seen in His temple the Ark of His Covenant, and there were lightning, and voices, and thunder, and an earthquake, and great hail.

Again, the lightning, voices, and thunder represent the power of God in judgment. The Ark of the Covenant is in the temple in Heaven. This is another reason why there can be no legitimate temple built before the Lord returns. Every earthly Jewish temple must have the Ark of the Covenant under the mercy seat. The Ark was never lost; it was taken to Heaven—when, we don't know. Jeremiah indicates that the Ark will never again be seen:

"And it shall come to pass, when you are multiplied and increased in the land in those days," says YHWH, they will no longer say, 'The Ark of the Covenant of YHWH,' nor shall it come to mind. Neither shall they remember it; neither shall they visit it; neither shall that be done anymore.

"At that time they shall call Jerusalem the throne of YHWH, and all the nations shall be gathered to it, to the name of YHWH, to Jerusalem. Neither shall they walk anymore after the imagination of their evil heart."(Jer 3:16-17)

The context is obviously the Millennial Age, so the Millennial Temple will not contain the Ark of the Covenant. Because the Lord Himself will be present, there will be no need for the Ark which bore within the symbols of the Exodus.

Some insist that the Ark in this verse is the original Ark in the heavenly temple which was the pattern for the Ark in Israel's tabernacle and temple. But there are no Scriptures that say this. When God gave Moses the pattern for the tabernacle in the wilderness, and David the pattern for the temple in Jerusalem, He merely told them to be sure to make everything after the pattern He had given them. He didn't say they were exact duplicates of what was in Heaven.

The idea that the tabernacle and temple in Jerusalem are fashioned after the temple in Heaven is erroneously gleaned from Hebrews 8:1-5:

Now of the things which we have spoken this is the sum: We have such a high priest who sits on the right hand of the throne of the Majesty in Heaven—a minister of the sanctuary and of the true tabernacle that the Lord pitched, and not man.

For every high priest is ordained to offer gifts and sacrifices. Therefore it is necessary that this man also has something to offer. For if He were on earth He would not be a priest, seeing that there are priests who offer gifts according to the Law—who serve as an example and shadow of heavenly things, as Moses was admonished by God when he was about to make the tabernacle. For He says, "See that you make all things according to the pattern shown to you on the mountain."

The wilderness tabernacle was a shadow of heavenly things, not in the sense that it was an exact copy of the temple in Heaven, but that it and all it contained were shadows and types of Christ Himself and His work of atonement. Thus, God gave Moses patterns to follow which bespoke the reality of salvation through Israel's Messiah. The Ark of the Covenant had over it the mercy seat which represented Christ Jesus specifically, because the blood of the sacrifice was sprinkled on it before YHWH. Within the Ark were the tablets of commandments, Aaron's rod and a jar of manna.

There is only one Ark of the Covenant God made with Israel. That covenant was replaced by the New Covenant in Christ, so the Ark is no longer of use. Thus, the Ark was taken to Heaven so that Israel could no longer have atonement for their sins apart from their Messiah whom they crucified. And without the Ark of the Covenant, there can be no temple.

SUMMARY OF THE THIRD REVELATION

The events of the third revelation transpire between the sixth and the seventh trumpets. This appears to be an interlude in time between the resurrection and the Lord returning with His saints—the time when the seventh angel sounds the last trumpet for the first time (vs. 10:7) and when he sounds the last trumpet the second time (vs. 11:15). The temple seen in 11:1 is the Millennial Temple, not a temple for the present age. The outer court is for the Gentiles, because natural Israel will again be the focal point of God's redemption during the Millennium for all who enter into it as mortal men, and who are born during the thousand years.

- The nations will tread upon Jerusalem for three-and-one-half years;
- During that three-and-one-half years, two witnesses (most likely Elijah and Enoch) will appear to torment anti-Christ's kingdom;
- When they have finished their testimony they will be put to death by anti-Christ;
- After three-and-a-half days they will be raised to life, and will be taken up to Heaven;
- A great earthquake will destroy one-tenth of the city of Jerusalem;
- The seventh angel again sounds the trumpet, heralding the Lord coming to set foot on the earth;
- The judgment of the dead takes place, and the saints are about to receive their reward;
- John sees the temple in Heaven opened, and the Ark of the Covenant revealed.

7

THE FOURTH REVELATION

The events that follow establish in different words and images the same events that transpire after the latter part of the first three revelations. They specifically address the second half of Daniel's seventieth seven, and detail the fate of the holy city and Israel during those three-and-one-half years. The Body of Christ—Jews and Gentiles—will have been caught up with the resurrected saints. Now comes the second half of Daniel's seventieth seven—the time of great tribulation upon Israel after she has seen the Lord receive His saints. They will then turn to Him, but by sight—not by faith—thus they are not able to be in the first resurrection.

REV. 12:1-2:

And there appeared a great wonder in Heaven: a woman clothed with the sun, and the moon under her feet, and on her head a crown of twelve stars. And being with child she cried out, travailing in birth and in pain to be delivered.

This is not the Madonna-and-child as the Roman Catholic Church interprets this sign. The woman clothed with the sun, and with the moon under her feet, and wearing a crown of twelve stars is Israel. The sun represents Jacob, the moon, Rachel, and the twelve stars the twelve tribes of Israel. This symbolism is confirmed in Genesis 37:5-11:

And he [Joseph] dreamed still another dream, and told it to his brothers, and said, "Look! I have dreamed another dream and, look, the sun and the moon and the eleven stars made obeisance to me!"

And he told it to his father, and to his brothers. And his father rebuked him, and said to him, "What is this dream that you have dreamed? Shall I and your mother and your brothers indeed come to bow down ourselves to you to the earth?"

And his brothers envied him, but his father observed the saying.

Jacob knew prophetically what the sun, moon and stars represented. Together they would come to comprise the woman—the nation of Israel that came from his twelve sons. During the Millennium, Israel will be reborn as a nation that is faithful to its God. The present Zionist state is merely the beginning of the birth pangs. (Many within it are not true Jews because their fathers are not true Jews. Today, Jewishness is reckoned according to one's mothers' lineage according to Halacha, Jewish law based on the Tanach, the Talmud and Rabbinic tradition.) There is much travail to come.

12:3:

And there appeared another wonder in Heaven, and look! A great red dragon, having seven heads and ten horns, and seven crowns on his heads.

The dragon is Satan (12:9). The seven heads represent seven of his kingdoms that have conquered Israel and/or Judah. The ten horns are ten successive kings over one of those kingdoms (cf., Da 10:20). The seven crowns are diadems, representative of authority, spiritual or temporal.

12:4-5:

And his tail drew the third part of the stars of Heaven, and cast them to the earth. And the dragon stood before the woman who was ready to be delivered in order to devour her child as soon as it was born. And she brought forth a man child who was to rule all nations with a rod of iron, and her child was caught up to God, and to His throne.

Satan and his angels (one-third of the stars) are cast out of Heaven to the earth, and in great fury he immediately seeks to destroy the man child.

The man child is not Jesus; he is the company of 144,000 future Israelites who are sealed with the name of God in their foreheads. This is borne out in 14:1-5. After a time, they will be taken up to Heaven in the same manner as the saints in the resurrection.

12:6:

And the woman fled into the wilderness where she has a place prepared by God so that they should feed her there a thousand two hundred and sixty days.

After the man child is caught up to God, Israel flees into the wilderness to a place God has prepared to protect her for three-and-one-half years. This three-and-one-half years is the second half of Daniel's seventieth seven—the same time period in which Jerusalem is trod underfoot by the Gentiles (the unbelieving nations), and the two prophets are bringing God's judgments on the world (Rv 11:2-3).

12:7-9:

And there was war in Heaven. Michael and his angels fought against the dragon. And the dragon fought, and his angels, and did not prevail; neither was their place found any more in Heaven.

And the great dragon was cast out—that old serpent, called "the Devil," and "Satan," who deceives the whole world; he was cast out into the earth, and his angels were cast out with him.

Verses 7 through 16 iterate in more detail verses 3 through 6. Until this time Satan will have access to Heaven as the accuser of the brethren. But the resurrection and the final stages of God's judgment leave no room for Satan to stand as the accuser any longer. Therefore, his purpose is ended, and he is cast out along with his angelic followers.

12:10-12:

And I heard a loud voice saying in Heaven, "Now has come salvation, and strength, and the Kingdom of our God, and the power of His Christ, for the accuser of our brethren is cast down, who accused them before our God day and night! And they overcame him by the blood of the Lamb, and by the word of their testimony, and they loved not their lives unto the death!

"Therefore, rejoice you heavens, and you who dwell in them! Woe to the inhabitants of the earth and of the sea! For the Devil has come down to you, having great wrath because he knows that he has but a short time!"

Satan can no longer accuse the brethren. Therefore salvation, strength, the Kingdom of God and the power of Christ are about to prevail on the earth. The true believers alive at that time will have overcome Satan by the blood of Christ, which cleanses from all sin, and they will have given up their lives for their testimony. While the heavens will rejoice, the earth will be in greater distress because Satan has been cast down with great anger; he knows the time of his end is near.

12:13-14:

And when the dragon saw that he was cast to the earth he persecuted the woman who brought forth the man child. And two wings of a great eagle were given to the woman so that she might fly into the wilderness, into her place, where she is nourished for a time, and times, and half a time, from the face of the serpent.

This is an iteration of Israel fleeing into the wilderness for three-and-one-half years. These verses may be aligned with verses 7-9. The wings of a great eagle symbolize swiftness.

12:15-17:

And the serpent cast out of his mouth water as a flood after the woman so that he might cause her to be carried away by the flood. And the earth helped the woman, and the earth opened her mouth and swallowed up the flood that the dragon cast out of his mouth.

And the dragon was angry with the woman and went to make war with the remnant of her seed who keep the commandments of God, and have the testimony of Jesus Christ.

What this means is open to speculation. It's possible that Satan's armies, sent to destroy fleeing Israel, are destroyed by natural catastrophes arranged by God just as Pharaoh's army was swallowed up by the sea after the Israelites had crossed safely. Satan, seeing that he is thwarted in his attempt to destroy Israel, will seek to destroy the remnant of Israelite believers in Christ throughout the nations. Israel will not have been fully gathered into the land as yet, and there will be many Israelite believers in Christ who are among the nations. They will begin to experience the wrath of Satan through persecution.

SUMMARY OF THE FOURTH REVELATION

The man child—the 144,000 Israelites—will be sealed in their foreheads near the start of the three-and-one-half-year period during which the Lord will be dealing with Israel. During that time, Israel will be protected in the wilderness. At some point, the 144,000 will be caught up to Heaven.

Israel will flee into the wilderness and anti-Christ will go forth to make war against the remaining Israelites who are living among the nations and who believe in Jesus.

8

THE FIFTH REVELATION

This revelation takes us back to the rise of anti-Christ and the false prophet, revealing in greater detail their functions under the power of Satan. We must keep in mind all the previous elements to the prior revelations, particularly the opened six seals and the seven trumpets.

REV. 13:1-2:

And I stood on the sand of the sea and saw a beast rise up out of the sea, having seven heads and ten horns, and on his horns ten crowns, and on his heads the name of blasphemy. And the beast that I saw was like a leopard, and his feet were like the feet of a bear, and his mouth like the mouth of a lion. And the dragon gave him his power, and his seat, and great authority.

This beast represents the anti-Christ kingdom embodied in the seven nations that have conquered, or will conquer, Israel/Judah—from Egypt to the final, anti-Christ kingdom. The ten horns are ten kings (emperors) of the sixth kingdom, Rome, but the beast appears as a leopard, which represents Greece, with the feet of a bear (Medo-Persia), and the mouth of a lion (Babylonia) (cf., Da 7:1-8). This will be seen in more detail as we progress. The ten crowns likely represent the demonic rulers over those ten kings.

Here we must take a lengthy diversion from the Revelation narrative to see the symbolism as revealed to Daniel:

In the first year of Belshazzar king of Babylon, Daniel had a dream and visions of his head on his bed. Then he wrote the dream, and told the sum of the matters.

Daniel spoke and said, "I saw in my vision by night, and, look! The four winds of the heavens strove upon the great sea [the Mediterranean Sea]. And four great beasts came up from the sea, different from one another.

"The first was like a lion, and had eagle's wings. I looked till its wings were plucked, and it was lifted up from the earth, and made stand on its feet like a man, and a man's heart was given to it.

"And look! Another beast, a second, like a bear, and it raised itself on one side, and it had three ribs in its mouth between its teeth. And they said this to it: "Arise, devour much flesh!"

"After this I saw, and look! Another, like a leopard, which had on its back four wings of a fowl; the beast also had four heads, and dominion was given to it.

"After this I saw in the night visions, and look! A fourth beast, dreadful and terrible, and exceedingly strong. And it had great iron teeth. It devoured and broke in pieces, and stamped the residue with its feet. And it was different from all the beasts that were before it, and it had ten horns.

"I considered the horns, and, look! There came up among them another little horn before whom there were three of the first horns plucked up by the roots. And look! In this horn were eyes like the eyes of man, and a mouth speaking great things." (Da 7:1-8)

Daniel sees only four heads, not seven, yet the entire vision is otherwise consistent with the revelation given to John of seven heads and ten horns. So why the seeming discrepancy?

Daniel was given a vision of the future from his time; John was given the revelation of all seven kingdoms including Babylonia and the two that preceded the Babylonian kingdom in which Daniel lived. The three prior kingdoms to the future four in Daniel's vision, all of which conquered Israel/Judah were Egypt, Assyria and Babylonia (remember, all prophecy revolves around Israel, particularly Jerusalem).

The seven kingdoms that conquer Israel/Judah throughout history, five of which we find in Nebuchadnezzar's dream, are as follows:

- Egypt: Prior to Daniel;
- Assyria: Prior to Daniel;
- Babylonia (the first of five from Nebuchanezzar's dream onward): Head of gold;
- Medo-Persia (the first from Daniel's vision): Chest and arms of silver;
- Greece: Stomach and thighs of brass
- Rome: (Daniel's fourth beast, <u>with ten horns</u>) Legs of iron;
- The last-days kingdom: Feet and toes of iron and clay.

Thus, we see that the next kingdom that came after Babylonia (a lion), was Medo-Persia (a bear), followed by Greece (a leopard), then Rome (different, with teeth of iron). Because of its many conquests and brutality, Rome is always represented by iron. So the feet and toes of iron and clay represent the last-days anti-Christ's kingdom comprised of Rome, which seemingly was wounded to death, but will rise in the last days to be united with the other nations (the clay), which should be the Islamic nations, also formed from the Babylonian kingdom.

It is important to note that only one of the kingdoms, Rome, has all ten horns (Da 7:6-8). The horns are not distributed among the seven heads.

We continue with Daniel's dream:

"I looked till the thrones were cast down and the Ancient of Days sat, whose garment was white as snow, and the hair of His head like pure wool. His throne was like the fiery flame, and His wheels like burning fire.

"A fiery stream issued and came forth from before Him. Thousand thousands ministered to Him, and ten thousand times ten thousand stood before Him. The judgment was set, and the books were opened.

"I looked then because of the voice of the great words which the [eleventh, little] horn spoke. I looked till the beast was slain, and his body destroyed and given to the burning flame.

"As concerning the rest of the beasts, they had their dominion taken away, yet their lives were prolonged for a season and time.

"I saw in the night visions, and, look! One like the Son of Man came with the clouds of the heavens, and came to the Ancient of Days, and they brought Him near before Him.

"And there was given to Him dominion, and glory, and a kingdom, that all people, nations, and languages should serve Him.

His dominion is an everlasting dominion, which shall not pass away, and His kingdom that which shall not be destroyed."

I Daniel was grieved in my spirit in the midst of my body, and the visions of my head troubled me.

I came near to one of those who stood by, and asked him the truth of all this. So he told me, and made me know the interpretation of the things.

"These great beasts, which are four, are four kingdoms, which shall arise out of the earth.

"But the saints of the most High shall take the Kingdom, and possess the Kingdom forever, even for ever and ever."

Then I would know the truth of the fourth beast, which was different from all the others, exceedingly dreadful, whose teeth were of iron and his nails of brass, which devoured, broke in pieces, and stamped the residue with his feet, and of the ten horns that were in his head, and of the other which came up, and before whom three fell—of that horn that had eyes, and a mouth that spoke very great things, whose look was greater than the others.

I looked, and the same [eleventh, little] horn made war with the saints, and prevailed against them until the Ancient of Days came, and judgment was given to the saints of the most High, and the time came that the saints possessed the Kingdom.

Thus he said, "The fourth beast shall be the fourth kingdom on earth, which shall be different from all kingdoms, and shall devour the whole earth, and shall tread it down, and break it in pieces.

"And the ten horns out of this kingdom are ten kings that shall arise: and another shall rise after them. And he will be different from the first, and he will subdue three kings.

"And he will speak great words against the most High, and shall wear out the saints of the most High, and think to change times and laws. And they shall be given into his hand until a time and times and the dividing of time [three-and-one-half years].

"But the judgment shall be set, and they shall take away his dominion, to consume and to destroy it unto the end.

"And the kingdom and dominion, and the greatness of the Kingdom under the whole heavens, shall be given to the people of the saints of the most High, whose Kingdom is an everlasting Kingdom, and all dominions shall serve and obey him." (Da 7:1-27)

Here we address the ten horns on the fourth beast, which are ten emperors of the Roman Empire, and the eleventh to rise among them.

Judea first came under Roman oversight when Pompey arrived in Jerusalem in 63 B.C. and entered the holy of holies. Although he withdrew his army from the Temple Mount and allowed the Jews to retain their authority over it, Judea was for the first time under Roman control.

Expecting to be made emperor on his return to Rome, Pompey found opposition, primarily from Julius Caesar. The two agreed that the empire would be ruled by a triumvirate which would include them along with a third general, Marcus Licinius Crassus. The triumvirate lasted only five years, after which Julius Caesar became sole emperor of Rome when he seized power from the Senate of the Roman Republic in 49 B.C.

The human rulers of the fourth beast (Rome) in Daniel's vision who ruled over Judea and Jerusalem were (including their dates of reigning):

- 1) Pompey (Non-emperor who first gained control of Judea in 63 B.C.)
- 2) Julius Caesar (First Roman emperor, 49 B.C. – 44 B.C.);
- 3) Augustus (January 16, 27 B.C. – August 19, 14 A.D.)
- 4) Tiberius (September 18, 14 – March 16, 37);
- 5) Caligula (March 18, 37 – January 24, 41)
- 6) Claudius (January 25, 41 – October 13, 54)
- 7) Nero (October 13, 54 – June 9, 68)
- 8) Galba (June 9, 68 – January 15, 69)
- 9) Otho (January 15, 69 – April 16, 69)
- 10) Vitellius (April 17, 69 – December 20, 69)
- 11) Vespasian (July 1, 69 – June 24, 79)

Vespasian, the eleventh, followed as Roman Emperor after the short reigns of Galba, Otho and Vitellius, all who died within the year 69, shortly after gaining the throne (they were plucked up by their roots).

That the horns are the spiritual rulers over these emperors, and not the emperors themselves is borne out in Daniel 7:24:

> "And the ten horns out of this [single] kingdom are ten kings that shall arise: and another shall rise after them. And he will be different from the first, and he will subdue three kings."

Vespasian did not subdue the three emperors before him. They all died shortly after attaining their rule. Spiritual authorities cannot die, but they can be subdued, just as the ruler of Persia was subdued to make way for the ruler of Greece (Da 10:20). There are evidently not only spiritual rulers over the nations, but also lesser spiritual rulers over the successive human rulers of the nations. The lesser horn that grew to subdue the three horns prior to him was the spiritual power over Vespasian.

Under Vespasian the temple was destroyed and the sacrifices taken away as the abomination of desolation stood in the holy place. The pagan idols on the Roman standards were placed in the holy of holies by Titus's troops in A.D. 70, and sacrifices were made to them. The Jews were dispersed throughout the nations for the last time, ending the time of Daniel's vision. The Roman emperors that followed had no dealings with the Jews as possessors of Jerusalem, thus they are not germane to scriptural prophecy regarding Israel.

How was Vespasian "different" and "smaller" from the previous Roman emperors? All previous emperors were of the Julio-Claudian Dynasty. Vespasian was the founder of the Flavian Dynasty, a new rulership, initially "smaller" than that of his predecessors.

We have shown that the coming of the Lord is yet future. So because Daniel says the last horn will rule until the Ancient of Days comes, that last horn must be the same spiritual one that ruled Vespasian. Spiritual principalities are attached to the rulers described in biblical prophecy. They are the true rulers or horns over the nations. The last principality to rule will take over where he first left off according to Daniel's seventieth seven. Just as the first half of the seventieth seven took place under the principality ruling over Vespasian's reign, the second half of the seventieth seven will take place under that same principality, although through the reign of the last-days anti-Christ. The Time of the Gentiles to be brought into the Kingdom of God is, again, an interlude within that prophetic history.

13:3-4:

And I saw one of his heads as if it were wounded to death. And his deadly wound was healed, and all the world wondered after the beast. And they worshipped the dragon that gave power to the beast, and they worshipped the beast, saying, "Who is like the beast? Who is able to make war with him?"

The beast represents the anti-Christ kingdom through the ages. The seven heads represent seven nations that have conquered or will conquer Israel/Judah. One nation was destroyed, but will rise again.

I believe this wounded kingdom is Rome which, at this time, is considered dead. When Rome is revived it will be joined in union with the

Muslim nations in order to again attain control over the Middle East (the feet and toes of iron and clay).

If the anti-Christ will be a Muslim, which is most likely, then his initial power will be over the Muslim nations of the Middle East.

13:5:
And there was given to him a mouth speaking great things and blasphemies. And power was given to him to continue forty-two months.

Anti-Christ will have power over Jerusalem for three-and-one-half years. This does not include the time he has dominion over other nations; all prophecies relate primarily to Jerusalem.

During those three-and-one-half years the Jews from Jerusalem will be in the wilderness and anti-Christ will tread Jerusalem underfoot. He will speak great things (Da 7:8), and great blasphemies.

13:6-7:
And he opened his mouth in blasphemy against God, to blaspheme His name, and His tabernacle, and those who dwell in Heaven.

And it was given to him to make war with the saints and to overcome them, and power was given him over all tribes, and languages, and nations.

Anti-Christ blasphemes God, God's heavenly tabernacle (Rv 11:19), and His saints who have been caught up to Heaven. It is at this point that the anti-Christ may gain power over all the nations.

These verses may be overlaid with 12:17. Satan will use the anti-Christ to persecute believers in Jesus—especially Israelite believers. In order to do so, his kingdom will be increased to the entire world for a season.

13:8-10:
And all who dwell on the earth whose names are not written in the Book of Life of the Lamb slain from the foundation of the world will worship him.

If any man has an ear, let him hear: he who leads into captivity shall go into captivity; he who kills with the sword must be killed with the sword. Here is the patience and the faith of the saints.

It is unclear at this point whether the mark of the beast will come before or after the Body of Christ is removed from the earth. As we progress, I believe we will find that it will come afterward. In any case, only those whose names are written in the Lamb's Book of Life will resist worshiping the anti-Christ when the time comes to take his mark. After the resurrection and the catching up of the living saints, those who survive until the Lord returns to the earth will enter the Millennium as mortals. Those who die during the Millennial Age will rise in the second resurrection along with all from previous generations who were not in the first resurrection.

13:11-15:

And I saw another beast coming up out of the earth, and he had two horns like a lamb, and he spoke like a dragon. And he exercises all the power of the first beast before him, and causes the earth and those who dwell in it to worship the first beast whose deadly wound was healed. And he does great wonders, so that he makes fire come down from the heavens onto the earth in the sight of men, and deceives those who dwell on the earth by the means of those miracles that he had power to do in the sight of the beast, saying to those who dwell on the earth that they should make an image to the beast that had the wound by a sword, and lived.

And he had power to give life to the image of the beast so that the image of the beast should both speak, and cause that as many as would not worship the image of the beast should be killed.

The first beast is the anti-Christ kingdom that has one of its heads (one kingdom) wounded and revived. The spiritual principality behind that kingdom is Satan, but as he is over all the kingdoms of the earth, this particular kingdom, represented by the seven earthly kingdoms, is possibly ruled by a lesser spiritual being who will be embodied in the anti-Christ. Or it may be Satan himself, the dragon with seven heads and ten horns in Revelation 12:1-17.

Now comes another beast who exercises the same power of Satan that the anti-Christ exercises. He has two horns like a lamb, but speaks like a dragon. He will appear pious, but will speak the words of Satan to deceive the entire world. Consistency requires that this beast be another kingdom, but with two rulers (the two horns). It remains to be seen, but this kingdom could be a religious kingdom, as it requires everyone to worship the first beast (Satan or his anti-Christ). Might it be the Vatican whose second of two successive popes in the last days may be the false prophet? The Vatican is the only religious nation state on the earth, and it's roots are in the Roman Empire. But, again, it remains to be seen.

The signs and wonders that the false prophet performs will convince the nations that he has power to resist the God of Heaven who has brought great plagues upon them. He will cause the people to make an image of the anti-Christ, which they will be compelled to worship. This is similar to Nebuchadnezzar's command to worship his image. Exactly what form the image will take is not stated, but it will be given the appearance of life. Even today we have seen life-like holograms of famous deceased entertainers projected onto stages to re-enact their concerts. It is not certain that these Scriptures are speaking of holograms, but man's science is accomplishing some startling things today.

13:16-18:

And he causes all, both small and great, rich and poor, free and bond, to receive a mark in their right hand, or in their foreheads, and that no man might buy or sell, except he who had the mark, or the name of the beast, or the number of his name.

Here is wisdom: let him who has understanding count the number of the beast, for it is the number of a man. And his number is six hundred, sixty-six.

The false prophet will require that all men, of every station in life, receive the mark of the anti-Christ in their right hands or in their foreheads as part of their religious duty. It may be that there will be six distinct marks depending on the particular class of person who receives it:

In the right hand: the mark of the beast; the name of the beast; the number of his name;

In the forehead: the mark of the beast; the name of the beast; the number of his name.

One's rank in the anti-Christ's kingdom may determine where one receives the mark, number or name, and which of these three he receives.

The number of anti-Christ will be 666, which is the number of a man. The number six in biblical typology is said to represent man, created just below God, whose number is seven, denoting perfection.

There is no end to the speculation of just what this means,but it will not be revealed until the anti-Christ comes.

There is also much speculation as to what nationality the anti-Christ will be. Some say he will be Jewish because he will be accepted by Israel as the Messiah. But there is no scriptural evidence he will be a messiah figure.

Thinking that Russia will attack Israel, Some say he will be Russian. Again, there is nothing in Scripture to prove this.

Some say he will be the coming king of England, possibly Prince Charles, because England has the last major monarchy in the world, and has been the dominant power of the dispersed Roman Empire.

Those who erroneously believe the United States is Babylon might say the anti-Christ will be the president of the United States.

Others say he will be Syrian, because Syria is Israel's old nemesis from the north.

Still others say he will be Greek, for no apparent reason. That he will be Turkish is another viable hypothesis because Pergamum is said to be where Satan's seat is (Rv 2:13). That is my personal position for reasons stated earlier in this book.

At this point, no one can say for sure. He will be revealed in his time, and only the diligent true believers in Christ will recognize him when he does appear. And only those left on the earth when his image is set up will recognize the mark of the beast. One thing is certain: the mark will not be imposed without a clear demand that those who receive it do so because they worship the image of the beast. There are some who fear that they might inadvertently receive the mark should the government implement some form of personal identification system such as a microchip or national identification card. No one will inadvertently receive the mark of the beast. They will have to make a conscious decision to receive it. They will seek to preserve their lives and choose anti-Christ over the true Christ.

SUMMARY OF THE FIFTH REVELATION

This revelation chronicles in detail the rise of the anti-Christ and the false prophet, and their warfare against the saints of God during the last half of Daniel's seventieth seven.

The beast (anti-Christ) rises to power;

One of his kingdoms that was destroyed comes back to power;

He will have power to conquer Jerusalem for three-and-one-half years;

He blasphemes God and the saints in Heaven;

He persecutes the saints and kills many of them;

The false prophet arises and causes all the earth to worship the anti-Christ;

The false prophet performs signs and wonders to deceive the nations;

The false prophet causes all the nations under his rule to take the mark of the beast;

Those who do not receive his mark will be put to death, or at least will not be able to buy or sell.

9

THE SIXTH REVELATION

The sixth revelation describes in more detail the destruction of Mystery Babylon and the reaping of the earth by Jesus and His angels. It begins with an account of the 144,000 Israelites and describes their holiness and ministry to the Lord.

REV. 14:1-5:

And I saw, and, look! A Lamb stood on Mount Zion, and with Him one hundred forty-four thousand, having His Father's name written in their foreheads.

And I heard a voice from Heaven, like the voice of many waters, and like the voice of a great thunder. And I heard the voice of harpers harping with their harps, and they sang as it were a new song before the throne, and before the four beings and the elders. And no man could learn that song but the hundred and forty-four thousand who were redeemed from the earth.

These are they who were not defiled with women, for they are virgins. These are they who follow the Lamb wherever He goes. These were redeemed from among men, being the first fruits to God and to the Lamb. And there was found no guile in their mouths for they are without fault before the throne of God.

Now we see the identity of the man child birthed by Israel. He is the company of 144,000 Israelites who are sealed with the mark (the name of the Father, Yahweh [Rv 7:1-8]) before God pours out His final judgments upon the anti-Christ's kingdom. At some point they are caught up to God (Rv 12:5) and here they are seen on the heavenly Mount Zion. They have a special place in God's Kingdom.

Detractors who believe these are not necessarily Israelites because "the Church" has replaced Israel say that no one knows which tribes any Israelites belong to. But God knows, and that's all that matters.

Significantly, verse 4 tells us they are the first fruits unto God and to the Lamb. Some might think they must be caught up before the resurrection and the Rapture. After all, how can they be the first fruits if they are caught up after the resurrection and the Rapture? But the timing of this event wherein the 144,000 true Israelites who had been sealed with the Father's name in their foreheads (Rv 7:3) is after the resurrection and the catching up of the living saints at the Lord's next appearance. So again, how can they be the first fruits to God and to the Lamb?

Jesus is the first fruits of the resurrection; these are the first fruits from among the saints of Israel in the last days. There are three different classes of first fruits: 1) Those resurrected with Jesus (Mt 27:50-53) were the first fruits of Israel (the graves were opened with the earthquake, but they certainly didn't rise before Jesus who is the first fruits of all the resurrected); The first fruits from among the saints of the present age—Jews and Gentiles—will be presented to God after the first resurrection. The 144,000 are the first fruits from among the redeemed of Israel at the close of the nation's prophetic history—the last half of Daniel's seventieth seven. They are not resurrected, but translated to immortality.

14:6-7:
And I saw another angel fly in the midst of the heavens, having the everlasting Gospel to proclaim to those who dwell on the earth, and to every nation, and kindred, and language, and people, saying with a loud voice, "Fear God, and give glory to Him, for the hour of His judgment has come! And worship Him who made the heavens, and earth, and the sea, and the fountains of waters!"

This is an angel who goes forth to proclaim to all men the need to repent and give all glory to the true God of Heaven. There will no doubt be many left who will escape having to take the mark of the beast. These will enter into the Millennium as mortal men, women and children. They will be ruled by Christ with a rod of iron, meaning that His righteous decrees will be rigidly enforced. Not everyone who survives the judgment at the end of this age will be enthusiastic about the new government of the Lord. Many of those born during the Millennial Age will resist it.

14:8:

And there followed another angel, saying, "Babylon, that great city, has fallen—has fallen because she made all nations drink of the wine of the wrath of her fornication."

This is the first mention of Babylon in the Book of Revelation, and it is in the context of the very last days. There are those who believe the actual city of Babylon will be rebuilt and become the center of commerce over all the earth. If that were possible, it would require a long and arduous recovery that could take centuries considering the current conditions in Iraq.

However, "Babylon" in this case could mean something else, perhaps even Rome, the city that has committed spiritual fornication by being unfaithful to the Christ she claims to represent. This is much as Jerusalem is called "Sodom" and "Egypt." The Holy Roman Empire which spawned Roman Catholicism has operated in the spirit of Babylon. Alexander Hislop's *The Two Babylons*, though somewhat flawed, demonstrates how the Babylonian mystery religion has lived on through Roman Catholicism.

Babylon had its origins in the city of Babel built by Nimrod, the son of Cush. Although Scripture does not specifically say so, Babel is considered the first great rebellion against God after the Flood, and it is from there that the ancient mystery religion of Babylon was formed. The similarities between Babylon's mystery religion and those of Egypt, Assyria, Medo-Persia, Greece and Rome lend credence to this understanding. They may be summed up in the term "Mystery Babylon," which is named in future chapters.

14:9-12:

And the third angel followed them, saying with a loud voice, "If any man worships the beast and his image, and receives his mark in his forehead or in his hand, the same shall drink of the wine of God's wrath which is poured out without mixture into the cup of His indignation! And he shall be tormented with fire and brimstone in the presence of the holy angels, and in the presence of the Lamb, and the smoke of their torment ascends up forever and ever, and those who worship the beast and his image, and whoever receives the mark of his name, have no rest day or night!

"Here is the patience of the saints; here are those who keep the commandments of God, and the faith of Jesus!"

This angel sounds a warning after the one proclaiming the Gospel calls all men to repent. Therefore it will take place at the time the decree goes forth for men to take the mark. Before they take the mark they will be warned not to do so. There will be a special, terrible torment for those who take the mark of the beast. They are forewarned; there will be no excuse.

14:13:
And I heard a voice from Heaven saying to me, "Write, 'Blessed are the dead who die in the Lord from henceforth,' says the Spirit, 'yes, so that they may rest from their labors. And their works follow them.'"

Just as those who receive the mark of the beast will receive a special punishment, those who die in Christ rather than take the mark will receive a special reward.

14:14-16:
And I saw, and, look! A white cloud, and on the cloud sat one like the Son of Man, having on His head a golden crown, and in His hand a sharp sickle.

And another angel came out of the temple, crying with a loud voice to Him who sat on the cloud, "Thrust in Your sickle, and reap, for the time has come for You to reap. For the harvest of the earth is ripe."

And He who sat on the cloud thrust His sickle into the earth, and the earth was reaped.

On the white cloud sits Jesus who is told by an angel to thrust in His sickle and reap the earth. To reap the earth means to take out of it the good produce. This is the final separation at the end of this age. The context of these verses, which is after the 144,000 are caught up to Heaven, is good reason to believe that the mark of the beast will be instituted after the resurrection and catching up of the saints at the end of the present age, but before Daniel's seventieth seven begins.

This is the event to which the Lord alluded in His parable of the wheat and tares as recorded in Matthew 13:24-30:

He put forth another parable to them, saying, "The Kingdom of Heaven is likened to a man who sowed good seed in his field. But while men slept, his enemy came and sowed weeds among the wheat, and went his way. But when the blade sprang up and brought forth fruit, then the weeds appeared also. So the servants of the householder came and said to him, 'Sir, did you not sow good seed in your field? From where then has it weeds?'

"He said to them, 'An enemy has done this.'

"The servants said to him, 'Do you wish, then, that we go and gather them up?'

"But he said, 'No lest while you gather up the weeds, you root up also the wheat with them. Let both grow together until the harvest, and at harvest time I will say to the reapers, "Gather together first the weeds, and bind them in bundles to burn them, but gather the wheat into my barn."'"

14:17-20:

And another angel came out of the temple that is in Heaven, he also having a sharp sickle.

And out from the altar came another angel who had power over fire, and he cried out with a loud cry to him who had the sharp sickle, saying, "Thrust in your sharp sickle, and gather the clusters of the vine of the earth, for her grapes are fully ripe."

And the angel thrust his sickle into the earth and gathered the vine of the earth, and cast it into the great winepress of the wrath of God.

And the winepress was trodden outside the city, and blood came out of the winepress, even up to the horse bridles, by the distance of a thousand, six hundred stadia.

Jesus receives His saints; an angel takes the ungodly for destruction. Here we see the judgment of those who took the mark of the beast. The vine of the earth is of no value in contrast to the fruit of the vine taken up by Jesus. The vine, along with its bad fruit, will be thrown into the winepress, which represents destruction.

That the winepress will be trodden outside the city indicates a final battle between anti-Christ's army and Jesus when He returns to set foot on the earth. The destruction of life will be so great that blood will be deep over the earth. Sixteen hundred stadia equal approximately one hundred eighty miles (one Roman stadium was equal to about 600 feet). How wide the swath of blood will be is not stated. The Valley of Armageddon varies in width from 14 to 20 miles, but it is only about 35 miles in length.

Whether this is literal or merely a metaphor for great bloodshed cannot be stated. It seems like an awful lot of blood to be about five feet deep over a distance of almost two hundred miles. But with God, anything is possible.

SUMMARY OF THE SIXTH REVELATION

- The first fruits of the redeemed from Israel, the 144,000 are seen in Heaven with a special ministry to Jesus Christ;
- Three angels fly through the heavens: the first with the Gospel, the second proclaiming the fall of Babylon, the third warning against taking the mark of the beast. (This demonstrates that the mark will not be received inadvertently; men will be given a warning, and will make an informed decision.);
- The mark of the beast is instituted;
- Those who resist the mark of the beast and are put to death will receive a special blessing;
- The Lord reaps the earth and receives His saints who are alive at that time;
- The angel of God gathers the ungodly and destroys them in the winepress of God. This indicates the physical death of God's enemies.

The evidence suggests that the mark of the beast will be instituted during the last three-and-one-half years of the anti-Christ's reign. The nations that enter into the Millennium will consist of those who did not receive the mark of the beast, but were not saved through faith in Jesus Christ

That there will be people left alive indicates that the mark of the beast will not be fully applied before anti-Christ is destroyed. All who take the mark will be destroyed. Those who are martyred for their testimony of Jesus will be with Him. Those left will have missed the opportunity to believe by faith; they must enter into the Millennial Age through obedience to the reigning King, Jesus.

10

THE SEVENTH REVELATION

The seventh revelation Jesus conveys to John takes place toward the end of the present age. It leads through the last of the tribulation upon Israel into the glorious culmination of history with the Lord's conquering of the nations.

REV. 15:1-4:

And I saw another sign in Heaven, great and marvelous: seven angels having the seven last plagues, for in them is filled up the wrath of God.

And I saw as it were a sea of glass mingled with fire. And those who had gotten the victory over the beast, and over his image, and over his mark, and over the number of his name, stand on the sea of glass, having the harps of God. And they sing the song of Moses the servant of God, and the song of the Lamb, saying, "Great and marvelous are Your works, Lord God Almighty; just and true are Your ways, You King of saints. Who shall not fear You, O Lord, and glorify Your name? For You only are holy, for all nations shall come and worship before You, for Your judgments are revealed."

The seven last plagues are reserved for the anti-Christ and his kingdom after the saved are received into Heaven. Those seen here are the Israelites

290 The Day of Yahweh
who have the testimony of Jesus (Rv 12:17) and resist the anti-Christ's mark, refusing to worship his image. They are not the 144,000 caught up previously, but they stand on the crystal sea, singing the song of Moses and the song of the Lamb, indicating that they are Israelites with faith in Jesus.

15:5-6:
And after that I saw, and, look! The temple of the tabernacle of the testimony in Heaven was opened, and the seven messengers came out of the temple, having the seven plagues, clothed in pure and white linen, and having their chests wrapped with golden belts.

As revealed in Rv 21:9–22:9, these are redeemed men:

And I, John, saw these things, and heard them. And when I had heard and seen, I fell down to worship before the feet of the messenger who showed me these things.

Then he said to me, "See that you not do it, for I am your fellow servant, and of your brethren the prophets, and of those who keep the sayings of this book. Worship God."

They are from among Israel's prophets, clothed in pure, white linen, which is the clothing of the saints. Here, the term *angelos* should be translated as messengers, rather than angels in order to distinguish between the two.

15:7-8:
And one of the four creatures gave to the seven messengers seven golden vials full of the wrath of God who lives forever and ever.

And the temple was filled with smoke from the glory of God, and from His power, and no man was able to enter into the temple till the seven plagues of the seven messengers were discharged.

The temple in Heaven is filled with the glory of God, so much so that even the redeemed cannot enter it until after the seven last judgments from God are dispensed upon anti-Christ's kingdom.

REV. 16:1:
And I heard a great voice out of the temple saying to the seven messengers, "Go your ways, and pour out the vials of the wrath of God upon the earth."

The voice must be the voice of God or an angel because no man is able to enter the temple at this point. The following judgments take place after the mark of the beast is instituted in the latter part of anti-Christ's reign. These judgments occur during and/or after the three-and-one-half years.

16:2-12:

And the first went and poured out his vial upon the earth, and there fell an evil and grievous sore on the men who had the mark of the beast, and on those who worshipped his image.

And the second messenger poured out his vial upon the sea, and it became like the blood of a dead man, and every living soul died in the sea.

And the third messenger poured out his vial on the rivers and fountains of waters, and they became blood.

And I heard the messenger of the waters say, "You are righteous, O Lord, who are, and was, and shall be, because You have judged thus. For they have shed the blood of saints and prophets, and You have given them blood to drink, for they are worthy."

And I heard another out of the altar say, "Even so, Lord God Almighty, true and righteous are Your judgments."

And the fourth messenger poured out his vial upon the sun, and power was given to him to scorch men with fire. And men were scorched with great heat, and blasphemed the name of God who has power over these plagues. And they did not repent to give Him glory.

And the fifth messenger poured out his vial upon the seat of the beast, and his kingdom was full of darkness. And they gnawed their tongues for pain, and blasphemed the God of Heaven because of their pains and their sores, and did not repent of their deeds.

And the sixth messenger poured out his vial upon the great river Euphrates, and its water was dried up so that the way of the kings of the east might be prepared.

"The way of the kings of the east" suggests that Asian nations, possibly China, will become involved in the anti-Christ's kingdom at some point. But it may be that the Asian nations will eventually withstand him, though this is not clearly stated.

Up to this point in this seventh revelation we see the judgments poured upon the anti-Christ and his kingdom. We then leap in time to the Lord's actual return to set foot on the earth.

16:13-14:

And I saw three unclean spirits like frogs come out of the mouth of the dragon, and out of the mouth of the beast, and out of the mouth of the false prophet. For they are the spirits of devils, working miracles, that go forth to the kings of the earth and of the whole world, to gather them to the battle of that great day of God Almighty.

This is the battle of Armageddon (Rv 16:16) which will lead to the Lord's return to set foot on the earth. The battle is not anti-Christ coming against Israel, but his gathering the nations to fight against the Lord when He returns with His saints and angels. The Jews had already been driven from Jerusalem for three-and-one-half years. Now, God is going to deliver the city back into the hands of Israel for the Millennial Kingdom.

The nations will have seen the Lord take His people out of the earth; they will have experienced His wrath; they will know He is coming back. Their only course of action, after having taken the mark of the beast, is to stand with the anti-Christ in the hope that, somehow, they can win against the Lord, perhaps trusting in man's superior technology at the end of this age.

16:15:

"Look! I come as a thief! Blessed is he who watches, and keeps his garments, lest he walk naked, and they see his shame."

Here the term, "I come as a thief," refers to the Second Coming of Christ to the earth. The term also applies to His coming to take His people with Him to Heaven previously. He warns those who believe after seeing Him come for His saints to keep themselves from sin.

16:16-21:

And he gathered them together into a place called in the Hebrew language "Armageddon."

And the seventh messenger poured out his vial into the air, and there came a great voice out of the temple of Heaven—from the throne—saying, "It is done."

And there were voices, and thunder, and lightning, and there was a great earthquake, such as was not since men were on the earth—so mighty an earthquake, and so great. And the great city was divided into three parts, and the cities of the nations fell, and great Babylon came in remembrance before God, to give to her the cup of the wine of the fierceness of His wrath.

And every island fled away, and the mountains were not found.

And there fell upon men a great hail out of the heavens, every stone about the weight of a talent. And men blasphemed God because of the plague of the hail, for its plague was exceedingly great.

The seventh vial reveals the battle of Armageddon and the worldwide calamities that will accompany it. The earthquake is not confined to Jerusalem; it will be worldwide and will cause such destruction that man's cities and all his technology will be destroyed. The city called "Babylon" will be divided into three parts, suggesting that a great chasm will split the city. These events will pave the way for the millennial reign of Christ, during which man's technology will not be available to him. Society in the Millennium will be, for lack of a better term, primitive by man's standards.

There is no mention of how long a time period passes as these events transpire.

SUMMARY OF THE SEVENTH REVELATION

This revelation begins with the original plagues upon the nations under anti-Christ then moves to deal with the destruction upon anti-Christ's kingdom after the saints have been removed from the earth.

- The redeemed out of Israel stand on the crystal sea before the throne of God;

- Seven redeemed men come out of the heavenly temple having the seven last plagues;

- These men are given seven golden vials containing the wrath of God;

- The first vial brings sores upon those who took the mark of the beast;

- The second vial turns the sea into blood, just as Moses did to the Nile River. Whether this is the Mediterranean Sea, which Scripture usually calls "the sea," or "the great sea," or if it means all the seas of the world is not clear. It is possibly confined to the Mediterranean Sea because it is this sea adjacent to Israel. In any case, this is a terrible judgment because it destroys all life in the sea;

- The third vial turns the fresh waters into blood. These plagues are seen to be further judgments upon the waters which, previously, had been only one-third polluted by similar plagues;

- The fourth vial causes the sun to become unbearably hot. This is just the opposite of it previously being darkened by one-third;

- The fifth vial brings darkness like that which fell on Egypt under the plagues God sent through Moses and Aaron. Men will be in such pain from all the plagues that they will gnaw their tongues;

- The sixth vial dries up the Euphrates River to make a way for the kings of the east;

- The devils gather all nations to battle against the Lord when He returns. The nations will see this as their only possible means of escape. They will have no choice but to gather in the valley of Armageddon to fight against the Lord;
- This battle is not against Gog and Magog coming against Jerusalem, but anti-Christ against Jesus Himself when He returns to the earth. The surrounding of Jerusalem by Gog and Magog will be at the end of the Millennium, when the nations are deceived by Satan to think they can overturn the righteous rule of the King to whom they were forced to bring tribute for one thousand years;
- The seventh vial brings final destruction upon the cities of the world led by anti-Christ;
- Babylon is remembered by God, and He destroys the city. A plague of hail rains upon the people, but they respond by blaspheming God.

11

THE EIGHTH REVELATION

The eighth revelation given to John describes Mystery Babylon, the religious system that has allied itself with the world powers and has persecuted the saints of God. Mystery Babylon is described as a woman who sits on a scarlet-colored beast with seven heads and ten horns—the kingdom of the anti-Christ.

REV. 17:1-2:
And there came one of the seven messengers who had the seven vials, and spoke with me, saying to me, "Come here. I will show to you the judgment of the great whore that sits upon many waters, with whom the kings of the earth have committed fornication, and the inhabitants of the earth have been made drunk with the wine of her fornication."

This vision brings John into the wilderness of earth. (There is no wilderness in Heaven.) But from this point he sees Mystery Babylon, the religious system of the earth that serves the anti-Christ.

17:3-8:
So he carried me away in the spirit into the wilderness. And I saw a woman sit upon a scarlet colored beast, full of names of blasphemy, having seven heads and ten horns.

> And the woman was arrayed in purple and scarlet color, and decked with gold and precious stones and pearls, having a golden cup in her hand full of abominations and filthiness of her fornication. And upon her forehead was a name written, "MYSTERY BABYLON THE GREAT, THE MOTHER OF HARLOTS AND ABOMINATIONS OF THE EARTH."
>
> And I saw the woman drunk with the blood of the saints, and with the blood of the martyrs of Jesus. And when I saw her I marveled with great wonder.
>
> And the messenger said to me, "Why did you marvel? I will tell you the mystery of the woman, and of the beast that carries her, that has the seven heads and ten horns.
>
> "The beast that you saw was, and is not, and shall ascend out of the abyss and go into perdition. And they who dwell on the earth, whose names were not written in the Book of Life from the foundation of the world, shall wonder when they see the beast that was, and is not, and yet is.

The woman (Mystery Babylon) sits on a scarlet-colored beast having seven heads and ten horns. The beast was (it existed for a time), is not (will not be in existence during the time revealed to John), and yet is (will exist again during the last of the revelation). The last kingdom among the seven was ancient Rome (which was), seemingly destroyed (is not); but (yet is) will be revived as a weakened empire. The beast (the combined seven kingdoms) came out of the abyss when Satan's anti-Christ spirits formed the first of the kingdoms (Egypt) to conquer God's people.

Mystery Babylon—the ancient mystery religion that originated in Babel—will rise again to become the world's global religious system. New Age philosophy, largely spawned from the ancient mystery religion, permeates the world today, and has even infiltrated the churches to a large extent. It will replace the purity of biblical faith to become the anti-Christ's religious system.

Occult philosopher Manly Palmer Hall boasted decades ago that this would happen:

> Though the modern world may know a million secrets, the ancient world knew one—and that one was greater than the million; for the million secrets breed death, disaster, sorrow, selfishness, lust, and avarice, but the one secret confers life, light, and truth. The time will come when the secret wisdom shall again be the dominating

religious and philosophical urge of the world. The day is at hand when the doom of dogma shall be sounded. The great theological Tower of Babel, with its confusion of tongues, was built of bricks of mud and the mortar of slime. Out of the cold ashes of lifeless creeds, however, shall rise phœnixlike the ancient Mysteries.[1]

17:9:

"And here is the mind that has wisdom: The seven heads are seven mountains on which the woman sits."

The woman is the great city that reigns over the nations (vs. 18). This city sits on seven mountains. We see in Rv 12:3 that the beast (Satan) has seven heads, and in Rv 13:1 that the beast that represents anti-Christ has seven heads. This ties Satan and the anti-Christ to the city that sits on seven mountains. The seven mountains are not likely the seven kingdoms of the beast, because it is a specific city which must be situated in one nation. Might the seven mountains be the notable seven hills of Rome?

The seven heads also represent the seven nations under anti-Christ that have conquered Israel/Judah:

17:10:

"And there are seven kings: five have fallen, and one is, and the other has not yet come. And when he comes, he must continue a short time."

The five kings that had fallen were the spiritual rulers of Egypt, Assyria, Babylonia, Medo-Persia and Greece. The one that is (at John's time) is Rome. The one to come is the spiritual ruler of anti-Christ's kingdom which will conquer Jerusalem for a short time—three-and-one-half years.

17:11:

"And the beast that was, and is not, he is the eighth, and is of the seven, and goes into perdition."

The final kingdom is the eighth from among the seven—the principality over anti-Christ's kingdom—who must again rise to power:

And now you know what holds fast so that he might be revealed in his time. For the mystery of iniquity already works, only now holding fast until coming forth. And then shall be revealed that

---

[1] Manly Palmer Hall, *The Secret Teachings of All Ages, An Enyclopedic Outline of Masonic, Hermetic, Qabbalistic and Rosicrucian Symbolical Philosophy, Being an Interpretation of the Secret Teachings concealed within the Rituals, Allegories and Mysteries of all Ages,* (Los Angeles: Philosophical Research Society, Inc., 1962), p. XLIV.

wicked one whom the Lord shall consume with the breath of His mouth, and shall destroy with the brightness of His coming—him whose coming is according to the working of Satan with all power and signs and lying wonders, and with all deception of unrighteousness in them who perish because they did not receive the love of the truth so that they might be saved. (2Th 2:6-10)

17:12-13:

"And the ten horns which you saw are ten kings that have received no kingdom as yet, but receive power as kings one hour with the beast. These have one mind, and shall give their power and strength to the beast."

These ten kings or spiritual rulers cannot be the same ten spiritual rulers over the Roman emperors, ten of whom have already ruled and fallen (Rv 7:10). They come later, and will be revealed after anti-Christ comes to power.

17:14:

"These will make war with the Lamb, and the Lamb shall overcome them, for He is Lord of lords, and King of kings. And they who are with Him are called, and chosen, and faithful."

These ten rulers will be over the nations that lead the armies of the world to Armageddon in their attempt to defeat Christ when He returns. It will be a coalition of nations within the area held by the old Roman Empire.

17:15:

And he said to me, "The waters that you saw, where the whore sits, are peoples, and multitudes, and nations, and languages.

The city will have spiritual as well as temporal authority over many nations because of the power of the false prophet.

17:16-18:

"And the ten horns that you saw on the beast, these shall hate the whore, and shall make her desolate and naked, and shall eat her flesh, and burn her with fire. For God has put in their hearts to fulfill His will, and to agree and give their kingdom to the beast until the words of God shall be fulfilled.

"And the woman that you saw is that great city that reigns over the kings of the earth."

The ten horns—ten spiritual rulers over ten nations—will, through the human rulers over those nations, turn against Mystery Babylon.

Why would anti-Christ attack this city allied with him? I offer here a scenario that I foresee, although I am not calling this prophecy, but rather a prediction based on knowledge and study of both history and Scripture.

There is only one city on earth that fits the description of sitting on seven hills, having commerce with the entire world, having arisen out of the Roman Empire, and wielding spiritual power over billions of people. That city is Rome, and more specifically, it is Vatican City—the seat of the Roman Pontiff, the pope of Rome. The Roman Catholic Church, by calling the pope the Roman Pontiff, identifies itself with that city as the capital of all the world's religious, economic and governmental powers.

Roman Catholicism is the only religion that operates as a temporal nation, with a government recognized by virtually all other governments of the world. While there are many nations who have national religions, no religion has its own state except Roman Catholicism.

Throughout the early centuries of the faith, Rome was the seat of great persecution against God's saints. Even with the rise of Constantine, the bloody persecution of true believers continued under the banner of the bishops of Rome—the popes who used the power of the Roman state to impose their will upon what became Christendom.

The popes have committed fornication with the nations in return for great wealth and power. The reason the Vatican State exists today is because Pope Pius XII made a pact with Mussolini that the Catholic Church would not hinder his rise to power if he would grant the Vatican political autonomy.

It would appear by all evidences that the false prophet, then, will be the pope of Romanism at the time anti-Christ comes on the scene.

For centuries Christianity and Islam have been at war. The Crusades were in large part a response by Roman Catholicism to Islam's conquests in the West. Islam has never given up the quest to conquer the earth, and the West is its most treasured objective. Roman Catholicism was for centuries the dominant military and economic force within Christendom and will again assert its position as the Holy Roman Empire with the acquiescence of all other major Christian religions.

For a time Islam and Christianity will co-exist under anti-Christ because both wish to have Jerusalem for their own possession. They know that they must join forces in order to oust the Jews from Jerusalem. Once they vanquish the Jews, Islam's anti-Christ will turn against the pope in order to assert himself as sole possessor of the entire region. God will be behind the decision of anti-Christ to attack the city.

REV. 18:1-3:

And after these things I saw another angel come down from Heaven, having great power, and the earth was lightened with his glory. And he cried mightily with a strong voice, saying, "Babylon the great has fallen—has fallen, and has become the habitation of devils, and the hold of every foul spirit, and a cage of every unclean and hateful bird. For all nations have drunk of the wine of the wrath of her fornication, and the kings of the earth have committed fornication with her, and the merchants of the earth have grown rich through the abundance of her delicacies."

Rome, which had incorporated the mystery religion of Babylon and imposed it upon Christendom through the Catholic Church, is destroyed. Verse two speaks of the intrigue that characterizes the political power that resides in Roman Catholicism. Verse three tells of her betrayal of the true Gospel for the love of the world.

18:4-5:

And I heard another voice from Heaven, saying, "Come out of her, My people, so that you not be partakers of her sins, and so that you not receive of her plagues. For her sins have reached unto Heaven, and God has remembered her iniquities."

Do not suppose that this appeal to come out of the Babylonian religious system is for Roman Catholics only. All Christendom has partaken of her fornication to some degree. The ecumenical movement of today is leading many back to her authority. Notice that the Lord says, "Come out of her, My people," demonstrating that true believers are found within the churches that are committing fornication with the whore. This will take place after the rise of the anti-Christ and his alliance with the whore of Babylon. We must all ask where we stand at this time.

18:6-24:

"Reward her even as she rewarded you, and double to her double according to her works; in the cup which she has filled, fill to her double.

"How much she has glorified herself, and lived deliciously, give her so much torment and sorrow, for she says in her heart, 'I sit a queen, and am no widow, and shall see no sorrow.'

"Therefore her plagues shall come in one day—death, and mourning, and famine—and she shall be utterly burned with fire. For strong is the Lord God who judges her.

"And the kings of the earth, who have committed fornication and lived deliciously with her, shall bewail her, and lament for her when they shall see the smoke of her burning, standing far off for the fear of her torment, saying, 'Alas, alas, that great city Babylon, that mighty city! For in one hour has your judgment come.'

"And the merchants of the earth shall weep and mourn over her because no man buys their merchandise any longer—the merchandise of gold, and silver, and precious stones, and of pearls, and fine linen, and purple, and silk, and scarlet, and all thyine wood, and all manner vessels of ivory, and all manner vessels of most precious wood, and of brass, and iron, and marble, and cinnamon, and perfumes, and ointments, and frankincense, and wine, and oil, and fine flour, and wheat, and animals, and sheep, and horses, and chariots, and slaves, and souls of men.

"And the fruits that your soul lusted after have departed from you, and all things that were dainty and goodly have departed from you, and you shall find them no more at all.

The merchants of these things, who were made rich by her, shall stand far off for the fear of her torment, weeping and wailing, and saying, 'Alas, alas, that great city, that was clothed in fine linen, and purple, and scarlet, and decked with gold, and precious stones, and pearls! For in one hour so great riches have come to nothing.'

"And every shipmaster, and all the company in ships, and sailors, and as many as trade by sea, stood far off and cried out when they saw the smoke of her burning, saying, 'What city is like this great city?!'

"And they cast dust on their heads, and cried, weeping and wailing, saying, 'Alas, alas, that great city, in which all who had ships in the sea because of her magnificence were made rich! For in one hour is she made desolate.'

"Rejoice over her, you Heaven, and you holy apostles and prophets, for God has avenged you on her."

And a mighty angel took up a stone like a great millstone, and cast it into the sea, saying, "Thus with violence shall that great city Babylon be thrown down, and shall be found no more at all.

"And the voice of harpers, and musicians, and of pipers, and trumpeters, shall no longer be heard at all in you. And no craftsman, of whatever craft he be, shall be found any longer in you; and the sound of a millstone shall no longer be heard at all in you; and the light of a candle shall no longer shine at all in you; and the voice of the bridegroom and of the bride shall no longer be heard at all in you. For your merchants were the great men of the earth, for by your sorceries were all nations deceived.

"And in her was found the blood of prophets, and of saints, and of all who were slain upon the earth."

Rome has always been in the center of all commerce. Roman Catholicism has a hand in the world's wealth through its financial empire. The Roman Catholic Church owns a huge share of the world's wealth in its banks, insurance holdings, corporations, investments, real estate, influence in governments, and love of mammon. The ancient treasures in its cellars, including much obscene pagan art, are worth untold billions of dollars.

And certainly the blood of prophets and saints, as well as that of all who are slain in wars, can be found to have been spilled directly, or indirectly, through the papal office.

SUMMARY OF THE EIGHTH REVELATION

This revelation centers exclusively on the great Whore of Babylon, which I believe is Roman Catholicism and its economic, political and spiritual power over the nations. It chronicles her power, then her demise at the hands of the anti-Christ.

One possible reason anti-Christ will turn against the city, besides the desire to own Jerusalem outright, is because he will see that it is powerless to stop the plagues that God sends upon his kingdom. God's power will be seen to be far greater than that of Satan's.

The fury of evil men is often revealed in their turning against their allies even if the allies' failure is beyond their ability to rectify.

12

THE NINTH REVELATION

The ninth revelation begins where the eighth revelation leaves off—with the destruction of the whore of Babylon. Then comes the ensuing judgment of the anti-Christ's kingdom and the Lord's conquest of the nations upon His return. The scene takes place around the throne of God while exclamations of joy over the destruction of the world system are heard.

REV. 19:1-3:

And after these things I heard a great voice of many people in Heaven, saying, "Alleluia! Salvation, and glory, and honor, and power unto the Lord our God! For true and righteous are His judgments, for He has judged the great whore that corrupted the earth with her fornication, and has avenged the blood of His servants at her hand."

And again they said, "Alleluia!"

The cry of "Alleluia!" is found four times in the writings of the apostles, all of which occur in Revelation 19. In verses 1 through 4, the praises are for judgment of the false religious system, even more so than for judgment of the secular world. Religion has always been the worst enemy of God, particularly that which calls itself by His name. It is significant that the whore of Babylon will be an apostate Christianity/New Age occultism aligned with the anti-Christ's religion of Islam.

19:4-9

And the twenty-four elders and the four beings fell down and worshipped God who sat on the throne, saying, "Amen! Alleluia!"

And a voice came out of the throne, saying, "Praise our God, all you His servants, and you, both small and great, who fear Him."

And I heard as it were the voice of a great multitude, and as the voice of many waters, and as the voice of mighty thunder, saying, "Alleluia! For the Lord God omnipotent reigns! Let us be glad and rejoice, and give honor to Him, for the marriage of the Lamb has come, and His wife has made herself ready. And to her was granted that she should be arrayed in fine linen, clean and white, for the fine linen is the righteousness of saints."

And he said to me, "Write: 'Blessed are they who are called to the marriage supper of the Lamb.'"

The fourth "Alleluia!" in this chapter is for the Lord reigning, and for the coming marriage supper of the Lamb. The marriage supper of the Lamb will take place when the present earthly kingdoms are made to become the kingdoms of Christ. All the saints from all the ages will come to the marriage supper. These are blessed because they come through the first resurrection, and will not be subject to the second death (Rv 2:11; 20:6-14; 21:8).

19:10:

And I fell at his feet to worship him. And he said to me, "See that you not do it. I am your fellow servant, and of your brethren who have the testimony of Jesus. Worship God, for the testimony of Jesus is the spirit of prophecy."

This is the only place in Scripture where the terms "the testimony of Jesus" and "the spirit of prophecy" are found. Any true prophet inspired by the Holy Spirit will bear a true testimony that the Word of God did indeed become incarnate in human flesh in the person of Jesus the Messiah (Jn 1:1-14; 1Jn 2:22; 4:1-3). Therefore, Jesus is God, and worthy to be worshipped as the Creator.

That this person speaking to John tells him not to worship him because he is a fellow servant who has the testimony of Jesus indicates that the voice from out of the throne that has called for God's praises is that of a redeemed man, not an angelic being.

19:11-14:

And I saw Heaven opened, and look! A white horse! And He who sat on him was called "Faithful" and "True," and in righteousness He judges and makes war.

His eyes were like a flame of fire, and on His head were many crowns, and He had a name written that no man knew but He Himself.

And he was clothed with a robe dipped in blood, and His name is called "The Word of God."

And the armies that were in Heaven followed Him on white horses, clothed in fine linen, white and clean.

The Lord is riding on a white horse. This is a separate revelation from that in 6:2, dealing with a different period of time. Whereas in 6:2 the horseman, who could be some other spirit being, wages war at the end of the present Time of the Gentiles, these verses describe the Lord Jesus Christ upon His coming to the earth with His saints (clothed in white linen) to establish His millennial reign over the nations.

19:15-16:

And out of his mouth goes a sharp sword so that with it He would strike the nations. And He shall rule them with a rod of iron. And He treads the winepress of the fierceness and wrath of Almighty God. And He has on His robe and on His thigh a name written: "KING OF KINGS, AND LORD OF LORDS."

The idea that the Lord destroys His enemies by a sharp sword that comes out of His mouth is a euphemism, much as the flood that proceeds from the mouth of the dragon. In this case, the meaning is that the Lord will destroy His enemies by His spoken word.

Revelation 1:16 reveals the Lord Jesus having a "two-edged sword" proceeding from His mouth. Hebrews 4:12 tells us "For the Word of God is quick, and powerful, and sharper than any two-edged sword, piercing even to the dividing asunder of soul and spirit, and of the joints and marrow, and is a discerner of the thoughts and intents of the heart." Ephesians 6:17 calls the Word of God "the sword of the Spirit." Whatever the Lord speaks is the Word of God—a sword that bares men's souls.

19:17-19:

And I saw an angel standing in the sun, and he cried out with a loud voice, saying to all the fowls that fly in the midst of the skies, "Come and gather yourselves together to the supper of the great

God so that you may eat the flesh of kings, and the flesh of captains, and the flesh of mighty men, and the flesh of horses, and of those who sit on them, and the flesh of all men, both free and bond, both small and great."

And I saw the beast, and the kings of the earth, and their armies, gathered together to make war against Him who sat on the horse, and against His army.

This supper is not the marriage supper of the Lamb. It is for scavengers who clean the earth of carrion. Here in a different revelation is another telling of the anti-Christ's preparation for the battle of Armageddon.

19:20-21:
And the beast was taken, and with him the false prophet who worked miracles before him, with which he deceived those who had received the mark of the beast, and those who worshipped his image. These both were cast alive into a lake of fire burning with brimstone.

And the remnant were slain with the sword by Him who sat on the horse, which sword proceeded out of His mouth. And all the fowls were filled with their flesh.

The anti-Christ and the false prophet will be cast into the lake of fire, after which the Lord will destroy their armies by His spoken word, just as He created the cosmos by His spoken word.

REV. 20:1-3:
And I saw an angel come down from Heaven, having the key of the abyss and a great chain in his hand. And he laid hold on the dragon—that old serpent, which is the Devil, and Satan—and bound him for a thousand years, and cast him into the abyss, and shut him up, and set a seal on him so that he could no longer deceive the nations till the thousand years should be fulfilled. And after that he must be loosed a little season.

This Scripture makes clear reference to the "thousand years." During the Millennium, Satan will be bound in the abyss. The nations will have neither the will nor the means to resist the righteous rule of the Lord Jesus Christ and His saints. The angel John saw may well be the Lord Jesus Christ who has the keys of Hell and Death (Rev. 1:18). It would be appropriate for the Son, on behalf of the Father, to personally send the great rebel to his prison—the bottomless pit.

20:4:

And I saw thrones, and they sat on them, and judgment was given to them. And I saw the souls of those who were beheaded for the witness of Jesus and for the Word of God, and who had not worshipped the beast or his image, nor had received his mark on their foreheads, or in their hands. And they lived and reigned with Christ for a thousand years.

All the faithful will be resurrected to live with Christ for a thousand years, ruling over the nations of the earth.

Some say these are "tribulation saints" who did not escape in the pretribulation Rapture. But we have already shown that the Rapture doesn't occur until the sounding of the last heavenly trumpet. The Rapture and the resurrection of the dead are concurrent:

> But I would not have you be ignorant, brethren, concerning those who are asleep, so that you do not sorrow as others who have no hope. For if we believe that Jesus died and rose again, even so those also who sleep in Jesus, God will bring with Him.
>
> For this we say to you by the word of the Lord: that we who are alive and remain until the coming of the Lord shall not go before those who are asleep. For the Lord Himself shall descend from Heaven with a shout, with the voice of the archangel, and with the trump of God, and the dead in Christ shall rise first. Then we who are alive and remain shall be caught up together with them in the clouds to meet the Lord in the air, and so shall we ever be with the Lord. (1Th 4:13-17)
>
> Look, I show you a mystery: not all of us shall sleep, but we all shall be changed in a moment, in the blinking of an eye at the last trump. For the trumpet shall sound, and the dead shall be raised incorruptible, and we shall be changed. For this corruptible must put on incorruption, and this mortal must put on immortality. (1Co 15:51-53)

The first resurrection is the resurrection of all those who have died in Christ since the time of Adam. The first resurrection actually has three stages. The first stage was a limited resurrection of the dead when Jesus rose:

> And, look! The veil of the temple was torn in two from the top to the bottom, and the earth quaked, and the rocks split. And the graves were opened, and after His resurrection many bodies of the

saints who slept arose, and came out of the graves, and went into the holy city, and appeared to many. (Mt 27:51-53)

It is possible that this resurrection brought forth the twenty-four elders who sit on the thrones in the midst of God's throne. There may have been others as well, but Scripture isn't clear on this. Some think these saints went back into the grave, but Scripture doesn't tell us that either. Certainly those who rose with Jesus were not compelled to die again (Heb 9:27).

The second stage of the first resurrection will occur just prior to the Rapture, after great tribulation on the whole earth (as opposed to the great tribulation on Israel afterward) as described in Matthew 24:29-31; Mark 13:24-37; Revelation 6:12-17.

The third stage of the first resurrection will take place at the end of the anti-Christ's rule, when Jesus returns to the earth.

Those who would dispute the idea that the first resurrection has these three stages must first reconcile the chronology of events and the prophecies that relate to the resurrection, which otherwise would be contradictory. The Lord was the first fruits of the resurrection, so all who follow Him are considered part of the same resurrection, including those who rose with Him (Jn 53:52-53).

20:5:
But the rest of the dead did not live again until the thousand years were finished. This is the first resurrection.

The "first resurrection" refers to verse 4. The rest of the dead will rise in the second resurrection, some to reward, some to condemnation. All the resurrections prior to the Millennial Kingdom are part of "the first resurrection." All who are part of the first resurrection have been saved by faith in Jesus Christ, the Messiah of Israel. Those who enter the Millennium as mortals, as well as those born during the Millennium, will have to prove their faithfulness to the Lord by their gifts and sacrifices. They will not be resurrected until the end of the Millennium when the rest of humanity will be raised either to everlasting life, or to eternal damnation. Thus the following blessing is pronounced:

20:6:
Blessed and holy is he who has a part in the first resurrection; on such the second death has no power, but they shall be priests of God and of Christ, and shall reign with Him for a thousand years.

Here, the Millennium is spoken of as a literal one-thousand year reign of Christ on the earth with His saints. The amillennial and postmillennial concepts of eschatology are totally unscriptural and without merit. They are the product of a theology which exalts "the Church" and assigns to it conquest of the earth before the Lord returns. This belief, called "dominion theology," is easily discredited not only by Scripture but by the character of many of its principal proponents.

20:7-9:

And when the thousand years are over, Satan shall be loosed out of his prison and shall go out to deceive the nations that are in the four quarters of the earth—Gog and Magog—to gather them together to battle, the number of whom is as the sand of the sea.

And they went up on the breadth of the earth and encircled the camp of the saints about, and the beloved city. And fire came down from God out of Heaven, and devoured them.

This is the final battle when Jerusalem will be surrounded, not by the armies of anti-Christ, but by the armies of Gog and Magog as prophesied in Ezekiel, chapters 38 and 39, which I've cited earlier.

20:10-13:

And the Devil that deceived them was cast into the lake of fire and brimstone where the beast and the false prophet are, and shall be tormented day and night forever and ever.

And I saw a great white throne, and Him who sat on it—from whose face the earth and the heavens fled away, and there was found no place for them.

And I saw the dead, small and great, stand before God. And the books were opened. And another book was opened, which is the Book of Life.

And the dead were judged out of those things which were written in the books, according to their works.

And the sea gave up the dead that were in it; and Death and Hades delivered up the dead that were in them. And they were judged every man according to their works.

This is the second resurrection—that which brings to life all who have lived since the creation of man. Every man will be judged not by faith in Jesus Christ (those of true, living faith will have been resurrected in the first resurrection), but by whether their lives were lived in relative innocence, and particularly how they lived in relation to the Lord's saints:

When the Son of Man shall come in His glory—and all the holy angels with him—then He shall sit on the throne of His glory. And before Him shall be gathered all nations, and He shall separate them one from another as a shepherd divides his sheep from the goats. And He shall set the sheep on his right hand, but the goats on the left. Then the King shall say to them on His right hand, 'Come, you blessed of My Father; inherit the Kingdom prepared for you from the foundation of the world. For I was hungry, and you gave me food; I was thirsty, and you gave me drink; I was a stranger, and you took me in; naked, and you clothed me; I was sick, and you visited me; I was in prison, and you came to me.'

"Then the righteous will answer Him, saying, 'Lord, when did we see You hungry, and feed You? Or thirsty, and give You drink? When did we see You a stranger, and take You in? Or naked, and clothe You? Or when did we see You sick, or in prison, and come to You?

"And the King shall answer and say to them, 'Truly I say to you, inasmuch as you have done it to one of the least of these My brothers, you have done it to Me.'

"Then, also, He shall say to them on the left hand, 'Depart from me, you cursed, into everlasting fire prepared for the Devil and his angels. For I was hungry, and you gave Me no food; I was thirsty, and you gave Me no drink; I was a stranger, and you did not take Me in; naked, and you did not clothe Me; sick, and in prison, and you did not visit Me.'

"Then they, also, will answer Him, saying, 'Lord, when did we see you hungry, or thirsty, or a stranger, or naked, or sick, or in prison, and did not minister to You?'

Then He shall answer them, saying, 'Truly I say to you, inasmuch as you did not do it to one of the least of these, you did not do it to Me.'

"And these shall go away into everlasting punishment, but the righteous into eternal life." (Mt 25:31-46)

For there is no respect of persons with God. For as many as have sinned without the law shall also perish without the law, and as many as have sinned in the law shall be judged by the law (for not the hearers of the law are just before God, but the doers of the law shall be justified. For when the Gentiles, who do not have the law, do by nature the things contained in the law, these, not having the law, are a law unto themselves, who show the work of the law written in their hearts, their conscience also bearing witness, and their thoughts the meanwhile accusing or else excusing one another) in the day when God shall judge the secrets of men by Jesus Christ according to my Gospel. (Ro 2:11-16)

And He sat down and called the twelve, and said to them, "If any man desires to be first, the same shall be last of all, and servant of all."

And He took a child and set him in the midst of them. And when He had taken him in His arms, He said to them, "Whoever will receive one of such children in My name, receives Me. And whoever will receive Me, receives not Me, but Him who sent Me."

And John responded to Him, saying, "Master, we saw someone casting out devils in Your name, and he does not follow us. And we forbad him because he does not follow us."

But Jesus said, "Do not forbid him, for there is no man who shall do a miracle in My name that can lightly speak evil of Me. For he who is not against us is on our side. For whoever will give you a cup of water to drink in My name, because you belong to Christ, truly I say to you, he shall not lose his reward." (Mk 9:35-41)

There are billions of people who have lived throughout the ages. They have not had saving faith in Jesus Christ to inherit the Kingdom of Christ; they have not been evil in their hearts and in their intents, but their sinful nature and lack of faith in Christ for whatever reason has prevented them from entering into the Millennial Kingdom. But we are not speaking of the Millennial Kingdom now; we are speaking of eternity—the time when the New Heavens and New Earth will be populated by people who have by God's grace been restored to life.

There will be punishments and rewards for these people.

And this is where there has been a woeful lack of teaching. The Gospel has been only partially proclaimed in a manner that focuses primarily on those redeemed by faith in Jesus Christ. But few have taught about other classes of people who are not so evil to incur the ultimate in God's wrath—the lake of fire: 1) those who hold some belief in Christ but do not live in obedience to His Word in order to inherit the Millennial Kingdom; 2) those who have not heard the Gospel but must be judged according to their consciences; 3) those who have not been the enemies of Christ—who have treated His saints with kindness and mercy; 4) the mentally handicapped who cannot understand or discern between good and evil—who are like babes in their innocence; 5) the humble in spirit among those ignorant of the Gospel; 6) the billions of babies who have died in innocence, many through abortion. I believe the Lord's blood covers the innocent and ignorant.

This is not universalism which says that eventually all men will be saved in some fashion. The lake of fire still awaits those who are evil and/or intent on fighting against the Lord and His truth. Rather, these Scriptures demonstrate God's mercy toward those who are not called in Christ to inherit the Millennial Kingdom on earth and to reign with Him for 1,000 years.

If this is strange, or seems heretical because it is erroneously taken to mean denial of the blood of Jesus for salvation, let us not forget that our heavenly Father is not unjust. There will no doubt be some form of judgment upon all, but Scripture indicates that the second resurrection, whatever form it takes, will not be for the saints during this present age who are resurrected or translated to immortality at the Lord's coming. Those in the second resurrection are people who were not in the first resurrection; it is made clear by these verses that they will be judged by their works.

It is here that those who professed Christ but did not live for Christ will also be judged and will receive not only their rewards but some form of punishment for their failures:

"Do not fear, little flock, for it is your Father's good pleasure to give you the Kingdom.

"Sell what you have and give alms; provide yourselves bags which do not grow old, a treasure in Heaven that does not fail, where no thief approaches, nor moth corrupts. For where your treasure is, there your heart will be also.

"Let your hips be girded about, and your lights burning, and you yourselves like men who wait for their lord, when he will return from the wedding, so that when he comes and knocks, they may open to him immediately.

"Blessed are those servants, whom the lord when he comes shall find watching. Truly I say to you, that he shall gird himself, and make them sit down to food, and will come forth and serve them.

"And if he will come in the second watch, or come in the third watch, and find them so, blessed are those servants.

"And know this: that if the master of the house had known what hour the thief would come, he would have watched and not have allowed his house to be broken into.

"Therefore, you be ready also, for the Son of Man comes at an hour when you think not."

Then Peter said to Him, "Lord, do You speak this parable to us, or to all?"

And the Lord said, "Who then is that faithful and wise steward, whom his lord will make ruler over his household, to give them their portion of food in due season? Blessed is that servant whom his lord, when he comes will find so doing. Of a truth, I say to you that he will make him ruler over all that he has.

"But if that servant says in his heart, 'My lord delays his coming,' and will begin to beat the menservants and maidens, and to eat and drink, and to be drunken, the lord of that servant will come in a day when he does not look for him, and at an hour when he is not aware, and will cut him asunder, and will appoint him his portion with the unbelievers. And that servant who knew his lord's will, and did not prepare himself, nor did according to his will, will be beaten with many stripes. But he that did not know, and committed things worthy of stripes, will be beaten with few stripes. For to whomever much is given, of him shall be much required. And to whom men have committed much, of him they will ask more." (Lk 12:32-48)

These verses speak of inheriting the Kingdom. The unfaithful servant will not inherit the Kingdom (the Millennial Kingdom of Christ on earth), but will appear at the second resurrection to give an account of his actions. Those who knew to do the will of the Lord but did not do it will be punished in some way. How this will be manifested we don't know. But the important thing is that they will have missed out on entering the Millennial Kingdom and must await the second resurrection to receive their rewards and punishments. Those who call themselves by the Lord's name ("Christian") but live ungodly will suffer among those who are unbelievers. All unbelievers will appear in the second resurrection. They will not be judged by the covering of Christ's blood, but by how they lived their lives.

When Jesus says that all the ungodly will have their part in the lake of fire, it may be construed that the suffering of some will be greater than the suffering of others. Lacking details, we must leave the judgment of men to God. He is just and will do nothing unjust. Exactly how rewards and

314 The Day of Yahweh

punishments will be meted out is not stated, but the Lord, speaking analogously of His return, gave us a clue in Luke 12:32-48, quoted above.

Certainly not all men deserve the same degree of punishment or reward. Nor should we think that there will be no price to pay for lack of diligence in our service to the Lord. Exactly to what these "stripes" refer no one can say. However, one's salvation may entail a bit of shame along with the joy:

> For no man can lay another foundation than that which is laid, who is Jesus Christ.
>
> Now if any man builds gold, silver, precious stones, wood, hay, stubble on this foundation, every man's work shall be revealed, for the day shall declare it because it shall be revealed by fire, and the fire shall test every man's work of what sort it is.
>
> If any man's work abides which he has built thereupon, he shall receive a reward.
>
> If any man's work shall be burned, he shall suffer loss, but he himself shall be saved, yet so as by fire.
>
> Do you not know that you are the temple of God, and that the Spirit of God dwells in you? If any man defiles the temple of God, God shall destroy him, for the temple of God—which temple you are—is holy. Let no man deceive himself. If any man among you seems to be wise in this world, let him become a fool so that he may be wise. (1Co 3:11-18)

This Scripture is not saying we can live as we like and still be saved, though our sins will be burned up. The works to which Paul refers are not sin or good works, per se; they are service to the Lord. They are works built on the foundation of Jesus Christ. No sin is built on the foundation of Jesus. These are works done in the flesh; all such works will be burned up. And one may stand naked and without rewards in the day of judgment, entering the Kingdom of Christ ashamed.

If this runs contrary to one's theology based on "unconditional love" and easy believism, I'm sorry. Read these Scriptures until they sink into your soul.

20:14-15:

And Death and Hades were cast into the lake of fire. This is the second death.

And whoever was not found written in the Book of Life was cast into the lake of fire.

The lake of fire is reserved for those judged evil and enemies of God.

SUMMARY OF THE NINTH REVELATION

The ninth revelation describes the events from the Lord's final return to set foot on the earth until the end of the Millennium and the culmination of the Great White Throne Judgment.

- Praise is heard in Heaven for the judgments of the Lord upon the whore of Babylon;

- The marriage supper of the Lamb is prepared and the bride—the New Jerusalem—has made herself ready for Him;

- Heaven is opened and the Lord appears on a white horse with His army clothed in white linen, which is indicative of the saints;

- The Lord strikes the nations and prepares to rule them with a rod of iron;

- An angel calls together all the scavenger fowls of the skies to cleanse the earth of the bodies of those slain by the Lord on His return to the earth;

- The anti-Christ and the armies of the world gather to make war against the Lord;

- The beast and false prophet are cast into the lake of fire;

- Satan is bound in the abyss for one thousand years in order to prevent him from deceiving the nations during that time;

- The saints who are martyred for their testimony of Christ and who did not receive the mark of the beast are raised to life to reign with Christ for a thousand years;

- At the end of the thousand years Satan will be loosed from the abyss to deceive the nations again, bringing Gog and Magog to attack Jerusalem;

- Fire from Heaven destroys the armies of Gog and Magog;

- Satan is cast into the lake of fire;

- The second resurrection of all the remaining dead, both righteous and unrighteous occurs;

- The Great White Throne Judgment takes place;

- All who were not in the first resurrection are judged according to their works;

- Death and Hades are cast into the lake of fire along with all who are not found in the Book of Life.

13

THE TENTH REVELATION

The final revelation given to John discloses the refurbishing of the cosmos to bring into existence the New Heavens and the New Earth. The Bride of Christ—the heavenly city New Jerusalem—is described, as is the state of all the redeemed for eternity.

REV. 21:1:

And I saw New Heavens and a New Earth, for the first heavens and the first earth were passed away, and there was no more sea.

Sometime after the Millennium God will re-create the heavens and the earth. Peter compresses the entire scenario of the Lord's return and the New Heavens and New Earth into a few verses.

But the Day of the Lord will come as a thief in the night, in which the heavens shall pass away with a great noise, and the elements shall melt with fervent heat, the earth also and the works that are in it shall be burned up.

Seeing then that all these things shall be dissolved, what manner of persons ought you to be in all holy conduct and godliness, looking for and eagerly awaiting the coming of the Day of God, wherein the heavens, being on fire, shall be dissolved, and the elements shall melt with fervent heat?

Nevertheless, according to His promise we look for new heavens and a new earth, wherein dwells righteousness.

Therefore, beloved, seeing that you look for such things, be diligent so that you may be found by Him in peace, without spot, and blameless. (2Pe 3:10-14)

Because of the contraction of these events into these few verses, some insist that there will be no Millennium, but that immediately upon the Lord's next appearing there will be the resurrection which will coincide with the New Heavens and the New Earth.

This is a simplistic approach, not taking into account the great detail the Book of Revelation presents in separating the events that, together, combine to make up "the Day of the Lord" appearing in stages over a span of over one-thousand years, just as "the last days" addressed by Peter have already spanned the past two-thousand years.

21:2:

And I, John, saw the holy city, New Jerusalem, coming down from God out of Heaven, prepared as a bride adorned for her husband.

It is after the Millennium, and upon the establishment of the New Earth, that the New Jerusalem will descend from Heaven as the Bride of Christ. The present-day "Church" is not the Bride of Christ. All believers will have a part in the Bride of Christ, which is the New Jerusalem, including the saints who have lived through all the ages since Adam.

21:3-5:

And I heard a great voice out of Heaven saying, "Look! The tabernacle of God is with men, and He will dwell with them, and they shall be His people, and God Himself shall be with them, and be their God.

"And God shall wipe away all tears from their eyes, and there shall be no more death, or sorrow, or crying, nor shall there be any more pain, for the former things have passed away."

And He who sat on the throne said, "Behold, I make all things new."

And He said to me, "Write, for these words are true and faithful."

The entire creation will be made new, God will move His throne to His temple in the New Earth. All suffering will have passed away as the saints enjoy eternity in their resurrected bodies.

21:6-8:

And He said to me, "It is done. I am Alpha and Omega, the Beginning and the End. I will give from the fountain of the water of life freely to him who is thirsty.

"He who overcomes shall inherit all things, and I will be his God, and he shall be My son.

"But the fearful, and unbelieving, and the abominable, and murderers, and whoremongers, and sorcerers, and idolaters, and all liars, shall have their part in the lake that burns with fire and brimstone, which is the second death."

In verse 6 we see that the Father calls Himself Alpha and Omega. In this case Alpha and Omega is not the Son, because He says that those who overcome shall be His son. So Alpha and Omega—Beginning and Ending—is an attribute or name shared by both the Father and His Son, the Lord Jesus Christ.

21:9-14:

And there came to me one of the seven messengers that had the seven vials full of the seven last plagues, and spoke with me, saying, "Come here. I will show you the bride, the Lamb's wife."

And he carried me away in the spirit to a great and high mountain, and showed me that great city, the Holy Jerusalem, descending out of Heaven from God, having the glory of God. And her light was like that of a most precious stone, even like a jasper stone, clear as crystal. And it had a great and high wall, and had twelve gates, and at the gates twelve angels, and names written thereon, which are the names of the twelve tribes of the children of Israel—on the east three gates; on the north three gates; on the south three gates; and on the west three gates.

And the wall of the city had twelve foundations, and in them the names of the twelve apostles of the Lamb.

Again we see that the Bride of Christ is not "the Church," as the churches have been so eager to teach. The Bride is the New Jerusalem whose gates are inscribed with the names of the twelve patriarchs of Israel. The foundations have inscribed the names of the twelve apostles. Thus, the completion of God's salvation through the prophets first and then the apostles is made known. The Israel of Faith will consist of all true believers who have come out of every nation:

"For as the New Heavens and the New Earth, which I will make, shall remain before Me," says YHWH, "so shall your seed and your name remain. And it shall come to pass that from one new moon to another, and from one Sabbath to another, all flesh shall come to worship before Me," says YHWH.

"And they shall go out and look upon the carcasses of the men who have transgressed against Me, for their worm shall not die, nor shall their fire be quenched; and they shall be an abhorring to all flesh." (Isa 66:22-24)

Contrary to what the modern churches wish to think, God's salvation is contained within the Abrahamic Covenant into which all who have faith in Christ will enter. This is not the Mosaic Covenant restricted to Israel in the flesh; it is the original covenant God made with Abraham.

We Gentiles are a parenthesis in God's plan of salvation. This is not to demean our station, but to make clear that, as Jesus said, "salvation is of the Jews." The feasts and the Sabbaths are eternal, though suspended as a requirement for salvation during the present age.

It appears as if the redeemed will, at least at some time, be able to see the suffering of the ungodly.

21:15-17:

And he who spoke with me had a golden reed to measure the city, and its gates, and its walls.

And the city lies foursquare, and the length is as large as the breadth. And he measured the city with the reed: twelve thousand stadia. The length and the breadth and the height of it are equal.

And he measured its wall: one hundred forty-four cubits, according to the measure of a man, that is, of the angel.

A Roman stadium was approximately 600 feet. This would make the dimensions of the New Jerusalem approximately 1,400 miles square, with the same height. The city is not necessarily in the shape of a cube, but more likely in the shape of a pyramid or irregular in height. This suggestion should not be construed to mean that I believe the pyramids of Egypt were built by God, as some myths have it, but the pyramid would be the perfect shape for such a large city. Whatever the shape, the important thing is that it will be the final dwelling place of our Father.

Certainly the height of the city is mind-boggling. But we must not rule out the possibility that the New Earth will be of a greater size, capable of sustaining such a large city on its surface.

21:18-23:
And the material of its wall was of jasper, and the city was pure gold, like clear glass. And the foundations of the wall of the city were garnished with all kinds of precious stones. The first foundation was jasper; the second, sapphire; the third, a chalcedony; the fourth, an emerald; the fifth, sardonyx; the sixth, sardius; the seventh, chrysolyte; the eighth, beryl; the ninth, a topaz; the tenth, a chrysoprasus; the eleventh, a jacinth; the twelfth, an amethyst.

And the twelve gates were twelve pearls, each gate was of one pearl. And the street of the city was pure gold, as it were transparent glass.

The city will be built of gold and all manner of precious stones; nothing of it will be corruptible.

21:22-23:
And I saw no temple in it, for the Lord God Almighty and the Lamb are its temple.

And the city had no need of the sun or of the moon to shine in it, for the glory of God lighted it, and the Lamb is its light.

The Millennial Temple, with its sacrifices, will be done away with. There will be no need for anything like it because all the inhabitants of the New Earth will have been resurrected to immortality.

21:24-27:
And the nations of those who are saved shall walk in its light, and the kings of the earth bring their glory and honor into it.

And its gates shall not be shut at all by day, for there shall be no night there.

And they shall bring the glory and honor of the nations into it.

And in no wise shall there enter into it anything that defiles, or whatever works abomination, or makes a lie, but they who are written in the Lamb's Book of Life.

The nations will exist for all eternity and will be inhabited by redeemed men who will live in peace, bringing their abundance into the New Jerusalem. All the pain and suffering of this present life will have been forgotten:

For, look! I create New Heavens and a New Earth, and the former shall not be remembered nor come to mind. (Isa 65:17)

REV. 22:1-2:

And he showed me a pure river of water of life, clear as crystal, proceeding out of the throne of God and of the Lamb. In the midst of its street, and on either side of the river, there was the tree of life which bore twelve kinds of fruits, and yielded her fruit every month. And the leaves of the tree were for the healing of the nations.

We will still eat in eternity. The fruit of the tree of life will give health to the nations, providing sustenance, just as it was given to Adam and Eve before they fell in sin.

The Marriage Supper of the Lamb will take place when the Bride of Christ, the New Jerusalem, descends to the New Earth. It appears as if the New Jerusalem will be the habitation of all the saints from the time of Adam to the first resurrection. According to Revelation 22:12 the nations will still exist in the New Earth, so it seems as if they will be populated by those chosen in the second resurrection to inherit the earth—those who are accepted on the basis of their works. These will have missed the first resurrection because for one reason or another they lacked sufficient faith in Christ.

They will not inherit the New Jerusalem, but will have been counted acceptable to inherit the New Earth within the nations. Otherwise, why is it necessary for the water of life to flow out of the New Jerusalem into the earth in order to water the tree of life by which the nations will be healed? The Greek word for "healing" is *therapeia*, from which we get the English "therapy." If the inhabitants of the New Earth are all the redeemed from this present age there would be no need for healing. Recall these scriptures cited earlier: Ro 2:14-16; Mk 9:36-41.

Our God will not forget those who have been kind to His children, some of whom have risked and even given their lives to protect His children. They may not have had sufficient faith to inherit the New Jerusalem and be be counted within the Bride of Christ, but they will populate the New Earth after the second resurrection and will enjoy the Lord's blessings on a more mundane (or less spiritual) plane throughout eternity.

Knowing this should give us hope for those we love and who love us, but who lack faith in this age. This should not be an excuse to refrain from ministering the Gospel to them; if anything, it should give us greater boldness to assure them of the work Christ has done to effect the redemption not only of individual believers but of the entire creation.

Again, this is not universalism. There are those who will be eternally lost because of their evil deeds and hatred of the Lord. In relation to the

New Earth, I'm speaking of those who do not hate the Lord and who do not practice evil, but who have never heard of Christ, or who lack sufficient faith to inherit the Heavenly City.

This is what the Millennial Kingdom is about; it is an inheritance of the resurrected saints to rule and reign with Christ until the New Heavens and New Earth are prepared. Inheritance of the Millennial Kingdom and the New Jerusalem is a reward for faith in Jesus Christ during this age. The nations of the New Earth are for those who are not eternally condemned.

All the more reason to lead those we love to Christ; we want them to inherit the Kingdom with us.

22:3-5:

And there shall be no more curse, but the throne of God and of the Lamb shall be in it, and His servants shall serve Him. And they shall see His face, and His name shall be in their foreheads.

And there shall be no night there, and they need no candle or light from the sun, for the Lord God gives them light. And they shall reign forever and ever.

What a glorious vision of what lies ahead. All the cares of this world will have passed away. In their place stands our glorious Redeemer with whom we shall live forever.

22:6-7

And he said to me, "These sayings are faithful and true, and the Lord God of the holy prophets sent His angel to show to His servants the things that must shortly be done."

"Look, I come quickly! Blessed is he who keeps the sayings of the prophecy of this book."

Jesus is quoted by the man showing John these things, reminding him that Jesus is coming again. And, again, the Lord says that we will be blessed if we believe and obey the prophecies in this book.

22:8-9

And I, John, saw these things, and heard them. And when I had heard and seen, I fell down to worship before the feet of the messenger who showed me these things.

Then he said to me, "See that you not do it, for I am your fellow servant, and of your brethren the prophets, and of those who keep the sayings of this book. Worship God."

This is not Jesus. Nor, as it turns out, is it an angelic being. The *angelos* who held the seven golden vials are redeemed men from among the prophets. The translation would have been more understandable had the word been translated "messengers" in this case.

22:10-15

And He said to me, "Do not seal the sayings of the prophecy of this book, for the time is at hand. He who is unjust, let him be unjust still, and he who is filthy, let him be filthy still, and he who is righteous, let him be righteous still, and he who is holy, let him be holy still.

"'And, look! I come quickly, and My reward is with Me, to give every man according as his work shall be. I am Alpha and Omega, the beginning and the end, the first and the last.'

"Blessed are those who do His commandments, so that they may have a right to the Tree of Life, and may enter in through the gates into the city. For outside are dogs, and sorcerers, and whoremongers, and murderers, and idolaters, and whoever loves and makes a lie."

Again, the messenger quotes the Lord as Alpha and Omega, then speaks of the righteous and unrighteous. The latter are those judged unrighteous according to their works in the second resurrection.

22:16-19

"I, Jesus, have sent My messenger to testify to you these things in the assemblies. I am the root and the offspring of David, and the bright and morning star.

"And the Spirit and the bride say, 'Come.'

"And let him who hears say, 'Come.'

"And let him who is thirsty come. And whoever will, let him take the water of life freely.

"For I testify to every man who hears the words of the prophecy of this book: if any man shall add to these things, God shall add to him the plagues that are written in this book. And if any man shall take away from the words of the book of this prophecy, God shall take away his part out of the Book of Life, and out of the holy city, and from the things that are written in this book."

Here it is either the Lord Himself who speaks, or the man again quoting Him. His words do not mean that men may not comment on the Book of

Revelation, but that anyone who adds words to it as coming from the Lord, or who takes words away from it to hide what the Lord is saying, will be blotted out of the Book of Life, and will not be able to enter into the Holy City or receive the blessings that are written therein. Those who interpret the Scriptures erroneously for lack of knowledge, or for having believed teachers who themselves were in error will not necessarily be plagued. This refers to willful corruption of the words of this book. However, it behooves us all to handle God's Word with care, examining our hearts and praying for understanding.

22:20-21

He who testifies these things says, "Surely I come quickly."
Amen. Even so, come, Lord Jesus!
The grace of our Lord Jesus Christ be with you all. Amen!

SUMMARY OF THE TENTH REVELATION

This revelation, which covers the last two chapters of the Book of Revelation, has to do with events after the Great White Throne Judgment. God will recreate the heavens and the earth. The New Earth will have no seas. This will provide for an even, temperate climate throughout.

- The New Jerusalem—the Bride of Christ—will descend from Heaven to the New Earth;
- God's tabernacle will be with men, and God will dwell with us on the earth for eternity;
- There will be no more pain, suffering or evil of any kind on the earth;
- The river of life will flow from the throne of God throughout the whole earth, just as living water will flow from the temple of God throughout the Promised Land during the Millennium (Eze 47:1-12);
- Those redeemed as a result of their pure faith in Jesus Christ will inherit the New Jerusalem;
- Those in the second resurrection who are judged righteous according to their works will inherit the New Earth, but not the New Jerusalem;
- Those in the second resurrection who are judged unrighteous will be cast into the lake of fire.

I pray this book will help many understand the critical nature of not only the need to have faith in Jesus Christ in order to inherit the Kingdom of God, but the importance of our righteousness in Him to be manifested in the way we live our lives.

EPILOG

No doubt there will be those who have been startled by some of the conclusions I have drawn from the Scriptures. But I believe that I have been diligent in keeping everything in context. I do not profess to know all things. As always, I pray that if I have erred in any way, my errors will not take root in any heart, but only those truths that are of the Lord.

Those who disagree with my conclusions are welcome to say so. But first, read all the Scriptures thoroughly; keep everything in context, and do not be afraid to question the "accepted wisdom" of any theological system, tradition or popular theory. If Scripture is to be our final authority, let us not depart from it in order to indulge our preferences for comfort.

Some will be frightened at the prospect of the terrible future that lies ahead. No one really wants to think they will have to put their lives on the line for their beliefs. But that is the difference between belief and faith. The former is mental; the latter resides within the heart, reaching the spirit.

We must ask ourselves if we have merely mental belief in Jesus or if we have faith in Jesus. Because He will come again. And it is fitting that, at the very end of His writing, John is reminded by Jesus to warn the believers that when He does come He will come suddenly.

In conclusion, it is my hope that this book will not be an end in itself. It is meant to be a follow-up to my previous two books, *What Do You Believe; Why Do You Believe It?* and *What is the True Gospel?*

The purpose for this series has been to help all—believers in Christ Jesus and non-believers—to come to a more perfect understanding of the grace that God has extended to all mankind through the sacrifice of His only-begotten Son. If these writings amount to nothing more than intellectual ascent to the truth of the Gospel, I will have failed. My prayer is that they will bring the lost to Christ, and the believer to a closer walk with Him.

It is up to each of us to examine ourselves to see if we truly are in the Faith, and if we are faithful to the One who is the center of that Faith.

Whether or not one agrees with all that has been written herein, whatever lies ahead, let us echo John's penultimate words, "Even so, come, Lord Jesus!"

❖   ❖   ❖

Please check out other books available from this author on pages 356 and 357, as well as information about Media Spotlight Ministries on page 359.

APPENDIX A
WHAT IS "THE CHURCH"?

One may question why this Appendix is necessary to our study of eschatology. I believe it will become evident as we progress, that a proper understanding of what constitutes "the Church" as opposed to the Body of Christ is essential to understanding eschatology. This is because there are many errors in eschatological teachings that are based on a misunderstanding of what "the Church" is.

**EXCERPTED FROM THE BOOK, *THE HOUSE ASSEMBLY*
BY ALBERT JAMES DAGER**

When Jesus came the first time to Israel He proclaimed the Gospel of the Kingdom of God, also known as the Kingdom of Heaven. He demonstrated how the Kingdom came in the past, how it continues to come in the present, and will fully come in the future. There is an important detail to the Kingdom which must be addressed if we are to enter into it with understanding. One of those details has to do with a great apostasy (falling away from the faith) that occurred in the early centuries after Jesus came.

Because of that apostasy, which came in the name of Jesus and claimed to be the visible representation of His Kingdom on earth, the truth of the nature of the Body of Christ (the sum of believers in Him) has been obscured. One reason we have been left in the dark on this issue is that we have been taught to think of ourselves as members of something called "the Church."

Since at least as early as the fourth century, Christians have referred to themselves as "the Church." We have become accustomed to the word "church," without understanding how it came about or why.

The various English translations of Scripture use the word "church" for the Greek *ekklesia*. In truth, however, *ekklesia* is properly translated "called out." The word "church" is not a proper translation of *ekklesia*, but comes from another root word with a different meaning.

In reference to the word "Church," the *Online Etymology Dictionary* states:

Church - O.E. cirice "church," from W.Gmc. *kirika, from Gk. kyriake (oikia) "Lord's (house)," from kyrios "ruler, lord." For vowel evolution, see bury. Gk. kyriakon (adj.) "of the Lord" was used of houses of Christian worship since c.300, especially in the East, though it was less common in this sense than ekklesia or basilike. An example of the direct Gk.-to-Gmc. progress of many Christian words, via the Goths; it was probably used by W.Gmc. people in their pre-Christian period. Also picked up by Slavic, via Gmc. (cf. O.Slav. criky, Rus. cerkov).

The term "church" (Anglo-Saxon, *cirice, circe*; Modern German, *cirche*; Sw., *kyrka*) is the name employed in the Teutonic languages to translate *ekklesia*. But this is an error.

The Latin origin of "church" (*kyriake oikia*) meant "The Lord's house." At first glance this may seem a moot point. But the Lord's house speaks of the place of gathering (or the institution) rather than of the people themselves. *Kyriake oikia* came to be used by the developing hierarchical establishment of the world system to refer to itself and to the Christian "synagogues" or meeting places called "churches," "cathedrals," "chapels," "sanctuaries," etc. in which they plied their religious trade.

(The word "sanctuary," which is used even in non-Catholic churches as a name for the room where the congregation meets, means a holy place, or the place where God dwells. It was used for the Holy of Holies in the Hebrew temple. Yet Scripture says that each believer in Jesus is the temple of God; He does not dwell in temples made by hands [Ac 17:24; 1 Co 3:16]).

It's this erroneous usage that was adopted for the developing hierarchical system which eventually became the Roman Catholic Church. The carry-over of this error into the English translations of the Bible effectively keep the people thinking of themselves as members of their particular institutions rather than members of the larger Body of Christ on one hand, and part of autonomous local assemblies on the other hand.

This may be denied by religious leaders, but what do they call their institutions but "churches"? Christians ask other Christians, "Which 'church' do you attend?" Every week they attend "church." When speaking of religious meeting places even Christians encourage people to attend their "church," "synagogue," "temple," or "mosque," equivocating the church with these other places of gathering. Church institutions are every bit detached from the identity of the individual as the *ekklesia*, or "called out" of God. Observe how they operate and you will see that most of these institutions exist for their own benefit above that of the people.

Although *ekklesia* may mean the "called out" for Christ in total, or as individual assemblies of the called out, it has no connotation of a religious system. The "churches," however, are part of a theological system which operates on a professional level. They are clergy-laity oriented. The rank-and-file are distinguished from the clergy who function as priests—the perceived oracles of God.

Outside the "high" churches such as Roman Catholicism, Anglicanism, Lutheranism, and the various Orthodox churches of the East, most Christians would say that their pastors are not priests. Yet they make the clergy-laity distinction by referring to them as "Reverend," "Bishop," or some other hierarchical religious term. Some pastors wear clerical robes that speak as loudly as words: "I am clergy; you are laity." Even the word "pastor" is suspect. Technically, the Greek word *poimen*, and the Latin word *pastores*, mean "shepherds." But Latin being the official language of the apostate Roman Church, *pastores* referred to its papal priests. We need not make an issue of this fact if some prefer the word "pastor." It just helps to know.

In the true *ekklesia*, all members are equal before God, although there may be some gifted by God as apostles, prophets, evangelists, shepherds and teachers (Eph 4:11), who are to function in specific manners strictly from a motive of love. They may receive some honor or support for their service, but it is better for them to work with their own hands so that they not be a burden to others (1Th 4:11). Professional clergy often preach only that which is popular or will ensure their financial security.

Over the centuries, *ekklesia* was usurped to mean the churches whose leaders rule the spiritual lives of their congregants through a clergy-laity system. Originally this was done to preserve the establishment of the Roman papal system. With the Reformation it was carried over to the Protestant religions. Today the word "church" is commonly used to denote the Body of Christ, which is an error. That error was propagated by the English translators of the "New Testament," who knew that the word "church" would cement in the minds of their congregants the legitimacy of their hierarchical establishments. So, too, the words, "bishop," "pastor," "preach," and other terms did not originate in the Greek Scriptures but in the apostate Roman Catholic religious system. All are incorrect translations of the original Greek.

This is not a matter of semantics. Those English words were included as a means to keep the people subservient to the hierarchical systems that produced their Bibles.

Yet we can thank God for using the apostate establishments to preserve the Scriptures for us. Had it not been for their power-grabbing nature, much of what we have in ancient manuscripts would have been lost to us today. They made possible the King James Bible and all subsequent translations in many languages for the average person. The truth is available to us if we but study the Scriptures diligently. While translations have their flaws—some more so than others—the Gospel can be found in most of them.

Because of the confusion wrought by the early apostasy, today virtually all churches hold that "the Church" was either a new creation by Jesus to replace Israel, or was created in addition to Israel as a separate entity. Both positions are based on the erroneous assumption that "the Church" was necessary to be the oracle of God because of Israel's unfaithfulness. The truth is that all the promises of God in both the "Old" and "New Testament" are only to Israel, and all believers in Jesus are heirs to those promises regardless of their national heritage. This is important to know if we are going to understand the true nature of the *ekklesia* of God and function in the manner He has ordained for us.

Read the following portion carefully and test it against the Scriptures. The truths of God's Word in relation to what is said here can set us free from the religious errors that have kept us blinded to our true inheritance in Jesus Christ.

Old And New Reconciled

It is supposed that the "New Testament" replaced the "Old Testament" for Christians. The word rendered "testament" is *diatheke*, which means "contract." There has been a problem created by those who compiled the Scriptures, particularly those within the Roman Catholic Church. Confusion exists in what is meant by the "Old Testament" and the "New Testament" as they relate to the Old Covenant and the New Covenant.

There is no such division of Scripture as an "Old Testament" and a "New Testament," except as invented by the apostate early "Church." Nor is there any such thing as different testaments. There is only God's Word given through His prophets who wrote prior to the coming of Israel's Messiah, and to His apostles and prophets who wrote after the coming of Israel's Messiah. There is one Testimony which is made up of all the prophetic writings, and it was given to Israel—the Testimony of Yeshua, HaMashiach (Jesus the Christ), which spoke of Him before He came (pre-messianic Scriptures), and related His life and teachings after He came (post-messianic Scriptures).

"The Church" separated these into two categories called "Old Testament" and "New Testament," then said that these are two different covenants for two different people—the "old" for the Jews, the "new" for "the Church."

While "testament" means "covenant," it was erroneous for them to separate the prophetic writings given before Messiah came, from the prophetic writings given after Messiah came, and call them the "Old Testament" and the "New Testament." This implied that all of the pre-messianic writings comprised the whole of what was done away with when Messiah instituted His New Covenant in His blood. The only parts of those pre-messianic writings that were done away were specific Mosaic laws given to Israel to keep them separated from the nations and to provide for atonement from sin until Messiah came. But it is not true of God's original covenant with Abraham, or of any other writings.

The pre-messianic Scriptures recorded many covenants with different people: Adam and Eve, Noah, Abraham, Isaac, Jacob, and others, including non-Israelites such as Hagar and her son Ishmael (Ge 17:20). So the "Old Testament" is really the record of many testaments (covenants) between God and men. All of those covenants were specific to those people. The Old Covenant in Moses, and the New Covenant in Jesus, were made specifically with the nation of Israel. The Old Covenant was sealed by keeping the Law by faith. The New Covenant with the house of Israel was sealed with the blood of Messiah.

All who come to Him enter into the covenant He made with Abraham. The Old Covenant with Israel through Moses has been done away and replaced by the New Covenant in Jesus' blood. Therefore, the only parts of the pre-messianic writings that do not apply to today's Israel of Faith are those that specifically related to Israel's sacrifices for sin and the ceremonial laws that pointed to the future coming of Messiah. Once Messiah fulfilled those laws they no longer had to be adhered to by faithful Israel. The wall of separation was torn down and the Gentiles were invited to enter into the New Covenant with Israel.

For centuries the Abrahamic Covenant has been misunderstood and/or ignored to the detriment of the spiritual growth of Christians. The New Covenant did not replace the Abrahamic Covenant; it supplemented it. And it pertains to Israel, not to "the Church." This is borne out in the Scriptures.

When Jesus told His apostles at His "Last Supper," "This is my blood of the new testament [covenant], which is shed for many," He was fulfilling a prophecy given through Jeremiah that spoke of a new covenant God would make with......Israel:

> "Look, the days are coming," says YHWH, "that I will make a new covenant with the house of Israel and with the house of Judah, not according to the covenant that I made with their fathers in the day that I took them by the hand to bring them out of the land of Egypt, which My covenant they broke, although I was a husband to them," says YHWH.

> "But this shall be the covenant that I will make with the house of Israel: After those days," says YHWH, "I will put My law in their inward parts, and write it in their hearts, and will be their God, and they shall be My people. (Jer 31:31-33)

This prophecy pertained to Jesus at His first coming. It is specific to the tribes of Israel and the tribes of Judah. That specificity means it cannot be construed to mean it is for something called "the Church," which replaced, or was created in addition to, Israel. This is affirmed in the post-messianic Scriptures, especially in the writing to the Hebrew believers in Christ. Speaking of Jesus as the perfect High Priest of Israel, the writer says:

> But now He has obtained a more excellent ministry, by how much also He is the mediator of a better covenant that was established upon better promises.

> For if that first covenant had been faultless then no place would have been sought for the second. For finding fault with them, He says, "'Look, the days come,' says the Lord, 'when I will make a new covenant with the house of Israel and with the house of Judah, not according to the covenant that I made with their fathers in the day when I took them by the hand to lead them out of the land of Egypt, because they did not continue in My covenant, and I did not regard them,' says the Lord. 'For this is the covenant that I will make with

the house of Israel after those days,' says the Lord. 'I will put My laws into their mind, and write them in their hearts, and I will be a God to them, and they shall be a people for Me, and they shall not teach every man his neighbor, and every man his brother, saying, "Know the Lord," for all shall know Me, from the least to the greatest. For I will be merciful to their unrighteousness, and I will no longer remember their sins and their iniquities.'"

In that He says, "a new covenant," He has made the first old. Now that which decays and grows old is ready to vanish away. (Heb 8:6-13)

The Old Covenant spoken of here was that which God made with Israel through Moses and the giving of the Mosaic laws. That covenant provided for animal sacrifices which could not fully remove the sins of the people. These were types that pointed to Christ.

The New Covenant is a more perfect one based upon the shed blood of Jesus. Both the Old Covenant and New Covenant are said to be made with "the house of Israel and the house of Judah." Thus, the imperfect was replaced by the perfect for the benefit of Israel which, in its totality, included Judah and Benjamin—the house of Judah. There is no mention of "the Church."

God's covenant with Abraham through Israel still stands; only the aspects of the covenant given through Moses and pertaining to sacrifices for sin, and those meant to keep Israel separate from the nations, are done away.

While the Mosaic laws pertaining to the sacrifices and other things necessary to demonstrate righteousness before God were done away, it remains that God's covenant with Abraham, operating through Israel, carries through to the disciples of Jesus. This is part of the Gospel: we are joint heirs with Christ as promised to the father of our faith, Abraham. This is affirmed in the post-messianic Scriptures:

Therefore, know that those who are of faith, the same are the children of Abraham. And the Scripture, foreseeing that God would justify the heathen through faith, proclaimed the Gospel to Abraham earlier, saying, "In you shall all nations be blessed."

So then those who are of faith are blessed with faithful Abraham. For as many as are of the works of the Law are under the curse, for it is written, "Cursed is everyone who does not continue in doing all those things that are written in the Book of the Law."

But it is evident that no man is justified in the sight of God by the Law, for the just shall live by faith. And the Law is not of faith, but the man who does them shall live in them.

Christ has redeemed us from the curse of the Law, being made a curse for us (for it is written, "Cursed is everyone who hangs on a tree") so that the blessing of Abraham might come on the Gentiles through Jesus Christ, so that we might receive the promise of the Spirit through faith.

Brethren, I speak after the manner of men: although it is but a man's covenant, yet if it is confirmed, no man annuls or adds to it.

Now the promises were made to Abraham and his seed. He does not say, "And to seeds," as of many, but as of one, and to your seed, who is Christ. (Gal 3:7-16)

Thus, we enter not into the Mosaic Covenant, but into the Abrahamic Covenant. The Mosaic Covenant was interspersed to keep Israel separate from the nations until Messiah came. Through faith in the Messiah, Jesus, believers from out of the nations are melded with the faithful of Israel so that out of the two, God has made one people for Himself (Eph 2:15). God's covenant in Abraham's faith was not annulled by the covenant of law later given through Moses to Israel:

And I say this: that the covenant that was confirmed earlier by God in Christ, the Law, which was four hundred and thirty years after, cannot annul that it should make the promise of no effect. For if the inheritance is by the Law it is no longer by promise. But God gave it to Abraham by promise. (Gal 3:17-18)

To whom was the promise of a better covenant given? Israel. Yet all who come to Christ by faith, whether born naturally to Israel or to the other nations, are heirs of the Abrahamic Covenant:

For you are all the children of God by faith in Christ Jesus. For as many of you who have been baptized into Christ have put on Christ.

There is neither Jew nor Greek; there is neither bond nor free; there is neither male nor female; for you are all one in Christ Jesus. And if you are Christ's, then are you Abraham's seed, and heirs according to the promise. (Gal 3:26-29)

God proclaimed the Gospel to Abraham before it was fulfilled—that through Abraham all nations would be blessed (Gal 3:8).

Isaiah, speaking prophetically to the Messiah, said He would be a light to the Gentiles:

And he said, "Is it a light thing that you should be My servant to raise up the tribes of Jacob, and to restore the preserved of Israel? I will also give you as a light to the Gentiles so that you may be My salvation to the ends of the earth." (Isa 49:6)

Simeon, seeing the child Jesus in the temple referenced Isaiah:

"Lord, now allow Your servant to depart in peace, according to Your word, for my eyes have seen Your salvation which You have prepared before the face of all people—a light to enlighten the Gentiles, and the glory of Your people Israel." (Lk 2:29-32)

As the Messiah of Israel, Jesus is a light to the nations. He came to break down the wall of separation between Israel and the other nations:

Remember, therefore, that you, being in past times Gentiles in the flesh who are called Uncircumcision by that which is called the Circumcision in the flesh made by hands—that at that time you were without Christ, being aliens from the commonwealth of Israel, and strangers from the covenants of promise, having no hope, and without God in the world. But now in Christ Jesus, you who were once far off are made near by the blood of Christ. For He who has made both one, and has broken down the middle wall of partition between us, is our peace, having abolished in His flesh the enmity—even the law of commandments contained in ordinances—in order to make from two, one new man in Himself, so making peace, and that He might reconcile both to God in one body by the cross, having by it slain the enmity, and came and proclaimed peace to you who were far off, and to those who were near. For through Him we both have access to the Father by one Spirit.

Now, therefore, you are no longer strangers and aliens, but fellow citizens with the saints, and of the household of God, and are built upon the foundation of the apostles and prophets, Jesus Christ Himself being the chief cornerstone, in whom all the building fitly framed together grows into a holy temple in the Lord, in whom you also are built together for a habitation of God through the Spirit. (Eph 2:11-20)

The Gentiles, without Christ, are alienated from the commonwealth of Israel and are strangers from the covenant of promise. In Christ they are bonded to the commonwealth of Israel and partake of the New Covenant God made with Israel and Judah through Christ (Heb 8:8). This is a mystery that was hidden throughout the centuries:

> And you who were once alienated and enemies in your mind by wicked works, He has now even yet reconciled in the body of His flesh through death, to present you holy and faultless and approved in His sight if you continue in the faith grounded and settled, and are not moved away from the hope of the Gospel which you have heard, and which was proclaimed to every creature that is under the heavens, of which I Paul am made a minister, who now rejoice in my sufferings for you and fill up that which is lacking of the afflictions of Christ in my flesh for the sake of His Body, which is the Called Out, of whom I am made a minister according to the stewardship from God that is given to me for you, to fulfill the word of God—the mystery that has been hidden from ages and from generations, but now is revealed to His saints to whom God would make known among the Gentiles what are the riches of the glory of this mystery, which is in you, Christ the hope of glory. (Col 1:21-27)

So sacred is the truth that God has made of two people one in Israel for His glory, that Paul condemns those who would try to erect again the wall of separation torn down through Christ's sacrifice:

> But when Peter came to Antioch, I withstood him to his face because he was at fault. For before certain came from James, he ate with the Gentiles, but when they came he withdrew and separated himself, fearing those who were of the circumcision. And the other Jews, were in concert with him, insomuch that Barnabas was also carried away with their hypocrisy.
>
> But when I saw that they did not walk uprightly according to the truth of the Gospel, I said to Peter in front of them all, "If you, being a Jew, live after the manner of Gentiles, and not as the Jews do, why do you compel the Gentiles to live as the Jews do?"
>
> We being Jews by nature, and not Gentile sinners, knowing that a man is not justified by the works of the Law but by the faith of Jesus Christ, we have believed in Jesus Christ so that we might be justified by the faith of Christ and not by the works of the Law. For no flesh shall be justified by the works of the Law. (Gal 2:11-16)

From the very beginning, Satan tried to undo what Christ had done. He tried to drive a wedge between Israel and the Gentiles, devising false teachings that treated the two as something distinct.

Roman Catholicism proved his perfect foil to accomplish this. Using the military power of Rome, that religious system—a hybrid Christian-pagan hierarchical "church"—imposed upon kings and their subjects the belief that the Kingdom of God had come through the Roman pontiff as the Vicar of Christ on earth. Its leaders claimed that Israel was no longer the inheritor of God's promises; "the Church" was.

Thus, "the Church" drove further the wedge between the two through persecution and a bloody pogrom that still reeks today.

Although God has managed to preserve individuals—even among the leaders—in the religious systems, the fact remains that those systems are all illegitimate usurpers of the promises made to the Israel of Faith. They do not proclaim the full Gospel of the Kingdom as the Lord commanded. Rather, they claim rewards and promises distinct from those of the Israel of Faith. So doing, they cut off their hearers from blessings.

It pains me to say this. I know wonderful men who are pastors of these churches. I would not question their love for the Lord. They also are victims of the deception, having been trained in particular theological systems. I fear I am wounding them by my words. All I can say is I'm sorry. But as I understood these things, I felt the same as when the true nature of the Roman Catholic Church—which I loved—was revealed to me in 1964. I gave up what I loved for Him whom I loved more. With understanding of the truth comes responsibility to the truth.

To be sure, we are not saved by this knowledge. We are saved by grace. We are saved by our faith in the Messiah of God. But God's grace does not come without consequences for those who receive it. One of those consequences is conviction by the Holy Spirit to surrender our very thoughts to His thoughts. Although we recognize this vital truth about "the Church," we must regard as saved by grace our true brethren in Christ who are still in the churches, content under the tutelage of even the most errant pastors. We must likewise regard as saved those pastors who labor out of a motive of love for God's flock. We cannot be puffed up, as knowledge often does to people. Our eyes may be opened now, but they were closed for too long before. Let us have grace toward those who do not see these truths at this time. Some may resist until the end—until they are cast out of the synagogues called churches today. Some pastors will be cast out by their congregations when they begin to really minister the truth as well.

Were Jesus' words for "the Church"?

So successful has Satan been in erecting again the wall of separation through the churches that there are some who even say that Jesus' words were not meant for "the Church."

They assume that, because the Lord related His teachings to the Law, they were meant only for Israel. And since the Law was done away, they do not apply His teachings to "the Church." They assume that Israel was saved by keeping the Law while "the Church" is saved by grace merely through affirmation of faith in Jesus. They have misconstrued the meaning of grace, lacking understanding of how grace came to Israel through the Law. Thus, they have established an inadequate gospel as a means to salvation.

Let us be clear about this very important truth: there is nothing man can do to earn his salvation. Salvation comes by grace through faith, and that is a gift from God (Eph 2:4-10). But God's gift of faith is available to all who seek truth with an honest heart:

> O Lord, open my lips, and my mouth shall show forth Your praise. For You do not desire sacrifice, or else I would give it to You. You do not delight in burnt offering.
>
> The sacrifices of God are a broken spirit; a broken and a contrite heart, O God, You will not despise. (Ps 51:15-17)

Many focus on the idea that man's heart is utterly corrupt, and that no semblance of goodness can be found in it. And it is true that there are several Scriptures that attest to the deceitfulness of man's heart. Yet man, bearing the image of God, does have an innate goodness, even if that goodness of itself cannot save him. Even Jesus acknowledged the possibility of a good heart. When explaining the parable of the sower, He said:

> But that on the good ground are they, which in an honest and good heart, having heard the word, keep it, and bring forth fruit with patience. (Lk 8:15)

So whom do we believe? Jesus or some theological system? I suppose we should correct the Lord?

We are saved by God's grace, not by our own works of righteousness. But our response to God's grace reveals the condition of our hearts. We are not robots to be forced against our wills into the Kingdom of God. We have the ability to choose Christ or reject Him. Otherwise there would be no such thing as love on our part toward our heavenly Father and Jesus. Love is an act of one's will. And God desires that we love Him with all our hearts, souls, strength and minds.

It is important to know that God's grace as the only means of salvation did not apply only to "New Testament" believers, but also to "Old Testament" Israel. Israel was never saved by keeping the Law; God's grace has always been at the heart of His dealing with men even from the creation of Adam. The moral law was given as an expression of God's grace to show man what God required of him in order to be in fellowship with God. It was never meant as a way to be saved.

True faith involves a desire to obey God's moral law, which must be kept by faith in what it teaches us: that God has made us His workmanship, created in Christ Jesus to do good works in which God had ordained us to walk. One cannot break God's commands and claim to love God. Jesus said, "If you love Me, keep My commandments" (Jn 14:15).

"But," some say, "Jesus never spoke to the Church, He spoke only to Israel." Yet what did He say immediately following these words?

> "If you love Me, keep My commandments, and I will ask the Father, and He will give you another Comforter so that He may abide with you forever—the Spirit of Truth whom the world cannot receive because it does not see Him, nor know Him. But you know Him because He lives with you, and shall be in you. I will not leave you orphans; I will come to you.
>
> "Just a little while, and the world sees Me no longer, but you see Me. Because I live, you shall live also. In that day you shall know that I am in My Father, and you in Me, and I in you.
>
> "He who has My commandments and keeps them, it is he who loves Me. And he who loves Me shall be loved by My Father, and I will love him and will reveal Myself to him." (Jn 14:15-21)

To whom has the Comforter—the Holy Spirit—been sent? To Israel, or to "the Church"? We cannot have it both ways. Those who claim Jesus' words are not for "the Church" want to claim this promise of the Holy Spirit for themselves, but they do not want to assume the responsibilities required to receive that blessing.

The Holy Spirit is sent to Israel and to all who are grafted into New Covenant Israel by faith in Jesus. So, in that sense the Lord's words were only for Israel. For we are all Israel by faith if we have been baptized into the New Covenant which was promised to Israel. Thus, all of the "New Testament" writings are for the Israel of Faith, not for the apostate religious system that came to be known as "the Church." Those Israelites who do not believe in Jesus as their Messiah are cut off from Israel.

It is only those who believe in Jesus as Messiah who are allowed to claim the promises of Israel, whether they are Jews or Gentiles. Abraham's faith is what is at issue here. And only those who have the same faith Abraham had may enter into the Kingdom of Heaven.

Does "The Church" Exist?

The truth is that there is no such thing as "the Church" in God's economy. All of the churches that exist today are descended from the original apostate system, no matter how far from the original they may have progressed. As long as they think of themselves as something other than a company of people within the Abrahamic Covenant and as distinct from Israel, they are in error. This does not mean that all individuals in those churches are not saved, or do not love God. It merely means that they have not been taught properly who they are in Christ. God did not create a new entity to replace Israel; nor did He establish a new creation in addition to Israel. There is only the Israel of Faith.

Before the Covenantalists or the dispensationalists pick up their stones, I ask that they please hear me out.

All who would be saved, whether Jew or Gentile, are of one and the same company through faith in the promise to Abraham:

Now the promises were made to Abraham and his seed. He does not say, "and to seeds," as of many, but as of one, and to your seed, who is Christ.

And I say this: that the covenant that was confirmed earlier by God in Christ, the Law, which was four hundred and thirty years after, cannot annul that it should make the promise of no effect. For if the inheritance is by the Law it is no longer by promise. But God gave it to Abraham by promise.

How then does the Law serve? It was added because of transgressions till the seed should come to whom the promise was made, and it was ordained by angels in the hand of a mediator.

Now a mediator is not a mediator of one, but God is one. Is the Law then contrary to the promises of God? It cannot be. For if there had been a law given that could have given life, truly righteousness would have been by the Law. But the Scripture has concluded all under sin, so that the promise by faith in Jesus Christ might be given to those who believe.

But before faith came we were kept under the Law, kept from the faith that should afterwards be revealed. Therefore the Law was our schoolmaster to bring us to Christ so that we might be justified by faith. But after faith comes we are no longer under a schoolmaster. For you are all the children of God by faith in Christ Jesus. For as many of you who have been baptized into Christ have put on Christ.

There is neither Jew nor Greek; there is neither bond nor free; there is neither male nor female; for you are all one in Christ Jesus. And if you are Christ's, then you are Abraham's seed, and heirs according to the promise. (Gal 3:16-29)

Thus, all believers, whether born to natural Israelite stock, or from other nations, grow together on the same tree—faithful Israel.

For if the first fruit is holy, the lump is also holy. And if the root is holy, so are the branches. And if some of the branches are broken off, and you, being a wild olive tree, were grafted in among them, and with them partake of the root and fatness of the olive tree, do not boast against the branches. But if you boast, you do not bear not the root, but the root you.

You will say then, "The branches were broken off so that I might be grafted in."

Well, they were broken off because of unbelief, and you stand by faith. Do not be proud, but fear. For if God did not spare the natural branches, beware lest He also not spare you.

Behold therefore the goodness and severity of God: on them who fell, severity, but toward you, goodness if you continue in His goodness. Otherwise you also shall be cut off. And they also, if they do not still live in unbelief, shall be grafted in, for God is able to graft them in again.

For if you were cut out of the olive tree which is wild by nature, and were grafted contrary to nature into a good olive tree, how much more shall these, which are the natural branches, be grafted into their own olive tree?

For I do not want, brethren, that you should be ignorant of this mystery lest you would be wise in your own conceits, that blindness in part has happened to Israel until the fullness of the Gentiles has come in. And so all Israel shall be saved, as it is written, "There shall come out of Zion the Deliverer, and He shall turn away ungodliness from Jacob, for this is My covenant with them, when I shall take away their sins." (Ro 11:16-27)

Read these Scriptures carefully. You will see that there are not two trees, but one. God did not create a new tree called "the Church," but grafted into the existing tree, Israel (not natural Israel, but faithful Israel), all who have faith in Jesus Christ and obey His commandments by faith.

We are not members of something called "the Church." We are members of the Israel of Faith.

The concept of replacement theology is a terrible deception. It boasts against the natural branches. It states that God has completely finished with Israel with the coming of Christ, and that He has replaced Israel with something called "the Church," which word is not found in the original Greek Scriptures. As we have seen, the Greek word mistranslated "church" is _ekklesia_, which merely means "called out." Israel was called out from among the nations to present the Gospel to the world. This is why Paul calls the faithful of Israel the elect of grace (Ro 11:5). This is a term "elect" we often hear applied to "the Church," but it initially applied to the believing remnant of Israel. If Paul referred to Israel as the elect of grace at a time when "the Church" was supposed to be in operation, why has the concept been discarded?

Satan's hatred for God's people caused him to devise a religious system that would confuse those who come to Christ, and obscure their understanding of the great promises that are theirs if they will be faithful.

But didn't Jesus say to Peter, "on this rock I will build my church"? That must prove that "the Church" is the legitimate institution of Jesus.

No. At the risk of being redundant, Jesus said He would build His _ekklesia_ (His "called out") on the faith exhibited by Peter when he stated that Jesus is the Christ (Messiah), the Son of the living God (Mt 16:15-20). Jesus was not going to build something new called "the Church." He was calling out the faithful of Israel, this time to be built on the New Covenant in His blood. His "called out" were called out from among Israel's apostate religious system known as Judaism.

When Jesus' disciples gathered for fellowship they met in their homes. They were "called-out" from not only the nations, but from unfaithful Israel. They recognized that the Body of Christ is a family. Family meetings were for only the family members unless non-believers were specifically invited in so that they could be witnessed to. The believers did not take a census of their community and ask what the people wanted to hear, what "needs" they wanted met, or what programs would fit those "needs." There was no psychological counseling or mysticism.

However, the believers did continue for awhile to go to the synagogues in order to witness to the Jews as a company. They did so up to the point that they were cast out of the synagogues.

Today, the Israel of Faith has been in captivity to pastoral Christianity for the past 1,800 years, just as it was in captivity to rabbinic Judaism for centuries before Messiah came. In many ways pastoral Christianity is much the same as rabbinic Judaism. A remnant of rabbis followed their Messiah when He came. Most rejected Him. A remnant of pastors strive to remain faithful to the Lord. Most do not. And most in both companies have made the Scriptures of no effect in the lives of God's Israel through their traditions. If there are two distinct companies they are Judaism and Christianity, both of which are part of the world's religious system. Many of today's Christian leaders do not realize the degree to which worldly tradition has taken over their belief systems.

The messages in many churches are fraught with anecdotes and psychobabble in place of God's Word; programs take the place of discipleship; entertainment takes the place of worship. But should we be surprised that they are sliding into apostasy, considering that they originated in apostasy?

What is written in these pages is not a "new revelation"; it is not extra-biblical "knowledge." It is just better understanding of the knowledge already contained in Scripture.

Certainly others must have seen these truths. Perhaps some in the messianic congregations have seen them, although most do not consider biblical Christianity a continuation of biblical Judaism. (Actually, there is no such thing as "biblical Christianity" or "biblical Judaism." There is only the Faith once delivered to the saints.) The churches think it is their duty to make "Christians" out of Jews and bring them into "the Church"—their institutions.

On the other side, many messianic congregations believe that God has two ways of dealing with His people: one way for naturally born Israelites, another way for those grafted into Israel by faith in Messiah Jesus. They want us to believe that they are our mentors because of their natural heritage. Yet what they offer is not the true Faith alone, but a Christianized form of rabbinic Judaism, some even insisting on the keeping of the Law, at least for those born as natural Israelites.

It is permissible to put themselves under the Law in order to win those under the Law as Paul did (ICo 9:19-23). But that is the extent of having any legitimate thing to do with the Law. As one in Christ, let us keep the Covenant in His blood as one people.

So both the churches and the messianic congregations are re-erecting the wall of separation that Jesus tore down. As long as they teach that Israel and "the Church" are distinct entities they are hindering the Gospel of the Kingdom.

I am certain that many who read this will be alarmed. It's as if the very foundation for all they have believed since coming to Christ has been taken out from under them. That is how I felt when the truth about Roman Catholicism was revealed to me. At that time I determined to leave that place of comfort—of beloved priests and comfortable ritual. I knew that I could not remain there and be faithful to the Lord because of the truth I had attained.

Should You Leave Your Church?

Now the question is certainly in the minds of some whether or not they should leave their churches and all the comfort they provide. They love those with whom they fellowship. They know that salvation is in Jesus, not in the church they attend. They love their pastors, and rightly so. They should not forget the true servants of God who have labored in the churches these past centuries—some still today. But they also know that the church system is part of the world's religious establishment, its various elements at worst controlled by Satan; at best they are influenced by him.

I would say that each must make up his own mind what to do, provided his church is not overtly apostate. However, for those with knowledge the purpose for attending should shift from what they can receive from the churches to what they have to offer to the churches in the way of sharing the truth. We should treat the churches as the Lord's disciples treated the synagogues. Recognize that few in them hold a genuine faith in the Lord, but demonstrate the love of Christ to all.

However, we should not be naïve to think that we will be welcomed. Jesus told His disciples that He was sending them out as sheep among wolves (Mt 10:16-17). He warned that they would be cast out of the synagogues and would even be killed by those who think they are doing God a service (Jn 16:2).

It is difficult to face the prospect of giving up one's church. The churches provide a sense of community; they give an air of security; they are lovely places. And there are many sweet brethren in them. But the cost of following Christ is to be willing to give up one's own life for Him. Yet I am not suggesting my brethren do anything more than I have done. I know the pain that arises with separation from those we love.

Frankly, you need not leave your church; just bring the hard truth and most likely you will be escorted out.

It must always be our hope that God's truth will prevail in the hearts of His people.

APPENDIX B
The Twenty-four Elders

My conclusion that the "elders" in chapters four and five of the Book of Revelation are men (KJV) rather than angels (implied in modern English translations) is based on a number of factors:

- The idea that these are angels is primarily a teaching among amillennialists based on references to the principalities and powers of Ephesians 1:21, Colossians 1:16, and 1 Peter 3:22. But there is nothing in Scripture to link these with the references to elders in the Book of Revelation, particularly as a class of angels sitting on thrones;

- Modern English translations do not conclusively state that these are angels; they merely speak in the third person ("them"). So it cannot conclusively be determined that they are angels;

- Most modern translations of the apostle's writings are based on the Westcott-Hort compilation of diverse Greek texts, largely the Codex Sinaiticus and Codex Vaticanus, as opposed to the Byzantine text on which is based the King James Bible (KJV). I am not "King James Only," but there are issues with modern versions that touch on higher criticism which is in opposition to true faith in Jesus. Higher critics overwhelmingly prefer the Westcott-Hort Greek texts, and consider them "the best" manuscripts, primarily because they are deemed of older origins, and contain discrepancies that allow for questions of serious doctrinal concern. There are thousands of such discrepancies from text-to-text within the Sinaiticus and Vaticanus texts. The Byzantine text which formed the primary basis for the *Textus Receptus* (Received Text) of the KJV was used long before the discovery of Sinaiticus and Vaticanus, beginning in 1516 with Erasmus (in Latin). Luther based his German New Testament (1522) on the Byzantine text, as did Tyndale (1526), the Great Bible (1539), the Geneva Bible (1560) and the Bishop's Bible (1568). B.F. Westcott and F.J.A. Hort first published their Greek text in 1881, and it was received with enthusiasm by the higher critics. Since then it has become the standard for modern English translations;

- Nowhere in Scripture are angels called "elders" (Gk: *presbuteros*). All references to *presbuteros* have to do with elders in the Body of Christ;

- The descriptions of the elders fit those that Scripture uses to identify the saints of God: a) they wear white clothing (admittedly, so do angels); they wear crowns (*stephani*, which are rewards, as opposed to *diadema*, which denote royalty); the song they sing (Rv 5:9) is one of praise for redemption, which would be reserved for the redeemed among men;

- It may seem that the four creatures also sing the song of redemption, but Greek syntax is different from English syntax, and the "they" could refer to only the last subject (the twenty-four elders), apart from the previous subject (the four living creatures);

Why could these not be redeemed men taken to Heaven with the Lord after His resurrection? Many of the saints were resurrected with Him:

> When He had cried again with a loud voice, Jesus yielded up the spirit. And, look! The veil of the temple was torn in two from the top to the bottom, and the earth quaked, and the rocks split. And after His resurrection the graves were opened, and many bodies of the saints who slept arose, and came out of the graves, and went into the holy city, and appeared to many. (Mt 27:50-53)

> Therefore, when He ascended up on high, He said He "led captivity captive, and gave gifts to men." (Eph 4:8)

That these are redeemed from all nations suggests they are yet to be resurrected. So was John seeing something still in the future? Whether these are men redeemed from among the nations prior to and relative to the nation of Israel (resurrected with the Lord), or men yet to be resurrected, we cannot tell. But the evidence is compelling that they are men and not angels.

Index

rapture 11-12, 27-28, 31-33, 37-38, 155, 229, 242, 243, 256
replacement theology 22, 88, 188, 189, 344
Revelation 11
Roman Catholicism 23, 142-143, 215, 285, 299-300, 302, 331, 339, 346
Roman Empire 23, 65, 67-68, 139-140, 142, 143, 166, 179, 220, 225, 277, 280, 282, 285, 298-299
Russia 121, 179, 183-184, 281

S

Saddam Hussein 67, 252
Satan 17
Scofield 27-28
second-temple era 111, 112
seven seals 234-235
Solomon 89, 94, 112, 115
Sproul, R.C. 82-84
Spurgeon, Charles Haddon 28
Syria 134, 136-137, 140, 282

T

Tanakh 41, 42, 47, 61
technology 17, 18
Thermopylae 135
Thief in the Night 10
Third Reich 15
Tiberius 277
Time of the Gentiles 5, 48, 54-55, 59, 70, 73, 108, 112, 128, 134, 139, 145-147, 150-151, 153-160, 162-165, 190-191, 196-197, 247, 255-257, 261, 262, 278, 305

Titus 70, 108, 146, 148-149
Tower of Babel 13, 16, 297
Turkey 142, 184-185, 208

U

United Nations 16
United States 15, 20, 56, 68, 143, 160, 179, 185, 203, 254, 282
universalism 312, 322

V

Vatican 68, 177, 280, 299
Vespasian 70, 146, 148-149, 196, 204, 277-278
Vitellius 277
Vulgate 11

W

Warren 177
Westcott-Hort Greek texts 349
World Trade Center 143
World War I 15
World War II 15
World-Christian Movement 177
Wright brothers 15

X

Xerxes I 135

Z

Zadok 111-112
Zerubbabel's temple 108, 260
Zion 42, 45-46, 55, 83, 93, 96, 100, 104, 115, 140, 141, 191, 283, 284, 343

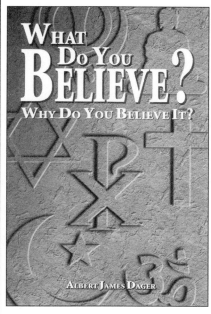

WHAT DO YOU BELIEVE? WHY DO YOU BELIEVE IT?
102 pages

What you believe is important. But can you give a reasoned explication for why you believe what you believe? Can you say for a certainty that your belief is superior to all other beliefs?

The author challenges you to examine the reasons for your beliefs, at the same time offering reasons for why he believes the way he does. You can accept or reject what he has to say, but at the very least you will be able to assess your own belief system and either give a reasoned defense for it, or, perhaps, see the need to reassess what you believe.

Are you willing to take the challenge?

B-1075 Paperback $10

WHAT IS THE TRUE GOSPEL?
110 pages

Today we are witnessing the development of a great apostasy based largely on the traditions of religious institutions. The many gospels emanating from pulpits, radio, and television often differ significantly from the Gospel proclaimed by Jesus and recorded in the Bible. As a result, we are left with half gospels based as much, or more, on theological suppositions as on the Scriptures. This book points the reader back to the Bible in order to be able to grasp the significance of that true Gospel of the Kingdom. The author urges you to test all things, including this book, by the Scriptures.

B-1081 Paperback $8

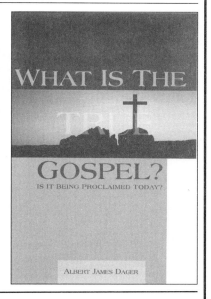

WHY MEDIA SPOTLIGHT?

Media Spotlight is a ministry to the Body of Christ, bringing understanding of the ways in which the world shapes our thinking and lifestyles—particularly through the influence of the mass communications media, both secular and religious.

When Media Spotlight began in 1977, we were the first ministry on an international scale to specifically address the ungodly nature of the secular media, particularly motion pictures, television, toys, games and myriad other problems that contribute to Christians living no differently than the rest of the world.

The mass media have impacted the Body of Christ as much as they have society. Many Christians are so dependent on the media that they aren't aware of how lukewarm they have become. We have many testimonies from readers who tell us that, because of Media Spotlight, they no longer compromise their love for God with the need to be entertained. They have become aware of the effect the media have on their thinking, and are now more selective in their choices.

But the problem of ungodliness is not exclusive to the secular media. One of our major concerns is the religious media which present messages contrary to God's Word. Media Spotlight addresses the impact that religious teachers have on believers in Christ, whether for good or for evil.

It has escaped the understanding of many Christians that what they believe is more often shaped by the teachings and traditions of religious men and institutions than by Scripture. Yet the wisdom of the world is no substitute for God's Word, even if offered from the pulpit or in the Christian media.

Jesus tells us in Matthew 24:24 that in the last days false christs and false prophets would arise and would show great signs and wonders, "insomuch that, if it were possible, they shall deceive the very elect." He also states in Matthew 24:12 that at the same time, the love of many toward Him would grow cold because evil would increase in the world. If we believe Him, then we would be foolish not to guard ourselves against deception. There is little time to waste in the short span of life granted us by God. We must choose today whom we will serve. ❖

For a free subscription to Media Spotlight, write to:
MEDIA SPOTLIGHT
PO BOX 290 - REDMOND, WA 98073-0290
or go to: www.mediaspotlight.org